THE
EAGLE
AND THE
CROSS

JOHN L. SULLIVAN

authorHOUSE®

AuthorHouse™ UK Ltd.
1663 Liberty Drive
Bloomington, IN 47403 USA
www.authorhouse.co.uk
Phone: 0800.197.4150

Published by AuthorHouse   06/07/2013

ISBN: 978-1-4817-8547-1 (sc)
ISBN: 978-1-4817-8548-8 (e)

The Black Eagle has a sharp, distinctive gaze and is renowned for its total commitment to its mate.

The Black Eagles of the Matopos Hills have been part of systematic observations and study for many decades and are reported to have the highest concentration of territories in the whole world.

Each season's surviving hatchling is carefully reared and trained and then dispatched to its own life and a new territory.

Father Odilo Otto Weeger CMM

THE EAGLE AND THE CROSS

This is an account of the full and exciting life of a missionary priest, some of his own experiences and the impact he had on the many people with whom he worked. Born in a farming village in Bavaria, he left Germany during the rise of Nationalism, to work in Rhodesia.

For nearly seventy years he experienced, and was part of, what happened in Zimbabwe - its economic development, as well as the troubled times before the country changed to Zimbabwe. He lived through the post-independence rise and then most of the spectacular man-made collapse that followed, but he did not live long enough to see its renaissance.

Father Odilo Weeger's dedicated service as a missionary and citizen of his adopted country was recognised in many quarters. Germany decorated him with the Cross of Merit, First Class, and he was variously honoured by the City of Bulawayo, Rotary International, the Boy Scouts Association and others. He also served with the Knights of da Gama and was inducted into the Order of Saint Lazarus of Jerusalem.

By John L. Sullivan

With illustrations drawn by Leigh Hogan

FOREWORD BY
THE ARCHBISHOP OF BULAWAYO

There are pioneers in every field of life. Some dare more than others. Father Odilo Weeger CMM was such a daring man of his time. He was ever determined to achieve what he wanted trusting in the power of the Almighty. Nothing could stop him until he achieved his goal. He took his personal and his missionary mandate, *"go into the whole world and proclaim the Good News to every creature"* (Mk. 16;15), very seriously. He accepted this freely leaving his home country to work in Zimbabwe for Zimbabweans. The numerous places he worked, the number of baptisms and other sacraments that he celebrated, the number of hearts he won is a clear testimony to his dedication.

This book by John Sullivan, a long-time friend and companion of Father Odilo, clearly narrates the adventures and missionary challenges he encountered during his life time here in Zimbabwe. It is a true testimony. I highly appreciate and applaud the hard work John Sullivan has put into writing this book.

The title of the book, "The Eagle and the Cross", very appropriately depicts the life and ministry of Father Odilo. This is a highly motivating and inspirational book for all Catholics and for many youngsters. I personally have been very much inspired by this book.

+Alex Thomas
Archbishop of Bulawayo
01.05.2013

The Cross that overlooks the road to Victoria Falls and the Lukosi River

DEDICATION

To all Missionaries, but especially in honour of those who have done such truly good things for the people of Africa, in respectful gratitude for their dedication and committed service to God and mankind.

To Father Odilo Weeger, CMM, and his Arberg family who gave him to all of us. His own recollections provided the detail and outline for this book, and he gave me generous access to his precious time, sharing photo albums and extensive memoirs.

To my mother, Doreen, who was determined that this story should be told; she made it one of her life's missions. She searched for an author, before one day being convinced that she was directed to have me write this book. A mother's wishes have great power and she followed up with her supporting presence and encouragement. She died on 29th August 2003 having lived an example of tolerant love, with a saintly prayer life and a rock-solid faith.

To my father, Larry, a truly great self-made man, who lived his whole life with enormous drive and determination, and provided the wherewithal to unselfishly rear and educate all of us seven children. He was an active and interested father, grandfather and great-grandfather until he died on 22nd July 2012, just 3 days before he would have been 98 years old.

I am truly grateful to Leigh Hogan for her wonderful illustrations that bring the book to life, highlighting notable scenes and events.

I extend my sincere thanks to Robin Doust and others who kindly perused and pointed out errors in my manuscript and made practical suggestions towards this book. I thank my colleagues and friends, who encouraged and helped me to complete this record.

Contents

PART THREE

PREFACE

This era, and our African continent, suffers from confused and often very dishonest teachings and philosophies. Politicians, terrorists and academics 'tilt at' cultures and people they envy. Propaganda prevails when audiences and observers are poorly informed, and people's perceptions are distorted, not simply because of minor cultural patterns and associated habits of thinking and judging.

The greatest problem in our developing world is poverty, not a surplus of people. Just as the Benedictines helped Europe develop its agriculture and downstream industries, good missionaries help people to raise themselves up through honest education and productive activity, while becoming better persons in their own personal lives.

Father Odilo lived through some of the madness and anti-Semitism of Hitler's era but he also witnessed the human greed and dishonesty that has unfortunately become the stereotypical image of African rulers. True leaders bring benefits for all their subjects and make changes that set countries on paths of progress and improvement.

As the rich-poor gap widens greedy people use fear and terrorism to hijack opportunities and frustrate real development. Breaking and building are very different processes, involving very different motives and skills. Abraham Lincoln cautioned that 'you cannot build up the poor by bringing down the rich'. At one of my old school's board meetings a Christian Brother observed that rich children can indeed be very poor.

News media emphasise the worst of what is happening; but I contend that good is growing more than evil in the world. Sadly, many 'better-off' people don't get around to dumping their less important pursuits and attachments, in order to pursue the in-built spiritual hunger that guides us towards inner peace.

I enjoyed the time spent with a man who was like a 'second father' in encouraging and passing on his wisdom; he has helped countless people in similar ways during his years of service as a Roman Catholic Missionary Priest.

INTRODUCTION AND
ACKNOWLEDGEMENTS

The lives of many Catholic missionary priests are a rich source of human inspiration, and I had the unique opportunity to observe and draw upon his wisdom, his memory, his understanding and his skills of observation and description. Many people, here and all over the world, have fond memories of Father Odilo. People were the focus of his life and work, and he took a genuine interest in the lives and well-being of all of us who know that he was our friend.

Pope John Paul II was one of the greatest witnesses to the manly dedication of the Catholic Priesthood. Father Odilo also emerged from an oppressive and evil regime to expend himself in total dedication, touching thousands of lives in a meaningful and beneficent way.

Despite their cultural, scientific and industrial brilliance, Germany succumbed to the anti-Semitic and unchristian evil of Nazism. Escaping this, Father Odilo and his fellow-German missionaries arrived in British African territory as war broke out. Undaunted, he lived and worked for the betterment of the people, keeping true to his vows of poverty, chastity and obedience. He mixed widely in Zimbabwean society, endeavouring always to be respectful and loving in all he did.

Christian Missionaries have been at the forefront of the very best that was brought to undeveloped countries, presenting the Word of God all over the world. They have brought untold benefits and improvements in the lives of hundreds of millions of people, sometimes literally giving their own lives for this. When history is one day presented with greater balance and kindness their role will be clearly recognised and applauded.

The Congregation of Mariannhill Missionaries, (CMM), and their founders give an inspiring example, and have continuously done wonderful work in Africa and elsewhere in the world. The Southern African origins and history of this Order make it unique. Their priests and brothers, helped by their sister order, have greatly enlightened and empowered their students and followers.

In this human drama we see many terrible parallels between Germany's crimes under a hate-filled Hitler, and some of the criminal rule in Africa and elsewhere in the world. On a higher plane, though, God has held mankind in His loving care through it all, offering His message of Truth, Love, Justice and Peace. The Bible itself records the history of God's Love for Mankind, in the Creation accounts and the Covenants that He made with His Chosen People. God has never stopped loving mankind, and our destinies as His followers, Christian, Jew, and even Muslim, are inseparable. Understanding and respect for all people of good will, and their different faiths, are lessons still to be learned.

Father Odilo was one of those great Catholic priests, driven by a spirit of dedication and self-discipline. There are many other examples of good missionary and religious life, as well as martyrs of old and recent history, and yet each life, each person, each situation, is still totally unique—just like our own fingerprints, or the striped pattern on each zebra's coat, or the shape of each mountain, or the architecture of each cave in the Matopos Hills.

A brief record of some of the other CMM missionaries and martyrs is included, one of whom, Father Johannes Banning, used to join us in our home for dinners. He survived, and bravely returned to the country, after narrowly missing martyrdom at his mission near Plumtree.

The terms and language have been kept true to the periods for which events are portrayed. Although the main content has come from working directly with Father Odilo, it is natural that the way I have written was influenced by my own experiences, education and perspective. I apologise if this gives offence to certain people, for that is not my purpose, but it would be dishonest to distort history and dialogue styles to suit a passing mindset. Many of the characters are indeed real people, and are named correctly. Some names are not those of real persons, alive or dead, and a few names have been changed, while making every effort to maintain authenticity.

PART ONE

"Festina lente"

"Eile mit Weile"

"Hasten Slowly"

CHAPTER 1

THE NEST IN ARBERG

A STORM IN THE SAND-FOREST

He woke up with a sudden start. The atmosphere tingled with warning. The darkness was pitch-black. He blinked his eyes, but could see absolutely nothing. He leaned over and parted the hessian that covered the window. The African night was crisp and clean, but the sky was thickly clouded; there was not even a hint of starlight.

He was alert and ready, but for what? He had been dreaming something. What was it? What strange sensation had disturbed him? Something was definitely amiss, but what? His mind was now in a whirl of thoughts.

Here he was, trapped on his way back; stopped by a swollen river again; the wide stretch of brown water had been frothing and raging as it tumbled menacingly across his track through the bush. It flowed much stronger and more dangerously than any of the rivers in which he had swum in Germany.

How long before the river would go down? He wanted to get back; the new roof sheets had to be put on quickly; he needed to get these roofing nails to them; he was also on his way to give catechism classes; would the people come back after the rains, or must he start all over again? Would the river subside tonight, or would he have to wait for days?

"Stop this," he said to himself, almost out aloud. "You must either get back to sleep, or you must halt this cycle of pointless thinking." But it didn't work. His usual self-discipline was not enough. The coldness of the sandveld forest was giving him goose bumps, and he pulled the rough, smoke-filled blankets around himself. He simply could not snuggle up and get back to sleep.

Suddenly, there was a humming blaze of fierce light. The electric-blue aura was all around him in an instant. An eerie force pervaded all his surroundings. His hairs bristled, and he felt a peculiar sensation of being stung, just as he experienced the sharp crack of the lightning strike. The chrome and black of his bicycle lit up as if a powder-flash had gone off for a photo.

Almost immediately, there was a deafening, thunderous roar. The walls of his mud hut shook and trembled. Bits of plaster dropped to the floor around him, and a fierce tearing sound came from the dark forest. Everything shook menacingly, and the shaking went right through him. But he knew he had not been hit. "That was close! Too close! Somebody was certainly looking after me!"

The air had a crisp sweet smell. He remembered that smell now; he had experienced the same electric odour many years ago, when a bolt of lightning had just missed him and his sister. He remembered the comforting feel of her hand, walking home that day, when they were young children. Now, though, he was completely alone.

He was already out of the blankets, standing looking through the unsealed window, opening out under the overhanging grass roof. He pulled on all the clothes he could manage, and stepped outside. Another flash of lightning lit up the sky, but the sound came at least a second after. "Thank God," he calculated, "the worst must have passed." He thought gratefully of his guardian angel, and recalling the life story of Saint Thomas Aquinas, he thanked this patron saint for protecting him. 'How often would he have to confront lightning and storms in his own life?', he wondered. Saint Thomas had escaped unscathed, but his baby sister had been killed by lightning in their bedroom.

In the lightning glow he had seen the huge tree next to his hut with half of its rounded top dropped down like the jib of a derrick crane. He looked towards the nearby hut and wondered, "How do the Dube family all sleep through this?" He certainly could not see any movement, even with the occasional glow of the receding lightning flashes. "Did they sleep? Perhaps they had been hit! No," he realised; they were further than he was from the strike. They might be cowering there in terror, at this new warning from their dark forest. The light rain was gently ticking away on the leaves and dripping rhythmically off the roof around his hut.

He went back inside and rekindled the fire to make some coffee. He coughed to clear the smoke in his lungs, and watched with satisfaction as the water in the little tin pot started to bubble. Just a month ago today, he had enjoyed a birthday supper with his colleagues. Birthdays were not very important events now, but still the thought brought back flashes of the past; more things to stop him sleeping.

He drew the blankets closer around him, as he squatted on the dirt floor. He poured some hot water onto the coffee in his waiting tin cup, and stirred in three spoons of sugar. The first sip nearly burnt his lips, but he took a small and fast suck, and let it cool in his mouth. It tasted good, and now he was fully awake anyhow. He had come far from home, but God was with him as always.

OTTO'S BIRTH IN ARBERG—THE MOUNTAIN OF THE EAGLE

It had been a cold day, with a bleak and cloudy sky; now the late afternoon winds were stirring the dry leaves that carpeted the forest floor. A pair of eagles was soaring high above, sharp-beaked heads moving, as their keen eyes flickered over the landscape, taking in the distant villages and hamlets on the gentle hill slopes below. Far-off, familiar sounds were drifting through the heavy evening air; axles creaking from the tilled fields, and livestock, some with bells, coming in from the meadows. The little streams were cheerfully ambling towards the rivers, and the smaller birds were chirping and fluttering through the firtrees, on their way to their nests.

The eagles circled down and dropped back into their tangled nest, high in the pine trees. From their stronghold, the eagles felt the heat of the day fade as the sun went down, and night settled over the hills. For a while, the people noises of the distant farm and village life rose and filled the air. Slowly they settled down for the night.

October was a pleasant month; the autumn colours were thinning out now, as some of the trees began to shed their foliage for the harsh winter which always lay ahead. The sun was setting sooner on each day when it shone, and the clouds were still gentle and friendly. They came and went on alternate days, like the sort of friends whom you are happy to see, and you know will be back when they say "aufwiedersehen".

In the close community of Arberg village, many of their neighbours thought about the Weeger family. Some were already waiting with them in the Gasthaus, while others were within easy calling distance, a few houses away. Josef Weeger himself was pacing the corridor anxiously. He stared at the patterned carpet, as he kept passing the closed door of the bedroom. He listened attentively for any change in the sounds within.

What he was straining to hear was just as worrying as before, even though it was so familiar to him. He had listened to sounds like these before, for the birth of each of their five children.

Now, he thought about his wife, Julianna. He knew her very well; so well, that he could anticipate almost everything she would say when they were talking together or with friends. He knew the things she did every day of their lives as she busied herself caring for their family; he also knew when to help and how to step in if needed. There were times when he had to exert his manly authority, and hold her in check. At other times he just noticed supportively the way she would begin a fresh task.

But right now, what she really went through, behind that door, he could only guess at. He had no place there by her side, once her sisters and the wise village ladies took over. The farmer simply had to wait, and every now and again he silently prayed, but with great urgency.

Suddenly, there was a new buzz of anticipation. Matronly voices could be heard among other sounds of activity in the main bedroom.

"Push, Julianna, push . . . push . . . ." he heard through the door. The older children, further along in the corridor, had become completely silent. They waited as the tortured sounds from their mother grew more worrying.

"Was she dying? How much pain can she handle?" the little ones wondered, as they heard her muffled groans and occasional shrill outbursts, from far down the long corridor of their Gasthaus.

The youngest Weeger, Josef, heard her cry out, and he began to sob, looking up in alarm. Distracted from their own concern, the others soothed their little brother. The children all sat there together, waiting out of sight, while the adults kept watch near the door. They were silent and alert, a bit like puppies that are tracking a bird, watching it hop among the branches above them.

The gas-lights hissed quietly. Suddenly, their expectations were answered. There was a loud, final scream, which struggled its way from Julianna. Then silence. "What had happened?" they strained to know. At last, Aunt Maria came out beaming, and hugged their father.

When she spoke, his shoulders sagged in a relieved slump. At last, the agony and waiting was over. He turned to them, his eyes moist with emotion, and told them, "You have a little brother." Another little baby was born on 14th October 1912 into the Weeger family home.

Josef was kept waiting for ages, and when they allowed him in, he pushed his way through to Julianna's side. She was exhausted, perspiring and dishevelled; damp locks of her long hair clung to her face; but when she looked at him, she was radiant with happiness and pride. There was their baby, wrapped up and cradled in his mother's arms. A father again, he was holding back a flood of emotions, which he simply could not understand, as he took his first look at their new baby.

Those infant eyes were so alert, and they held Josef's gaze. It was only for an instant, but it was enough time for Josef to wonder, in the way of a man who trusted in God's Providence, "so frail and delicate now, but what has God in store for this bold little boy?"

This miracle of creation filled him with awe; it was one of those rare and blessed moments in life; breaking through the armour of the role destined for him as he lived out the manly role of his times. Josef was a solid and practical man. He was used to applying himself to the serious tasks that he simply had to handle. Now, though, he allowed his mind to wander off. His thoughts drifted poetically into another world, and to future times; with surprising clarity, he could see so many happy times and great things ahead.

Julianna soaked up her husband's happiness. She knew that it was she who had brought the tears to his eyes and this wonderful display of deep gratitude and love. "Oh God," she thought, "You have done great things for me. Thank you, thank you . . . ."

She had never felt closer to God than at this amazing moment, just as she had felt with each of their children's births before. This gift of life was her most powerful proof that God is good and that He was truly present in her life.

Josef didn't have to say the words; his expression said everything. His watering eyes conveyed the greatest message in life, "I love you." They were silent for a while, until Josef asked hoarsely, "what name should we choose for him?"

It was a surprisingly quick and easy decision. He agreed promptly when Julianna suggested confidently, "we must call him Otto." Of course, one automatically thinks of Otto von Bismarck who had been a powerful figure in German history. This man had branded himself an image of power and results, and the name had a strong feel to it. So much so, that most Germans overlooked the means he used to get his way; and even how arrogantly he had treated the Church when it got in his way.

They also thought about the former kings, named Otto, but the Otto who meant the most to this couple, was their own medieval bishop of Bamberg. Bishop Otto had left such a strong legacy and had such a rich influence on the church and the legends of Bavaria. Josef could not yet understand at that moment, why the name just felt so right, but he concurred so easily that he was surprised at himself.

Celebrations

Julianna needed to rest, and Josef was ushered out of the room, into a good-humoured ambush of neighbours who, within minutes, had joined the closer circle at the Gasthaus. The comfortable smell of tobacco smoke enveloped them as they all congratulated Josef loudly and most heartily.

He was a very popular man, and he had so much to do with the village. He was a man of many parts; a farmer, a butcher, an innkeeper, a baker, as well as being an active member of the village council. He was a man whose ideas were listened to and considered carefully. He certainly had many of his own unique opportunities to study human nature at work, with his inn and Gasthaus being a centre of the village social life.

As the mood grew more jovial, Josef poured out extra glasses of schnapps for all these relatives and friends, and the party grew even louder and happier. "Well done, Josef," they chorused from time to time, and glasses were steadily re-charged. On the wall of the bar, there hung a picture of Josef's grandfather. His stern gaze was now fading into a benevolent smile, and Josef could almost hear his voice saying, "I am proud of you, Josef."

Their house was almost in the very centre of the village, just near the Altmuhl River. It was only a short walk up to the church, and the parish priest soon joined the merry group. Josef led him away from the crowd and up to the bedroom, where he saw the little boy lying asleep in his mother's loving arms. This was a sixth child for this good family, and he had his own wondering thoughts, "what does the future hold, for this busy household, and this new child?"

"I bless you in the name of the Father, and of the Son, and of the Holy Ghost", he said, as he made the sign of the cross and sprinkled Otto with holy water. Otto got a shock and shuddered at the feel of cold water on his skin; then he began to cry. Julianna soothed him gently, holding him close and crooning to him. "Where will these tiny little legs take you?" she thought. With her great faith in God, she knew he would grow strong, and that she would be proud of everything he did.

Growing up

Right from the start, Otto had a firm gaze. His eyes were alert and he took in all that was going on around him. There was so much to assimilate, and there were so many interesting and exciting things going on in his home. Josef was watching him one evening, while he was gazing off far into the distance.

Then, some sound or movement in the corridor startled him, and he turned his head sharply. He seemed to be more alert and curious than one would expect for the few weeks of life which he had lived so far. With so many brothers and sisters, he was probably expecting yet another person to come into the room. There was a constant stream of family who still came in quite often to check on him. Perhaps they also wanted to remind Julianna that there were other children in her life as well.

There were so many sounds in the Gasthaus, and Josef realised that little Otto must be taking note of them all. "Whatever goes on in that tiny little mind?" he thought to himself. His alertness reminded Josef of the eagle he had watched earlier that day. It was high up on the dry branch of one of its favourite perches.

Josef had watched while it stood there and preened itself. It gripped the branch with the firm talons of one leg, and was as steady as a rock. First it balanced on one leg, and then on the other, while it used its talons to scratch and clean itself. Every so often, it just stopped and looked out intently. Its eyes were so piercing and alert, and it was capturing even the slightest of movements. Its head responded quickly, swivelling to and fro, while it seemed to be assessing what was happening in its territory. He had watched for a good fifteen minutes, before he had snapped out of his reverie. "A man must work hard and honestly, all day," was the thought that pricked his conscience. He was soon at the barn, helping his older sons, Max and Karl, as they pitched hay into the stalls, and placed the pails of water in each stall.

Otto was the second youngest of seven children, four boys and three girls. When he was born, they were a family of three brothers and two sisters, Karl, Rosa, Juliana, Max and Josef. Later, while he was a toddler, his little sister, Marie, was born.

He was too young to be directly affected by the huge First World War that Germany had fought and lost. But it affected his country and family; the proud German people had been defeated and humiliated; they had even lost their colonies in Africa and elsewhere. Now there was poverty and suffering all around, and the reparation costs demanded by the victors left very little for rebuilding their shattered and destroyed country.

A TOUGH AND DISCIPLINED UPBRINGING

Despite everything, the Weegers were a happy, hard-working family. "Hard work never hurt anybody", his father used to repeat constantly. And working hard was what they all did. The family looked after their Gasthaus/inn, the farm, their butchery and the bakery, and there were numerous chores to be shared by all. There was hardly ever a period of complete silence or rest. There was always so much life and activity around their home.

They used to all sit down at a long table for their main meals together. Josef sat at one end and Otto's mother at the other, nearest the kitchen. Then grandfather sat near his mother, and all seven children had places allotted by age. It was an informal, but well-established seating plan; the eldest got the most elbow-room, of course.

The discipline was clear, and understood from an early age. Josef and Juliana ensured that their children knew what was right or wrong, and the children understood either the stern or the approving looks and words, which they used to keep control of the active family. Otto loved his parents. Years later he saw how the disciplined upbringing was to stand him in good stead, as if Providence was preparing him for his later life as a missionary.

There were no luxuries in their home. They had to draw water in buckets from wells, as there was no running water in the house. At bath-time, there was only one tub, which they filled up and then everybody used the same water in turn. The Weegers relied on candlelight, or paraffin lamps, as there was no electricity at that time, in their village.

Not only was the Weeger family big and bustling, but there was also a constant stream of friends and guests in their lives. Their house was open to friends and family always, and they visited out of friendship. Such guests were never expected to pay, but they would often bring some little gift, like the barometer that Josef hung proudly in his living room.

HIS BELOVED GRANDFATHER

Otto also loved his grandfather. He was stooping with age now, but was still a tall and proud looking man. He always wore his formal clothes, even with a tie or scarf. The kindly old man was never happier than when he was answering questions or telling Otto stories from his own life. He was old now, and one day he fell seriously ill. Young Otto didn't understand things like that, and he missed his grandfather.

One evening, he found a long box in the living room. It had a big lid and lots of shining handles. He moved a chair across and climbed up to look in, and then he got a big surprise! There was his grandfather, hiding in the box, and he had fallen fast asleep.

"Grandfather," he cried out happily, "I've found you. Where have you been?"

There was no reply. He leaned over and prodded his grandfather. "Wake up, Grandfather. It's me, Otto." He was shaking his grandfather, more persistently now. "Why don't you talk to me?" his parents heard him asking. When they rushed into the living room, they found him right inside the coffin, hugging his grandfather and trying to wake him up.

Julianna lifted him off and comforted him. Otto simply could not understand that Grandfather had died. He realised that death was what had happened to the old horse, the one that they had put down when he could not walk properly any more. However, this was not like that at all. His grandfather was a real person, somebody he talked to and loved. It was a long time before he stopped asking, "Where is grandfather?" There was a huge hole in his life now, after his first encounter with mortality.

Adventures at School

Otto was soon sent to the little school in Arberg, for his basic schooling. He was a handsome young boy already. He had quite a forest of curly, blonde hair, and a look of great character about him. He used to walk into his class, all bright and chirpy, and he was not the sort of boy who got away with not being noticed.

The school classroom in Arberg

The village school was just on the other side of the road, so he did not have to go far at all. It was very convenient for the Weeger family. He was usually well behaved, and even considered himself to be quite a "good little man". However, there were times when boyish pranks just had to happen.

One day in grade five, Otto had made himself a little peashooter, or pellet gun, out of a goose quill. With a bit of practise, he had become quite accurate, and the little potato pellets could hit his classmates with quite a sting. When Mr. Wieland walked passed, one morning, on his way to the blackboard, it was just too much to resist.

Otto watched as he passed, and then drew the shooter to his lips. The potato bullet popped out with a quiet hiss and shot through the air. His friend, Alois, sitting at the desk with him, clamped his hand over his mouth to stop himself from bursting out laughing. The bullet hit the teacher sharply on his neck, and obviously gave him a nasty sting. His hand shot up to rub himself, and he swung around with eyes ablaze, to search for the offender.

Alois now kept perfect control, and all the little faces around were quite still. Their gaze was riveted on the blackboard, except for Otto; his control left him, and he began to turn a red and then a purple colour. He could actually feel the colour change spreading over him, but nothing would stop it. He knew his guilt had been revealed, and when the teacher asked, "who did that?" he answered with his raised hand. It was not so much out of honour, but just from realising the futility of trying to deny it.

Otto was marched up to the front of the class. "Bend!" ordered Mr Wieland. Otto was soon sprawled over the front desk, and the cane was raised high above him. (One of his classmates, Hans, used to get a beating at least once a week, and was quite experienced now. Hans was a bit of a cry-baby, and would be just about in tears even before he was hit, so he used to only get one or two lashes at the most.) Well, Otto braced himself, with great determination, and clenched the cheeks of his little bottom as he lay there, waiting.

With his pea-shooter

The cane whistled as it came down, and he felt the sting even before it hit him. He gritted his teeth firmly, and refused to yelp. The next lash came quickly after, and it was harder still. Then the next swing of the cane came whistling down on his already stinging bottom, and the next. He could taste a bit of blood in his mouth, and wondered if the cane had cut him. Perhaps the "cuts" caused him to bleed everywhere.

As his pain turned to some sort of numbness, he realised that he had bitten his cheek and his lip. Finally, it was too much and he cried at last. Mr. Wieland relented, having at last managed to get a reaction. Otto found it very painful to straighten up; it felt as if his poor little tail would almost fall off as he walked back very awkwardly to his seat. But the worst was sitting down. "Sit down, and behave yourself, young Weeger. I shall be reporting this to your father, and we shall see what he has to say about this behaviour," hurled Mr. Wieland, adding more fear to the whole painful episode.

On another occasion, Otto's classmate, Franz, pinched him hard in class, and he let out a sharp, "Ow!"

Herr Hummel swung around to see who it was, and his eyes quickly fixed on Otto. "Come out here!" he roared.

"No, I am innocent," explained Otto, quite convinced that it was Franz who should own up to the offence.

"What? Did I hear you correctly?" boomed the angry teacher.

"I did nothing," was Otto's worried reply. He knew well what stepping out in the aisle meant, and he was positive that he had done nothing wrong, so why should he be punished? Later, he would think of such injustices, and this was an early lesson in life—it is not always fair.

Herr Hummel was a man of action, and he soon grabbed Otto by the arm, and began to drag him out by force. But it didn't work! Otto clung to the legs of the desk with fierce determination. "Let go and come with me," he shouted, but to no avail. It looked as if Otto was going to win this little battle, but of course, that could not happen, and he relented. His obstinacy simply earned him an extra good hiding, for resisting his punishment. When he got home, his father, (who assumed that all teachers were fair and just, and men and women of integrity), was waiting for him.

He was standing there in the sitting room, with a fierce expression in his eyes. He looked like a lion, ready to pounce on his victim. Otto knew that he was in for a severe punishment. "How could you dishonour our family like this? First by your naughtiness, but even worse by running away from your punishment," shouted Josef.

Otto prayed to God that his dear mother would come to his rescue. She always understood and comforted him when he got hurt, or things went badly in some way. Meanwhile, his father carried on, "You have brought shame on the whole family. The honour of our Weeger name has been tarnished. How could you misbehave in that way? What got into your head to make you refuse to accept your punishment?"

Just then the door opened and his dear mother put her head around the corner. He breathed a sigh of relief. "Phew!"

Relief quickly changed to total disbelief, when she asked, "Father, do you want the big riem or the small belt to knock some sense into this disgraceful son of ours?"

Otto could only wonder how reports could get so distorted, and he still felt bitter at the injustice of having to submit to the teacher's punishment. And all he had done was to let out a yell, "Ow!" That was hardly a hanging offence! Anyway, he got the extra beating, and Josef said, "And what is more, Otto, you will have no food today just to help you remember how naughty you have been."

That was quite unnecessary, after his bottom stung from two hidings already, but that was the way it was to be. His stomach was aching with hunger as he went outside and huddled up behind the water trough. If ever food seemed desirable, it was then, and he certainly needed some consolation for the pain.

The water-trough and the Linden tree at the
Weegers' Gasthaus, in Arberg

His older sister had heard and watched it all, and when the coast was clear she went out the side door and sat down next to him at the water trough. From her dress she brought out a piece of bread and offered it to him. He could not form words, but his sad little face said everything. He took the bread, and slowly took a bite. After a second bite, which he chewed very slowly, he managed to say, "thank you, Juli."

She slipped her arms around his little shoulders and held him close to her for a while. Every now and again, she felt a little shiver as he gradually settled down. It was not long before he seemed fine again. "Are you all right, Otto?" she asked.

"Yes, I'm fine," he said more confidently now. "I just don't think it was fair at all!" he said indignantly. Then he started to sob quietly again, as he thought about it all over again. "It wasn't my fault. Franz did it."

"That happens, Otto," Juli said wisely. "I have had the same sort of thing happen to me, so I know what you mean."

"But why didn't father believe me?" he carried on, his lip quivering slightly still. "I tried to explain but he didn't want to listen!"

"It's grown-ups, Otto," she said. "They will always believe each other before one of us—even if we are their own family."

THE COUNTRYSIDE AND NATURE

Otto's home village, Arberg, was close to the big city of Nuremberg, and he grew up knowing that Bavaria is the most beautiful part of Germany. Arberg gets its name "the mountain of the eagles", from its position, built below the slight hill slopes, from where the eagles look out over vast areas of meadows, forests, tilled lands, rivers and, about sixty towns, villages and hamlets. It was a beautiful scenic ride to the north to reach the town of Ansbach.

As he grew up, Otto often noticed the eagles in the sky. They would soar high above, and their flight was graceful and free. He loved to watch them, sensing how they enjoyed just gliding about in the thermals or making display flights, as they hunted and defended their territory.

Otto loved it when the weekends came. After he had tidied his bed and cupboard, and done his chores at the Gasthaus, he would slip away on the old black bicycle with the wheels which were too big for him. He had to stand up to pedal, as he could not reach from the saddle, and he would go off towards what seemed like high mountains above the church. It was hard work, cycling up there, past the old castle and to the top; but he loved the views and there were so many different animals and birds. Coming back was easy, and he would cycle at great speed, sitting perched high on the saddle this time.

Otto had lots of direct and vivid contact with nature. He had the chance to play with and really fall in love with animals. His favourites were the new-born lambs, and he loved the kids and piglets on the farm. When a little lamb was born, he just wanted to hold and hug the cute little thing. "You have to give it back to its mother," Max explained. "If you keep it too long, the mother won't take it back, and then it could die from not having its mother's milk." Well that worked, and it was hard to know what would happen if Otto insisted on keeping the little lamb for too long.

Josef was fascinated by the weather, and used to talk about it often. "Look at that sun going down tonight," he said to Otto. "Tomorrow it will be raining again in the morning."

"How do you know, father?" Otto was intrigued. Josef found it hard to give simple explanations like barometric pressure changes, but he did his best. There was, of course, in the sitting room, a barometer, hygrometer and thermometer. He looked at them regularly, with great interest, and always asked his father to tell him what the weather was going to be. He was nearly always right.

His uncle gave Otto a weather-frog, which lived in a big glass with a little ladder. The frog would sit on the top rung when there was good weather, or descend when it was dull and miserable. There were only three rungs out of the water, and the rest of the ladder was submerged. The frog was really quite a good weatherman for forecasts, agreeing with his father's predictions most times. Otto was fascinated at how the frog and the instruments said the same things.

In winter, he had little snow battles, rode on the bob-sleighs, and went skating on the village lake. He joined in when the children built snowmen and snow-castles, and he took great pleasure in making and hurling snowballs, at his older brothers especially.

The forests grew right down into their village, and Otto only needed to walk a hundred metres from the house and he was in among the trees, with their birds, squirrels and deer. He often went off on his own little picnic outing, sometimes with one or two of his school-friends, but mostly on his own.

When it was cold and the birds could find no food out there, he fed the birds that came into their yard. Sometimes they could not fly properly because of the cold, and he was very sad when he discovered cats catching them. He soon decided he did not like cats. He chased them away and saved some birds, but often it was too late. The cats teased the birds; they pounced on them, then let them hop away wounded. Then they would spring back and spin around with the helpless little bird in their claws. They seemed quite evil in the way they made the poor birds suffer.

The Gasthaus

The inn had all sorts of visitors. Builders and carpenters were very good customers, and they drank huge amounts of beer. He watched one ruddy-faced man with a big beard one evening, as he drank tankard after tankard from a whole barrel that his friends had bought for him. Otto was positive that he saw his stomach swelling up, and it had to; where else was all that drink going? "How does he keep all that in?" he wondered.

He knew that he needed to go to the toilet when he was full, but this man seemed to be like a bag filling up, as he gulped down each glass, letting out loud burps every now and again. His friends all cheered him on, and clapped on his back when he had finished the whole barrel.

On Sundays, after attending Holy Mass at St Blasius, people would gather at the inn. He watched how some of them would down one beer after another. Most of them showed no signs of being drunk, though. They were all cheerful and friendly, and the inn was a loud and happy place. This was a man's world, and the women didn't really drink. They would come and go, but it was the men who stayed and kept his father and brothers busy.

It was clear that drinks were for celebrations. Sometimes these celebrations carried on for a long time, and he knew his father was very tired. He would never chase them out, though, and patiently kept on serving the guests, as they ordered, "more drinks, please!" Although they did not come there to get drunk, one or two sometimes left looking as if they might get lost on the street on the way home. Sometimes it was just one fellow who stayed on. Then, Julianna and everybody would become impatient. "Just one more drink," he would insist.

"Why can't Josef just tell him to go?" they would murmur. Whatever, they thought, though, they never interfered. Eventually the man would leave, and he could hear his father locking up, and his mother sometimes said, "at last; now come to bed, Josef. You must be exhausted."

One evening, Otto watched his father downing a glass of schnapps, and he asked him, "Why do you drink those smelly drinks, Dad?"

"It just warms my stomach," his father replied innocently. Later, he locked the cabinet and put away the key in the drawer of his beer wagon. A little pair of eyes had seen this all, and Otto waited until there was nobody around. It was a very cold night, and he fumbled as he got the key out of the drawer. Carefully, he put it in the cabinet and turned it. The door seemed to make a loud squeaking noise as he opened it slowly, and he waited. All was quiet. He twisted the cap off the schnapps bottle and brought it to his lips. Then he closed his eyes and took a big swig of the foul-tasting medicine.

He waited to feel the warm effect for himself. Suddenly, he felt sick, and his stomach wanted to bring up the drink he had just gulped down. He sat down in the chair, in the corner, and waited. There was no warm effect . . . ! His head now started to feel strange. He felt a bit dizzy."

"That schnapps is terrible," he decided. "I feel rotten." Then he stood up, but his legs were not listening properly. He managed to lock the cabinet, and got the key back into the drawer, but he did not go to kiss his mother good night, as he soon made his way to bed. The bed seemed to be spinning and he felt as if he was falling.

"Nobody must know," he kept reminding himself, and eventually he managed to get to sleep.

"Otto, did you see anybody go into my cabinet last night?" his father asked next evening. Well, he hadn't so he did not go into any details, but he never attempted to warm his stomach like that again! In fact, he always looked at his father with a curious expression when he saw him drinking schnapps.

"I don't know how it works for him, but I am certainly not going to try that again," he vowed to himself. Perhaps the abundance of alcohol and this experience of it were useful lessons to enable him to keep alcohol in perspective throughout his life.

A GHOST STORY

Travellers would often come in and tell tales. Otto was sitting behind the railing one evening, when a huge man from Berlin told his drinking companions that he was running away from a ghost. He had been chased out of his house, and he could not walk around near his home without being attacked by this fierce ghost, even in the wide streets.

"Oh, it's not true," they teased him, but he assured them in an ominous whisper. "You don't have to believe me, but be careful. There are ghosts in every town." They were subdued now. "I am sure somebody here has died and is not at rest," he said, as he could see he had their attention. "Maybe, even as you walk home this evening, he is watching you." Otto's eyes were wide, and he had a strange prickling sensation down his back. He shivered.

Two nights later, Julianna sent him down the road to sleep at his Aunt Wilma's house. The Gasthaus was full and some family had arrived and needed to be put up. "It's only for tonight," she told him, "and Maria is there already waiting for you." He went off with his little bag of clothes, but as he stepped out into the dark street, he felt scared.

He had often gone there before, and the darkness had never worried him before. It was very close, and all he had to do was cross the street and walk about three houses along. Tonight, everything felt different. He looked up and down the street, and then made his way across quickly.

Suddenly, he heard a scratching sound. He froze in his tracks and then pressed up against the wall. It was nothing, he decided after a short while. He whistled a tune as he made his way, and then he started to sing a little song he knew from school. Maria stepped out from the gate of the house and he was startled. "Why are you singing?" she asked.

"No reason," he said, and then he added, "I like that song."

"You are afraid," she said teasingly.

"Oh no, I'm not," he retorted, thrusting out his little chest defiantly. She did not press the point, but they went in together, and he was never so pleased to have a door close on the night behind him.

Farm Machines

One night he woke up in a fright, with a yell that brought Aunt Wilma to his room. When she came through to him, he was curled up, with his knees tightly tucked in. She sat down on the bed. "Was ist los?" she enquired comfortingly.

He realised he had just had a dream, but it had been so vivid. He hated that chopping machine in the stadel. He understood how the horses turned it, (or sometimes they used cows), in the yard below. He had climbed up and looked at the machine on the first floor, and seen the huge cogs and axles that drove it somehow. Karl and Max were feeding in the lucerne and silage from the pile they had mixed and tossed up from below onto the wooden floor.

Every now and again, it seemed to make a rasping noise, and Karl would bend low and push silage deep into the narrow opening. He saw his hand so close to the blades that were chopping everything up into fine pieces. "Be very, very careful of this machine," his father warned him. "You have seen Klaus and Fritz. That's how they lost fingers and hands."

One day Karl faked an injury, pulling his arm out of the opening but tucking it in so it looked as if he had nothing from his elbow. He hopped up and down and clutched his arm with a red cloth that he had concealed. Otto was devastated, and ran to the house crying for help.

Now, he had dreamed that it had happened to him. His brothers had been there and told him it was his turn to clear the blockage and he had caught his hand in the blades. When he woke up, it even felt as if his arm was still in pain. "My arm, my arm," he said.

"There, there," she soothed, as she examined it. "I think you were lying on it and you have 'pins and needles'. It's fine. Nothing is wrong."

A LIGHTNING FRIGHT

When he was about seven years old, Otto was walking home through the forest one afternoon with his sister, Maria. The sky was dark and ominous and soon a thunderstorm began. The earth seemed to shake with the rumbling. Lightning was arcing from the clouds to earth and sending long fingers of electric light across the sky. He held Maria's hand tightly as they walked along the road on the way home.

There was a strange smell and suddenly his hair seemed to stand on end; at the same time there was a terrific bang and a bolt of lightning shot right between them. "Yow!" they screamed in unison, as they reeled from the shock. They felt its heat and electricity, and were momentarily blinded by the sharp light. How had it missed striking them? It had shot right between them, but not even burned them! What a close shave!

His mother, Julianna, did not like lightning at all. "Be careful of the lightning," she often cautioned them. "Come inside, and get away from the lightning," she would say, or "don't touch anything with iron when the lightning is about." When they were out walking and a storm was in the air, she would warn them, "keep away from the trees. "When you see lightning, you must never run under a tree for shelter. That is the first place the lightning will aim for." Her protective instincts were at their strongest with lightning, and she certainly wanted them to always be prepared.

Arberg had a lot of thunderstorms, and storms featured strongly in his life as a child and later on as well. Several times as he grew up, lightning struck trees near him, and roofs of buildings in the village, but he was never harmed. All the same, it was a powerful demonstration of some almighty power, such a fierce outburst of nature at its most dangerous. He would feel the same again later when it happened to him in the African forests.

ANIMALS ALL AROUND

Otto grew up in this natural and rural community, with lots of animals, agriculture and the pleasures of watching life close at hand. They kept sheep, pigs, cows, dogs and horses. All of them needed to be herded and fed, so Otto had his share of the duties as he grew up. The animals sensed his love for them, and seemed to communicate with him, or at least he felt they understood a lot more than grown-ups thought they could.

He stood watching the little calf as it quickly ran to its mother. It gave a little bounce, and did a playful sideways movement. Reaching its mother, she nuzzled its head, and then the calf dived under her and grabbed a teat with its mouth. Soon there was a sucking and releasing sound, and the calf swung her rear around towards the cow's head, pushing her tummy firmly against the cow's foreleg

Her tail swung joyfully backwards and forwards and the suckling continued. When the first teat was emptied it moved to the next. Suddenly, it released its grip, and gave a huge head-butt to her mother's udders. Reflexively, the cow lifted her leg, as if in painful reaction; but the milk flowed better, and the little tail was swaying vigorously back and forth, hitting the cow's neck. She attended to her fresh little daughter's clean-up, licking her everywhere, as only a devoted mother can.

The farm animals were part of his growing up experiences

Another duty he enjoyed was to exercise the big horse. It was a huge animal in his young eyes, but had a special intelligence far greater than the other animals. It was powerful, but he sensed how it was ageing; just like his grandfather had been. He noticed how it seemed stiff when he first took it out of the stadel, and he was careful not to hurt it. (Much later on in life, a hip injury of his own would remind him of this strong old horse.)

Summer came and he was fascinated by the young European storks that he used to see, in their nests on the village chimneys. They waited patiently there while their parents were finding food in the marshes along the rivers. Sometimes he saw the huge birds walking stiff-legged in the fields, especially when there were lots of frogs about.

As the leaves changed colour and began to fall from the trees, the storks flew in little flocks and he often saw them high in the sky. The time came when they began to move in large flocks, migrating south. Their necks and legs were stretched out like darts, and their big wings with the black tips, seemed to hardly ever flap as they sailed in the supporting air.

He was intrigued as it was explained to him at school. "They travel a long way, so that they can spend winter far away in Africa."

"Why do the storks go there?" he asked.

"It is warm in Africa, and it gets very cold here in winter," the teacher replied. "Storks would never survive our winters in Germany or Europe." Their winter weather was setting in, and he thought, 'Africa must be a very nice place!'

Their migration was quite a sight. The flocks would gather and gradually groups of them began taking to the air, as they set off on these enormous journeys. As he visualised the warm African sun, he wondered if the frogs were bigger there.

Storks flying overhead, migrating from Europe's winter

After supper, he was in the living room with his father. It seemed a good chance to talk, and his older sisters and brothers were not around to ridicule him, because somehow he often found that they knew these things already. "How do the storks know where to go?" was one of the questions Otto asked.

"I think that they have some sort of built-in magnetic compass," suggested Josef.

"How far do they have to fly?" was the next question.

"They fly six or seven thousand kilometres, but they do it in a period of days or even weeks," Josef explained to his fascinated listener. "They use the winds which blow in the right direction for them, high up in the sky."

Then there was a whole string of questions which he had not had the nerve to ask at school, as he attempted to understand this amazing phenomenon.

That night, Otto went to bed wondering if he could fly somehow. Furthermore, if he could fly, would he make such a long journey, to darkest Africa? What would he find there? Nature was a big part of his life, but his real love of nature really grew in later years, when he followed those birds. Perhaps it was these storks which first made him think of far-off Africa.

FUTURE COMMITMENT

Herr Mayr looked old and weary, sitting quietly on the bench outside the church, while the sun was setting. Otto had finished his errand early, and knew this man was a good friend of their family. "Hi, Otto," he was greeted warmly. "What are you doing with your holiday?"

"Nothing much, Herr Mayr. I'm mainly helping my father and brothers with the animals," he replied cheerfully. There was a pause, the sort of thing a child can't ever allow. "Where do you work?" Otto asked.

"Oh, I work in the textile mill, over there," he pointed out.

"What do you do, Herr Mayr?"

"I am a weaver; we weave threads to make it into cloth," he replied. "It's a tough job, you know," he added as an after-thought.

"Why?" Otto asked innocently; and then his jaw dropped as he received the full blast of Herr Mayr's pent-up frustrations.

"Well, I have to get up very early, and walk to work. Usually it's very cold or raining, so I get there, feeling quite rotten. Then, I have to set and watch the big machine. It is a dirty and noisy place. I can't hear anybody speak over the noise; and we don't stop for even one minute for the whole day. If the machine ever stopped, I would be in big trouble, and they would fire me!"

"That sounds terrible," Otto sympathised.

"It is very bad, and what is worse, I get paid almost nothing at all for all my hard work and suffering."

"Then, why don't you go and get a better job?" he asked in logical surprise.

"What!" Herr Mayr exploded. Otto sensed that he had made an outrageous suggestion, and Herr Mayr explained, "I have worked for this company all my life, from when I was fifteen years old. They have paid me everything I have earned. I wouldn't dream of working for anybody else. They are my employers." This was said with such force that Herr Mayr must have presumed he had settled the issue without any room for the slightest option. "And besides, that's what life's all about; you have to give your full commitment to your employer."

"I see," Otto relented quickly, but not really with wholehearted conviction.

After family supper that evening, he asked, "Father, will I have to make a full commitment to my employer one day?"

"What are you talking about?" Josef responded, wondering where such an unusual question had originated.

As usual, the explanation followed, "well, Herr Mayr was telling me about his work, and that's what he said. He said you can never go and work for somebody else."

"Oh, Herr Mayr," Joseph nearly dismissed the topic. However, something else occurred to him, and perhaps he sensed that Otto needed to find a career of his own away from their farm and Gasthaus. "Well, I think it's true," he said. "There is no point doing anything at all in life, if you don't do it with your full commitment. Whatever you do, you must dedicate yourself to it, and give of your very best. And when you find the job you intend doing, you stick to it and give it your very best always. You certainly don't want to live like the gypsies."

Otto nodded and was silent. A fleeting vision came to mind, of the circus gypsies and their animals, tricks, music and gymnastics, and that seemed quite exciting, despite his father's assumption. He quickly banished the images, as he heard his father's voice.

"Why are you asking about work? Have you thought what you want to be when you grow up?"

"Not yet, but I will do it well, father," he replied.

HIGHER STUDIES

When it came to decision time about Otto's High schooling, a hard choice had to be made by Josef and Juliana. They had been through the anguish of deciding what was best for Josef, and they had sent him off to Lohr for his High schooling the year before. He was quite homesick at first, but he was managing now, and he was quite academic and serious.

But Otto was different. He, too, had shown great promise at school, but he was so keen and adventurous. Did he need to be controlled more? It costs a lot to educate a child in the classics, and sending him away costs an extra amount, because they must pay for boarding and travelling and so on.

Their home was very full, there was so much work to do in the businesses, and there were many pressures on the family finances. The girls accepted that they had to learn practical, domestic skills, including sewing and cooking and the like. The older boys both trained in trades, learning the skills of butchery, baking, farming and carpentry. Josef had been given the chance to go on to Higher Studies, and now they both realised they had to make the necessary sacrifices to send a second child away to use his intellectual skills.

Parents—Joseph and Julianne Weeger

CHAPTER 2

THE FLEDGLING MOVES ON

WHICH WAY WILL HE GO?

During the summer holidays, Josef sat with Julianna one afternoon, catching up on a rare chance to be alone, amid the constant flow of guests and family, and the hard routine of work on a busy farm. "Otto is growing up to be a fine young boy," commented Josef. "Look how strong he has become already, and he is not even twelve years old."

"He had better be a bit careful, though," Julianna pondered aloud, "I have seen the way Karl looks at him when he pushes his luck a bit too far."

"I don't think Otto will be pushed around like a baby brother for too many more years," replied Josef. "I am afraid that I can see ahead to a day when there will be fighting among the boys."

Quickly changing the subject, Julianna said, "it is time we made the bookings for his senior schooling. We have to decide where he should go."

"He is certainly bright enough to go on to university." Josef said wistfully. "Of course it would be great to have another son helping me here, but perhaps it is best for him to go away and study further." Josef waited for the response, ready to weigh up Julianna's motherly instincts. She was a good wife and mother, and she knew each of their children so well that he was not at all obstinate about listening to her ideas on this subject.

Fortunately, she did not intrude or overdo things; she knew many women whose husbands did not take at all kindly to a wife trying to push her husband along.

"He is a very devout young boy, and I think he could even have a calling to serve the Church in some way, perhaps even to follow his older brother Josef, and become a priest," was Julianna's opinion. "He could go to Lohr-on-Main, and study there."

Luggage—ready to travel to Boarding School

"Do you think he should become a priest also?" asked Josef, a bit alarmed now.

She smiled, as she looked him in the face. He was such a good man, so practical and human. "Only if it is God's will, but somehow I do not see him taking that step," she replied with a re-assuring voice.

"Well, where would he stay?" asked Josef practically.

"Young Josef has been there for three years now, and he has been happy enough at the Aloysianum boarding house. He would just be one of the boarders, but it is close enough to walk." Julianna continued, "And we know that he will be well cared for by the Mariannhill fathers."

There was a pause as they both let things sink in to their minds. 'Why was Otto so different?' wondered Josef. 'His older brothers have their lives mapped out, following in my footsteps and continuing the businesses which generations of Weegers have nourished . . . . except for young Josef, who is studying to become a priest.'

Then there was the cost to consider. "However, Julianna, we have to understand what we will be letting ourselves in for. We shall have to pay over thirty marks a term, and that is just for Otto's fees and lodging," worried Josef.

"As I have said before, we could certainly do with some extra help here. There is so much to do on the farm, in the Gasthaus, or the butchery. Is it fair on Karl and Max? Look how they are helping me now. And, of course, Rosa and Julianna are wonderful with the Gasthaus and the bakery."

"I don't know, either. He just seems so different; I don't mean he's afraid of work," said Julianna. "In fact, I think he would be our hardest working son if he stayed and joined the family here."

"He could certainly be a great scholar or a well-educated leader; and we will certainly need more people like that, especially the way I see things developing here in Germany," mused Josef.

"I certainly agree with you on that," said Julianna, "but we must think what is best for him, now."

"And what is that?"

"We don't know yet which way he shall go, but he always seems to love learning new things. We simply have to make the sacrifice. After all, that is our principal responsibility in life—to develop our children. We don't have to build things up and pass them on to the children. They can all fend for themselves once we have trained them."

"You are nearly always right," he said, reaching for her tender, but hard-working hands.

"I have really missed Josef, being away so much. He is our great gift to God and the church, and I feel as though we have lost the right or the chance to influence and help him. I will really struggle if we must let Otto go away as well," she went on.

"My wife, I know all those things, but we both know that he is different," he went on gently. Then Josef behaved like quite a different person, as he went on, "you know, I think he is like a young eagle, one that is ready to learn how to fly. In him this sticks out more than in any of our other children, really."

Julianna looked at Josef in surprise, as he continued, explaining, "he is also quite used to being independent. Look how often he goes for long cycling trips. He also hikes and climbs all over the countryside around here."

"That's true enough. He loves the outdoors, and he definitely is the most adventurous of all our children." Again, she came back to his academic side, and said, "he deserves whatever we can manage, and he is certainly a very diligent and self-disciplined young boy. He will not disappoint us, and I think Higher Studies are what he needs."

The parents had reached an agreement of minds, after testing and challenging one another. They just needed to check if they had both been thinking it all through. Once that was done, the rest became easy. "It's not that far away if he needs anything, and we will see him during all the long holidays. He will not have any of his classmates with him, but I think he makes friends easily," Josef added.

"Josef has already made a lot of good friends, and he will be there to guide Otto as his big brother," said Juliana.

"I already know more or less what it will cost us, but we shall look at our finances again, and we can make a final decision before the end of summer holidays," Josef concluded the discussion.

ASKING QUESTIONS

Josef junior came home from Lohr-on-Main for part of the summer holidays. Otto could not get enough time with him; there was so much to do, but he grabbed every moment he could get; or as much as a big brother would allow in among all the activity and chatting of home. Josef was such a sociable brother, always talking and with so much knowledge and a wonderfully descriptive talent. He described people like the teachers to perfection, and often with such great humour. The way he spoke about them kept Otto in awe, and sometimes in bouts of unstoppable laughter.

"Why did you decide to become a priest?" Otto asked one evening.

"Otto, you probably would not understand yet. There were many things," he said warmly. "I think I somehow just knew that God wanted me to become one of his workers."

"Isn't it a hard life? Otto asked him.

"Yes, and no." Josef replied. "Firstly, you have to give up girls; but you are not worrying about that just yet," he said with a smile. "But once you've decided, everything seems to make sense."

"Can anybody become a priest?" asked Otto.

Josef looked closely at his younger brother now. This conversation was no longer about him; Otto was asking serious questions for a young boy. It seemed to Josef that they might be too serious, and he worried about influencing an impressionable little brother. "It's certainly not the life for everybody," he answered. "In fact, I don't think there are very many people who can survive. I just hope and pray that I can."

Otto sat silently, with respectful admiration, partly distracted by deep thoughts of his own as his older brother continued, "Already, I have realised that I must study very hard. Then, I shall have to live a very disciplined life, getting up early every day to pray and say Holy Mass. I have to be available to all my parishioners, when their children die, or when they are sick. I have to listen to their sins in confession and give them guidance and penances." Otto seemed to be drifting off in thought and he sensed that he was probably overdoing the details now. He stopped and looked at Otto, full in the eyes, with a kindly expression. He asked, "Why do you want to know?"

"Nothing, really." Otto answered, and then he continued, "but I just wonder what it would be like, you know, if I also wanted to be a priest." Then he looked away and continued swinging his little legs, as he sat on the bench next to his brother. Before Josef had time to respond, he had another question and out it came. "Why did you not choose to become a missionary priest, and go off to Africa or South America?"

His ready response to Otto's earlier chatter had been easy, but now, he had to think for a while. "I am not sure if I could have made such a big choice," he answered. "It means leaving home and family for ever; and I am not that bold. Also I would have had to start my studies last year, so I am too late now. But it's also great fun, studying; you should see some of the characters who teach us. You think Herr Hummel looks funny, but one of our lecturers has long hair like a woman, or an olden-days nobleman. Another one has a head that shines like that pot over there; and his nose is huge, like a big turnip," and he demonstrated with his hand.

Otto burst out laughing as he always did when his brother started describing people. He could almost see them right there in front of him, as Josef went on to describe the tricks they played sometimes, or to make up thoughts of what must be going through the minds of the lecturers as they stormed down the passage to the classrooms. He felt deeply complimented by Josef, the way his older brother took time to chat with him, and he just loved the way that Josef was able to describe people and things, with such clarity and humour.

Farm Chores and Home Life

The next morning, the children were all pressed into service, while the women chopped cabbages into strips and pieces, and tossed them over the edge, into the huge wooden vat. Once the first layer of cabbage was deep enough, salt was added and they were called. "Come along, children; in you get."

They jostled one another as they climbed the steps set up at the side of the tank, and lowered themselves, one at a time, over the edge, into the deep wooden tank. They started moving around slowly, squishing the soft leaves with their bare feet. "It feels all slimy," Otto said to his cousin. More cabbage was flung in, and more salt was added, and they began to warm to the mood, kicking and holding onto each other, as they began to move faster and faster.

More cabbage was added, and more, and around and around they went. The leaves became softer and squishy, and they sank to their calves. Salt again, and more leaves, and they were finding it harder to move around as they sank deeper into the sauerkraut vat.

It was fun, though, and there was a closeness of contact, something that a young boy found enjoyable, but strange. He found that it was especially nice to be bumping into his cousin, Rosie, and her little friend, Anna. He didn't mind that he was getting tired, and he could have kept going for as long as was required.

It was soon lunchtime, and they stopped for a well-earned rest. His feet were certainly clean, but very wrinkled from the moisture. As they sat on the benches, eating delicious wurst and bread, his father came and sat beside him.

"What do you want to become when you grow up?" asked Josef.

"I want to be a farmer, or a doctor, or a lawyer, or an engineer, or a teacher, or an accountant . . ."

"Whoa!" his father stopped him. "You will have to choose one of these, you know. You cannot do all of that in one life." He looked deep into Otto's eyes as he asked him, "what about going to Lohr-on-Main, and joining your brother for studies? Then you can see what is possible, and make a decision later on."

That sounded very exciting to Otto, and more than he could ever have dreamed of.

FAMILY SUNDAYS

Sunday was always the same. No matter what else was going on, with visitors, the farm duties, the weather or what was happening around them, Sunday was an island of continuous security, like the family photos and confirmation certificates, hanging in the passage. This day was always the same, and was set aside as the day of the Lord. It was a time for strict fasting before Mass, and Otto's tummy often cried out for food and drink. No matter what he thought about—something like a simple little slice of bread, or a small glass of milk—he always knew and accepted that today it was impossible!

The whole family dressed up in the best clothes they had, and they walked or ran, more or less together, up the village road, to attend the solemn, High Mass. The church of Saint Blasius had been finely built and it was beautifully decorated; it had the history of centuries adding to the atmosphere of God's presence. A red sacristy lamp hung from a high chain in front of the altar, and the candles burning on the ornate altar and the statues helped Otto to feel deep reverence, as they sat there together in their family group. Sometimes they were allowed up into the gallery at the back, from where he could look onto the congregation and the art below. The gargoyle with a red tongue frightened him a bit, but he would walk down past it quickly.

After Mass, there were still chores that had to be done. The house and Gasthaus had to be cleaned. Animals had to be fed, and were already complaining when it was late. Meals had to be prepared for themselves and any guests they had. Then they would go for a walk and visit friends and relatives in the village. Sometimes the friends would come to them for something to eat and drink. Sundays were very sociable and active days.

NATIONAL PRIDE

Bavaria was never conquered by the Roman Empire; the Romans gave up and built a tall and thick stone wall to mark its defensible boundary. Some remains of these '*limes*' were close to Arberg, a proud reminder of their strength and indomitability. Apart from its rightful pride in German arts and culture, and a claim to being the best-educated nation in the world, severe difficulties had begun to cripple Germany economically. "What are these reparation costs all about?" he asked his father one day.

His father shot him an angry look, but settled down after a few seconds. "Well, we were eventually over-run by all their armies that came against us and the French and British demanded that we must pay them back what they call 'reparation costs'; it is like a punishment, to teach us a lesson. The Versailles Treaty imposed huge penalties on us. Who has ever heard of paying back one hundred and thirty two billion gold marks? This is what is crippling our German industry. What is more, for over ten years, we have not even been allowed to build our own submarines, warships, planes and guns."

Young Otto caught the gist of what his father told him, but he felt deeply out of his depth, and was a bit worried about this sort of conversation with his father. He didn't enjoy the strong emotions that were building up and it even seemed to be somehow directed at him. 'It was not my fault', he knew, but this was clearly an unpleasant subject.

Germany had actually been quite fortunate with the limited amount of damage that had been done to it, even though it had been violently repulsed from occupied France. Now, the French were arrogantly parading their military strength on its borders, and enjoying the fruits of mandates over confiscated German colonies.

A cocky little agitator, called Adolf Hitler, had just been imprisoned in Landsberg, and had apparently been silenced by the Bavarian government that he had tried to overthrow. Germany had also just signed the Locarno Pact that guaranteed its frontiers with France and other nations, and this had helped to restore trade with the major powers. Now welcomed into the League of Nations, Germany was sure that its pleas for fair treatment would soon be heard, and relief would come to its battle-scarred economy.

Time was moving on, and forces were at work that few outsiders fully grasped. Germany's Chancellor, Stresemann, was scoring convincingly against the weak successors of France's Clemenceau. Furthermore, on a military front, a strong trio of French generals was fading from the scene, and their successors would prove soft targets for the new Germany.

MILITARISATION

It was impossible to suppress the deeply ingrained German military instincts, and much was already beginning to happen behind the scenes. German airmen were even being trained in secret for the day when a powerful Luftwaffe would seize control of the skies. Military leaders were not prepared to take defeat as final and binding.

For a while the ideals of the Weimar Republic had appealed strongly. Hopes faded, though, and a view was already formed and being fanned, that all the wealth and economic power was being wielded by the Jews. (Jewish establishments were known for offering their wares at just a fraction below the other shopkeepers' prices.) Times were getting tougher, and competition conquered other loyalties.

Those who kept losing business to Jews in this way fostered these resentments. They did not think that money was their own drive; however, to them it always seemed to be the chief Jewish ambition and driving force—a false idol down through the ages. The Chosen People, whom God promised never to forsake, still suffered the hatred of some people who did not want to forget whose ancestors had crucified their own Messiah, somehow forgetting that Jesus himself, and the earliest Christians were mostly Jews. Misguided church leaders added confusion to this vexed question, the crux of Christianity, still thought to be unforgivable in the hearts of so many.

A new, proud, German spirit was forming again, one of hope and, with it, a spark of rebellion. Damaged national pride was being revived again. Oswald Spengler wrote a book, "Third Way", which introduced the concept of the Fuhrer, a man who would be a charismatic leader, and especially as one of the pure race, the Volk.

And sure enough, one soon arose who seemed to fit the description. "It is time to shake off the yoke of oppression," they heard the strutting young Adolf Hitler urging, soon after he had come out of Landsberg prison.

In the meantime, Lenin died, and the ruthless Stalin had inveigled his way into taking over full power, but now with an ominously more firm grip, and a cruel streak which he began using right from the start. America and Britain appeared to be changing policy in favour of lending finance and other resources to German business. These were assets that they desperately needed to rebuild their once-mighty industries. The Ruhr again had the potential to be a mighty centre of real production.

Gymnasium

As the leaves on the trees lost their greenness, Otto began to realise what it would mean to leave home. There were so many things that he enjoyed and which made him very happy at home. He was used to a routine of family meals and prayers. He had family and friends who loved him and he spent time with them. He knew his surroundings in great detail, and this all added up to 'being home'. These feelings always passed, but he experienced some strong twinges of apprehension, and a foretaste of loneliness and discomfort.

Fathers soon feel the pain that must come somehow with sons, when they fall from their own lofty pedestal; and sure enough, one day Josef carelessly killed a lizard. "What are you looking at me like that for?" Josef exclaimed, as he saw Otto's expression. "It is only a creature with no life or soul." Otto was shocked and deeply saddened.

That was certainly not the way he saw things, and he thought of the other lizards and the squirrels that he fed with breadcrumbs and seeds. His mind flashed back briefly to an unjust punishment he had once been given. This view of the lizard didn't fit the image that he had built up of his father.

He was saddened and felt a hot, deep anger. He never really got over this, or forgave his father for the way he killed the lizard; it was so off-hand, without any care or regrets. (At the time, there was also a lot of careless hunting going on in places like Africa, although it was treated as brave exploits, and the hunters were heroes to most people.) This incident cauterised that male instinct in him, and he just could not kill carelessly; his love of nature grew more protective, and remained with him all his life. (Later, when he had to do it sometimes, in Africa, he used to regret killing creatures like snakes and scorpions, even though they had the potential to do him severe harm.)

When the day came to go to Lohr-on-Main, Otto knew he was leaving everything he was used to; his family, his home, his pets, his farm, his friends, his safe little world. However, he was also quite excited, and he looked forward to his new school with great intensity. He bravely said goodbye to his mother and father, and boarded the train with his big brother. It was quite an adventure, and these thoughts helped him to overcome his sadness at going, as the train pulled out of the station, and they rode quietly in the carriage together.

Lohr-on-Main is a beautiful little city, and the Aloysianum Boarding Establishment was right on the bank of that idyllic river—with its boats, canoes, ferries and cargo ships. The Gymnasium was one of Germany's best, and everybody in Germany knew their education system was the best in the world. Otto was happy and proud, and he knew that he had been given a unique opportunity.

Many of his friends would still do their six years of schooling, and go on to qualify as professionals, or men with trades. He, however, had this chance to study in the classical tradition. Nine years lay ahead of him, and he was excited and determined to absorb all he could. He would not waste a moment of this time, and he certainly knew it was a great gift from his parents. Otto was determined to do more than the average person does, in everything that he tackled.

He was not fully aware of what it meant to be sent to Gymnasium. This was definitely the education preferred by those who could afford it, and involved a long and thorough training with standard compulsory subjects, (history, geometry, mathematics, physics, geography, drawing, painting), plus classical training.

What he found to be the most difficult subjects were the classical languages, Latin from fourth year and Greek from sixth year. However, he did very well in languages and was well ahead of his classmates in these. Otto also took French and Italian, although he hardly used them later on in life.

The school was mixed, and there were a few girls among the mainly boys who had this education. Some of them were quite noticeably attractive, and Otto was just beginning to realise that there was something quite stirring about the sight or thought of a girl's charms.

He noticed the way their skirts concealed but revealed their shape, when they walked ahead of him, or sat on their chairs in front of him; he was captivated by their beauty, as he looked into bright shining eyes and generous lips, with glowing hair that swung so invitingly as they looked away in shyness or teasing. But life was busy and active, and he didn't have too much time to slip into daydreaming about them.

Their day began at the boarding establishment when they rose at five thirty, and shortly after that they gathered for morning prayers, Holy Mass and then breakfast. After that there was the long walk to school.

Otto was soon at home here, and he had plenty to keep him fully occupied. His Catholic faith had been deeply instilled into him already, and the Aloysianum built up further on this. Through the prayers and Holy Masses, he felt strongly guided and supported by God.

He often prayed when he was alone, in appreciation for all that he had. He also prayed for guidance and help in choosing the right vocation, and living a good life.

Sport and its Hazards

Exercise, physical training and sport were an important part of the curriculum, and Otto enjoyed and practised a lot of gymnastics. He continued to develop his great strength, and the parallel bars, rope or pole climbing and many other exercises all developed his manly characteristics to the full. He enjoyed football and volleyball because he loved the team participation that all young men need; and he loved to swim in his free time.

The rivers were beautiful for this, especially as it drew closer to summer, although he swam all year round, and even in winter he would jump in and navigate his way through big ice floes. In summer, the cabins and jetties along the riverbanks were perfect for swimming and socialising. One afternoon, he dived in from the jetty and had a good swim up the river, pitching his power against the current. When he was tired enough, he made for the shoreline, and rested on the grass for a while.

Heinz came dashing down the path in his swimming costume, and yelled, "hey, come on in. I will race you to old Spengler's jetty!"

Well, that was a challenge, and Otto didn't give it a second thought. "You have no chance," he shouted, and he was up and chasing in a flash. As he ran in, and launched himself into a racing dive, he suddenly felt a sharp pain under his right foot.

He had definitely stood on something among the stones, and he had done so with all his weight and thrust. He pulled up short in the water and lurched back to the bank, where he sat down on the grass. Then he looked down at his foot and saw the blood pouring out through a deep gash. He splashed water on to try and clear away the blood. He looked at his foot in horror, and nearly fainted when he realized the damage he had done. It must have been an old bottle he landed on, and it had punctured deeply, nearly slicing his foot in half.

Heinz looked back; he soon saw that there was no longer any contest, and he swam swiftly back to see what was wrong. He let out a yell, "Mein Gott! Otto, what have you done?" Quickly, Otto bound up the wound with his trousers, and together they limped up to the path. Fortunately, a group of men passing by took pity on them, and bundled them both onto the back seat of their van, sitting on their drenched towels and clothes. Making their way up from the river, they were soon at the hospital.

"Young man, you are very lucky. Another half centimetre and I would not have been able to fix your foot to move again," reprimanded the surgeon who stitched him up.

"I am sorry, sir," Otto replied respectfully.

"Ah, these things happen. I am sure it is very painful now, is it?"

"Yes it is," Otto admitted.

"I don't know how you managed, but you just missed severing the main tendon. Now you must rest your foot well, or you will still lose the movement. You will have to stay here tonight, and I want to check your foot again tomorrow before I let you go home."

After noon the next day, he was discharged. Plastered up tightly, and with a new pair of crutches, Otto headed back to the boarding house. His classmates cast admiring looks at this plaster cast, it was the equivalent of a duelling scar for young boys, and Otto was one of those who had achieved a suitable injury with flying colours!

It was many weeks before he was off the crutches, but he took good care. Somehow he knew full well just how important his feet would be for the rest of his life. Soon he was taking part again in all the sports he could, including football, classical training in fencing, and horse riding.

One day, while they were enjoying a wild snow battle, he was hit on the right eye with a hard snowball. It was so sudden and so intense that he instinctively reached back with his hand, as if he was going to pick up his eyeball at the back of his skull. He was in great pain for a while but he didn't realise then how he had damaged the retina. (The effects on his eyes were felt many years later, when surgery was needed[1], and accelerated his failing eyesight towards the end of his life.)

He had another mishap at High School. He was a good and keen athlete, but on one occasion he lost his grip whilst swinging on the horizontal bar and came right down on his head. He was lying there stunned and paralysed for a couple of minutes, and thought he must have broken his neck. However, he soon got up and carried on normally. About thirty years later, though, he realized that serious damage had been done to several vertebrae and he began to suffer from sharp neck-aches and other pains coming from pinched nerves. (One of the discs was even displaced so much that it could easily be felt protruding, a small lifelong injury.) That was to be one of the crosses he had to bear, and he did so without complaining about it.

He loved horses and rode them with great strength and understanding. They seemed to sense that he liked them, and would respond willingly to his firm controls. Although still a young boy, he sat a horse with his back rigidly upright, in a comfortable harmony with his horse. He had poise and a commanding air about him, like some of the statues of famous men, at the fort on the hill.

At times he would even swim with the horses in the river. It was an enjoyable way to give them their washing down.

Time passed quickly, and the terms were broken by the trips and holidays home to Arberg. He loved the summer days; later only would he come to understand and appreciate how those extra hours of daylight make Europe so special. Of course, summer was a time of work, and he pitched in with his brothers and helped with the many duties on the land, and in the barns or animal stalls.

---

[1]   In his later years when he found his eyesight fading, his right eye gave him noticeably more trouble. At 92, he would begin the day with reasonable reading ability; by the time he had said his morning office and read a few other things he could soon barely make out the letters.

SIBLING RIVALRY SETTLED

On his first short holiday at home, the Christmas presents were all given out from under the tree, and he received a fine shirt. The next day was Sunday, and shortly before time to go to church, Max appeared in the barnyard, wearing Otto's new shirt. Max was well dressed, with his winter jersey and trousers with breach stockings. He was a fine, handsome young man, but he was in Otto's new shirt!

Otto was very angry. "Take off that shirt; it was my Christmas present," he commanded his older and much bigger brother.

"You cheeky little so-and-so. Who do you think you are, talking to me like that?" yelled his big brother.

"Take it off right now, it's mine," Otto stood his ground.

"You cheeky kid. I will kill you," was the sudden angry response.

"If you can!" Otto retorted.

That was the last straw for older brother, and off Max went into the butcher shop. Suddenly he was at the door, holding a huge butcher's knife on high, and threatening Otto. His eyes were not the same, and he really looked fully capable of a fierce fight.

"Go ahead!" was the brave reply, as he stood there with his little knees perceptibly trembling. He was sweating now and could feel the perspiration in his trousers, but he ripped his shirt open and bared his young chest, daring Max to make good his threat.

Suddenly, light seemed to flood back into Max's crazed eyes, and he was totally disarmed by his little brother's gesture. "I'm sorry, Otto," he said, "here is your shirt back." A whole new respect grew from then on, and Max suddenly stopped looking upon Otto as merely his baby brother.

THE BEAUTY OF LOHR

The walking distance from the Aloysianum to High School was about one and a half kilometres and it took about twenty minutes. It was a daily chore, but he came to enjoy walking through the beautiful gardens along the way, strolling on paths built centuries ago, on the banks of the Main River.

Through summer it was very pleasant, but when winter came, the temperature dropped right down to between minus five and minus ten degrees Celsius. The morning was bitterly cold at seven thirty and he looked with fascination at icicles that formed on some peoples' beards as they made their way along the paths and streets. It became so cold that birds could barely hop along the ground, weakly seeking food. They often fell easy victims to the street cats; he still hated the way cats played with their helpless prey, before finally running off to tear it apart and devour their meal.

One day, a bird flew into the glass pane of the dining room, and fell stunned to the ground. He rushed outside and picked it up as it lay fluttering its wings weakly. Its eyes were open, but its neck was limp. Blood started to flow from its beak, and he had a bad feeling about this one. Often they flew away after being stunned for a while, but this bird had flown in hard. It was warm, and he could feel its little heart beating. He looked into its eyes and tried to console and encourage it.

He prayed that it might revive, so that he could let it free again. Its left eye was more closed than the right. Its feet had been gripping his finger tightly, but the grip relaxed. The bird was still warm, but its heart beat more slowly. After a while that stopped, too. He knew it was no good, and now he wondered if he should have spared it the pain by twisting its neck. "No, I think it felt my love and I am sure I helped it pass on happily with my prayers," he consoled himself, as his eyes watered a little.

Otto loved the outdoors and he would often go into the Spessart, one of the most famous forests in Germany—where the kings and princes hunted deer and wild boar in the Middle Ages. The sights, sounds and smells of the forest would envelop him, and there was never a shortage of trees or hills to conquer.

He would set out and hike, usually with a few friends; sometimes he would also just head out on his own, and then he could stop and think or pray. Some days Otto would walk to Maria-Buchen (Mary of the Beech Tree), a popular shrine situated in majestic beech and oak forests, about five kilometres away. It was an exciting time of life, with so much to do and to master. "Where will I be in ten years time?" he wondered. "I wonder what God has planned for me."

Otto also had a good ear for music. He learned to play the violin and the trumpet, and had a natural Bavarian love of music and singing, of which there was always plenty in their Gasthaus.

Drama and acting were a normal part of their life, and there were often plays in the village or at school. In one of the play productions at the Aloysianum, he played the part of a Franciscan missionary in a pagan country. In another, he was given the role of an Arab philosopher from Granada, a wise and intellectual Mohammedan. He played the part of a holy and hard-working monk in another play.

A Man in his Brother's Eyes

He took great delight in challenging his older brothers and rising to any of their challenges. He could soon do anything that they could. Gathering in the two or three hay harvests was hard work, and they used to pile the wagon high with hay to re-stock the barn.

He did less farm work than his brothers did because he was away at gymnasium, but when he was there he gave it his very best effort, and always tried to outpace his brothers. They were definitely still stronger than he was and he used to wish he had Karl's strength as he watched him climb the steep and narrow stairs, loaded with heavy sacks of grain.

Ploughing on the farm was done with horse or oxen

Sometimes, Karl could not help feeling a few twinges of jealousy. He saw how his two young brothers, Josef and Otto, were being given the opportunity of this expensive education. Meanwhile he stayed and worked hard to run the farm and other business interests. "You fellows with your books and fancy learning," he ragged one day. "You can't even use a pitch fork or carry a sack of flour up to the loft."

The teasing soon developed into a tussle and a bit of a wrestling match, one which Karl would have expected to win comfortably, with his age and exercise advantages. But Otto was no pushover now, and had reached a turning point. He was no longer the little brother who would take whatever cheek his older brothers chose to hand out. He had also learned a thing or two at High School, and suddenly, Karl found a strong grip around his waist, and he was being hoisted in the air so that he could not get his feet back into position for him to use his strength.

"Hey!" he yelled, surprised. But, try as he did, he could not get out of the grip. Otto clung on fiercely, pressing home his advantage all the way, until Karl relented, "Okay, okay." When he was back on his feet, he turned around, and offered his hand. "You are a good man," he acknowledged Otto for the first time. A further something had changed, and their relations would never be the same again. Karl still teased Otto, but he now considered him "a good man" after this experience.

Chapter 3

The Call of the Wild

Eagles and Their Young

Young eagles soon learn the skills of flying. After watching over many weeks how their parents launch from the nest, one windy day they stretch their own wings, feel the lift and hop up to glide on the invisible air, making it safely to rest on a perch some distance below. Encouraged and watched all the time by their parents, they soon extend their flights, and within a few weeks they are using the natural lift of thermals to sail the skies. Their sense of identity is suddenly propelled to new levels, and they revel in the feel and joy of flying; as they become more adventurous they learn to fly up higher and higher on the rising air. Copying their parents they tuck in their wings and gather speed like a downhill ski-racer. Growing ever more skilful and confident, soon they are able to hunt for themselves, and to lead their own existence. Sometimes they lead quite a solitary life for a while.

With their fantastic flying skill and the range that they can travel, there comes a call; it is something which lures them out of their nest area, and away into the unexplored, their wilderness. Later there will come a time when the nest and home territory is not for them at all, and this is their preparation.

This is just a fact of life for eagles, but young Otto also had a sense of calling; he needed to make some choices and to find a deep purpose that was somehow destined for him. Adult eagles actually chase their young ones away once they have matured so that they can fend for themselves. The feeding and caring instincts of eagle parents only lasts for as long as necessary and they make way for the next nesting season, quite indifferent to the wonder of creating life, which human parents never really recover from.

SEARCHING FOR DIRECTION

Once again, Otto sat with his older brother, only now his feet reached the floor quite comfortably, and there was something approaching an atmosphere of equals. At fourteen, the three years between them seemed to have shrunk, and their respect for one another was evident in their conversation. "Otto, you have done very well at Gymnasium; have you decided what to do next?"

"Do you remember how I asked you why you did not become a missionary?" he followed up.

"Ah sure. That was a few years ago already; are you thinking of that for yourself?" he asked, having guessed the reply.

"Yes, I would love to go to Africa. I have been so interested in it, ever since last year's geography. It is a huge continent, and mostly inhabited by pagans. They live in grass huts, have almost no clothes, and certainly very few ever get a chance for any education. They don't even read or write."

"Yes, that may be true enough, but where do you see yourself in this?"

"I would love to bring them schooling, medicine and civilisation. But most of all, they do not know Jesus; the greatest thing I can do with my life is to bring Christianity to them."

"Do you know what that will mean, now?" Josef asked.

"I understand what I am giving up," he answered. He felt embarrassed, but now his brother was nearly a priest already, and so he felt he could talk about more intimate subjects, more than he would with Karl or Max. "Josef, I think girls are the most beautiful creatures, and I must admit that they do more than just stir my thoughts up." He was blushing slightly at his admission, but he continued, "The early apostles managed that; some of them even left their own loved ones behind when Jesus asked them to follow him and become fishers of men."

"True enough, but they had Him right there with them; I think that made it a lot easier," answered Josef.

"I look at you, and our parish priest, and the other priests, and I think, 'what could be a greater thing to do with my life?' I don't get any other answer, except maybe that I am drawn to go even further. I have always liked that Gospel of Matthew's, "Go forth and teach all nations . . ." and I think that is what missionary work is all about."

"Well, you will certainly find that example if you go on to Pius the Tenth," Josef agreed, sensing that Otto was likely to follow him to that seminary in Wurzburg.

INSPIRED BY THE EXAMPLE OF ABBOTT FRANCIS

While Otto was at the boarding establishment in Lohr-on-Main, he had many opportunities for inspiration from the Mariannhill Mission Society. The Society had been European in their original form, with a very powerful and dramatic history as they transformed and responded to the needs of Africa. The "phenomenon of Mariannhill" was a relatively new order in the Catholic Church; it was vibrant and inspiring. The missionaries who taught young Otto had been working in Africa, and especially South Africa, and he soaked up their story and developed awe-filled respect and admiration for his mentors.

As a student, Otto read the story of Francis Wendelin Pfanner, the founder of the Mariannhill order. He listened keenly when the older priests and brothers spoke of him; he could see that they had actually met and known him, and had been strongly influenced in their own dedication and achievements.

As a boy, Pfanner had been mischievous; he had later enjoyed their tradition of wrestling called Hosenlupfen, and prematurely became a village champion, when he beat the much bigger grocer's boy. This had appealed to Otto, and fuelled his own passion for wrestling and strength sports.

Pfanner's search led him to join the Trappists, a contemplative, working monastic order, with a most severe regimen of prayer and austerity. At Mariawald, he was given the new name, Father Francis, and settled into a period of peace and spiritual studies. To resolve a little power struggle that developed, he was sent to establish a new monastery in Austria. He also endured a period of dark confusion. One day, at Trifontani, in Rome, he helped an old man with snow-white hair, who directed him to Bosnia, and then mysteriously disappeared.

Off went Pfanner; he negotiated a half-price land purchase and set up the Maria-Stern monastery on the river Vrbas. He had to contend with suspicious politicians and discontent within, and he handled these with humorous skill and wisdom. War came and he became quite well recognised as a hard-working medical improviser. Later, in Bosnia, Francis Pfanner had built up a new Trappist monastery, with eighty monks eventually.

Francis Pfanner's life story was a series of escapades and challenges, and he had a zestful nature that struck a chord in Otto. He foiled thieves and extortionists, physically outmatching them. On one occasion while assigned to the Convent in Zagreb, Croatia, he had saved the community from a fire, by climbing on the steep and high roof and stuffing the chimney to cut off the airflow that the fire needed to fuel itself. He had marshalled the rest of the fire-fighting operation, and the nuns had all seen what a true hero their chaplain was.

When he attended an Abbots' meeting one year, nobody volunteered in response to a request from Bishop Ricard for help in South Africa, so he stood up, with his eyes blazing, and said, "If no one else will go, then I will." And that was how he ended up going off on a new adventure, and a three-year commitment that did not quite run to plan.

On arrival, after a tempestuous sea voyage, the funds that they were initially given and a site in Dunbrody, in the Cape's Port Elizabeth diocese, were nothing like suitable. After two and a half years of frustration, working this useless piece of dry land, without waiting to obtain formal permission they trekked to Natal by ox-wagon. It was a decision their Abbot took, sure that he was doing the right thing.

Many things along the way would have completely dispirited a lesser band, and they were sometimes on the point of despair and failure. They overcame that, and just pitched up in the Durban diocese. The Bishop, Jolivet, soon realised he was dealing with a man of great fire and energy!

ABBOTT FRANCIS SET UP HIS TRAPPIST MONASTERY IN NATAL

A phenomenal amount of work went into establishing their monastery in Natal, with facilities and expertise in all sorts of impressive practical disciplines. The Zulu people needed schooling, trade skills training, agriculture and animal husbandry, and all sorts of other practical help; and here they were, a community dedicated to silent prayer and meditation, although admittedly working and developing farmlands and other productive facilities.

Soon the strong reality of Africa's pressing needs hit Abbott Francis in a powerful way. He ended up remodelling his Trappist community to engage in active missionary work—much later,
the Mariannhill order was born out of his forcefulness and vision combined with God's guiding hand. Meanwhile, he brought out women missionaries from Europe as well, and he managed to get local people to join in as missionary helpers.

There were those who opposed him, sincerely considering that it was their duty to remain as contemplatives, who were not allowed to engage in mission work. Abbott Francis, however, was far-sighted and felt strongly that they were called to do more.

The Abbott insisted, despite opposition; and so began a change which revolutionised their mission and led to a whole new order being created to meet the needs that he saw.

He was a witty and brilliant speaker, captivating his audience, and usually persuading them to help or agree with his plans. He stood up boldly against the emerging threat of communism as far back as 1891! He saw how to welcome both poor and rich, the former in obvious need of respectable opportunity and the latter as benefactors, for their own good.

He rode around in his white habit, on horseback, with a wide-brimmed hat, a long beard, and a large crucifix hanging prominently from his neck. Cruel press efforts criticised them for spreading German influence, but he was quick and effective in responding that the work they did was for God, not for Bismarck.

Mariannhill grew into a wonderful village of its own, complete with useful industries and practical schools, productive farmlands and housing. Prayer and spiritual life was always kept foremost, and must surely have been what fuelled this success story. Never wanting any form of self-aggrandisement, Francis Pfanner nevertheless saw the benefits of the great colourful ceremonies of the Church, and how they reached out to the natives.

The Bishop in the Cape had not been flexible enough to fit in with or understand their needs, and had expected them to make a paradise out of absolutely nothing, at Dunbrody! Meanwhile, Abbot Francis displayed the same single-mindedness now, as he put their monastery at Mariannhill to work.

They engaged in training and missionary work, in addition to their very full routine of prayer and meditation. However, this led to trouble, and libellous accusations were soon relayed to Europe about financial and even spiritual matters. Rome appointed somebody to investigate Mariannhill, but really to take over, and Abbot Francis left his missionaries, humbly cast aside.

Undaunted, he continued working for his order, from a small mission nearby, called Emmaus. This remained his silent base, and in years to come, became world-renowned for its cheese. As an eighty-year old Abbott, he was able to see the developments that he began in Africa, spread to China and many other parts of the world. He was truly an inspiring leader and a vital figure, giving deep inspiration to followers for decades to come.

He stood up to officialdom and obstruction. When he had set up the Maria-Stern monastery in Bosnia petty officials pressurised him over everything they could, but he still succeeded. Years later, he met Cecil John Rhodes in the Transkei, after a long horseback ride of three days to catch up with his rail wagon. With his persistence, he secured a grant of thirty thousand acres for a mission farm in the vast new territories, over fifteen hundred miles away.

Rhodesia was a Jesuit mission territory, but they made room for the Mariannhillers. In 1895 Father Hyazinth Salomon, a Pole, built their first mission there, near their later site, Triashill. The next year, the Mashona Rebellion threw everything into turmoil, and the mission was abandoned. In 1908 they began again at nearby Monte Casino, close to the newly built railway line.

MOTIVATED BY THE DEDICATION OF MARIANNHILLERS

Otto read whatever he could find about Abbott Francis, and his Mariannhill priests and brothers. (He had also established the Congregation of the Precious Blood Sisters.) Their spirituality was clear, and he was inspired by its power. Meeting the missionaries first hand at the High School had inspired him even more, and ignited the fuel that was waiting in him.

"I want to share our Catholic faith with those in most need," he affirmed, when discussing his motivation with the spiritual director. "If only we can reach all those pagan people, and show them what God has done," he mused further. Otto was to become one of these men, and like those before him, he was led in a way that he accepted, without lots of questioning and waiting—he simply got on with it!

He told his brother, Josef, "I know why I want to join them. It is the dedication of these Mariannhillers, to Mission work in foreign, "pagan" lands. This has made a very deep impression on me and the idea has grown from a thought to a determination, and I simply want to join this noble band."

"Otto I can see that there is a deeply planted adventurous streak in you. You also have the urge to travel over the seas to foreign lands, and this will enable you to reach out to people of totally different cultures," his brother said.

Otto found that he listened attentively whenever the missions were discussed, and he read many of the books and stories of missionaries, and especially the founders of this congregation who were teaching him now.

Throughout this time, he grew in happiness in his own strong faith. "I really would like to share my faith with those who did not have faith," he told his spiritual adviser. "I want to give my life like Abbott Francis and those missionaries working in Africa."

"How would you feel about working here in Germany?" he was asked.

"I would do it happily if that was what I was directed to do," he said. "But, Father, I would far prefer to help those who do not know Jesus Christ at all. I think that is how I am being called."

"Otto, have you studied the other missionary orders?" he asked dutifully, and with a little less conviction.

"There are many, some much older and with excellent records of missionary work. The Jesuits have set high standards of work and spiritual life, and the Oblates of Mary Immaculate have been very successful. I like the Franciscan ideas, but I do not think I am called to be one of them. The Redemptorists have a great call to evangelise, but they don't seem to be for me either."

"All right, Otto, I think you have probably given quite a bit of thought to this. You must not make a hasty decision, though. This call is for a long lifetime of total commitment and dedication; and it will certainly not be easy. I believe you will be a great asset to God if you decide to join the Mission Congregation of Mariannhill. Keep reading, praying and observing; there is time to make up your mind, and only you can do that."

The surroundings of the Boarding School also had a deep influence. There was a superb school chapel in the baroque style adorned with beautiful paintings. It was a healthy, disciplined way of life, walking to the High School every morning—in summer and winter, heat and cold, swimming even in winter, in the ice cold rivers.

There was a routine of simple good meals and regularity of study, sport, recreation and social activities, and contact with fellow students from throughout the German territories. One of these was a young man named Adolph Schmitt, whom he had met before. He was now in his final year. This senior spoke to him in a friendly manner, which made a deep impression on him. He conducted himself with dignity and yet he was not aloof from his juniors; he was free of the seniority complex which many institutions breed into their students. Later, he came across him at the major seminary, and their paths would cross in a powerful way, decades later.

There were also teachers and professors of great stature, conviction, and vision. They all contributed to making up his mind to decide upon a life of sacrifice, service and dedication, but also venture and adventure.

Otto had a strong sense of adventure and took a keen interest in other people. He was fascinated by the history he learned, and delved into this subject with gusto. He learned all he could about famous emperors and periods in history, and enjoyed some of the discussions which allowed them to wonder how life might have been changed, if outcomes had not been influenced by some of the chance events which had such an effect on the future.

History lessons also sparked off discussions about politics, and this was a tough time for Germany. Poverty and injustice were clearly evidenced in the streams of unemployed men, and their desperation. Nazism had begun to make its influence felt, and discussions about politics overlapped with loftier principals about ethics and moral positions. The colonies that Germany had lost in Africa were fascinating places, and he viewed Africa itself as a continent that was still almost totally undeveloped.

His interest grew into an over-powering desire to go abroad, and to do so in the highest calling which he could think of—to serve God as a missionary. Again he listened to Matthew's reading after Easter, "go, therefore, make disciples of all nations"; it seemed to have special significance and a noble purpose.

It became clear and obvious to him; this is what he was meant to do. He would enjoy it to the full, and he wanted to be a great missionary like Abbott Francis and many others of whom he had read and heard so much. The people of Africa hardly knew anything of Christ and the faith, which St. Paul had spread to so many pagan lands.

There were also the saints whose life stories he read avidly. One of his favourites was Saint Teresa of the Little Flower. She lived a life of humble simplicity, and died very young, of tuberculosis. At her canonisation, unexplained showers of roses came down from the heights of Saint Peter's. Many miracles have been worked in her name, often announced with roses in some mysterious way, and just as she had asked of God. Her deep faith inspired many Mariannhillers and other missionaries to endure and achieve so much. "I am sure she has been responsible for more conversions than even Saint Francis Xavier," one of his teachers told the class. "That is why we have adopted her as the patron saint of missionaries, even though she never left Europe."

A Second Son Declares His Calling

Even if they had thought gymnasium might lead to a vocation to the priesthood, it still came as a surprise and they responded with natural parental concern. They wondered if he was making the right decision, and they cared for him, much as they accepted that God's work was the most important thing any one could do.

It was Julianna who was beside herself with doubts and worries, at first. "Why did we send him to Lohr? He would have been fine here, and he could have learned a trade. He is excellent with animals, and very practical with his hands. There is so much he could do here."

"My wife, he is now ready, and he is making choices, for his life," Josef soothed her.

"I would so love to see him happily married. He would give us some more beautiful little grandchildren. God knows that he is one of my most handsome sons. You have seen how quite a few of the girls have been keeping an eye out. They have been attracting his attention, and I can see he responds. How can a man give all that up? It is not natural. He will not be able to manage . . . ."

Josef was more practical. "He is a fine son, and he knows what he will be giving up. I would love to have him here with us, but if he truly has a calling from God, it would be a great sin if we did not encourage him and do all we can to make it possible."

"We have already offered up his older brother, Josef. He is nearly finished training to become a priest," reasoned Julianna just one more time, before really understanding and accepting that this was really meant to happen.

Away from Home

There had been something exciting about being away from home and family. At Boarding School, he had been able to free himself gradually from the very strong bonds of family. This was not easy, as he realised that the Weeger family was very happy and closely-knit.

He used to go on long train journeys and undertook very strenuous, wide-flung cycle tours into unknown areas. All this had contributed to his "emancipation" from those very close ties of immediate family and friends.

He loved the sports at Gymnasium. He was strong and dedicated, and he mastered a wide range of sports with determined self-discipline. At the finale of the athletics season he was crowned with the Eichenlaub, the victor's wreath. He was proud of his accomplishment, and could not help feeling the admiration from the beautiful girls who watched, especially Professor Imhoff's daughter.

"Life is precious, and there are so many options. I could happily marry and have a family," he said as he confided to her. "But you know, I am happy to serve God. I really do want to share this with others," he continued shyly, and he watched her beautiful face to see how she reacted.

"I think you have far too much longing for adventure," she answered with a cheeky laugh.

He grew serious, though. The conversation had made him realise how he was determined to do more than the average. Something at work within him, and these ongoing inner experiences finally led to a final decision, "I simply must dare the jump into the unknown".

His was a very interesting education, especially at the beginning as the new subjects opened up so many ideas. Otto was fascinated by what he learned about words and their origins and meanings; like ornithology, paradigm, and so on . . . Then there were all the clear-thinking and thought-provoking Greek philosophers, Plato, Aristotle, Cicero and even a few quite surprising renegade poets like Aristophanes. He revelled in this classic terminology and language and the arguments had a logic he appreciated.

Otto pricked up his ears as the professor explained how Plato was over-awed by the complexity of creation. "But how do you get that message across to people?" he asked.

"Take this example that he used so well," he suggested. "Plato's opponents claimed that a creator god was *not* logical and he wanted to refute this. He said, 'let us say that you gather enough random letters of the alphabet to make a book. Now put them haphazardly into a drum and then roll it around and around. Now take out the letters, simply as they come out, and put them together one after another until you have made a book. What are the chances that a sensible book would emerge? How many times would it take for that to happen? Could this really be done enough times to succeed?' Plato asked."

He paused while the concept sank in. Otto was deeply impressed at this simple example. Even a simple man-made thing like a book could not possibly evolve in this way, so how much more unlikely is it for the cosmos to just happen?

When he went to Saint Pius X Seminary, in Wurzburg, he again came across Adolph Schmitt, now Father Adolph. He had been in the missions in Rhodesia, and had been brought back to the seminary as Vice-rector.

He was an inspiring man and Otto already had great respect and admiration for him from the time when he was at the Aloysianum. He saw how this young priest carried himself with the same old dignity he had seen before, and he had a great air of refinement about him. He was refreshingly humble, though, and Otto appreciated the way he still conversed so easily with the young seminarians, with no pretensions or complexes.

Otto loved the old villages nearby, and they were rich with art, culture, history and inspiration. He stopped and read the inscription at an old village faucet one day. Under the old tap the sign spoke of giving of itself, as the instrument, although not the source; the source was somewhere else, the well or spring, from which the water came.

"I really enjoy poetry and literature," he said to one of his colleagues. "I find the words so powerful and inspiring. Take this little poem, which I copied from the plaque on the village faucet." He offered the piece of hand-written paper. "Read it and tell me what you think."

His colleague read it over and over a couple of times to himself.

Ein alter Brunnen spendet leise	An old well freely gives
sein Wasser taeglich gleicherweise.	its water daily happily
Wie segensreich ist doch solch Leben,	rightfully just such a life
geben, imer nur geben.	giving, ever more giving.

Mein Leben soll dem Brunnen gleichen,	My life will mimic that well
Ich leb, um andern darzureichen;	I live to thus serve others
doch geben, geben alle Tage.	only giving, giving all my days.
Sag Brunnen, wirds dir nicht zur Plage?	Say spring, are you never troubled?
Da sagt er mir als Jochsgeselle,	There's more than just fooling about
Ich bin ja Brunnen und nicht Quelle.	I am that well and not a spring
Mir fliesst es zu, ich gebs nur weiter,	It's coming to me; I only pass it on
drum klingt mein Platschern froh und heiter.	That's why my splashing sounds gay and bright
Nun leb ich nach des Brunnens Weise,	Now I live like a well
zieh still meine Segensreise,	And silently go on my soul vacation
was mir von Christus fliesst ins Leben,	What I receive in life from Christ
das kan ich muehlos weitergeben.	I can easily impart it now.

"I agree. We should aim to be like that water-font, serving by delivering God's teaching, like water from a hidden source, the wellspring. It is a powerful metaphor, so rich in symbolism," he summed up his thoughts.

Otto expressed his own thoughts: 'the font was happy dispensing water, just as a priest could pass on the gift of God's love.' (Many years later he would remember that poem, when he received a card from a fellow-priest, who used it as his own motto, saying, "So schoen und einfach ist mein Leben, Geben immer nur Geben!" It means, 'so beautiful and simple is my life, giving, always only giving.')

Another story that struck him with sadness, was Schiller's story, "die Glocke". The apprentice had struck the molten flow for casting the bronze bell before the master had ordered him to do this. In his anger, the master killed the apprentice, but afterwards, when he sounded the bell it produced the most perfect tone that had ever come from his foundry in all his years! And he had killed the apprentice for pouring it early.

Their literature professor opened Otto's mind to Goethe. "His writings are like an antidote, to lift our minds above some of the mob appeal which is making its impact on us. We are being told to forget ourselves, for the sake of the nation," he explained, as the oratory of nationalism was attracting its following. "How is that going to help the seven million people who are unemployed? We need people with ideas of their own, to inspire us and save us from losing our identity; or worse, from following leaders with absolutely no credentials or nobility."

However, many people became like hopeful mice, following the Pied Piper, and the crowds swelled at the public meetings. "I was reading a report about this Doctor Schweitzer," he went on to explain. "He is warning us about how little the individual is being extolled in all this. Where are we heading?" he asked rhetorically.

Later, Otto's history teacher reminded them; "great civilisations produce individuals not a crowd of mindless serfs."

However, Schweitzer's words helped strengthen the thinking of some, like a Prussian Pastor called Dietrich Bonhoeffer. When he came back from a time in London, in 1935, he campaigned for his seminary students to be individuals. He urged them not to collapse as well. "Even some of our own German religious community have stopped resisting this totalitarianism. Our churches are now being subjected to state control and interference. How can the Church lead us to God when this happens to them? It is dangerous to rely too much on state subsidies, and they have lost their integrity in the process." He began to work with the resistance movement, but was soon arrested and then hung by the SS at the concentration camp in Flossenburg.

The Jewish philosopher from Vienna, Martin Buber was another strong mind and voice, but he fled to Jerusalem in time to save his life. Pierre Teilhard de Chardin, a French Jesuit priest, travelling and exploring in China at the time, was becoming a world citizen. He held strong views, as he worried for the future of the world. "I think his Le Milieu Divin is a great work; have you read his treatise, "Spiritual Power of Matter?" one of Otto's more erudite colleagues asked him.

"I don't know how you get the time to read all these things," Otto answered. "I just never get around to it; so tell me what he says."

"He says many things, but reverence for life is one of his strongest themes. It makes so much sense, especially in these times," was his summation.

GERMANY'S DILEMMA

There were many problems confronting the people at this time, and all around Otto witnessed the suffering and shortages. Thousands of people were out of work, desperate for something to do, to earn a living and simply to eat. The German Chancellor, Bruening, appealed to the League of Nations, asking for some respite from the reparation costs that were crippling Germany and this new generation. The Pope saw the reality of their plight and added his own voice, but their appeals were ignored. Britain and France were adamant, and it seemed to these young students, that they were bent on a path of revenge, determined to make Germany suffer, just as much or more than it had made the rest of the world suffer in the War.

Otto had been writing his Matriculation exams at Lohr-on-Main, when an important election took place. Hitler, with his promise of jobs and a decent life, won by a very narrow margin, fifty one per cent of the vote. His well-drilled supporters had gone about with great jubilation, and greatly exaggerated this close but fateful victory.

By now, some people considered that things could not get any worse. Furthermore, a teacher assured them, "if Hitler does not perform properly, we shall just elect somebody else."

"There are three main camps now," the priest was saying to them one day. "There are those who see clearly and simply that Hitler is bad. They contend that he is evil; and we should have nothing to do with him, let alone grant him the powers he now has."

"Yes, but there are many who consider that he has done so much to uplift Germany," a student could not resist saying.

"Well, that is the second group. They are not worried about how he has done it. They can see he is a rousing demagogue, and how he has influenced so many of our young people, school children and older. He calls out to us that we must regain our honour and respect." He carried on, "listen to how they are saying that Hitler is the only one who can save Germany. We have to ask ourselves, 'What have the others done?'"

"The Bishop of Freiburg, Bishop Doctor Groeber is one of those supporters. He is Passionate in his support of Hitler, but he is a renegade, turning his back on our Catholic teachings about justice."

"Then there is a third group. Most people see Hitler as the lesser of the evils, and think he can be removed if things do not go right."

He said, "they are uncommitted, but they are willing to give Hitler a chance. To them, he seems to be the right man for the moment."

Hitler was soon requiring every young German to perform three years of compulsory labour service, and many were employed building railways, autobahns and public works. He had started training people even before he came to power and now they had to serve two years in the army. He was also introducing rallies and sporting meetings on Sundays, doing everything possible to make people feel that they were being unpatriotic if they preferred to keep their Sunday observances. And the tide was gathering momentum; the crowds swelled to the promises and fervour of a new young leader, strutting with his pretended credentials. He brashly rubbed shoulders with the cultured and aristocratic leadership of Germany, and wasted little time in using, and then doing away with them.

The victors of the Versailles treaty failed to react when Hitler began to completely ignore its terms, conscripting about half a million into the new armed forces; feeble French protests to the League of Nations were the sort of weakness which he began to thrive on. After Britain's Liberal Foreign Minister, Sir John Simon, visited Berlin, their professor burst out, "what did that stupid Englishman expect to do, flying to Berlin to have tea-time chats with Hitler?"

In the meantime, Hitler organised his Youth League with military discipline, although he himself had only been a corporal in the army. The youth had no weapons at first, and just performed lots of marching and drills.

The Jewish minority wielded significant economic power and Hitler's obsession grew as he fanned sparks of hatred and resentment; the Jews and the Anglo-Franco alliance became the scapegoat for all the troubles of Germany.

Hitler encountered considerable opposition from many Catholic and Lutheran clergy and other sectors, but was absolutely resolute in ignoring or disregarding resistance. Many good people, like Cardinal

Faulhaber of Munich, and Bishop Ehrenfried of Wurzburg, were arrested and imprisoned on Hitler's commands.

Their professor commented one day, "our Lutheran brothers may be more accepting of Hitler, but more and more Catholics also think they see benefits in Hitler's rule. It is tragic, and where will it lead us?"

One day they heard the news about Cardinal Faulhaber's 'arrest'. A troop of Nazis was sent to the Cathedral to arrest him. When he opened the door to them, he summed up their orders and asked, "Have you come to arrest Herr Faulhaber, or Cardinal Faulhaber?"

"We have come for Cardinal Faulhaber," was the clipped reply.

"Very well. Just wait a minute," he said as he closed the door. Within a few minutes the door opened and there he stood; he had donned his cardinal's robes, and even put on his bishops' mitre. Somehow this stunned and confused them, and they went off leaving him unharmed, this time anyway.

Despite eleven attempts at assassinating Hitler, he prevailed and it was soon realized that people who spoke out against him were quickly disposed of or suppressed. His support grew with his success at providing employment and restoring dignity. Many who opposed him were swiftly dealt with; they were beaten up, imprisoned or even killed. He generated immense fear, and this was soon his strongest influence on people, together with the restoration of some hopeful, national pride. Unseen by most Germans, their prisons were soon to develop into concentration camps.

CHAPTER 4

FEATHERING OUT

NOVITIATE IN THE NETHERLANDS

For the next stage of his training, at the age of twenty, he was moved to a very flat country. At first sight this was quite charming for a Bavarian. The fields were beautifully manicured, and the ditches ran in perfect straight lines, with no need to look for any contours or gradients. Everything was green, and the cattle munched with a very contented look about them. The roads went straight and level for as far as he could see, interrupted only by the bus stops, homes and shops along the way. The railway line ran alongside, raised slightly. People cycled around with ease.

Every few kilometres he came across a windmill; it reminded him of the famous story of Don Quixote and Sancho Panza. There were dragons and all sorts of evil things out there, but he trusted that God would keep him tilting at the right things. "Almighty God," he prayed as they drove along in silence, "I thank you for your hand in my life so far. Please guide me now. Shape me so that I shall be a good servant, a brave but wise knight."

The novitiate, Saint Paul's, near Venlo, had a special feel to it. This was a house where many great and holy Mariannhill Missionaries had begun their studies. Right now, it was also a haven from some of the confusion that was manifesting itself in next-door Germany. Here, he and his colleagues could study and prepare for their first vows. The

Holy Spirit could be felt in the atmosphere of the church and the whole seminary where they stayed. There was an atmosphere of peace, but in it there was a purpose.

Otto was now ready and eager to take up whatever cross or task he was given, and he wanted to receive all the graces and spiritual preparation that his chosen life had to offer. They were a proudly new congregation, but there was a vitality and determination that so suited his nature.

This was a monastery, and there were numerous daily chores, which had to be done. He would join his fellow-novices in the fields each day, cutting hay, baling it, loading, hauling, packing hay into the barns, planting potatoes, harvesting, trimming, moving and carting soil or many other farm tasks.

They went to study further in the land of windmills

His older brother, Josef, was already well on his way to becoming a priest. He was training to become a secular, or diocesan priest, and would stay at home in Germany, in a parish close to his family, no doubt. Otto found that he was drawn even more to the Mariannhill order, and realised it was missionary work that attracted him. He felt he could do so much in distant Africa; he remembered how he used to watch the storks as they began their annual migrations to Africa.

It was fascinating how they could travel that huge distance, in search of warmth and good feeding during the harsh European winter; he knew he could make the journey to put himself at God's disposal. "Go forth and teach all nations," often echoed in his mind, and that was a command he wanted to obey with all his heart mind and soul.

When the year was up, he took the solemn decision to take his temporary vows, of poverty, chastity and obedience.

"There are sound reasons for these disciplines," explained their spiritual director. "In its wisdom, the church calls you to make these ascetic choices, and commit yourself entirely to God."

The class listened attentively, aware of the gravity and permanence of what they were undertaking. The vow of Poverty was not so difficult for many of them but some had come from homes with most of the things life could provide. However, the effects of recent years, and the suffering that they had seen around them, right here in their own country were vivid reminders of how unimportant material things really are.

Otto knew what it meant to see and appreciate the beauty of girls; this was a very real giving up of something that his instincts called for. He knew he could have become a good husband and father, and he would have loved the intimacy of a soul-mate, a wife and mother for a family of his own. "In taking the vow of chastity, you will be turning your back on many things. We have been over these issues several times, but I want to remind you of one aspect. In choosing celibacy, you dedicate your whole life to God. You give Him the gift of your manhood, with all of the natural desires and instincts that entails.

But when you receive the title, Father, you will realise that it means precisely that. You will have many spiritual children, the converts you make, the parishioners that you guide, those who unburden their sins to you in confession. You will be giving life in such a special way that you will know you are a father in a different sense from being the father of an ordinary human family." A few of the men were moving on their seats; this was a serious issue. Otto let every word sink in. He could see this sacrifice as a gift, and the way to serve God better.

"There have always been people who say you cannot live without a wife. However, you all know of the long history of saints and holy people who have managed this; and their lives reflect the way they committed themselves totally to serving God. For that matter, there have been holy people in other faiths, especially the Asian cultures who see this purity of calling as a vital part of drawing closer to God."

He was still thinking about this subject, when he realized that the topic had swung. ". . . and whatever he says, you are bound to accept in obedience."

Otto knew he had curbed and controlled his individualistic nature, although this had not been without difficulty. Accepting the brotherhood of his confreres with all their individual personalities and idiosyncrasies was not that difficult for him; a large family upbringing introduces variety and acceptance, even if certain judgements and decisions are taken about what one likes or does not like. His own father and mother had instilled a sense of obedience in him while he was under their authority, and he never rebelled against them. Now he had to accept the total authority of his superior, his bishop, and the Church. He was confident that he could do this, although he could visualise that there would be times when he would be sure his way of doing things would be better.

"Incidentally, you recall from your psychology studies that we have three basic desires—what are they?"

"Sex, money and power," one student responded.

"Precisely! And it is precisely these natural urges that you are subjecting to your vows; you are ordering these desires, these forces and desires of your human nature. You will not be freed from the urges, or from the temptations—that would be unnatural, inhuman. You are accepting that they are part of your make-up, but you are accepting and imposing controls by way of your vows."

He strode to the board, and chalked a circle on it. He drew two lines across it, and said, "This represents you. You are a whole, a being created by God. At the top, in our day-to-day conscious living, we are experiencing things; your thoughts, perceptions, senses are at work here. This is life, a vital part of life, but it is not everything. Below this lies our sub-conscious. This is where our urges reside, and this is where our unique characteristics lie."

"Our inherited talents, skills, instincts and drives have formed us. Many factors have influenced each of us; our parents, our homes, and the communities we live in. What we see and read influences us, and we have a whole spectrum of reactions to people and situations."

"To give a silly example, some of you on seeing a blonde-haired girl, may think she has certain characteristics because those have been present in somebody you knew well, or your ideas have been influenced by stereotypes. But another one of you when seeing the same person will consider her in a totally different way."

"Isn't it wonderful, how unique, how individual we all are? Anyway, I am sorry; I have started to ramble a bit; we are talking about your vows."

"You will not have sex, and you will control your thoughts and instincts, keeping your soul chaste and focused on God and spiritual matters. Deeper down, here," he pointed to the lower part of the diagram, "is your soul, your spirit, your communion with God. You are called to direct your energies and your talents to serve God, and unite your soul with God in the most wonderful way which is humanly possible—in your calling as a priest."

Later, at his individual interview, the novice-master asked, "have you chosen a name by which you will now be called?"

"Yes. I wish to be called Odilo," he replied solemnly.

"That is a good name; please explain why you have chosen it." He related what he knew of the life of Bishop Odilo and how the story of this person had made such a big impression on him.

The new names that they adopted symbolised for him the big change that he was now undergoing. He was foregoing the life of a layperson, giving up the opportunity to marry and have a family of his own. He was turning his back on a career and the sort of income and comforts that he could expect. He was turning his life over to God, to put himself at God's service, and use his life, his talents and his best endeavours to become one of those special people who "go forth and teach all nations."

UNIVERSITY AND MAJOR SEMINARY

The next stage of his training began when he commenced University at Wurzburg, on the Main River. He stayed at the seminary, Saint Pius X, and went to the University for lectures. There were many similarities to the period when he had stayed at the Aloysianum and studied at Lohr-on-Main High School. He was still on the Main River, but now he was on the left bank of the river and about forty kilometres upstream. The Main River wound its way around and to the East of the mountains.

Pius X Seminary now represented a definite commitment. He already led a disciplined and spiritual life, and this was a natural progression. The major seminary had a routine, beginning each day with morning devotions around six a.m., followed by meditation and Holy Mass. Breakfast was served at seven a.m.

The day itself was divided up further by prayer periods, especially the noon and evening prayers. He liked the routine, and was able to discipline himself to adhere to it easily. It gave life a structure, and in so doing kept him free to concentrate on what he was studying and on his prayer life.

Saint Pius X Seminary in Wurzburg

There was no time to vacillate and waste, making decisions about what to do next. He established habits and routines which people respected. In these routines he provided for exercise. He loved the parallel bars, and his friends all knew that he would be on the bars at nine fifteen each morning. His friends knew how strictly he set aside time for this exercise. It was so regimented that they claimed they could set their watches by him. "Hey, Otto, you are fifteen seconds late today. What happened?" he was teased.

With the exercise, and his virility, Otto felt his strength increasing and he enjoyed using his muscles and his powerful grip to fling himself up, hold a position, and execute exercises which relied on great strength and timing.

At midday, they all made a church visit, which included a short examination of conscience. He would review the day so far and assess how he was doing in his spiritual and educational progress. "Lord, I ask your forgiveness for my wanderings and distractions. Keep me always disciplined and in control of my thoughts and dreaming," he prayed.

He kept fit and developed great strength through gymnastics

At times, a classmate tried his patience, and he confessed, "Lord, I have failed in human charity. Help me to understand all my fellow men, and see in them the spirit and soul which you have given to each of us. I was harsh and judgmental today, when I became impatient with my friend's arguing. Please forgive me, and help me to make amends, all of this in serving You, through the people whom I encounter along the way."

The afternoons were for more studies and for sport. He looked forward to the sport, and it was an important balance to the deep thinking and mental work, which was piled upon them each day. Evening prayers were said in the church before supper, with a spiritual reading. Then there was a period when they were able to socialise for a few hours, before going to their rooms for the night.

At the seminary he received thorough and disciplined teachings in philosophy, theology, pedagogy, nature study, morality, the bible, literature etc. There was so much to learn about, and his mind was like a sponge, absorbing all he heard and read.

He often thought again about Francis Pfanner, the founder of their Mariannhill Congregation. This was a holy man, but a man of action. He had become a contemplative Trappist monk, to be close to God, and to pray for the world and all of its people. However, in South Africa, teaching trades to people—skills like carpentry, masonry, and so on, he had seen other needs. There was a continent, with so many people who didn't know God, and who had no education to read or learn with. He saw these needs and the poverty of the people. Eventually, he could not carry on only as a contemplative monk, and he was determined to help people more. He was sure God had not brought him there to stand by and not get involved where he could see how much he could do for these simple, but happy Africans.

Odilo remembered the school plays that he had performed in, and the call to free people from ignorance and bring them to God. He knew he was following a calling, and that it was right for him. If only he could do it well, perfectly; "that is what God wants from me," he was certain now.

CONFRONTING THE BIG QUESTION

The deeper spiritual training was also a way of testing his vocation. Their teachers knew what they would have to contend with in the future, and what they had to give up now, at the age of twenty-five. "You have to be absolutely sure before you take your final vows," the rector reminded him often. "It is no use going out to Africa forever, and then thinking you can change your mind." He assured them all, "you can leave at any time until you make your final vows. That is three years away, so we are not rushing you. God will soon tell you, or us, if this is not your true calling."

When he went home for his first holidays, he could not help noticing that his sister, Rosa, had some very nice girl friends. One of them was Gustie Vierling, a beautiful girl, with fine blond hair and lovely eyes that he found so fascinating. She was hard to forget, after he had met her and spoken with her.

At night he would sometimes lie awake with troubling thoughts about her or other beautiful girls. Their hair, their eyes, their mouths, their ears, and above all the feminine curves and mystery concealed but revealed by their cotton dresses; a boy is designed to respond to these attractions. "How can I give up something so wonderful?" he questioned himself. He understood the sensual experience of being close to or touching a girl.

Wherever he went, there seemed to be girls who drew his eyes, and his thoughts strayed. The beauty and appeal of women was so powerful that he almost relented. He remembered how he was assured that, as a man, he would continue to be tempted. Watching a moth fascinated by a candle flame one evening, made him think of the power of desires; he knew that he must take control of his thinking, though, in order to resist what he had chosen to stay away from.

"If God wants you to become a priest, He will give you the grace you need to control your thoughts and desires," his confessor assured him during a very honest and direct confession. "Becoming a priest is not easy, and remaining faithful to your vows is beyond you as an ordinary person. Keep busy, distract your mind with sport and study. And, most of all, pray. Pray for God's guidance and strength of purpose."

"What if I do not have a vocation, Father?" he asked humbly. "What if I do not have the strength to take the vow of chastity?"

"Well, my son, that you alone will know and decide. God has led you this far, and He will not fail you if you listen to Him. Have faith, and stick to your training and study," he urged. "None of us are beyond temptation; but if we stay close to God, He will not allow us to fail. Now, make a sincere act of contrition, and for your penance, I want you to say a full Rosary, meditating on the Virgin Mary, and her role in our salvation. Jesus assigned her in a most special way to be the guide and comfort of His apostles and priests."

"Yes, Father," he accepted.

Something made the kindly old priest add a personal bit of advice. "You will find your priestly life a very tough calling; it is not meant to be easy. One of the hardest things you have to cope with is purity. There are many temptations for a man, but you must resist them with great determination. I have found that one of the greatest helps has been my devotion to Our Blessed Mother. In Our Lady we have the perfection of womanhood. Infinitely pure, yet beautiful like no other woman who ever lived. When I am tempted to harbour impure thoughts, or my desires begin to well up in me, I stop and pray to her. I ask Our Lady to strengthen me, and I think of her as the perfect woman. It helps me not to debase women by thinking impure thoughts, thoughts which are most improper for a priest." He paused in his monologue, and asked, "Does that make sense?"

"Thank you, Father," Odilo said. "You have given me something very special. I shall always remember your advice, and pay great heed to my devotion to Our Lady."

Alone in his own bedroom, he read, studied and prayed. Still, the dreams of a young man are not suppressed by commanding them to go, and Odilo learned to accept them for what they are, and to persevere in his calling. He met a wonderful girl, Maria Lecheler, on his home visit from university in 1938. Again, his vocation was tested, and she was clearly attracted to him as a man. She soon came to understand how deeply he was committed to his vows, and they became and remained good friends. Odilo never lost his enjoyment of female company, and always had his fair share of admirers, but he had excluded the option of sex from his own life.

When it seemed that he might start to daydream, he would call to mind the beautiful statue of Our Lady at Marienburg; he prayed Hail Mary's and thought of her role in salvation and accepting the Incarnation of Jesus Christ. She had carried Him in her womb, and given birth to the Messiah, God the Son. To be called upon to do that, she was surely so perfect in every way. Sinless and pure, his image of her was soon so strong that he saw girls and women in a wonderful way, their motherhood and femininity were such a wonderful gift from God.

WURZBURG WAS FULL OF INSPIRATION

There were lots of inspiring religious sites and splendours in Wurzburg. Many of the beautiful churches dated from the pre-Napoleonic times when princes were bishops, and bishops were princes. The great splendour and wealth of the churches and monasteries originated in the piety of the age.

He was fascinated by the grandeur of the Marienburg Castle and the baroque La Residenz. Everywhere he went, he came across an abundance of art, and it was of the finest quality. Artists like Tilman Riemenschneider had left a rich legacy of detailed wooden carvings over four hundred years before.

On the far side of the river, there were life sized Stations of the Cross. The way of the cross was made up of about two hundred steps, and he soon came to know most of them quite well. There was also a wonderful view over the seminary, and the Main.

"Lord, you surveyed Jerusalem like this from the Mountain of Olives," he prayed. "Please strengthen me with your love and divine grace, for I fall easily. I am impatient and very human. You suffered out of great love for all creation, and we rightly give you thanks and praise. Help me to fulfil the calling that you have given me. Keep my thoughts from straying, but may I always appreciate and enjoy the company of all the people You have placed in my life, now and in the times ahead of me."

There were thick, dark clouds in the sky, and the air was charged and ready for a huge storm. As he hurried down the steps, to cross the Main River, he passed a crucifixion scene, and he thought of Jesus, and how he had crossed the Kedron stream.

He had often prayed at the fourteen Stations of the Cross, on the hill, and his thoughts and prayerful moments flashed through his mind. He was going up to the mountain, like Moses, and when he crossed the river, he was following in the footsteps of Joshua. He thought of that passage where the scouts returned and demoralised the people, saying that they felt like grasshoppers, while they were confronted by defenders who were giants. One of the lecturers had spoken of how the devil loves to discourage us; it is a powerful weapon, and we are easy victims to this deceit.

"But, we are not grasshoppers!" He explained, "The Chosen People were soon victorious under Joshua, because they took courage and fought, with God's help, following His orders."

He was offering himself to God now, in a humble way. "Dear Jesus, allow me to join my life with yours. Let me spend my life for you and your people." He knew at that moment that he was doing what God wanted of him. He was never more convinced than now, that becoming a missionary was God's calling for him.

TEACHERS AND SUBJECTS

At High School, Odilo had been very good at History and languages. He was okay at maths, but had been hopeless at drawing; for which he only got a five; he would actually have scored a four if he had not made the desperate mistake of copying something from his neighbour!

One day, his professor questioned him about his Certificate results. "How many firsts did you get?"

"Seven" was the reply.

"And how many seconds?" he asked.

"Two", he replied.

"How many thirds?"

"None."

"How many fourths?"

"None." At this point, he dropped the next question, assuming he had covered all the likely answers; thus Odilo never had to lie or reveal the truth about his failed Drawing. What a relief!

Professor Merkle, a Swabian, taught him Church history. Merkle was a very courageous man. He was huge, leonine and very impressive, with long hair. He was quite open in pointing out the faults of the Catholic Church, where these had been made, and he expected his students to be critical. Some of those in authority did not find it easy to accept this aspect of his teaching. However, he was also very good at discrediting the critics of the Church, most of whom spoke without full understanding, or knowledge of the facts.

"Now, let's look at Martin Luther," he began one day. "We don't have to agree with everything he said, but he certainly had reasons for some of his rebellion against the Church."

'What can he be saying?' thought Odilo, for this sounded almost as if he was supporting a heretic.

"The Reformation started in 1516. Do you know how he became a priest?" he asked, rhetorically.

"Luther was out walking in a thunderstorm," he carried on. "There was fierce lightning all about! Luther said to God, 'If I am not killed by this lightning I will become a monk.'"

"Of course, God saved him, and that's what he did. He became an Augustinian monk." He paused to let that sink in. "Now, the Church was morally lax at this time. Some of the clergy even had mistresses. They lived princely lifestyles, and there were lots of worldly influences on the clergy and the Church."

"How did this come about?" Merkle mused loudly. "Emperor Otto the First had intended well, when he involved the priests as princes and advisers. They were considered to be men above material desires, and their advice would be for the best good of the people. However, the earthly authority they were accorded soon diverted and corrupted some of these churchmen. Moral standards in the church were lowered. Princes soon became avaricious for money and power."

This was not the sort of lecture Odilo expected to hear at seminary. The Church had always been extolled and defended in his home and school, and he found it hard to accept this bold man's obvious lack of faith and commitment. 'Should he be lecturing like this?' he wondered. 'Should he be lecturing at all? Perhaps he has been sent to confuse us, and is not a true follower of God.'

His attention came back to what was being said. "Luther saw this happening even in Rome, and he was shocked and enraged. A Dominican monk, called Tetzel preached here in Germany, offering indulgences and all sorts of things, but he expected the penitent to pay a price."

This was shocking stuff, and still Merkle went on. "He probably went way too far, and various things were reputed to have been said about the ways of the Church. It became a popular comment that, 'as soon as the money clinks in the collection bowl, the soul will come out of Purgatory.' Of course, this was untrue, but it was one of the typical accusations which were levelled against the Church at the time."

'That certainly must have been a terrible thing if it really happened,' agreed Odilo inwardly.

"The Pope could have been much more diplomatic in dealing with Luther. He was too over-bearing in his reaction," Merkle continued.

"Furthermore, some of the German secular princes wanted to get hold of the Church's property. And why not? The Benedictines were the finest agriculturists and developers of Europe. Imagine how effectively about a hundred monks at a time could clear and plant lands and forests."

"Anyway, Luther was captured and held in custody, to prevent him having any dialogue with the Pope. By the way, Luther also made some very bad statements about the Jews. Why do you think they are so easily persecuted here in Germany now?"

There were no answers from the class. "Jews have been stupidly blamed for many things, but Goebbels has to be the biggest liar I have ever come across," he added boldly, noticing how a few students looked about them.

The Jews were seen to be the biggest influence in commerce, and they were blamed for the many shortages and business failures. There was so much Jew-baiting going on, right now, all over Germany, and even here in Wurzburg, that this was an important thought. "What did he say?" one of the students asked curiously.

"Well, let me quote you from one of Goebbels' statements. 'Their synagogues should be set on fire . . . for the honour of Christianity . . . their homes should be destroyed . . . their rabbis forbidden to preach under threat of death. Let us drive them from the country for all time. If this advice does not suit, then find a better one that we may be rid of this devilish burden—the Jews.' What do you think of that, then?" he asked his students.

"I just know it's getting worse," one of them answered. "And what are we doing to stop it?"

The lesson took a diversion for a while, discussing the posters and literature which had proliferated, like that schoolbook, 'The Poisonous Mushroom'. They discussed the Old Testament origins of the sacrificial symbol and the term 'scapegoat', and how Hitler was blaming the Jews for all Germany's woes. He reminded them of a statement by Pope Pius XI, "It is not possible for Christians to take part in anti-Semitism. We are all Semites spiritually."

Gradually, Professor Merkle came back to the Reformation and how Adolf Gustav of Sweden came onto the scene, and the Thirty

Years War, which followed, against the Church. "This did great damage to the faith. However, the King of Bavaria stuck firmly to the Catholic faith, as well as some staunch believers in the Rhineland, like the great Jesuit, Peter Klaver."

The next lesson was with Doctor Pascher, who was another of their greatly respected professors. He strode in with a comfortable air of self-assurance, a fine, clean-cut man. Father Odilo admired his ascetic look; it was not excessive, but he clearly was not a man ruled by his passions. His demeanour and bearing made a deep impression on all his students, and unknowingly many adopted some of his style and mannerisms. He was very knowledgeable on a wide variety of subjects, including science, where some of his observations were quite prophetic, as later scientific discovery proved.

One day, he told them, "There is no such thing as dead matter. Everything is alive, and made of tiny moving particles." He had great vision and a powerful desire to know more about God's wonderful creation.

HELPING HIS OLDER BROTHER!

In the meantime, Odilo's brother, Josef, was having a serious problem with learning new languages, in particular Hebrew. In fact, he realised that he had absolutely no chance of graduating unless a miracle happened, or . . . . unless he had somebody else who could pass his exam for him. Their Hebrew Professor was one of those men with thick-lensed glasses. He struggled to see very far, and often stumbled as he walked slowly up the university steps; the perfect plan occurred to Josef one day.

"Otto, I have a very important request to make of you. You have to sit my oral exam for me," he appealed.

"Oh no, I cannot do that," said his younger brother. "It is dishonest, and besides Professor Braun would know it is me anyway."

"No, he wouldn't. I am sure he would never know the difference. Please, Otto. I have no choice; I have been studying so hard and I have passed everything else. But if I do not pass this Hebrew course, I cannot become a priest," was his older brother's logical appeal.

"You are mad, man" he blurted. "I cannot do that!"

"If you do not, I am finished," replied Josef. "Look here, it's not such a bad thing. I know what I am doing, and I will be a good priest, but this could stop me completely. You simply must help me. I assure you, that old Braun is blind as a bat. You are about my size, and you are a Weeger. You don't even have to lie."

On and on went the discussion, until an odd scripture came to mind—he had been troubled by the story of Jacob impersonating his twin brother, Esau in order to secure that all-important blessing from Isaac, in Genesis 28. Despite the wrongness it had clearly been God's plan for the blessing to pass on to Jacob and the people of Israel who followed. Otto finally relented, seeing how desperate and determined Josef was.

When he presented himself for the exam, which was an oral examination, he was called up, "Weeger, your turn. Come forward." So far so good, and their confreres were not letting on as they all knew Josef's problem. As he sat down, too close to Braun for his comfort, he was asked, "Are you Weeger?"

"Yes, I am Weeger," was his relieved reply. He was sweating now; he could feel perspiration dripping down his legs in his trousers.

"Funny, I don't recognise you," he said, peering through his thick lenses straight at Otto's eyes.

"OOPS", he thought, "I am done for". But, screwing up his determination, he went on, carefully doing all he could so that he would not actually be telling a lie. "Herr Braun, if I sit far back in a big class like this, with your thick glasses, it must be hard to see clearly."

"Well, let's get on with it then," Professor Braun demurred. The questions flowed and Otto answered well enough. His voice and general appearance were close enough to Josef's, and he was never actually asked if he was Josef Weeger. At the end, Braun said, "Good, I congratulate you; you have passed. But I still don't know you, Weeger."

NATIONALISM AND THE CHURCH

The country was in a muddle, and Nazism was gaining ground all over Germany. Hitler had stirred up the unemployed and desperate people; and those who had been clutching for opportunities, gave him their loyalty. The Catholic Church was in a difficult position, and some of its strongest leaders were persecuted, imprisoned or even killed as enemies of the state. Spies were everywhere, and an unguarded comment was quickly reported to the ruthless and ever-present SS.

Rome's objections were totally ignored by the all-powerful new state, as it deliberately phased in more and more Sunday sport and cultural meetings, whilst removing the rights of catechism and Catholic teaching at schools. The Pope knew and loved Germany, but was horrified at how this madness was taking root, and turning people, often in fear of their very existence. He was slow to speak out with force, and had to be very careful for the safety of his clergy and flock. Individual bishops and priests spoke out and suffered the most severe consequences. The Catholic Church was not alone in its protests, but many were made submissive and silenced.

'How can the Church speak out and endanger more of its priests and people?' was a deep worry, especially among the bishops.

Until one day, on 14th March 1937, something dangerous and dramatic took place. As the seminarians sat back in their seats, the rector made a surprise announcement. In a solemn voice he said, "the Holy Father has issued a special letter to the Catholic Church throughout Germany, which is to be read today. Its subject is the Church and the German Reich, and begins with his expression of deep anxiety; he has headed it *mit brennender Sorge*, with burning and urgent concern."

"It is a long letter, and I ask you all to listen with ears of faith. Pope Pius XI has a deep understanding and love for the Church here in Germany, but he is very concerned at some of the things happening here, in Germany," he said by way of softening the mood. There was a strong sense of apprehension, and they sensed that something momentous and also dangerous was about to be proclaimed.

"We are all proud of our country, and I know we do not all have the same views about certain things. When in doubt, though, we must go back to the basis of our faith, and this letter reminds us of that principal. Our Pope has been patient, even when the 'concordat' he signed with our leader has been twisted and trodden underfoot. Our faith is being excluded from school classrooms and compulsory Sunday activities are attempts to cut us off from Jesus Christ himself."

"Our Catholicism is truly being derided and cast aside by nationalism, and the racial pride that is being fostered is leading to evil consequences. The Holy Father points out many things for the good of our souls, among them a reference even to Cicero's observation on basic natural law as well; 'Nothing can be useful, if it is not at the same time morally good.' I ask you all to sit with your eyes closed, and let these words sink deep in your mind so that you can understand and follow the advice and teaching which is being given here."

Odilo Weeger listened in some pain and concern, as the words that were read out struck home. It was a very strong and brave message, to resist the false teachings of worldly leaders, and to be obedient to the natural and spiritual laws of God, and the teachings of the Church of Christ.

He knew that it was very true; the Pope did not say things that were not true, for a start. This letter was a definite attack on the rulers of Germany, their nationalism and disregard for others who differed, and especially the Jews, who were suffering persecution and even being interred in concentration camps. The call to stand up to evil was powerful, but intimidating; everywhere Hitler's youth, his brown-shirts, his soldiers and his voice were being idolised.

"Phew!" he exclaimed as they walked down the steps from the church. "That's going to cause a lot of trouble. Nobody has dared to stand up to Hitler like that before!"

"He can see things which we can't, you know," the giant Elmar said. "However, the Pope's timing is just so wrong. There is going to be a big backlash for sure. You see, he doesn't understand us Germans; we secretly all want Hitler to lead us to great victory. Deep down, we all believe in avenging what has been done to us by Britain and France, and Russia."

"What he said about tolerance of others, though; that is important," Ernst said. "We have no right to look down on others, even the Jews. Jesus called us to love everybody. Nazism thinks that only pure Germans are the perfect people, the master race!"

"Well, what's wrong with that?" one of the students jibed jokingly.

Later, Professor Merkle said, "I know this is hard to consider. However, Hitler is basically an evil man. He has no faith. He is a communist himself. He has no respect for life—even good German lives. Above all, his hatred of the Jews is of the devil himself."

"Professor, I want to ask you about the Jews," ventured one of the bolder seminarians.

"Go ahead," he allowed.

"Well, I come from a small town and my father used to have a shop there. He was doing quite well many years ago. Then a Jewish man came with his family. His name was Feinberg, and he set up a shop, just like my father's."

"That is a fairly normal Jewish thing and anybody's right," Professor Merkle commented gently.

"Yes, but he charged less for everything. He would just drop his price by a half Pfennig; but that was enough. Everybody started buying from him, and pretty soon my father had to sell his shop. In fact, he sold it to another Jew-boy, who came from Austria."

"That is a sad story," Professor Merkle said, "but is there anything morally wrong with what happened?"

"No. I mean, well, yes. I think there is. My father had that business from his father, and his father before him. He worked hard. He was educating us children. He was bringing us up, as was our right, as good Germans." He paused, to gather his thoughts, and the others waited respectfully. The story was a familiar one, in any case. "The thing I don't like is the way foreigners can come in and take over like that, destroying good, honest German businesses. My father now works for a clothing factory, as a bookkeeper. It is just totally immoral and unjust."

"I understand your feelings. I also sympathise; I have had similar experiences among my own family. Now, firstly you must remember that not all the problems are because of the Jews. Our country has suffered terribly because of the war. To add to our problems the reparation costs are too huge for us to recover."

"But, and this is an important point, wars damage economies. It can seem as if we are very busy and factories are working well, like they are starting to do now. But, what are we making that is useful to society? Bombs, bullets, tanks, guns? Pha! They are not real things. Their purpose is destruction only. If we made machines for our factories or bricks and tiles for more houses that would be a better way to use our efforts." He paused as he realized he was 'lecturing'; these were now seniors; no they were all grown men now. He knew he could speak with them as equals.

"Don't think I don't have my anger and disappointments about what has happened to us. I love Germany. I have deep respect for our glorious history. We are a great nation, and we have done great things for the world, in culture and science and all sorts of areas. But, we are being misled because we are desperate now. We are crying out for a leader with strength, somebody to restore our pride and put Germany back where we want it."

He got up, and went to the board. He sketched Europe and filled in Germany's borders. "We are the heart and might of Europe, as you can see. You know from your history how we have controlled most of Europe at one time or another. So, Hitler comes along, and he appeals to our pride."

"The devil does that, by the way. That is his favourite tactic—'tickle their pride, and they will go wrong, coming my way,' he thinks. Well, who is Hitler anyway? Why should we look up to him, a man with 'short-man syndrome', if some of our shorter men will excuse me saying it? He comes from an uncultured family; he has no worthwhile learning himself."

The class was starting to become uneasy, and Odilo could see some of them looking around, checking for spies. "It is not safe to speak out too loudly against him," one of them said carefully.

"Who can stop him, then?" asked Merkle. "I have often told you about my theory that one drop of honey is better than a whole barrel full of vinegar, if you want to coax somebody to do the right thing; but this is not such a case. Here is a leader who has fanned up tremendous support, but he is basically a tyrant. You watch; he will be rounding up bishops and priests before the end of the week."

He paused and paced back and forth for a moment. "I am sorry. I lost my thoughts for a while, there. We were talking about something else. You raised the question of Jews, and their businesses taking over. Firstly, I think we know they are steeped in business from an early age. It is spoken about at meals, even in their synagogues; it is their life. Perhaps it is their false god, just as sex and other things can lead people to ignore the one, true, God. The fact remains that they are good at business; they also work very hard at it. How often do you see them at the Bierhalle?"

"Secondly, our economy has been in a state of collapse; many businesses, like your father's were probably doomed already."

"Thirdly, they support one another. Their family links and the way they help one another puts us all to shame. How many German shopkeepers would think of helping another German competitor if he was going out of business? If you are honest, you will admit they might even be waiting smugly; they will think, 'Ah, good. If he closes, then his customers must come to me!' Not so?"

There were gestures of acknowledgement.

"And fourthly, they believe in God. They still believe in the God of the Old Testament, but they believe. The Jews still believe that the messiah is yet to come. They could not accept Jesus; he did not fit with their stubborn pride. Their messiah had to come with pomp and glory, and place them at the pinnacle of the entire world."

"Jesus came to redeem us from that sort of thinking, the sort that had them making a golden calf, just after they had agreed to worship one God only and before all else. Can you see their problem?" he paused as he looked at his nodding and attentive students.

This had been an exceptional class, and he was sorry that they would soon be leaving; but he expected great things of them. "But never, never, think they are godless. One day, they will all come together with us, in God's time. He has no intention of abandoning them—I assure you of that. The Jews still have every right to say they are the Chosen People—but so do we, as Christians."

"But, they are in control of our country," one student still murmured aloud.

"In what way?"

"They control the banks, the businesses, everything!" he said in exasperation.

"I am afraid your next lecture is about to begin, so we shall have to stop there for now. I just want you to remember what Jesus said about being a good shepherd—finding and bringing back a lost sheep means more to the shepherd than even caring for the obedient ones."

Hitler had reacted to the Pope's letter almost immediately. His spies reported the reading, not just in one church but across the whole length and breadth of Germany. "This is a direct attack on me!" he fumed. "Just who does that little Italian Pope think he is?"

"Mein Fuhrer," one of his accompanying officers stammered. "It will be forgotten soon. It is only the church leaders who pay attention.

The people are all loyal to you," he said in a placating voice. (Who knew what Hitler was capable of when seized by his mad frenzies? He remembered how Hitler had personally overseen the slaughter of seven thousand Germans who were loyal to Ernst Roehm, and potentially opposed to him in Munich. That was some years ago now, and his grip was constantly tightening.)

"I cannot allow this. It is an insult and invasion. It is an attack! The Pope has declared himself my enemy. Those people who choose to follow him must soon know the consequences! Their priests must be removed," he said sinisterly. "Be careful, though; do not let them have somebody prominent to rally around."

Students at University, even seminarians, were forced to take part in marches; if they refused they would be expelled from studies in the state-run institutions. They used to join in, but secretly they made jokes and commented critically among themselves; they were certainly not intending to show any support. They had no practical choices, and had to go along when it was imposed on them in this manner. Hitler could close them down completely and have them imprisoned, and he was already behaving with total disregard for any religion or ethics.

"I think the Pope is over-reacting," one of Odilo's colleagues said. "My father is in the army, and he knows what is really happening. Hitler is building up the nation again, just as it should be."

"My older brother has decided to join as well," admitted Odilo. "Apart from anything else, it is a paying job."

"Shame on you both," Ernst, the radical, intervened. "This whole country is being led into evil by that man. We all know he has no time for religion."

"Well, the Pope signed that concordat with him three years ago," Klaus reminded them, hoping to put an end to this delicate debate. It was not healthy to talk openly about Hitler in any disparaging way. Somebody could report it.

Undeterred, Ernst said, "can't you see how he manipulated the Pope into agreeing to a *concordat*? Cardinal Pacelli thought he would stick to it. He certainly hasn't. Hitler thinks he is above any rules or agreements. The day it was signed, he made a big fuss saying he had the Catholic Church in support. It was just for the votes, and then look what he did! He has broken every condition one by one, and never worried the slightest bit when the Pope made his protests. He knew the Pope could do nothing about it."

"Ah, sure. Well, we shall see," Odilo demurred. They were all concerned that they were getting so involved in this tedious subject again. Besides, it was becoming quite dangerous to express views like these.

Hitler's Youth and Bullies

As Nazism became more entrenched, Hitler's youths and brown-shirts were urged to greater displays of loyalty to the fatherland. They grew bolder, knowing that they would not be punished, and their intimidation tactics evolved with new nastiness. Anti-Semitic incitement was now more and more public. One day in 1937, Odilo was walking on the pavement with his colleagues when straw puppets, or effigies, of Jews were dragged through Wurzburg and people were encouraged to kick and mock them, to symbolise their attitude towards the Jews. The young men looked on, and even forced half-hearted smiles; looks of disapproval would invite a challenge from the brown-shirts and the mob that they had with them.

Those priests, and anybody else who objected strongly to Nazism, were taken away and interrogated. Others were sent to concentration camps. The Church was in a difficult position, and Hitler somehow sensed that many honest scholars of history, and most of the church leaders, were not in favour of him, or his more obvious evil personality.

"He is a tyrant," one lecturer spat out. "He is the worst leader Germany has ever had in all its history, and we will grow to be deeply ashamed of electing him."

"I see they have just arrested Niemoeller. He stood up for the Jews, all right. I expect he will be shipped away to a concentration camp to silence him," somebody reported.

"You know, I don't like Hitler at all; but look what he is doing to improve conditions for Germany. He has given people jobs, incomes and dignity. He is restoring a sense of national pride; something the French and British have been trying to annihilate," reasoned his colleague.

"We all thought that, at the next election, there would be a chance for change," his father said to Odilo. "But it doesn't look as if he intends giving us that chance!" (Many years later, and far away from Germany, Odilo would find himself faced with similar, despotic rule which would remind him of these terrible times.)

His superiors took a wise and fortuitous decision. It was providential, and had a big influence on their lives and destinies. The young men now took their solemn vows for life, swearing themselves to poverty, chastity and obedience. Nine priests out of their class of twenty-five were to be sent to Mariannhill in South Africa; there they would be able to complete their studies and embark on their missionary life. Some stayed in Germany to teach, and others went to the United States of America to teach.

Those in the class behind, which included Father Edmar, and Father Guntram, were no longer allowed out of Germany, and it was ten years before any missionaries would come from Germany again, or go back to visit either.

CHAPTER 5

FLIGHT TO NEW TERRITORY

LEAVING BAVARIA AND FAMILY

That last Sunday at home in June 1938, had to rate as the most emotional and tumultuous day of his life. All the villagers of Arberg were there for the parade and Holy Mass. The brass band led them marching prayerfully through the village.

Strong Bavarian voices were raised in unison, praising and thanking God for all He was doing in their lives. Father Odilo walked solemnly and yet so many things distracted his thoughts. As the parade turned the last corner before entering the church, he saw his mother and father walking close to each other.

He thought he knew his father well. He could always keep such a stern manner about him; but now he could see from the expression on his face how much he was struggling to control his deep emotions.

Josef's lips were pinched tight together so they would not betray the flutter, just like the feeling which he was also experiencing again himself. His eyes were moist and shining, and he could see that his father was trying so hard to avoid embarrassing himself with visible tears.

Julianna was not succeeding, however. Her eyes and even her cheeks were red from the regular deluge of tears, and she kept dabbing at herself with a large white handkerchief. It was beautifully embroidered, as if that would distract observers from a handkerchief's true actions.

The band struck up the powerful chords of the hymn, *Grosse Gott*, Great God.

> *Holy God, we praise Thy name;*
> *Lord of all, we bow before Thee!*

Both of the priests walking with him sang out with rich and faithful voices, and suddenly Father Odilo found his own voice failing him. He had to cough as he concealed his emotions. 'Oh Almighty God,' he thought and prayed, 'You are truly great and loving. I could never deserve what you do for me, and for all of us. I promise you, I will always be faithful and strong in carrying out your work. Keep me in your love and strengthen me with your grace.'

> *All on earth thy sceptre own,*
> *All in heaven above adore thee,*
> *Infinite thy vast domain,*
> *Everlasting is thy reign.*

'That puts things in the right perspective,' he thought. 'Nothing on earth comes close to God's glory and power; even the might which we see paraded by the leaders of Germany or America, or anybody.'

> *Hark, the loud celestial hymn,*
> *Angel choirs above are raising;*
> *Cherubim and seraphim, . . .*

'You know how much we all need your mercy and graces, in these troubled times. Please Lord, come to our aid. I thank you for the rich blessings of acceptance into your priesthood, and I ask you to be with me in Africa, amidst whatever dangers and troubles I may encounter,' he prayed during the end of the hymn. He had heard or sung this hymn on many occasions. All the words of the hymn were filled with meaning, even more today than ever before.

As they entered the familiar village church of Saint Blasius, he looked at the Crucifix above the altar, and it was an image which burned itself into his memory. It was funny how it often came back to him, years later, in times of trouble or when he needed strengthening and guidance.

Jesus Christ had allowed Himself, Almighty God, to be torn apart and humiliated before dying such a stark death, such an incredible testimony of His love for mankind, His creation. What human could ever come close to such a statement of love, and who but God himself would ever try to tell us what He had done, in this last deed in the human body, which He had fully accepted and loved?

The celebrant introduced Odilo Weeger. "It also gives me great pleasure to introduce Father Josef Weeger. He has joined us today for the special occasion of his younger brother's farewell mass," explained the parish priest of Arberg. "What a great honour it is for the Weeger family, to have two sons ordained as priests. And what a great honour for our village of Arberg! We are all truly proud of you both, true sons of Bavaria. May God bless you both. Please address us now, Father Josef, for the sermon."

"The Church was charged with carrying Jesus Christ's message of salvation to all nations, everywhere in the world," he began in a solemn voice that clearly was leading to some important observations. "We are all especially proud to have Father Odilo, my young brother as one of those who has heeded this call.

He has great courage and I know that he will be a wonderful missionary. He has heeded the call of Our Lord, to go off to foreign and far-off lands, to carry out that command. God knows how much we need His help right here in Germany, and Europe, but in Africa there are countless thousands of people who have not yet heard of God, much less of Jesus Christ."

Everything was charged with emotion, and the whole congregation felt deeply stirred by the sacrifice and the heroism, which another of their young man was making now. The fact that he was one of them, one of their village children, and a son of their friends and colleagues, the Weegers, brought his action close to them. They lived through it as well, and vicariously benefited from what he was now doing on their behalf.

At the consecration he raised his new chalice, and thought of his relatives as he looked prayerfully at its broad base. He had carefully chosen Isaiah's words in response to God's question, 'whom shall I send?' with *Ecce Venio²*, 'here I am', engraved on the upper ring. The lettering on the outer perimeter ring said, *Sanguis Christi inebria me*, 'Blood of Christ, permeate and control me'. His family had given this chalice[i] to him when he celebrated his first Holy Mass, in Arberg on 8th May 1938. Father Odilo thought of God, and the work that he was now embarking upon. All of this was to be for the Kingdom of God. This was the whole purpose of his life, and this calling; he would often remind himself of this in the years ahead, as he went about his duties in Africa.

Again he clearly remembered the passage when Jesus had commanded[ii], 'go forth to the whole world, and preach the gospel to everybody.' All this painful emotion and wrenching himself far away from his family, and those he knew and cared for, could be borne because of this motive.

SAYING GOODBYE

In the bright sunshine outside, the crowd was overwhelming, and every single person was keen to make sure he knew they had greeted him and wished him well. "You are a great man, may God bless and protect you," was the gist of all of the greeting and well-wishing.

Of course, there were his own brothers and sisters, and there were also two girls who had held places of special regard in his life. How they must have wondered at life's ways! Wiltrud, with her lovely head of dark brown/black hair, patted her beautiful eyes, and smiled weakly as she knelt to receive Holy Communion.

She knew her thoughts were not on receiving Jesus at this moment, but she also knew He would forgive her and understand. This man was off to serve God in an unimaginably distant place. It was so far away that it was as if he was dying, for surely this was what bereavement must feel like. Any thought she may have had, that things could turn out differently simply had to be pushed aside now. Only she knew that she would never stop loving him; he would always be in her thoughts and constant prayers, and she could not think at that moment of finding any man who came close to Otto.

---

² Isaiah 6:9, 'Here I am, send me.'

The Weeger Family at his Farewell in 1938

There was a pretty blonde girl in the congregation, who watched his every move and expression, as if looking into his soul. She was trying to understand this wonderful boy, who was now a full-grown man; and he was leaving her life forever. A petite and glowing Elfi flung her arms around him as he stood and greeted his friends and family at the door.

"Aufwiedersehen, Father Odilo," she managed to say, before her soft and rich voice broke slightly, and she flung her arms about him and squeezed him tightly, as if to help suppress her aching heart.

For a while she savoured feeling how strong and manly were his muscled arms and back. She had once had hopes that they would be lovers, be married and have a family, here in Bavaria. She had kept those hopes alive, even as he took his first vows, and then his final vows.

But now there was no ignoring reality. He had made his choice forever, and he was God's servant, he was wedded to the church, in a way that would never be shaken. As a true friend, she would keep in contact whenever possible and she hoped he would feel and know her support, no matter how far away he was from her.

"Aufwiedersehen, Elfi," she heard his strong voice. "I shall keep you always in my prayers, and I ask you to do the same for me." Any hint of deeper feelings was now well hidden, and Odilo, the priest, was off on a life where he knew how much he was offering up for God. He hoped sincerely that she would find a wonderful man who would love and care for her.

A CELEBRATION FEAST

There was a big celebration luncheon after mass, for family and friends. Everybody hurried to the Gasthaus zum Loewen. A strong band and choir rang out the music. It was powerful, and the music was fantastic. His emotions soared with a great sense of love and gratitude. He felt humbled as well, 'I am not worthy of this great honour, God,' he prayed. 'But I shall do all in my power, with Your grace and support, to carry out Your will.'

The mayor, the parish priest and the headmaster of Odilo's school made speeches. His father rose to reply. "My dear friends, I and my family are deeply touched by the wonderful words of praise and encouragement, which have been said today, for our beloved son, Otto, now Father Odilo. He is now off to be a missionary to Africa. We are filled with the deepest of sorrow as we have to say good-bye to Otto, now Father Odilo," he repeated, and Josef had to pause here to bring himself under control. "Sorry," he stammered.

"Otto has been a wonderful son, a fine man and an inspiration to all of us in the family and our village. He has always been a dutiful and respectful son. He has worked and studied with great dedication. He has been a great athlete and sportsman, and I am sure his strength and health will see him through whatever Africa throws his way. We ask you all to join us in wishing him God's richest blessings, and keeping him safe from harm."

Father Odilo rose to his feet, in his neatly pressed cassock, perfectly groomed and standing in his characteristic posture of well-controlled manliness. "Thank you, Father, Mister Mayor, Father Rector, and Herr Braun," he politely acknowledged the speakers.

"I am sad to be leaving you all. But I thank you for everything you have done for me, and I assure you of my great love for you all, and that you will always be in my thoughts and prayers. Please keep me in your prayers. I shall need God's help and guidance, but I go to Africa with confidence. I have great faith in God's divine providence.

There is a great need in Africa, with thousands, millions, who do not know about God. I often think of Jesus' instruction, "go forth and teach all nations," and I know that I am privileged to be called to help as a missionary. God has brought me this far, and He must have a purpose and work for me to fulfil. So I shall go, and I shall carry it out to the best of my ability. I know it is a call for life; and in accordance with the rules of my order, I do not expect to ever see you again."

DEPARTING ON HIS LIFE JOURNEY

When the car was loaded, and every last detail had been attended to, Father Odilo shook his father's hand and hugged him for the last time. Josef was so proud of his son that his heart was bursting, but no words formed in his mouth, as he clung to his once-little-boy, and passed on his love in the longest embrace he had ever given any of his children. He had so much admiration for him. He had a priest son, second to none, and a missionary on top of it all.

He could relate to the strong Weeger courage, from his bloodline, brave enough to go into distant Africa, facing the lions, leopards, crocodiles, elephants, raw tribes-people and living in a jungle. Who knew what he was letting himself in for? He felt sad; he was torn apart with strong emotions. This was not just "Auf wiedersehen!"—it was goodbye, forever. This move was for life!

Julianna knew this even more deeply, and no amount of self-control for her son's sake, could hold back the sobs rising and choking in her chest. She hugged her son lovingly, and her body heaved and sagged with loving sorrow. Father Odilo hugged her back with great love and understanding, and his own heart was breaking in pieces, as he knew this would be the last face-to-face exchange with his mother.

She had borne him, and reared him, watched his every step as he grew through infancy. Julianna had taught him and spoken with him, and listened to all his news and thoughts as he grew from childhood to manhood. 'Holy Mother Mary,' thought Father Odilo, 'I know you must have loved Jesus as much as my mother has loved me. Please help me to step back without acting like a baby, and to say farewell as I must now.'

He hurried into the car, and composed himself to wave and say goodbye. Some instinct, surely one every person clings to, made him hope, 'I will be back some day, God willing.' The villagers cheered and waved him on his way; a true son of whom they were all proud; he was part of them, but now he was to be no longer. He saw the storks' nests in the village chimneys, and now his own journey to Africa had begun.

Train Journey to Hamburg

They drove to Wurzburg by car, and then spent Sunday and Monday nights there as they all assembled. They were taken to the railway station, and waved off on their trip to Hamburg.

He soaked up the sights and smells of his homeland, knowing that he would never be returning. The train passed through Lohr and over the Main River, bringing back many happy memories. Most of the journey was now through the night, with a short stop in Gottingen before reaching Hanover, where some passengers disembarked. New passengers hurriedly took their places and the train clattered on, further and further from his home.

Although the sun was shining, they had been traversing dull and grimy plains for some hours, all so unlike the clean beauty of Bavaria. As they came closer to the port, the little villages had been closer together, and there were many more trucks on the road, and people walking, often with a barrow or a load on their shoulders.

They rattled loudly past factories and workshops, smoking their waste into the wet air. There was an atmosphere of storing and squirreling, perhaps for hard times, or the prosperity and boom times that the pending war was sure to bring.

They soon came to the outskirts of Hamburg and the train rumbled across the Elbe River, halting in the main railway station. They had tidied up and were ready, and took it in turns passing their trunks and bags out to one another, as they alighted on the crowded platform. The worst thing about travel is always the luggage that has to be moved with you, but Father Odilo and his contemporaries had less than most. They ferried the trunks and bags along the platform to the entrance where they hired a taxi to take their luggage to the docks, leaving them with only hand luggage for the rest of the day.

In their sightseeing they visited many famous places in this very prosperous city/state. Hamburg was the heart of the Hanseatic towns and city-states, controlling all freight and movement.

Later they arrived at the platform adjoining the huge harbours, where a giant forest of cranes and derricks was stooping to pluck loads from the ships, like water birds, feeding from the swamplands. The waiting ships were buzzing with activity; stevedores were directing and stacking the cargo in the holds.

The Watussi

Close by, there was a huge ocean liner, with streamers and fashionably dressed ladies and gentlemen gathered on the decks, hanging over the rails, and waving and shouting last-minute farewells to families and friends below. There were lots of uniformed men in evidence, their uniforms perfectly pressed and every centimetre of their bearing spelling out their importance and purpose. These were the men who would be ushering in the brilliant future for their homeland; women could sense this, and gave their allegiance and lots more to these brave new men.

The strange name *Watussi* was painted in fresh black paint high on the side. "The people in our colony Burundi are called the Watutsi," he was told.

A man with a bristling moustache was shouting angrily at the stevedore as he watched his sleek black motor car being lifted up and spinning in the air. The rope cables slung down around the crib of steel and timber looked far too light for such an important and shiny-new car, which had probably come straight off the latest tooling and designs of this year's record-breaking production line. The operator ignored him with the disdain of a craftsman, and with undue haste, soon had the vehicle almost plummeting into its hold, out of sight and earshot of the anguished yelling of its owner or his dutiful agent.

Over twelve hundred people were on the list for this sailing. Some of the places were taken for troop movements, but there were many people coming and going between Germany and Africa, and those moving between Germany, Holland, France and England. A crewman said, "You should see how much furniture we have to carry; this is the busiest moving trip I have ever been involved with, and I have been sailing for over forty years now!"

The evening sunshine persisted until the last passenger had been squeezed aboard. The rector from their seminary stood alone on the fading shoreline, as the *Watussi* blew hard on its whistle and took over from the tugs, which had pulled it out into the busy sea-lane. It was Providence that they had been sent off on this ship, for they were to be the last group of missionaries who were able to leave Germany.

The *Landratte* on a Sea Voyage

The nine young priests followed their leader, Father John Lignau. Father John explained, "It takes seven weeks from Hamburg to Durban. We will stop and load up at Bremen first. Then we go on to Amsterdam and Rotterdam. We have a short stop at each port, and go on to Antwerp next. After that we have to land in England, at Southampton; don't expect too much there after a giant port like Hamburg. We stop at Las Palmas on the Azores Islands, just off the African coast."

"Will we see the shore?" asked Father Gerwald.

"Most of the time we shall see nothing, just sea. I think by then you Landratte will have found your sea legs."

The rolling and rising of the ship had been making Father Odilo feel queasy and he had to admit that he was a mountain man; he was not at all experienced in sea travel.

When they crossed the equator, the ship broke into a festive mood with wild traditional ceremonies, including an "Equatorial baptism". He thought of their old colony, Tanganyika, right across on the equator, on the other side of Africa. They sailed past the Congo; this had been considered as the Belgian King, Leopold's personal property or territory. Then they travelled for six or eight days with no coastline in sight.

The dolphins soon broke the monotony, swimming alongside with such verve and love of life. They saw shoals of flying fish on several occasions, and sharks that swam about menacingly. One evening, after the sun had already set, Father Odilo suddenly saw a flash of light and then several more, darting about below. Later, he mentioned this to a seaman, who quickly said, "Oh, yes, I have seen them many times. You know, I've seen them most often in the Red Sea. They have phosphor on them, that's why they shine."

South of the Equator

The stars were now different, and he was intrigued to see that Orion looked as if it was upside down. Late one evening, he was looking for the promised Southern Cross, and he said, "there it is; I can see it."

"Oh no," a lady's voice corrected him from further along the railing. "You must wait a bit longer to see the Southern Cross." She smiled beautifully at him, and he was looking at the face of a lovely lady, with her little daughter at her side. He realised how much he had been missing the companionship of women.

"Hallo," the girl said shyly. "I am Wiltrud; who are you?"

'Well, that was a straight-forward introduction,' he smiled to himself. "I am Father Odilo Weeger. I am pleased to meet you."

Mrs Hiller introduced herself and the rest of his confreres soon joined him as she offered, "Would you like to see the Southern Cross?"

"Yes, please," they chorused.

"Well, we are having dinner first, and it won't be up for at least an hour. "I will happily show you before Wiltrud and I retire for the night."

It seemed a longer supper than usual, and Father Odilo was pleased when the many courses had been served and cleared.

He stood watching the shadow of distant horizons. Slowly people came up on deck, and then, Wiltrud called out, "there he is, mother, over there."

"I trust you enjoyed your dinner," she greeted him. "I noticed you slipping out early."

"Oh yes, indeed," he replied, "I was keen to learn about the Southern Cross."

"Well, there it is," she pointed. "It has come up there, on the port side, way over Africa; and just below it you can see the two pointers emerging as well."

"How long have you lived in Africa?" he asked.

"Just about all my life," she answered. "In the desert, the stars have an extra beauty. And, you can always find your way easily with the

Southern Cross," Mrs. Hiller explained, going on to detail how, with intersecting lines the South position on the horizon was always the same. "These stars appear to rotate about that point, as they change position. Sometimes, they appear late or completely disappear during the night. Tonight was perfect timing to see them come up after dinner."

They enjoyed the ship-deck company of this young German family from South West Africa, a lovely and very interesting family.

The ship docked at Lobito, in Angola and later the captain pointed out the Skeleton Coast as they continued further south. The ship docked the next day, at Walvis Bay. Mrs Hiller explained, "this is where we disembark. We live over there, in Swakopmund," she said as she pointed North up the flat coastline. "Walvis Bay is a very interesting place, and I am sure you will enjoy it; this is the last place in Africa where the people all speak German."

They exchanged addresses and he promised to write when he was settled down. He waved goodbye, and watched pensively for a while; that was the sort of family life he had turned his back on when he took his vows, a beautiful and cultured wife and a lovely young daughter. Once they had loaded their luggage into their car at the side of the dock, he watched them drive off, past the tall sand-dunes; the dust blew up behind for a long time on the desert road. He felt a strong sense of sadness and wondered when or if they would see one another again

Walvis Bay was a busy little fishing port, and did not have many big buildings. They were soon bustled off and reached their destination. "Well, here is the church," Father John said. "Let's go and meet the priest."

"I am Father Morgenschweiss," he announced, and welcomed them into his little home. "Would you like some schnapps with that coffee?" he offered. Nearly all the heads nodded approvingly, and the glasses were laid out.

"You were lucky," Siegfried soon pulled the priest's leg; "you must have had to pay a lot extra for the "W[3]" in your name."

---

[3]   This saved him from being named Morgenscheiss, during the *emancipation* time!

They all laughed heartily at this brilliant observation and their host laughed as well. He had not had such jolly company for some time. There was a note of sadness as he seemed to think about that period of Jewish Emancipation, and the names that were given, but it was old history now. However, Father Morgenschweiss realised how much he needed some laughter and spirit, with so much worry and foreboding in the air.

The next day they experienced a terrible storm for themselves as it lashed and pounded the ship, as they were sailing to Luderitzbucht. The waves and swells were enormous and the raging seas kept up their assault for two days and two nights. Despite some of his own discomfort, Father Odilo was dying to get a good snapshot of the ship cutting through these twenty metre high waves. Despite the captain's order confining all passengers below deck, he could resist no longer. As he was taking his photograph the sea reared up high above him, and he was almost swept overboard as a mighty wave picked him up and flung him across the deck.

Again, his guardian angel was working overtime; if he had been washed overboard nobody would even have known what had happened to him. "The sea nearly took me away, but I got an excellent shot with my camera!" he said, as he patted his Voigtlander.

He pondered that evening, on God's Providence and how he was saved from being swept overboard. 'This was a warning to take more care of my life,' he thought. 'My studies and vocation will be useless if I die early, and I still have many duties ahead of me.'

They celebrated Holy Mass early every morning, in a room set aside on the ship, while the ship rose and fell gently and ponderously on its voyage. They had breakfast afterwards, and soon had their own different routines of exercising and walking about for a while.

"Okay Fathers, the first one to sight Table Mountain will receive a reward," Father John promised. They were assembled on the port railing, quite accustomed now to the rhythmic rise and fall of the ship on the swells. It was hard to tell, but there seemed to be a slight cloud on the horizon.

"There it is," Father Elmar shouted first. Perhaps his height gave him the extra advantage. As their ship drew nearer, the mountain took shape, with its flat table-top, and the hills on either side of it.

It was a magnificent sight, and one of the priests commented, "This is much more imposing an entry to port than any we have experienced on the way." The mountain backdrop was silhouetted against an almost clear sky, and they stood at the railing, fascinated as its features could slowly be seen more and more clearly.

"Cape Town must be totally unique; no other port can look like this," mused Father Elmar.

A View of Table Mountain

On Dry Land, in Cape Town

The shrill seagull calls heralded approaching land, and the air was teeming with them. The wind was blowing quite stiffly, and the crests of the waves were breaking in white foam splashes and patches of bubbles that quickly melted away as they passed them.

The ship passed the long, flat, Robben Island on their left, with the mountains forming the most dramatic of backdrops. "On the left, is Devil's Peak. Then, of course, that is the unmistakable Table Mountain. I am not sure that I can make out why that one is called Lion's Head," Father John contemplated awhile. "I suppose it takes shape as you look at it more." He paused for a long time watching as they drew closer. "Over to this end of it, the rump really, is Signal Hill."

"After all this time on ship, I just can't wait to get out there and climb up that mountain," said Father Odilo. The green slopes leading up to it merged into horizontally layered cliff faces, but he could see places where it looked quite easy to make a way to the flat top.

"I feel homesick for mountain climbing. Let's make that our first day's task," Father Elmar urged, as they all murmured their assent.

Father Lignau had been there before, so he guided them all as soon as they had descended the gangway to the dockside below. Their first task was to book into a hotel and dispose of their luggage.

Then he took them out on the wide, open Grand Parade. "I want you to visit the Cathedral first," he directed them. It's not far, you can see it up there on the left," he pointed out. They set off, enjoying the land although it still seemed to roll gently beneath their feet.

Cape Town was alive with electric tramcars busily plying the roads, their steel wheels screeching on the tracks, while the overhead catenaries were sparking sharply as the electricity kept making and breaking contact. They wanted to exercise their legs, but later the trams came in handy. There was a variety of mostly British-made petrol taxi-cabs and horse-drawn carriages.

The group of young priests all wore their Roman collars and priests' attire, and made a fine looking group of men, proudly Catholic, and walking with happy sea legs, jauntily striding among the welcoming and friendly mix of faces, responding to their smiles on the streets of Cape Town.

A cold wind was blowing, and the clouds promised a wet day, as they made their way towards their beacon, the tall spire of Saint Mary's Cathedral, with castle-like crenelated walls and roof of the cathedral. They came to a statue of Louis Botha, mounted on his horse, in a proud pose that would have looked good in any German town.

They took shelter from the wind, as they entered the historic church. He noticed that the church was dedicated to Our Lady of the Flight into Egypt. High above him was a beautiful wooden roof, and he genuflected as he looked upon the red lamp glowing before the marble altar; it hung from a long chain suspended from a carved boss where the timber trusses curved down and met. Father Odilo knelt in prayer and gratitude. He asked God's blessing upon his new life in Africa, as a missionary, and presented himself for duty. "Here I am, Lord," he was saying inwardly again.

He looked at the ornately carved wooden pulpit on the left, and could see a beautiful statue of Jesus just behind one of the huge pillars, which supported the five or six tall arches along each side. His eyes swept around, taking in each of the bright and clear stained glass windows, and the carved Stations of the Cross. On either side of the entrance, the double-sided wooden confessional booths were set in below the huge organ, which he would have loved to hear playing on the landing above.

The Bishop received them warmly in his house, greeting them, "welcome to South Africa." He shook hands with each of them; Father Odilo noticed his genuine smile as he looked back into his eyes. "Thank you, my lord," he responded. "It is good to be on firm ground again."

"Yes, I am sure; you have had quite a voyage. I sometimes think of Our Lady's flight into Egypt when I welcome new priests and sisters to Africa."

"In what way," asked Father John respectfully.

"Well, at this time, there is so much hatred and anger in Europe. Our Lady had fled with Saint Joseph and baby Jesus, to escape Herod's army. They obediently followed God's command, and in so doing, protected and ensured the spread of the faith. Anyway, we are a bit like that haven or beachhead here, the Church in Cape Town. From here, the whole of Africa is waiting for you to go forth and be a light to the nations."

Some of the window titles were in French and he told them how the French Crown Prince had been killed in Zululand. The Church had secured and looked after the body, and offered up many prayers and masses for the prince's soul. "The Queen was very grateful; some time later she had a special painting done and gave it to us. You must have seen it over the altar."

After a polite tea, Father Odilo slipped back into the church, and knelt down. The huge painting of the Crucifixion intrigued him, and the suspended lamp in the middle was very similar to that in his own home church of Saint Blasius. As always, Jesus on the Cross reminded him that his calling was about serving and sacrifice, even though it was nothing close to what Jesus had endured to show His love and forgiveness. Elmar came and called him. "Come, we must get moving, Odilo. There is a lot to see and do."

'Thank you for bringing me safe this far. I am off now to enjoy Your Creation,' he excused himself from God, and genuflected, walked to the back of the church, blessed himself with the sign of the cross, and stepped out onto the panoramic view over Cape Town sprawled below the entrance on Roeland Street.

Soon their party was walking again; they turned left towards State House, and went along a path to the old Company Gardens, now a botanical garden; this was how Cape Town was established, as a place where the Dutch trading house, VOC, grew fresh vegetables for their ships passing this way on their long journey to the rich East.

An Incident on Table Mountain

"There is a way up, via Platteklip Gorge, you see that deep cleft over there," they were told by a local. "It is the source of the Fresh River, and goes past the old Slave Walk; washerwomen still do their work there. You could also go up on Smuts' Track; it goes up through Skeleton Gorge, over there. One of the approaches is up from the cable car station and you could find your way up from there; you can see that it's very steep nearer the top, though. If you have time, you should walk across to Maclear Beacon, when you get to the top."

"I think we must take the direct route, straight up along the cable car line," Father Odilo prompted. "After all that time on board ship, we can do with the exercise!" There was no objection, and five of them set off energetically. The rocking of the sea was still with them, and when they paused in their tiredness, it felt as if the mountain was rising and falling like their ship.

"These rocks are hundreds of millions of years old," a guide was telling some tourists, as they walked past on their way up to where the Cable car started, rising gently on a long cable strung to the edge of the mountain-top. These three men certainly had no intention of paying to ride up the easy way! "Let's go around that way, Father Elmar suggested, and off they climbed, up and to the right of the cable-car. As they neared the base of the cliff faces, Siegfried took the left fork and Odilo and Elmar carried on to the right.

As the slope grew steeper, Elmar headed off further to the right, while Odilo kept on going straight ahead, to get up as fast as he could. Eventually, he could just see the white top of Elmar's shirt about two kilometres in the distance, as he searched for better access. Father Odilo came out near the block-like structure of the cable house.

He looked all around but could not see Siegfried anywhere. Father Elmar arrived after a while. "Where is Siegfried?" he asked.

"I don't know. I lost sight him of ages ago in that sudden, very dense mist. I am very worried about him; he could easily have fallen down one of those cliffs or down a deep crevasse. They were right when they warned us that this is a dangerous mountain."

They called and called for Siegfried, and searched in different directions, before coming back to the cable car station. The sun was setting over the sea, and the evening glow was fading already. Eventually, there was no choice. "We have to go down, or we will all be lost in the dark as well," Father Elmar said.

Sad and worried, they headed back down to the lights below. There was no sign of him on the way, and nobody they met had come across him. At their hotel, there was a silence among them and it was ages before they went to their beds. Siegfried arrived much later, to all their relief. "Thank God, you were not killed! We did not know what had become of you. Sit. I will get some coffee and bread."

Siegfried explained how he had gone further to the right, and admitted he had become lost. He did not say he had been afraid, but they could see that he was relieved; some of his assurance left him that night, but he had survived.

TOURISTS AND ORIENTATION

They slept in late the next morning, but made sure they took the opportunity to take in the many sights of this beautiful and historic city. The harbour itself was bustling with activity. Despite all the ports they had seen already, this harbour was still very interesting to them all, probably more so because they had all grown up far inland.

They visited the Promenade and the Pier, and enjoyed walking about along the Grand Parade. They chatted to the local priest and enjoyed the church again; it was magnificent and seemed as if a bit of

Europe was firmly and purposefully rooted here on the southern tip of Africa.

Time went fast, and they devoted another day to seeing the museums and other churches. They were deeply impressed at all the evidence of a society, which appreciated Culture, especially music and arts; there was a magnificent Opera House and Theatre.

"You can clearly see our German influences here," Father Odilo noted.

The Castle of Good Hope was a huge fort but they did not have much time to tour and explore it fully. They wandered about in the exotic Malay quarter, the Bo-Kaap, on the slopes of Signal Hill; it was already falling into disrepair, and some of the buildings were being demolished. A regular meeting spot was agreed upon whenever members of the party went off in their own direction for a while, and they chose Cartwright's corner.

They strolled along and enjoyed the ambience of Adderley Street and the old Heerengracht, a main street, which had been named after Gentleman's Canal in Amsterdam. The colonists had pressurised the British to send a convict ship onward to Tasmania instead of discharging its criminals in Cape Town, but a British Member of Parliament, Sir Charles Adderley had championed their cause; the street name was changed in his honour.

They visited Greenmarket Square, and admired Saint George's, the solid stone-built Anglican Church. The Dutch Reformed Church also had their impressive and solid Groote Kerk. The famous buildings of the Houses of Parliament were close to the Company's Gardens and they paused and pondered at the statue of Cecil John Rhodes.

They learned that the South African Prisoner of War camps had held twenty thousand people. Father Odilo thought sadly of the Concentration Camps that were now holding those Hitler hated so much in Germany.

The old slave tree had only recently been cut down, after standing for over two hundred years. Who were the people who had sold their own kin, and what had he remembered hearing about Fort Jesus in Mombasa? Africa seemed to have only recently escaped the grip of such disrespect for God's people. New visions and opportunities were unfolding, and these missionaries were a vital part of it.

Hearing their German, a curator directed them to some woodcarvings done by Anton Anreith, who came from Riegel. There was a magnificent lion head that he had carved out of teak for the water-spout/gargoyle at the old pump-house. He had also mischievously carved a very tired looking lion and a mock British crest on a triangular gable at the back of the old Supreme Court.

"Come and look at these," Father Elmar called him. "These sections of wooden water pipes are amazing. They are teak and it says they date back to Simon van der Stel's period, in the Seventeenth Century."

Something they found difficult to get used to, was the British system of money. Their pounds, shillings and pence were divided in a most odd way, so unlike the simplicity of their Marks and Pfennigs.

They looked in at the magnificent Mount Nelson Hotel, and strolled down past the Great Synagogue. "Are there many Jews in South Africa?" Father Elmar asked.

"I think about forty thousand Jews came to South Africa before the War, mainly from Europe, of course. Some of them lived over there, in District Six; it was a sort of ghetto. Recently, some more have been coming as refugees or settlers again, of course," Father John explained.

They were stretching and re-acclimatising their legs and breathing in the atmosphere of South Africa. Father Elmar expressed their feelings as he said, "it is a pity we only have these three days before our ship sets off again for Durban."

The next day they made their way back to the Watussi. Soon the tug-boat had them in tow, and they were on their way out to sea again.

They watched as the range of hills called the Twelve Apostles was outlined against the receding horizon. It made a memorable impression, as they sailed off on the last stage of their journey. In Port Elizabeth, near where Abbot Pfanner had struggled with the Dunbrody site, they called on an elderly Bishop McSherry, who gave them a warm and encouraging welcome. From there they went on to East London and, eventually sailed into the docks of Durban.

MARIANNHILL

They disembarked at this busy port, and some priests met and took them to Mariannhill by car. There was a big welcome for this large contingent of nine new priests, who had come to do missionary work in Southern Africa for the rest of their lives. They were introduced to their new confreres; some of the older monks who had originally been Trappists, were still alive, and they had a chance to learn first-hand about more of the history of Mariannhill, that famous Mission and cultural centre of their Congregation in Natal.

They spent the next nine months there. Here they received their first real introductions to the African way of life, and their new territory. Their task at Mariannhill was to learn English and Zulu.

Besides studying, Father Odilo made frequent excursions into the beautiful countryside of Natal, practising his new languages with the local inhabitants. The same three became a regular trio, walking ten to twenty kilometres after lunch and arriving back just before supper. Being a very strong and sporty young man, one day Father Odilo had a friendly wrestling match with one of his colleagues, but left him with a couple of broken ribs. There and then he decided that was to be the last wrestling meeting of his life!

He loved Natal and soon hoped to be able to stay there. They completed their studies and were told about what to expect in their new countries, in his case, Southern Rhodesia. Nearly a year after leaving Germany, now aged 27, Father Odilo was assigned to Bulawayo with his big burly friend, Father Elmar. Two others went to Umtata, in the Cape, and five of his confreres stayed on at Mariannhill.

Chapter 6

Land Of Needs

On a Train Going North

The rains came to a halt, at last. It was a busy time for the villagers around Mariannhill, reaping their crops, tending their cattle and goats, and repairing the grass roofs of their homes. The dirt roads and paths were a mess; the mud and erosion gullies made them almost impassable to the struggling donkey-carts, but life continued as if nobody minded.

The patience of Africa was something Father Odilo had already come to accept, although it went very much against his own nature. He had fumed inwardly, at first, 'how can people tolerate the delays, and simply accept things as they are?' Instead of fixing the damage, he saw how people simply detoured around obstacles, like fallen trees or puddles on the dirt roads, and made even bigger areas of damage for the next rainy season. 'Tomorrow was another day,' and besides, it was not anybody's particular duty or responsibility to alter these natural occurrences.

The two young priests, Odilo and Elmar, boarded the train at their very own railway station, at Mariannhill. Johannesburg was the destination written up on the platform list of passengers, and they easily found their second class compartment, as they helped one another to haul their limited belongings aboard through the window.

"I wonder when we shall see this place again," Father Odilo mused aloud.

"It will be many years, I am sure," answered Father Elmar. "At last, we can begin our mission work. I can't wait to get on with things."

The train gave a sudden lurch. After a pause of a minute or so, it lurched again and then began a slow build-up of speed. "Aufwiedersehen! Good-bye," they waved and called, as they departed from their fellow priests and brothers on the platform.

Father Odilo stood at the window in the passageway for a long time, watching the little village receding out of sight. The lush green hills of Natal reminded him of home, and he thought back to that journey when he left home and began his voyage to Africa. Many things were very similar, and yet it was all so different. The trees, the flowers, even the grass were African, but they made him think of his trees, and flowers and grasses, in the rolling hills and forests of home.

'It will never be home again,' he realised. 'I have chosen this continent, and these people. Mother Mary, help me to fulfil your Son's wishes. Guide me and strengthen me, and hold me always in your loving care.'

He spotted a large flock of European storks at the edge of a marshy patch, and it reminded him of home. Things had been getting worse there, and he was sorry for his family and friends. He almost felt guilty, here in the sunshine and peace of South Africa, as if he had deserted the horror and chaos of Europe. But he knew that was not why he had come—the train was clattering on its way, to take him to his work as a missionary.

The storks were picking their way along the edge of the water, occasionally straightening and retracting their necks as they swallowed something. This was not their nesting territory, he knew; they came here to feed and survive the season, part of the borderless world of nature. Now that he had made the voyage himself, he was even more impressed as he realised what a huge distance they had travelled.

So much had happened since he left Arberg. He felt as though he was a completely different person now. He was no longer the young and impetuous man who had just been ordained. He had known then how he must take leave of his parents to follow the calling, which God had made upon him.

He had travelled the seas and arrived in Africa. Here he had met real African people, not those whom they acted out in their plays at the seminary. He had learned how to speak their Zulu language and he had known for certain that he was doing the right thing. Despite their simple life-style and poverty by comparison with German or European standards, Africans had great dignity and culture. "Respect is the most important thing," was what he had heard time and again at Mariannhill, and he had realised just how true that is.

"You know," Father Elmar said, "we are probably the last German missionaries who will be able to come here. Nobody is allowed to leave Germany at the moment. Something bad is happening at home, and I think Hitler is stirring up to make war. I wonder when others will come; it could take many months still."

"I have a feeling it will take many years, not months," Father Odilo replied. "That idiot Hitler is already making a complete mess of Germany. I can only look back and think how wrong we were when we thought he couldn't be all that bad. Pha!"

"Ja Ja. That's true enough. Everybody was desperate for jobs, and most of us ignored lots of things about him. He is completely anti-Catholic—he is even anti-God. Look how he treated our Bishop! And, what was the name of that other priest from Munich? Do you remember? But he still managed to squeeze in; he won, even it was with only a tiny one percent over the fifty percent."

"You know, he made people feel proud again, though. We were being hammered into the ground by France and England. But, what amazes me, is how my brother-in-law can be so fired up and passionate about being an officer working for a man like that," he responded. "There must be many more like him, all following that strutting little dictator. With the army he has built up he could certainly win some great battles; perhaps he could even conquer Eastern Europe and Russia, but what is he doing it for?"

SURPRISING NAMES

There was a lot of time to think on a train journey, and often they were each deep in thought. At the small stations along the way, they would get out and stretch their legs. Pietermaritzburg was a scenic stop, and quite a big town, but there were not many other big stops along the railway line.

They crossed the Mooi River, as the train snaked its way out of the hilly country of Natal, with the Drakensberg Mountains to their left. After Ladysmith, they wound their way up through the steep hills of Van Reenen's Pass, and stopped to take on more coal and water at Harrismith.

"Over there, you can see one of the blockhouses; they were set up during the Boer War," the conductor showed them proudly. "The British had to put those up all along the frontier, but they couldn't control the commandos. Eventually, they put all their families into concentration camps; that's how they beat us, you know."

As they steamed out of Harrismith, there was a road sign on the right, pointing to Bethlehem. "Pha! Surely they are not serious," Father Elmar said in amazement. "From here, it must be thousands of kilometres."

The old man in their compartment was quick to help him out. "It's a small town, just about sixty miles away. We travel almost due west from here, and go through it on the railway line; it is on the way to Bloemfontein if we carry on straight now."

"How did it come to be called Bethlehem?" asked Father Odilo.

"I don't know," he replied. "The Voortrekkers were a very religious people, though. They were convinced that God had brought them to this land, and I am sure they had a good explanation. I am sorry, I just don't know enough about their history," he apologised.

Again they stopped, but they did not have time to go far from the train so they left none the wiser about this town's origins. The locomotive had been changed over, and they were soon heading north again. Even more amazing, was the name Frankfort, which they came to about two hours later, after crossing the Wilge river.

As the land opened out into the plains of the Transvaal, he thought of the immensity of God's creation. There seemed to be such a wide world, open and waiting for man to harness and manage it as he had been directed in Genesis.

There were farmhouses here and there, and little clusters of grass huts from which children would sometimes spill out and wave cheerfully at the passing train. Father Odilo waved back and felt the fulfilment of his calling. Train trips had a special effect on him, he realised. "I see so much from a train," he thought. "It is as if the whole country is paraded before me, while all I have to do is watch and absorb its atmosphere."

They had been travelling on the flatter plains of the Transvaal. Alongside the train route, they saw occasional cars and lorries, making their way in both directions. The farmlands were looking healthy, "but how under-utilised," he thought. "If my brothers could see these huge stretches of land to farm, what would they think?"

They stopped in a town called Heidelberg, now becoming quite used to the German names, which made them feel quite proud and welcome. After taking on coal and water again, the train steamed uphill again, and soon they were passing through Germiston.

Their journey had taken them a distance of six hundred kilometres, and they rose from near sea level to an altitude of nearly eighteen hundred metres.

MOUNTAINS OF GOLD

"Come to the window. Quick!" Father Odilo called to his companion. "Just look at those mountains. They look as if they are made of gold."

"Amazing," was all Father Elmar could say.

"It is surely true. This is where nearly all of the world's gold is coming from," Father Odilo mused. The train had come in from the south of Johannesburg, and the first mine dumps to the left of the train soon gave way to dumps on both sides. They shone a sunflower yellow colour in the setting sun. "Even the sand they are throwing away still has so much gold in it."

"This must be a rich country," pondered Father Elmar out loud. "How many tonnes of rock have they had to dig out and crush to make those dumps?" They watched in amazement, as the train rumbled past the high golden mine dumps.

"Think of all the Africans who have to go deep down and dig it out," he continued. "It must be terrible work, down there, dark, hot and dangerous, too."

"Yes, but it is the best pay in the country. There are plenty of Europeans doing the digging as well. When you remember how many Europeans had no work here only a few years ago, it seems not so different from Germany."

"At least they have not had to dress everybody up in soldiers' uniforms to keep them busy," Father Elmar philosophised cheerfully.

"That's true, but did you see that big army camp we passed on the way up? I think it was even called Heidelberg, wasn't it?"

"Ja, I saw it. They don't really need much of an army here in South Africa," he said. "I don't think they would ever want to get involved in the troubles of other countries, and people seem to have pretty good relations here nowadays."

A steam train took them North towards Bulawayo

It seemed such a short time, and then the train pulled into Johannesburg railway station. The station was surrounded by tall buildings, and grimy with smoke, but nobody worried; it was alive with activity. There were several other trains on platforms, and the whole station was teeming with people. People were unloading luggage, and trolleys were helping them to and from trains. Well-wishers were bunched around departing or arriving passengers, all getting their last or first words in. The newspaper-seller walked along the platform, yelling, "read all about it. Late news! Read all about it!"

Their stopover in Johannesburg was a relief. They got to stretch their legs, and get over the motion of the train, which was so drummed into them that they went to sleep feeling as if they were rocking and lurching still. What a busy city! There were trams and buses all over, and people rushing about on the pavements or crossing the busy streets. Some of the buildings were very impressive, and they wished they had more time to see the sights and understand the city that was the economic heart of South Africa. All the big mining companies were headquartered here, together with every sort of industry that supported mining and the people who worked on the mines.

STEAMING NORTH AGAIN

As they passed through Braamfontein, they could see the cemetery on their right. They went out past Roodepoort and Krugersdorp, and through the Magaliesberg Mountains. They were going west again. "Why don't we go north to get to Rhodesia?" Father Odilo asked their new companions.

"Aah. That's a long story," a wizened old man was quick to venture. "It was all to do with Rhodes and his Cape to Cairo dream." He proceeded to give them an account of the man's life story, how he had come to South Africa, penniless almost, and with a weak heart condition. In a few clever moves he had teamed up with a Jewish businessman, Alfred Beit, and soon had bought up most of the new diamond fields in Kimberley.

"He became governor of the Cape and made huge decisions about South Africa. It was around then, with the Boers owning the Orange Free Sate, that he decided to change the borders; he had to secure his diamond-fields. This caused a lot of trouble, and he later had to keep well clear of the Transvaal if he wanted to push his railway line north. So, he routed it to the west, and that is why we are now going to go all the way to Mafeking, so that we can turn north and join his Cape railway line."

He explained a lot more, and was a mine of information and opinions, which he freely gave. He told them how, when gold was discovered on the Witwatersrand, Rhodes had bought most of the gold claims and so on. "He was the world's highest income earning man, after J. P. Getty at one time."

They soon reached the hills of Swartruggens, just as they had begun to travel a bit more to the north. Now they turned sharply west again, and stopped at Zeerust to take on coal and water. This gave them a chance to stop and stretch their legs.

As they steamed off again, they were confused by the setting sun. "How can that be?" Father Elmar asked? "We are going north to Bulawayo, but we have to see the sun set on our right as we go."

Bechuanaland

At Mafeking—whose name that was made famous by the siege in 1899, and from nearby where Leander Starr Jameson had led an abortive raid, apparently to rescue the *uitlanders* on the gold mines from the Boers—they were disconnected from their locomotive. After being shunted about, they were coupled to a new train with a harsh jolt. This was the train, which had come from Cape Town, and they were now on their way north again.

They enjoyed a superb dinner in the dining car, with magnificent Rhodesia Railways silverware and crockery. The stewards and waiters were impeccably dressed and well trained, and the meal could easily have been at one of the top hotels in Germany. The night sky was unbroken by lights of towns or housing, and the train clattered on like a strange snake through the darkness. The stars were brilliant, and twinkling or glowing distantly. The air was warm and clean, and Father Odilo breathed in deeply as he savoured the feeling, the peace and stillness, and the smell of Africa. He was close to his destination, and he struggled to sleep when he settled down on the upper bunk for the night.

The heavy steam locomotive gave a shrill blast on its whistle and the train began to pull out of Francistown's dusty and dirty little station. Africans ran alongside, still selling their beads and fruit. They were just about naked, usually only covering essential parts with old-looking cloths. They were much lighter-skinned than the Zulus, but they all had the same wonderful white teeth and eyes when they smiled. They were a happy and cheerful lot, joking among themselves, and very pleased when they had made a small sale.

The little bit of money they got was something to open the doors into another world. You could see Haskins' store from the train, as it gathered momentum, and Africans were already milling about the entrance, desperate to exchange their cash for some threads, knives, tin pots, hammers and all sorts of wares which must have been unthinkable only fifty years ago.

The white steam clouds hissing from the sides of the engine kept the people a respectful distance back, and the tempo gradually built up as the pistons punched the drive rods back and forth. The stationmaster waved, and three European men stood and watched as the engine passed them, fascinated at how steam power was being transferred through the offset pins to make the four pairs of 4ft 6in steel wheels[iii] rotate. The driver skilfully applied only enough power so as not to cause the wheels to lose their traction and spin freely, on the polished steel rails that threaded off into the far distance.

CROSSING THE RAMOKGWEBANE RIVER

A dry riverbed marked the border to his new "Promised Land". Shortly after the train rode over the Ramokgwebane River, they reached the station. "Plumtree, Plumtree. Passports please," yelled the conductor, as he made his way up the passageway. Looking out the windows on either side, there had been quite a remarkable change in vegetation. The trees were tall and green, and the grass was tall, perfect for the thatched huts they passed along the way. The trip through Botswana had been flat and almost uninteresting. But Father Odilo never failed to see the beauty in everything he saw.

"Well, I wonder where this famous plum tree is," Father Elmar quipped, as they both stared together out of the passage window. "Passports, please," they were interrupted.

Arriving at Plumtree Railway Station

"Oh, our two priests from Germany," said the conductor, as he helped the Southern Rhodesian official stamping passengers' passports. "It's not far to Bulawayo now. Welcome, you are now in your new country."

Father Andrew Baussenwein was on the platform to greet them. He was not hard to find, with his roman collar clearly evident, as were theirs. They had changed into fresh clothes and had been looking forward to seeing their first priest in Southern Rhodesia. "Welcome," he said, shaking each of their large German hands vigorously "Come with me. We can have some tea and lunch before you have to move on."

"Should we bring anything?" asked Father Odilo.

"Oh no, just leave everything in your compartment. It's totally safe; nobody would think of stealing, especially not from a priest, you know."

Later on they came to Figtree, and the quip came from Father Odilo this time, "I wonder where their fig tree is."

The train was moving very slowly as it puffed its way through the Mpopoma Township. Lots of little African children ran alongside, smiling and playing with one another. "Sweets, sweets," they chorused.

The train puffed its way between the curved tracks and came to the platform. Father Odilo was looking out the window, when the conductor said, "this is the longest rail platform in the whole world, you know." Bulawayo was certainly a new boomtown. It even had electric streetlights already, and the population, measured in whites, was over nine thousand people.

They were looking out of their windows to see who would be there to meet them. Once again, it was easy to spot their new bishop, in his clerical dress, with two priests accompanying him. They stepped down onto the concrete platform, and walked up to greet him. Bishop Arnoz asked, "What was the trip like?"

"It was fine, your grace, but what a long way. I feel as if I have crossed the whole of Europe!" answered Father Odilo humbly.

"Elmar you will be at Saint Joseph's, and Odilo, I want you to help me here at the Cathedral for a while, until you are assigned to a fresh parish," Bishop Arnoz announced almost immediately.

"Certainly, your grace, I look forward to beginning my duties."

"You both need to learn to speak iSindebele properly, though. I bet that you have studied your Zulu well, but you will find there are quite a few little differences. People will soon see if you know their language properly or not."

The Chapel at Plumtree Boarding School

PART TWO

Having grown up and studied in Bavaria, this young German priest arrived in Rhodesia at the beginning of World War II.

Then, with dedication and charm, he overcame many obstacles, and lived through the years of economic boom and the troubles leading up to and beyond its transition to Zimbabwe.

"ITE MISSA EST"

"GEHET HINAUS"

"GO, YOU ARE SENT FORTH"

CHAPTER 7

OLD WORLD ABLAZE

SAINT PATRICK'S MISSION

The town of Bulawayo was laid out with great care and skill, on a North-South grid, with carefully measured city blocks, even though the surveyor had only used fencing wire to measure it off some fifty years before. The railway platform was proudly claimed to be the longest in the world. He walked past the tax offices, and then up Tenth Avenue, to reach the Cathedral along Lobengula Street. The order and cleanliness appealed to his German background, as did these streets, which he was repeatedly told were wide enough to turn an eight-span ox-wagon.

He settled in to his duties assisting Father Joseph. After his first winter, with a few days of surprising cold, the dryness set in and then he had to cope with the relentless heat of his first October in Bulawayo.

He had to overcome his language and pronunciation differences, not to mention his German origins and nature itself. However, everything was new and interesting to him, and people responded well to his curiosity. He soon resolved to always delve deeper for understanding and information, and he enjoyed people's help and their varied but unique interests.

He found out a lot on his hospital visiting rounds and one of the patients told him proudly, "Bulawayo was one of the first cities in the world to have electric streetlights".

He looked now with appreciation down the long Ninth Avenue, which descended slowly from the Cathedral into the town. He saw several kerb-side Jacaranda trees, some still in bloom, with their purple flowers like an older woman's head of hair that had been decorated for show. Already the orangey-red flowers of the flamboyant trees were in full bloom, their flattened canopies spreading out like colourful umbrellas under the hot sky. His partial colour blindness muted the redness for him, but there was more than enough effect there for him to be deeply impressed by the way God gives mankind beauty in his surroundings—a seemingly unnecessary gift, but a special joy and opportunity to be reminded of God's loving hand in His creation.

This was the time of build-up, those very hot months before the rains for which everybody waited so anxiously. He had already come to understand how important rain was here, where its timing and quantity spelled the difference between good crops and grazing, or a time of drought and hardship. 'How we take our rain for granted in Germany,' he thought.

That evening he went over to the double-storey Dominican Convent School, right next door to the Cathedral; he loved it when he had the chance to say Holy Mass for the nuns in their beautiful chapel. The high roof and the rounded apse of the altar were set off by two beautiful stained glass windows, flanked by statues of Our Lady and Saint Joseph.

Although he did not reveal it, he could sense that his manly young presence aroused attention. He was not to know until much later in life, how much of an inspiration he was to the happy and dedicated Sisters. This historic school was the first to be built in Bulawayo, and the first Dominican Sisters had come North with the Pioneer Column. Over the years, they had taught many of the young girls and boys of the growing town.

Only a few months before, Father Odilo had been assigned to Saint Patrick's Mission, less than two miles to the West of the Cathedral, right in the middle of the 'locations', as they were called. Father Joseph Kammerlechner, the priest in charge, was a zealous missionary who inducted Father Odilo into the task of caring for their eight out-schools, on long-distance bicycle trips.

"My last posting was at Empandeni Mission," he said. "They appointed me as rector when we Mariannhillers took over Matabeleland from the Jesuits. That was a very unpopular thing, the switching around of our territories. Those Jesuits always seem to choose the best for themselves!"

"When did you arrive?" Father Odilo asked.

"I seem to have been here a long time. Let me think now. The Jesuits set this mission up in 1902 and I came here some time in 1932."

"Was it already established?"

"Ja Ja. But not completely. The Jesuits built the church here in about 1910. A lot has happened since I came and settled into my little room here."

All around the mission, the African houses were built in neat rows, and the Bulawayo Town Council insisted that all houses had to be strictly brick walled with proper roofing of corrugated iron or asbestos/fibre-cement. There were no design variations, so building contractors were able to build large sections of houses quickly and efficiently.

"The African housing in Bulawayo is quite good by African standards," Father Joseph commented. He explained how a special department in the municipality was tasked with providing affordable but decent housing, as well as basic community centres and amenities. "The roads are also well constructed and even tarmac surfaced," Father Joseph had observed. "It's a long way from paradise, but each little house has clean municipal water supplies laid on as well."

He used to walk past the Police station across the intersection, with its British South Africa Police crest and flag, and he often went to the open field where donkey carts used to load up or disgorge their passengers and wares. Father Odilo mixed more and more with the people there, and tried out his new language skills.

The Zulu he had learned was not quite the same as iSindebele, but they were pleased with the way he made the effort to speak their language, and very tolerant of his early clumsiness with some of the more difficult clicks and pronunciations. Slight changes in the way he said things, like where the emphasis is placed could and did cause the meaning to change. However, they somehow knew what he meant and that he meant well. He soon became a familiar figure on his bicycle, always fully attired with his Roman collar and the strict uniform of a Catholic priest.

One evening over supper, Father Joseph told him, "I am very pleased to have you as my assistant. I think you will be a great missionary, and you are a sensible priest. I also find you very willing, in the way you share the workload."

"Thank you, Father Joseph," he answered respectfully. "I am happy being here with you." He prepared and poured out coffee, and they conversed long into the evening, trading experiences, and affirming each other in their tough vocation of Catholic priesthood.

He regularly had to cycle great distances to the outstations, where he needed to give lessons or say Holy Mass for their converts and parishioners, and the fast before communion was a very strict one. Catholics were not permitted to eat anything from midnight the night before, if they wished to receive Holy Communion. Even water was forbidden, so he would arrive parched and hungry to say Mass, sometimes after several hours of cycling.

He soon worked out that it was best to get up early and cycle while it was cool. There was no point waiting about to have a breakfast meal first—it was simply not allowed anyway. Early Masses also suited the people; they had to go and work in the lands afterwards, and it became hot quite quickly. The people came to know that they could rely on him pitching up, and attendances grew; it helped that he spoke their language quite fluently already.

THE WILDS OF MATABELELAND

He loved making his trips to out-stations, and some of the journeys took him as far as Gwayi and even Lukosi. The old strip roads were quite narrow and they really just followed the land, going up and down, over rivers, and taking a gradual swing around little hills which in later years would need to be levelled. There were often Kudu or small buck, like Impala, on the road, and closer to Gwayi it was common to encounter elephants.

The bicycle ride really was very uncomfortable when it was hot. He thought back to his novice years in Holland, where you could cycle for miles and miles without feeling the strain; it was so flat. Here, the ground rose and fell quite steeply. The relief of the downhill runs was never enough to make up for the long, hot struggle up the rises. Where he could he would stop and have a drink of water, or even make some tea, under the shade of the beautiful Teak and Mukwa trees, or the upside-down looking Baobab trees.

THE CROSS AT SAINT PATRICK'S

The crucifix at Saint Patrick's Mission had a shock effect on most people. Father Odilo had seen several crosses with a figure of Jesus, depicted in his full suffering as he had died. However, this thorn-crowned figure, with arms stretched apart and upwards, was the most vivid he had ever seen; strips of flesh were shown torn from the body, all over, and Christ's death was certainly not disguised as something peaceful and clean.

Jesus' eyes stared heavenward, but still seemed to gaze down at him, as if they were seeing into his very soul as he prayed before the cross. Those eyes were so lifelike that he felt as if he was transported to, and present at, Calvary. 'The very least I can do is to offer myself totally to You, O God,' he prayed. 'I am here to carry out the great command, the mission you have given me, to go forth and teach all nations.'

Praying before this cross also reminded him of the cross in Wurzburg, where he often stopped and prayed. He could really sense the great reverence and compassion that the artist must have had. He had honestly but lovingly depicted the pain and ugliness of this eternal sacrifice.

He was a well-organised and disciplined young man, and he soon established a regular routine of prayer, Holy Masses, visits and teaching. Bishop Ignatius Arnoz required his priests to report to Saint Mary's Cathedral frequently, and he took a keen interest in the work they were doing.

EUROPE TORN APART BY WAR

However, thousands of miles away things were far from well. Bishop Arnoz and the priests had gathered at the Cathedral, to hear an important radio announcement. Although it was not entirely unexpected, the news flash had a stunning effect. They had eaten dinner hastily that evening, and were waiting beside the radio set.

After detailing the British version of events, the Southern Rhodesia Governor had confirmed that, "since eleven o'clock this morning, His Majesty the King has been at war with Germany." Prime Minister Godfrey Huggins went on to appeal for calm and confident minds, and finished off with, "Let us be of good cheer, and let us never doubt that God will defend the right."

At first, there was not even a sound. Each one of them was deep in private thought and worries. Most of them had family and friends back home in Germany. They could each picture the village or town where they grew up and went to school. Adolph Hitler seemed to be unstoppable.

His evil totalitarianism was backed by ruthless military rule; territorial greed and power hunger had long since eclipsed any idealised effort to uplift the people, or to spare Germany from the devastation arising from paying huge reparation costs for its defeat in the Great War.

His Aryan race concepts and the way he had fanned up old prejudices and jealousies to hound and even murder Europe's Jews had grown into a monstrous thing which nobody seemed able to halt.

"Of course, much of the news must be exaggerated by the British and the French," one of the priests said. "I am sure things are not as bad as they say. The Concentration Camps are just a temporary thing; Hitler's madness will subside, and people can get on with their lives again."

"I hope you are right," Father Odilo mused sadly. "I have come to mistrust what I see or hear. Do you remember the way the crowds were mocking those Jews in Wurzburg just before our ordination? I was so ashamed of my own weakness. The SS were even goading people to go over and kick them to watch them fall over."

"It was his speech when he opened the Volkswagen factory which sickened me."

"Why?" asked Father Odilo.

"He's been very shrewd with the business and industrial people, you know. Well, he just could not get on with opening a factory to make cars. That would have been a good thing. Instead he launched into an attack on Jews again, and all the other cars in the world. We once thought he might do some good for Germany; but now look where he has taken us! He is crazy!"

Father Odilo visualised the bombings and fighting, in Poland and in the countries that surround Germany. "How sad," he heard the bishop say, "that Pope Pius XI died; he was trying so hard to bring about that conference."

Most priests knew about the plans he had made for an international disarmament conference, as a last-ditch effort to avert war. He had often repeated his calls for an end to oppression and the suppression of the Church, but these had met with increasing contempt from the Nazi rulers, slavishly taking their cue from Hitler himself. This was especially so when the Pope spoke out for the rights of the individual and the increasingly non-Christian education forced on the German youth.

When Hitler took over Austria, that had not seemed such an abnormal event; it had been part of German territory off and on over the centuries anyway. But now, Poland had been invaded. Hitler had such an efficient and well-organised army, air force and navy that all opposition quickly crumbled.

Hitler himself was clearly not a man of God. In fact, it had soon become apparent just how opposed he was to the Church, Lutheran as well as Catholic. Few people were speaking out; it was a dangerous thing to do. He quickly silenced most of them, one way or the other. Where was he taking Germany now?

The cruelty and pain of war was inexcusable. However, only some of the priests thought fighting might happen in or around their own homes; that seemed unlikely, in spite of what Chamberlain had just said. The BBC message was re-broadcast later, and his chilling words echoed from six thousand miles away, "now it remains for us to set our teeth and enter upon this struggle which we have so earnestly endeavoured to avoid, with the determination to see it through to the end." There was emotion in his voice as he ended, saying, "God bless you all."

A few days before, Hitler had issued a proclamation to his army, forcefully claiming that, "in order to end the intolerable madness of the Poles" he had no other choice but to answer force with force. "The Polish State has refused the peaceful settlement which I desired, and has appealed to arms. Germans in Poland have been persecuted with bloody terror . . . ." and so the deceitful message had continued.

They were a long way from home, and it was hard to know what was really happening. One part of them heard that German honour and people were being trodden underfoot by Germany's enemies. However, something reminded Father Odilo how Hitler had come to power, and he felt suspicious that Hitler could create incidents and fan up support, even from those who wanted no part of his trouble-making.

They all knew how the German army and Luftwaffe had become mighty forces, which no individual country could withstand. Hitler certainly had the power to sweep away opposition swiftly and easily wherever he chose, and so far the rest of the world had done almost nothing to challenge it; they must see its futility. Perhaps many were even welcoming the idea of a Third Reich; it might even turn out to be good for the world, but with a less brutal ruler in charge.

"A 'World War', he calls it! What is the world coming to?" asked one of the priests. "The war Germany is waging is surely just a war to sort out the injustices against Germany. What has it got to do with Britain, or especially Rhodesia, nearly ten thousand kilometres away? How is it getting so out of hand?"

"Pha! I still say Hitler was our big mistake. He seems to be a bit of an imbecile," shot out a response from Father Odilo.

"Well, we cannot ignore all the good things he has done, like getting the unemployed off the streets. Also, at last he has shown some guts. Who could ever expect us to carry on accepting that Versailles Treaty? The reparation costs were ridiculous and impossible!" soothed one of the priests.

"Well this is deadly serious now. Germany must be careful or it really will be up against the rest of the world, and I am not sure we can win such a fight," chipped in the huge, Father Elmar.

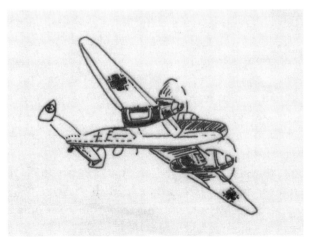

Germany had soon developed a powerful Luftwaffe, (Air Force)

"You know, I still can't work out what I truly think about his campaign against the Jews," pondered Father Joseph. "They certainly seem to control everything; their god appears to be money, and they certainly have most of the wealth and power. That can't carry on when you see millions of good Germans going without jobs, and becoming starving beggars in their own country."

He looked up into the questioning eyes around him. "Of course, I know that never gives him the right to imprison them like he's doing. It was wrong even to tell them to leave Germany; they have been there for centuries."

Father Odilo thought about the priest he had met in German South West Africa, on their boat trip out from Germany. His name was Jewish. He was a Jew; but Father Morgenschweiss was a good and holy priest. This persecution was not new. The Jews had suffered for a long time.

GERMANS IN BRITISH TERRITORY

In the meantime, the lengthy radio broadcast and discussion ended. The traffic and other noises on Lobengula Street, outside the Cathedral kept up a constant hubbub in the background. The Jacaranda trees had started to send forth new shoots, as the brief spring had begun, leading up to the hottest months of the year, the month of October, which was locally referred to as 'suicide month.'

As Germans, they knew there could be immediate action by the Southern Rhodesian authorities. The South African authorities soon arrested members of their own religious order and interned them in concentration camps, simply because they were German nationals. The fact that they were priests, and certainly not in the least bit involved on Germany's behalf in that war had meant nothing. The orders had been given that all Germans who came into South Africa after a certain date were to be arrested and detained, until screening was complete or until the war was speedily finished.

'Of course, this also means that no new priests will be coming now for certain; not for quite a while,' thought Bishop Arnoz. 'What a crazy, mixed-up world. Here we are working only to help people, and spread the Gospel of Our Lord, and this is what we get!'

The Rhodesians had been expecting this war. In fact, many had been totally appalled at their English Prime Minister's optimism when he had come back from the meeting with Hitler in Munich a year before. Despite the invasions of the Rhineland, Austria and the Sudetenland, he had returned to cheerfully proclaim that he had achieved "peace with honour. I believe it is peace in our time."

Only the dissenting voice of a backbencher, Winston Churchill, marred the parliamentary good spirits a bit as he growled back at them. What had then seemed like sour grapes and exaggerated gloom had come to fruition, and England was now truly "in the midst of a disaster of the first magnitude!"

To be Pope in These times

Pope Pius XII—the Church was in a most difficult position, but did a great deal to help those it could

Cardinal Pacelli had been elected as the new Pope, and he had a good deal of experience of the German situation; he had also been close to Pope Pius XI; perhaps these factors influenced his election. "What a difficult time to be Pope," Father Odilo said to his friend Elmar when he heard the news.

"If anybody can do something, he certainly can," Father Elmar ventured. "He understands German politics, but I think things have gone much too far to stop Hitler."

Right from the outset Pope Pius XII attempted to head off further warfare. Time and again he appealed for an end to the aggression and injustice. He also ordered his churches to do what they could do practically, in providing shelter and escape. He personally intervened to save as many Jews as possible, especially in Italy. The shelter and security of the Church enabled thousands to escape; Jews whom Hitler was intent upon capturing and sending off to the concentration camps. His pleas and injunctions were clear and wise, but he did not have temporal powers.

One scorching hot day, Father Odilo finished doing his rounds and sat down to go through his mail. In it was a copy of the Pope's latest encyclical, 'On the function of the State in the Modern World.' He retired to his room and read it fully, grateful that he was not disturbed by the doorbell for a change.

He couldn't help thinking, 'this Pope Pius XII is almost a revolutionary in the Church. He is a man worth listening to, and his words are so carefully weighed and chosen.' He was impressed at the way in which he confronted both totalitarianism and communism, and described the evils being inflicted upon the world. His reminder was, "today, venerable brethren, all men are looking with terror into the abyss to which they have been brought by the errors and principles which we have mentioned, and by their practical consequences. Gone are the proud illusions of limitless progress . . . ."

He wondered, 'how is my brother, Josef, coping as a priest in Germany? What is it like to be a bishop or priest in Germany now? How are ordinary Catholics coping in Germany? Their family security is under threat from ruthless enforcers, eager youngsters, others who have been unemployed, and fanatics who avidly swallow Hitler's words and grow in hatred of Jews and all who stand in their Fuehrer's way.'

"In these times, I think of Pilate's question, 'Truth! What is truth?'" Father Odilo reflected to his big burly friend, Father Elmar. "Of course, Pilate didn't really care at all. He was just an official carrying out his duties. The last thing he wanted to bother with was some religious issue that he simply could not make sense of."

"Well, what's your point, Odilo?"

"Simply that people are careless with the truth. Those who choose to twist it get away with it as a result. Is it true what they say is happening in Germany, for instance?"

"I don't know, and you are right." Elmar responded. "We do not know for sure what is happening. I just hope that what we hear here is not true. I must say, I am sure the British must be exaggerating to inflame emotions for their cause."

Throughout these war years, Father Odilo prayed constantly for his family, his country and friends. 'Almighty God and Father, I ask You to guide and protect us.' Calling to mind his own family, he pleaded, 'watch over them all. Protect them from harm. Strengthen them to resist evil and bullying. We have no power without Your grace and blessing.'

There was no way of even communicating with home now. He couldn't even find out if his beloved mother was alive. 'How is my father responding?' he wondered. 'Will he control his tongue?' He knew that he had said things against Hitler at the Gasthaus; if people heard him now, it would be very dangerous. You could not speak openly any more, even among close family and friends.

'How is my brother, Karl, now that he has to prepare to fight a real war?' he worried. This was no longer just a job being paid for in the army; he was now a soldier with all the risks of intense warfare. 'Are my sisters all right? Will Josef be imprisoned? Some Catholic priests have spoken out openly against Hitler and Nazism, and look what has happened to them!'

Royal Air Force Training in Bulawayo

Meanwhile, Southern Rhodesia was quick to enter the fray, loyal to Queen and country. The Empire Air Training Scheme was soon in full stride, and nine training schools were soon set up in Salisbury, Bulawayo and Gwelo. Construction had begun with amazing speed, and four bases were already hives of activity, preparing pilots to go off to combat, flying for the Royal Air Force. The boast of Goering, that Germany's Luftwaffe had total control of the skies over Europe, was soon to be tested.

Flying conditions in Southern Rhodesia were ideal, and the distance from the war zone ensured continuous training conditions; within six months new pilots could be trained enough to send them off to the war front. Soon a whole new community had been set up in Bulawayo, the training instructors and their support team, with the aspiring and passing-out pilots going through the system. Apart from those who came from abroad to be trained or to provide training, many Rhodesians became pilots or support crew and headed off to confront the Luftwaffe. One of these, Ian Smith, graduated as a sergeant-pilot in mid-1942, and was posted to Syria; he became a future Prime Minister,

The Red Cross offered their help and Father Odilo continued to try and find out about his parents and family through them. There was no direct contact at all, and these neutral parties were stretched so much in all they tried to do that the most one could hope for was that a few letters might get through to them. He tried desperately to send such letters home or to get word of his mother; he wanted to know how she was doing, and whether she was safe, and for her to know that he was safe and well. There was no way of knowing if any of the letters he sent had made it home.

'Fortunately,' he consoled himself, 'Arberg is not likely to be a major military target, although it sounds as if the whole of Germany is being hammered.' The news of food shortages and desperation was filtering out more and more. It was not long before the Chronicle began to report a turning of the tide. Waves of bombing and intensified effort were tightening the noose.

INHUMANITY AND CRUELTY

In Germany, the concentration camps became more sinister, and there were reports of atrocities and the worst forms of punishment for anybody who disobeyed or opposed Hitler and his elite SS. There was no authority above them.

Despite the evidence that was leaking out, things going on in the concentration camps remained largely under-estimated. Propaganda and counter-propaganda focussed mainly on military might and successes.

The Communist threat complicated matters, and Pope Pius XII was very conscious of this threat to Christianity, and indeed to civilisation.

In a major incident, the Soviet army had ruthlessly eliminated the pride of Poland's trained military leadership in Katyn. The Soviet announcers blamed the slaughter on invading Germans. Four generals, twenty-six colonels, one hundred and twenty-six lieutenant colonels, three hundred and sixteen majors, six hundred and forty seven captains were gunned down. In addition many Orthodox, Eastern Catholic and Jewish army chaplains were killed. Only a hundred survived, and probably only because a huge thunderstorm struck towards the end of the day's killings.

Good over Evil

Rhodesians were staunchly loyal to England, and the Union Jack flew from all government buildings. Concerts and bioscopes did not start until 'God save the King' had been sung.

Bulawayo's daily newspaper, The Chronicle, carried dramatic news of what was happening, and the horror of the war in Europe was its headline focus. London was being bombed, and over the English Channel, the Luftwaffe was constantly locked in combat with the Royal Air Force.

"How can God allow this?" people asked. "What is the Church doing to stop Hitler?"

Agnostics felt vindicated by things like war, as if this proved to them that God did not exist. "You cannot reason with people like that," Father Odilo said to one of his confreres. "To us it is so obvious; just the idea of creation, the universe, life and our own existence and free will are proofs. That's quite apart from the revelation of the Bible and Jesus' life, teachings, death and resurrection. God never said life would be free of war or troubles. In fact, He warned us there would be many crosses for us to bear; and wars and fighting are included."

"Well, I just keep on asking my parishioners to pray for peace and an end to the fighting," he replied.

"God will answer our prayers, somehow," Father Odilo responded confidently.

At the same time, he recalled Job's personal plight and complaints. He thought about how the Romans had ruled over what was then considered to be the whole known world, and the later persecution of Christians. He recalled something that Boethius had written, echoing some of the psalms, and it struck him how its theme had been copied by so many authors down the centuries:

> "Creator of the starry heavens,
>   Lord on thy everlasting throne,
>   Thy power turns the moving sky
>   And makes the stars obey fixed laws.
> Thou makest lesser stars grow dim
>   Before the moon's reflected rays
>   When opposite her kinsman bright:
>   Then closer to the sun she moves
> And loses all her borrowed light.
>   Thou the evening star dost make
>   Rise cold and clear in early night,
>   And change, as Morning Star, his reins
> To pale below the new sun's light.
>   When Winter's cold has stripped the trees
>   Thou holdest day in confines tight:
>   When Summer comes with torrid heat
> Thou givest swifter hours to night.
>   Thy power rules the changing year:
>   The tender leaves the North wind stole
>   The Spring West wind makes reappear;
> The seeds that Winter saw new sown
>   The Summer burns as crops full-grown.
>   All things obey their ancient law
>   And all perform their proper tasks;
> All things thou holdest in strict bounds—
>   To human acts alone denied
>   Thy fit control as Lord of all.
>   Why else does slippery Fortune change
> So much, and punishment more fit
>   For crime oppresses the innocent?
>   Corrupted men sit throned on high;
>   By strange reversal evilness
> Downtreads the necks of holy men.
>   Bright virtue lies in dark eclipse
>   By clouds obscured, and unjust men

Heap condemnation on the just;
No punishment for perjury
   Or lies adorned with speciousness.
   They use their power when whimsy bids,
   And love to subjugate great kings
Whose sway holds countless men in fear.
   O thou who bindest bonds of things
   Look down on all earth's wretchedness;
   Of this great work is man so mean
A part, by Fortune to be tossed?
   Lord, hold the rushing waves in check,
   And with the bond thou rul'st the stars,
   Make stable all the lands of earth.

Chapter 8

Where do I Begin?

Wankie Assignment

While the war in Europe was raging, Father Odilo's own life took a dramatic turn when he walked into the Vicar's office that December in 1939. This was not an ordinary summons to be directed to attend to a sick call, or say holy Mass for the sisters; he sensed immediately that there was something afoot. The Vicar was much more fidgety than his usual measured and disciplined self, and he quickly offered Father Odilo a chair at his desk.

"Father Odilo", the future bishop began seriously, "I have some important things to discuss with you this morning."

"Yes, my lord," Father Odilo replied respectfully, but with a bit of caution. Undoubtedly the time had come for him to be given another task. It seemed to come at just the time when he was settling into a happy relationship with his surroundings and the friendly people he met with whom he could enjoy and discuss so many things. His vow of obedience came to mind immediately.

"May God find me willing and able", he prayed quietly to himself.

"You know how Father Pancratius has left us, at Saint Mary's, Lukosi. Now Father Joseph has nobody to help him, and we have been struggling so hard to do more for the Africans in the Wankie area," he led on a bit further. "Well, I have decided that it will be good for you to go there permanently now; you can be with them, and work to develop the mission and to open schools around Lukosi."

Father Odilo knew something of the area, having made a few long trips on bicycle, going well beyond the boundaries of his Mission, and the Insuza and Gwayi areas. He had only been at Saint Patrick's Mission for about three months, and made two trips over two hundred miles from Bulawayo, where he had seen how much Father Joseph Ebert was in need of some encouragement and support.

The Wankie area was enormous, and he knew how Father Joseph was working there almost alone, hardly seeing a white face for weeks on end. Here he was now in the prime of life at 27, and although he had been appreciating his contact with people and the urban life of Bulawayo, he was ready for the more rural challenge. There, they would be surrounded by such pressing needs, of education, enlightenment and employment chances. "God works in strange ways," he acknowledged quietly to himself, and was starting to think about a lot of things. However, he realised that Bishop Arnoz had much more to say, and he paid attention respectfully.

"Of course, we have very little in the way of money, so you will have to be hard-working, careful and resourceful," he concluded after explaining some of the tasks he was dishing out. One of the points that struck Father Odilo strongly was the brief mention of a missionary strategy of building schools and out-stations, in order to reach the people further away from Lukosi Mission.

"Do you understand what I am asking of you?" he questioned, as he must have caught a glimpse of Father Odilo's mind wandering a bit; his attention quickly returned in full to the subject at hand.

"Yes, my lord, and I promise that I shall do my best for you and Holy Mother Church. This has all come about rather quickly, and I have not yet gathered my thoughts," he apologised.

"I have arranged for you to take one of the parish bicycles", Bishop Arnoz offered magnanimously.

"My lord, I look forward to this work, and I shall begin immediately with preparations," he concluded politely.

Father Odilo's excitement soon mounted. He was a man who wanted to get on and do things, and this was clearly such an opportunity. He would be many miles from Bulawayo, and he would be working closely with the African people, people to whom he had already become very attached, and whom he would happily teach whatever he could, and help in any way that God directed him.

His audience with the bishop was soon ended, and he walked out with an extra spring in his step. He could proceed with his mission, and undoubtedly, he would give it his best!

He strode on further, and reaching the heavy wooden side door to the Cathedral, he walked in. Genuflecting at the door, he made the sign of the cross, and prayed, 'Blessed Jesus, thank You for everything in my life. Thank You for this new task, and please strengthen me to do it properly, for Your glory, and for the good of all those poor African people whom Your gospel needs to reach.' He paused to collect his thoughts, and found it was hard to be truly prayerful right now. There was so much to arrange, and the bishop wanted him to catch the morning train on Sunday. And that was only three days away!

'Lord, please still my mind so that I may feel your presence. Guide my thoughts, and help me, as you always have. I will serve you faithfully, as I promised, and I only want to do the best I can. Make use of me, God, and give me your grace and strength,' he prayed quietly. Although he did not appreciate it at the time, the Hand of Providence had reached down again, and the loss of a priest created the opening for a whole new stage of his missionary work.

His mind slowly settled, and he brought himself into God's presence, before the Blessed Sacrament. He knelt for quite some time, before he was stirred again. The painting of Our Lady high in the alcove behind the altar depicted the Annunciation. He could feel Our Lady's gentle presence and acceptance, and he sensed her blessings as he prayed that she intercede and guide him also. 'I go to your mission, Saint Mary's, at Lukosi; please be my strength in times of trouble or doubt, and watch over me that I may bring Your Son to these poor people.'

He prayed the Joyful Mysteries of the Rosary, and as he thought about the Annunciation, he prayed fervently to the Holy Spirit, 'strengthen and guide me. Watch over and protect me. Give me courage and wisdom, to do your Holy will, and to gain more souls for Our Father and His Holy Catholic Church.' After resting in prayer for a while longer, he made the sign of the cross, got up, and walked to the front door. He dipped his fingers in holy water, and again made the sign of the cross, before exiting into the bright sunlight. There was a lot to do, but he would soon be ready for his move.

A GREAT SEND-OFF ON THE TRAIN TRIP TO LUKOSI

Steam train travels

The train journey was an experience of a lifetime. It was as if the Holy Spirit knew exactly how to raise Father Odilo's spirits to new heights, and charge him up to be fully alive for the people and the work ahead of him. A small crowd of well-wishers helped him onto the train, into his second class compartment; at least he had a coupe to himself; that was a lucky thing for such a journey.

As the train pulled out, several Europeans whom he had come to know well, all waved and wished him well. The train gathered speed as it began to slide endlessly past the very long rail platform of Bulawayo station. The larger crowd of Africans, many who had known him well from Saint Patrick's Mission, began to shout their greetings, "hambani kuhle, Baba," they chorused, and the ladies began to ululate joyfully. They had such happy and smiling faces. Perhaps they knew more than anybody else did, just where he was headed, and how much he would do in the two and a half years ahead.

And the greetings did not stop there. No sooner had they slowed down for the Mpopoma siding, than the noise of a large African crowd was heard again. Father Odilo crossed to the aisle window, and put his head out. Suddenly the chorus rose. "Salibonani Father," they called out, and their happy and encouraging faces were such a wonderful sight that it brought a lump to his throat. He could feel himself becoming quite emotional; just as he was about to face loneliness, he was greeted with deep love and friendship.

It is something that most Europeans just never really get to understand. Their emotions and reactions are strictly controlled, as if it is some shame to drop the pretences, or the expected styles of conduct; more so in Africa even, where they were expected to show the Africans how 'civilised' people should behave.

He could almost feel the rhythm, as the African ladies began to stamp their feet and dance about loudly, when the train came to a stop at the next siding, Luveve. "Sibongile khakhulu," they thanked him, and he realised just how genuinely they liked him, and he knew that his time among them had truly been worthwhile. What wonderful people! He stepped down and greeted the men-folk first, and then the women presented themselves, curtsying respectfully; they made sure that they kept their heads lower than his, as they offered him their hands to shake, in the traditional womanly greetings of Africa.

The train did not stay long at the siding and was soon on its way; steam was puffing away in clean white clouds, from the side and top of the majestic old Garratt locomotive, which pulled this long line of passengers and goods wagons. The large chunks of black coal were piled high behind the stoker, who casually tossed another shovel-full into the cavernous fire in front of the driver.

The train would go onto Wankie, the coalfield, where it drew its own fuel, and hauled back wagon after wagon for the power station at Bulawayo. It also hauled coal for the many factories, which had begun to spring up in this growing industrial centre.

As the train built up steam, and began to apply its enormous power to pull the wagons along behind it, the people chorused again, this time thanking him but also wishing him well for his journey, and his new mission station. "Hambani kuhle," they cried out, using the plural form of the verb to denote their very respectful attitude towards him, with his education, knowledge and status amongst them.

The next siding was Sawmills, and while they took on water these scenes were repeated again, with a smaller crowd. He waved his greetings and choked back his emotions. So much love and appreciation was a great tonic and a real surprise after such a short time among these good

Matabele people. His eyes were watered over as the train left them fading in the distance, and he turned back to look along the corridor.

He spotted a sidelong glance from a young European couple, a few compartments along on his carriage, and he glanced away to hide his embarrassment and awkward feeling, conscious of stepping outside the boundaries of accepted European reserve. Sitting down in his coupe, he got his emotions under control again. But as he thought about the happy people he had just left behind, he knew he was on the right track. He had work to do for them, and he would certainly give it his best.

'Thank you, God,' he prayed. 'You are mighty and powerful, guiding the whole universe, but You love me and all these people. I feel Your presence in their love, and in my life. Stay with me always, and watch over me in times of temptation and danger.' At the next sidings, Nyamandhlovu, Igusi and Sawmills, the scene was repeated again, although with smaller numbers of people.

These Africans had come from far away, from their kraals and villages, and they all offered their singing and cheering to encourage and thank him. Their appreciation was overwhelming, and deepened his resolve to work even harder for them all, and to bring them God's message of love and salvation.

The young couple in the carriage had taken to ignoring him by now, and seemed even a bit hostile; it was funny how Europeans seem to have such strict attitudes of decorum, and what is appropriate for them in African company.

By now he was gathering his composure, and each little stop became easier to handle. He spoke with the people, and asked about them and their families. Some recounted stories, reminding him of things like the time the bottom of his trousers were completely eaten away by white ants, when he left them lying on the floor of the mud hut where he had slept one rainy night.

They had a good laugh at these memories, and off he went again, the train chugging and grinding away in order to get its load moving. This wonderful tonic uplifted Father Odilo, as he savoured the pleasant thoughts, which his friends brought to mind.

This unexpected series of greetings had another side effect; perhaps it was an answer to his prayers on Sunday. His mind went back to Holy Mass. As he had offered up the host to God, consecrating it to become the body of Christ, he had offered himself with Jesus, 'take me God to do Your work. I know I am not worthy of Your divine presence in my life, but I promise to always do my best for You.' He had meditated after communion, and asked God, 'why must I move on so soon? What purpose do you have for me, and will I be able to fulfil it?'

The crowds stopped after that; this was no longer Father Odilo's district. Well, now he felt strengthened, and knew he could do anything God demanded of him. Furthermore, he was filled with a great sense of love for the African people he was called upon to serve. He loved their honesty, their happiness, and their freedom from the cares of city life. It did not matter to them how much money they had, or if they did not have the things they saw the Europeans bringing in to the shops.

They had the trees and the rivers, and their crops and their families, and they accepted the seasons as they came. It was as if they were truly close to God in His creation. It was easy to talk to them about uNkulunkulu, the great God, because they knew He had to be there. Their ideas of God had been formed by ordinary and simple life experience, and God was unquestioningly necessary; it was simply that they had not had any major revelations or inspirations, nothing like the Jewish people's Covenant experience with God, their journeys under Moses' leadership.

The culmination of it all fitted easily together, with Christ's salvation of mankind, dying on the cross, out of such incredible love for His creation, for mankind. It seemed a bit strange to them at first, but it was like a key to a puzzle which they had not really tried too hard to solve. Those missionaries who were able to explain and reveal the salvation story found a quick and ready audience.

He had plenty of time to ponder and pray as the train puffed its way through the teak and mukwa forests of the sandveld. The forests gave way to open vleis and pans and soon the baobab trees were in evidence, like upside-down trees, or giant vegetables, dwarfing their flimsy filigree of branches that only had a few leaves to testify to their 'treedom'. The people he saw were poor and uneducated, and he saw so clearly how much he could do for them; he also knew how good and decent they were.

The journey was over all too soon, and he watched the white clouds evaporating over the cooling towers next to a small thermal power station as the train snaked into Wankie. It shuddered to a halt at the railway station.

Lukosi—Saint Mary's Mission

Father Joseph Ebert, the rector at Lukosi, was delighted to welcome his new helper, as he stepped down onto the platform. Father Josef summed up his neat priestly attire, and gave an unconscious nod of approval to the Roman collar that marked him out clearly as a fellow man of God.

They drove back the short distance from Wankie to Saint Mary's Mission, in his vanette. Bishop Arnoz had told him, "he is a very holy man, and dedicated to his mission," and this fitted with his own picture of Father Joseph, as the two had met on several occasions, perhaps not expecting to be working so closely together. Father Joseph divulged how he had suffered a bitter disappointment when Father Pancratius had left, but that was behind now.

Strip Roads had been built in the 1930's, depression years and had soon become like twin ribbons throughout the country

Father Joseph had been a very active missionary, and done the pioneering work for this huge area. "At first they built the mission right down on the banks of the Zambesi River. However, that was too harsh and impractical an environment, and so we chose this site," he explained as they turned left onto a dirt road that took them steeply up the north-east bank of the Lukosi River. He stopped the vanette, and led Father Odilo to the edge of the hill. From this commanding position, high up on the sandstone hill, he gestured, "there you see it, the Lukosi River." He proudly pointed out the wide, sandy riverbed below them.

Looking across the riverbed, the brown hillside rose from the green riverine trees, tumbling with stones and scree that not even the baobab trees chose to climb. He could see that Father Joseph had chosen this site well, with the mission on the crest of a well-wooded hill. It had a scattering of indigenous fig trees and a wide assortment of other shady trees, including what he later came to see as mysterious 'pseudo-oak' trees, with their five-fingered leaves in a range of colours from dark green, through light green to a yellowish hue.

"Why did they build these roads in strips like this?" Father Odilo asked Father Josef.

"A very interesting story," he answered, and then proceeded to tell of what he knew of it, and how thousands of Europeans had gone onto relief in Southern Rhodesia. They were embarrassed but proud people, and were prepared to work at anything that would respectably keep their families alive.

"The roads department came up with this uniquely Rhodesian idea. It was an excellent plan; they were cheap and effective. Also, it gave people jobs during the 1930's. The government soon put people to work, with picks and shovels." He pointed out how men dug out two parallel strips of ground, backfilled them with gravel, compacted them well and then surfaced these strips with tarmacadam. By the time war broke out 2,000 miles of these roads had been built, becoming the backbone of Rhodesia's road system.

The stone-and-concrete drift at the mission carried an occasional car or truck over the sandy riverbed, while he was being given the tour. "There are plans to build a bridge over there," he pointed out. "We certainly need it; that river is impassable for weeks sometimes."

Cloud shadows drifted lazily over the full and leafy treetops. Father Joseph pointed out where he wanted to erect a large cross, near the road side of the mission. "All the cars coming from Bulawayo must be able to see it if they look up," he explained. "It is important to remind people of Jesus, and what better way than when they are on a journey like this; most of them are travelling to the Falls."

Then he led Father Odilo to the chapel and showed him the convent that he had built to house the six Precious Blood Sisters, and then lastly took him to the priests' house. "Welcome to your new home." The house was shaped like an 'L', with the bathroom/toilet in its corner and a covered patio on the inside edges of the L. Father Joseph's room was on the northern end, with a room in between him and the bathroom. Father Odilo had a room on the other arm, nearest to the bathroom, with one more room to his East.

At the top of the hill, a small to medium sized baobab tree stood just near their house, but it was already a prominent feature, a landmark. "Water is a constant problem, though," Father Joseph explained. "The biggest problem is that it has to be pumped from the riverbed so far below us."

He pointed past the baobab, saying, "We built that round brick reservoir next to the convent; it is at the highest place on the hill." Father Odilo was nodding as he took in all the details that Father Joseph was so keen to pass on to him. "The river only has water for a short time of the year, but we have set the extraction pipe into the sand and it gives us water most of the time, thank God. But the pump is often broken down and we have to watch out for sand getting into it, or blocking the non-return valve."

The next morning, Father Joseph took him to see the clinic which he had established there, to serve the community around them. "Who knows, one day this might even become a big hospital," he surmised. "There are certainly plenty of people in need around here."

After a few days, Father Odilo soon felt very much at home. He enjoyed his prayerful walks as he said his Divine Office, and found some beautiful places to sit or kneel as he did this.

Father Odilo was intrigued and one evening he commented, "there are some beautiful trees on that hill, and along the riverbank. The leaves look a lot like oak leaves, but quite a light green colour. Do you know what they are?"

"I am sorry, Odilo," he replied. "That is not something I know too much about. You might get more answers from old Mrs. Giese. I will introduce you to her one of these days." He pointed to the northwest, saying, "She lives just over there, about twenty miles away, and has been here ever since her husband discovered this coal-field."

Although Father Joseph himself had done a huge amount himself, he was agreeably surprised with his new assistant. The intensity, drive and determination, which had been bottled up in Father Odilo, burst out on Lukosi like a whirlwind!

The mission had very limited resources, and sometimes they differed and had problems over money matters. He had a chicken run, and the sale of eggs and chickens in Wankie was the only cash income they received. There was no money at all coming from Germany at this time, and the Church in Matabeleland was very poor. Father Joseph often objected to the cost of things that Father Odilo suggested. "How can we spend our money building outschools?" he reasoned. "We don't even have enough to run the mission station." But somehow they always found a way to make ends meet.

REACHING THE PEOPLE

Life was hard in this vast bush area, and he had to stay fit and determined in order to keep going. The heat became unbearable at times, and the insects buzzed around him incessantly for the slightest moisture that they could reach. No amount of swiping at them or brushing them away had any effect. In fact, it seemed to intensify the attraction, as if the odour of insects in distress signalled their companions to join in or take some sort of revenge. On many of the afternoons, the hot, dry winds would blow up dust-devils, tall columns of swirling sand and leaves; these would travel across the bush and the dry riverbeds like miniature tornadoes.

Father Odilo was soon very happy here and was filled with zeal to teach and convert these wonderful, but superstitious Africans. This was what he had trained for; it was his vocation. He saw and thought about all the poor people, mostly incapable of reading a single word, let alone understanding news, notices and letters. Most of them seemed still steeped in pagan beliefs, except for the few who had come to accept Christianity.

They certainly had a belief in a supreme being and some form of life after death. Ancestors were revered and relied upon to make or approve numerous decisions. These ranged from the choice of a wife, to healing wounds or sicknesses, planting times for crops and sorting out family or tribal disputes.

The people were primitive and poor, and their traditional clothing was scanty; it only had to cover what they considered to be the most private parts of their bodies. The women saw no reason to conceal their breasts, and these were used for their clearly intended purpose, of suckling infants.

During his teaching and services, young children would soon become fractious but there was no time wasted before the young mother would provide her baby with a breast to suckle. He sometimes watched fascinated at the way their tiny little hands and fingers stroked the mother, feeling the comforting brown skin of her breast, or her shoulder, neck, back, face or her curled up hair. The perfectly formed, chubby little fingers seemed to have a mind of their own as they probed her nose or her ears, and she would suddenly jerk her head as they felt an eye.

Before long, the child's eyes would begin to droop, and it would settle peacefully asleep in its mother's lap as she sat with her legs folded beneath her and partly to her side.

As Missionaries, they opened up more and more of this remote territory to both modern civilisation and Christianity, all the time creating opportunities to work with as many people as possible. In one of his reflective moments, he thought about the influence they had as missionaries. 'We have an effect on so many people and you can see the tremendous results—schooling, medicine and bringing the gospel of Christianity. Even the building work has been a perfect chance for contact and evangelisation. We have been able to give example and educate these Africans to new techniques and understandings in the process.'

Much of the work of the young priest was self-initiated; it was true pioneering work. He travelled far afield, and did not just stay put at the mission base. One of the difficulties was the fact that most of this travelling had to be done on foot or by bicycle.

On some of these trips, extending as far north as the Zambesi River, he encountered remote police patrols. Once, a European policeman asked, "where do you come from?"

He explained, "I am Father Odilo, from Saint Mary's Mission, at Lukosi."

"Gee, man! You are miles away! How did you get all the way here?"

"I use my bicycle, and sleep along the way," Father Odilo explained to the amazed men on their police patrol, and their suspicions were soon assuaged.

"Good luck to you, Father. Be careful the lions don't get you," they said, and bade him farewell.

A TRADITIONAL FUNERAL

One day, he was invited to attend a funeral, at Pongolo River. The first wife of the kraal owner had 'fallen'—it was considered indecent to say bluntly that somebody had "died". She was now about to be buried, obviously with all their traditional ceremonies. Father Odilo was by now coming to be regarded as a respected member of the local community, and so they asked him to attend. He gratefully and respectfully accepted the invitation.

When he arrived, he found that the grave had already been dug—it was of normal size, well over three feet deep, but there was something unusual about it. At the bottom, there was a lattice of sticks and branches so that the person would not lie on the bare ground. On both sides niches had been carved into the earth, and food and utensils were placed in these so that the dead woman would not go hungry. 'There alone is sure proof of their belief in the hereafter,' he thought to himself. He had found it difficult to follow some of the Ndebele explanations for ceremonies they performed, mainly involving their recent ancestors, but they most certainly did not believe that all life ended with death.

After all was prepared, the body, which was wrapped in blankets and cowskin, was carried from her hut to the grave. There she was buried with an elaborate and dignified ceremony, while the men and women lamented loudly and sorrowfully all the time. "She was obviously a well loved and special person," he said, and the men beside him nodded their agreement.

After the grave had been filled in, water was poured over the mound and the other wife and the daughters rolled and wallowed in the mud, grieving and wailing loudly, expressing genuine deep sorrow, their own, as well as that of the family and all their relatives and friends. This was all done with heart-rending wailing and sounds of distress that were truly African.

Father Odilo sensed the deep sincerity and grief, and was struck by their deep reverence and dignity. He found that he was deeply moved emotionally, and could not stop his own eyes from watering over; very soon his own emotions were flowing in sympathy with these loving mourners.

Cycling in the Heat

He cycled throughout a wide territory around Lukosi Mission. One of the remote areas he loved to visit was the Sebungwe District. This enormous territory included the present day districts of Binga and Gokwe. He established schools at Siyachilaba, Siyansale, and Saba. He also opened up new schools in the Matetsi area. His travels brought him to some of the natural hot-springs, at Mlibizi, Binga and Kabila.

People he met travelling by car were invariably on their way to or from the Victoria Falls; they usually waved a greeting and some of them even stopped to chat for a few minutes. The local people were very sociable, always willing to talk about things and curious to hear who he was and what he was doing. In true African fashion, they always said that the Victoria Falls were 'just down the road', making it seem very close by.

Early one morning, he set out on his bicycle to make a day-trip to the Victoria Falls. With the first streaks of dawn visible through the trees behind him, he cycled down their little hill onto the main tarred road, and began his journey. He planned to travel the sixty miles to the Victoria Falls and back.

On the way to Wankie, he looked closely at the huge sandstone rocks, remembering how Mrs. Giese had explained the layers to him. "They look like big boulders, but if you look carefully, you will see they are slabs that have dropped as the soft layer underneath has been washed away. This whole area is sedimentary, and that is one of the things my husband[iv] pointed out to me. He was sure this was a rich area when he was prospecting for minerals, like the coal-field he discovered here."

He had asked her about the undulating forestlands, and she told him, "Albert had a theory; he thought some of those hills were giant sand dunes, part of the Kalahari Desert; the teak and Mukwa trees, the forests, simply disguise the sand."

"I heard that he was the man who found the Wankie coal."

"Well, Albert heard from the Africans that there were rocks that burned hereabouts. I remember how he checked out the geology and was excited about the way it is all layered. He pegged his first claim here in 1894."

"How much coal is there?"

"Plenty. Albert used to say this could become the Ruhr of Africa."

He would have liked to stop for a cup of tea in Wankie, but there was no time today. He had set himself a tough target, to cycle to Victoria Falls and back, and he soon remembered that this was nothing like the level countryside of Holland. He cycled hard up the long hills, and really appreciated the down slopes on the other side. Because he was strong and fit he managed to keep up a good pace.

Occasionally the cars that passed the priest with his Roman collar gave a hoot and a cheery wave; they courteously moved one wheel off the road to allow him to stay on the tar. In some places, if he strayed off the compacted road shoulder, the sand was like treacle if he got into it. It was like the bush tracks, where he found it easier to walk the bike, especially if there was any sort of upward slope.

Mile after mile he noted the white concrete markers, counting down towards two hundred and eighty miles. He had just passed the two hundred and seventy mile marker, and as he crested the hill he saw the cloud of moisture, 'the smoke that thunders', rising above the tree canopy. It certainly was a cloud, but one that came from the earth, not one from above. He enjoyed cycling down the long hill to cross a river and then the railway line. The Falls were still a long way off, but after a strenuous uphill cycle, he was again able to freewheel down with the wide Zambesi River in sight, looking forward to his first sight of the Victoria Falls.

THE VICTORIA FALLS

Again he crossed the railway line, and looked to his right to see the famous Victoria Falls Hotel, with its own railway siding, the cloud above the Falls was so close that drops of cold water were falling on him as he cycled down-hill towards the Falls. He had to cross the railway line yet again as it snaked its way towards the arch-bridge over the Zambesi River.

Cycling as close as he could get, he rested his bicycle up against a rain-soaked tree. Then, he walked to the edge and stood in awe as he watched the world's largest body of falling water plunging over the edge.

'What a beautiful part of God's creation,' he stood thinking to himself, as he gazed over the edge of the deep precipice, into the thundering gorge below. A group of tourists was at the tall statue of David Livingstone, the first European to see the Falls. The base of the statue was dated, 1813 to 1873, and three simple words spelled out his life, "Missionary, Explorer, Liberator".

He stood and watched the water plunging about eighty metres into the invisible depths of what was aptly called the Devil's Cataract.

The water seemed like hundreds of tiny little divers, joyfully leaping with hands together, stretched out in front of their heads, just after their rough launch from the rockshelf. He watched for ages, fascinated by the droplets flying above the diving waves, shining and glistening in the sunlight. Each droplet was unique, and each group of droplets did something different. Every now and again a group would leap higher and further than the all the rest, but would soon join the inexorable plunge to their destination, a boiling and bubbling cauldron of tortured waters in the narrow chasm below, as the mighty Zambesi fought its way to the sea.

'Almighty God,' he prayed instinctively, 'thank You for this great wonder of Your creation. Thank You for my life, that I, too, may serve mankind as You commended. Like these waters, we are all on a journey, one that ends in being united with You when we die.'

Through the trees and thick ipamba vines, he looked down onto a perfect rainbow that hung shimmering in the spray. Its colours stayed fixed and perfect among the changing drops of water, an unchangeable reminder of God's promise to Noah, never to destroy the earth by flooding[4] it again.

Three English tourists were discussing where they thought Livingstone had died, and seemed to greet him warmly enough. "Good morning," he responded, and then he noticed a slight change of attitude;

---

[4]   Gen. 9: 8-16

he was quite accustomed to reactions to his German accent, but did not let it deter him in any way.

He was able to tell them some extra details of David Livingstone's life and death, and they soon accepted him as a fellow-missionary of Livingstone's. "We are staying at the Victoria Falls Hotel," the man said. "Please join us for tea if you are able to. We have just finished our little tour of the Falls."

"That is most kind of you," he acknowledged, "but I must make the most of the Falls before I cycle back to Lukosi."

"But that's even south of Wankie, Father. I shall happily pay for a room, and surely you didn't plan to cycle here and back in one day!"

"I am afraid so. The exercise will be great, and I have lots of work to do. So, thank you for your kind invitation, but I am sure you understand." By now they had walked back to where the view of Devil's Cataract was best. He assisted them by taking their posed photograph, and mused aloud, "there is something about moving water, but this is in a league of its own, far more captivating than I had ever expected."

"You are right, Father, and you have helped us appreciate it more. Have a safe ride back," the lady in the group said, as their paths parted and he continued along the edge of the Falls.

He thought the thundering water opposite him looked like giant tendrils of beautiful hair, but alive like nothing he had ever seen before. 'It was certainly well worth the strenuous bicycle ride,' he thought.

The roar of the plunging waters rose and fell with the changing winds it generated, and spray rose like upside-down rain, shooting upwards to great heights above him, before stopping and returning in obedience to the call of the river, to join its inevitable journey. In the interlude, these drops had joined in forming the continuous cloud, which he had seen from so many miles away. 'So,' he thought, 'the baobab tree is not the only thing that is upside down in this part of the world!'

Standing opposite a break in the Falls, sign-posted as Cataract Island, he looked north at the crest, where the smooth water, tinged with brownish streaks, was covering bubbling and frothing whitened layers. These instantly burst forth into snow-like plunging strands, gathering speed as they fell in a continuous curtain of roaring whiteness. It was so immense that it was impossible to view all of its seventeen hundred metres at once. He kept walking east, facing the Main Falls, which are over a hundred metres deep, and the sound grew louder as he went.

As he was walking on a path through the thick rain forest, a buck startled him slightly as it broke from cover. It stood still for what seemed ages, until it headed off, picking its legs carefully through the tangled undergrowth.

Short and tall palm trees contrasted with the rest of the bush, and the wet ground was covered in grasses, ferns and fallen trees. Thick tree trunks took fig leaves high into the raining air, and he clambered over a large trunk that had fallen across the path he wanted to take. Brushing his way through palms and ferns, he kept as near as possible to the Falls, near the roaring sound on his left, but careful not to go too close to the slippery edge of the chasm.

Breaking out into the open again, he noticed the sounds of birds and insects. The sun shone brightly on the tall grass there—the spiky seeds waving gently in the little breezes.

He wondered about the bright red berries he saw on a creeper— picking and squeezing them, a yellowish seed emerged, but its taste was less inviting than its colours. No doubt, the birds found them more appealing. Some of the palm trees also held sticks of yellowing fruit, too high to reach and taste.

The rain was soon drenching his clothing as he came out into an even more open area, treading carefully near the edge of the exposed basalt cliff, facing the Falls. The grass was glistening with rain, and the rock surfaces were flowing with water, but the sky above was bright and sunny except for the rising cloud. A sudden squall made him turn away and he stopped to admire another rainbow in the droplets.

Now the cloud became total and he could not even see the deeper sheet of falling water. Any hope of remaining partly dry was soon gone, and there were fewer trees to offer what was futile shelter anyway. He made his way back from the edge, but kept moving east.

Once or twice he almost lost his footing, but nimbly recovered in time to avoid slipping. Now he saw a brief break on the far side, an island, and another expanse of falling water, with a slightly dropped area in its middle. There the water was churned up and white before it tumbled over the precipice. He kept going until he reached the rocky tip from where he could look down into what was described as the Cauldron.

Here the waters from the east and the west arms of the Falls converged and squeezed their way together along the narrow gorge, passing south under the famous steel arch bridge spanning high over the Zambesi. That was an impressive sight and set him wondering and admiring such a great civil engineering achievement, built all those many years ago in 1905[5]. Somebody had told him how it had been built out from the two sides, but it did not meet exactly in the middle. He could not be sure if the story was true, that the English engineer had then despaired and committed suicide by diving into the river below. Whatever the difficulties, the problem had obviously been rectified, and he had heard a train crossing while he was at Livingstone's statue.

UNDER ARREST

Suddenly, two smartly dressed policemen appeared and asked, "who are you and what are you doing?"

He had hardly opened his mouth to explain, when they each grabbed an elbow and ordered, "come with us!" Quite stunned by this sudden turn of events, he found his voice quavering as he attempted to tell them he was a missionary priest from Lukosi.

"Yes, yes," they retorted rudely, "and you just cycled up here for the day, I suppose."

"Ja, that's true," he answered.

"I think we have one here for sure," the one policeman said. "Come with us to the police station."

"My bicycle," Father Odilo managed to say, as they marched past it, with an English couple staring at this arrest of an obvious villain.

The one policeman thought about it, then said, "We had better take it with; it could have some clues as to what this German is really up to. And so, there he was, a German Catholic priest, led off, with his bicycle, between two young English policemen who were sure they had arrested an infiltrator or an escapee, probably from German South West Africa. They had to walk up the hill, in full view of all sorts of people, over the railway line, past the shops, and up to the little police station on the left of the road.

The officer-in-charge asked him several questions, and then went into another office to phone the Cathedral in Bulawayo. Coming back

---

[5]   The Cleveland Bridge Company fabricated the steelwork and sent it out in pieces by ship and train.

to the prisoner, his attitude was completely changed. "I am terribly sorry, Father Odilo. This has been a dreadful mistake. I am sure you understand that we are at war, and so our men have orders; they are obliged to check anybody suspicious—not that you are really suspicious. It's just that we had a report that a German, wearing a priest's uniform was examining the bridge, and so . . . . I am sure you see how such a thing happened."

The two policemen at his sides had straightened up and had very embarrassed expressions on their faces. "Please accept our apologies. Can we do anything for you?"

"Gentlemen, I understand, but I hope this will be a lesson to you. Do not jump to hasty conclusions about people just because of their accent or skin colour. I have to cycle back to Lukosi, so I shall be off, thank you," he concluded crisply.

"That's impossible, father. It is a very long way; you cannot make it today. I shall be only too pleased to accommodate you at my home, if you will do me the honour," the officer offered.

"Thank you, but I know I can manage; if you have a cup of tea ready, that would be appreciated."

"Of course, Gibson, the pot is still hot. Pour our priest a cup quickly."

He drank his tea with his straight-backed posture, and then said, "Good day, gentleman," as he headed out, mounted his bicycle and began the long journey home to Lukosi.

He glanced back from the top of the hill, to appreciate this great and impressive sight that he had enjoyed, and glided down to cross the railway line and river again. Somehow, the memory of this arrest would always tarnish his attitude towards that great wonder of the world, though. Hill after hill rose to meet him, and by the time he reached the downhill to Lukosi it was nightfall, and he was utterly exhausted. Father Joseph asked, "Did you make it?"

"Of course," he replied proudly. "It is most impressive." He ate and had his tea, but he was in no mood to converse. He was asleep within minutes of climbing into his simple bed.

Making do and Making People do What they Can

"We have to build these outschools," he maintained. "There are so many people living a long way from our mission, and there is no other way to help them." However, seeing and doing did not always go easily together. He was encouraged when he thought back on the happy memories of his still-recent train journey, and was champing at the bit, like a racehorse, trying to get free of the stocks.

"I shall need to buy some tools, cement, timber, windows, doors, roof sheets, nails, glass, door handles and so forth," he approached his superior, Father Joseph Ebert.

"And how many chickens will I have to sell to pay for that?" was the response. "We can only arrange a limited amount of money, so you will have to revise those drawings you have, and make more use of local materials." The early missionaries and Father Joseph had developed a small chicken farm to raise some funds for the Mission, as they did not have anything like the income needed to cover even its normal expenses.

"I think I can do that," responded Father Odilo. "We can make our own mud bricks, and find thatching grass for the roof. The frame can be built of poles we cut in the area, and the same goes for the roof timbers. But it is essential that we have nails, wire, glass and doors."

"Well, I shall take in some extra chickens to sell on Wednesday, and see what I can get for them. You get started and make sure the Africans pitch in and help," Father Joseph urged.

The very next day, a group of men from Luseche's village were gathered around and squatting on the ground in front of this new young priest. "Do you want a school?" was the question he first posed.

"Yebo, baba," they responded enthusiastically. "We want our sons to learn, to read and write things on paper, to speak English, and to count properly. They must learn this well, so that they can get jobs."

"Well, madoda, it is also up to you. I can only buy some small things, but we have to make the rest. We can use the clay from the pans and the anthills, to make bricks. We must chop some trees for side poles, and for the roof. We need thatching grass, but that will have to come from far away; the grass here is too short, as you have let your goats and donkeys eat it all up."

Two days later, he arrived back on his bicycle, with his Roman collar very conspicuous but uncomfortable in this humid heat. He had two hammers, a wood saw, a tape measure and some string. By teatime, they had already cleared an area for the new classroom. The perspiration was dripping off Father Odilo's brow, and he was doing his level best to prove that one good German was able to do whatever two Africans could do in the same time.

Of course, he also had to contend with misunderstanding, deliberate or otherwise. It was one thing agreeing to have a school, but to actually have to make bricks, chop poles, and build it; well, that was a different matter. "I want these seven trees chopped down and trimmed before lunch," Father Odilo directed three men, strongly built, and young enough, he was certain. Agreement was nodded and the arrangements were well in hand now.

When Father Odilo came back after wandering off to try and find thatching grass, the three men had felled two of the trees, and were sitting in the shade discussing the rainy season and its effects on their crops. In his anger, he shouted, "what are you doing?" Are you like women, that you cannot do a simple job like this?"

His disappointed message required no great language skill for the people to understand what he meant. He was sure that Jesus must have felt like this, when he left the apostles to pray and keep vigil with him while he went further into the darkness of the Garden of Gethsemane; and when he returned, he found his apostles fast asleep!

Taking up an axe, he ripped into the closest of the trees himself. Within minutes, it was down, and then he attacked the next one with the same gusto! By now, Dumisani was wielding the other axe, and he soon had the next tree down. The next tree followed shortly after, and the men quickly trimmed away the foliage and branches.

"You see," he challenged them; "you can do the work easily. I am never going to do your work for you again. If you can do it, then it is up to you yourselves to do the tasks I give you."

The next morning, he arrived with Brother Basil Sofka. He was soon setting out the foundations, with his tape measure and strings.

Father Odilo held the end of the tape, while he made his arcs. He measured six yards, eight yards and then drew in an hypotenuse of ten yards to complete the right angle for the first corner. "Right, now we extend this to make the sideline," he said, as he marked off the twelve yards he wanted for the long side. He then repeated the process for each of the other three corners. He checked that the distance was exactly the same from corner to corner, and was satisfied that his foundation layout was perfectly rectangular before he drove in the final corner pegs. "There, now we can dig," he announced.

The soil was firm, but very sandy, and it did not take long before the second group of eight men who came to help with their school had dug the foundation trenches. Buildings soon sprang up, and the teaching was well received by keen pupils. (In some areas, Methodist schools had once been started, but were since abandoned. Perhaps the people realised what they were missing and were keener now.) The benefits brought by these Mariannhill Missionaries extended long into the future, and in ways that they could not even imagine.

There was so much to do and build, but Father Odilo was only granted ten pounds for each school that he built. Lukosi is ten miles from Wankie town, and he used to cycle there and back regularly, in spite of the heat and the hilly road. "I am still a fit young priest," he would proudly say when anybody asked why he did not wait for other transport. Father Joseph's vanette came in handy, though, when he needed to transport cement, wire, nails and other building materials for their new school sites.

THE MYSTERY OF WATER

Rain was always welcome in the land of the Amandabele / Matabele, and the birds seemed to lose all caution as they fluttered about after a downpour, pouncing on the myriads of flying ants that seemed to emerge from nowhere. People relaxed and smiled more as well.

Perhaps caution left them as well. One day as the clouds burst and a storm erupted, he innocently walked up and away from the bush track, to shelter in his raincoat under a large Mukwa tree. He saw how the rain was glistening as it slid down the dark cracked bark, and two other men came and huddled close to the trunk of the tree. There were some rumblings and lightning flashes, but they seemed far off.

Suddenly, he noticed a strange smell, like something from his gymnasium chemistry class. But, before he could give it any more thought, his body was tingling and he heard a loud bang and was enveloped in a blinding light. From the corner of his eyes he saw a huge bird flying through the air and landing with a solid thump about six metres away.

As his vision cleared he saw that it was not a bird at all, but one of the men who had taken shelter under the tree! He dashed over to him and started to ask him if he was hurt. The man leaped up, and babbled like a madman. "Leave me alone, leave me alone! I am dead, I am dead!"

After quite a while, the man calmed down, and Father Odilo persuaded him that he was still alive, but very lucky to be so!

The rains came down furiously and continuously, but as they abated the Lukosi River came down in flood. It was an amazing phenomenon. Father Odilo was intrigued as he saw a low line of frothing water rumbling down the river towards them, with sticks and all sorts of things ahead of it.

The river was still not flowing very deep, and then he watched wondering what the people were doing. There they were in the riverbed, with sticks and clubs, beating at the water. Looking more closely, he saw that barbel were jumping right out of the sand, as the water awoke them from their hibernation, only to be clobbered with knobkerries by the excited Africans. This was fishing with a difference!

They had to be quick, though, because the river grew in flow, and soon the Lukosi was flowing brown and strong, bank to bank and over the narrow drift, leaving people and vehicles stranded on either side. In the flow were trees and even cattle and other animals that had underestimated the might of the river. Only hours before it had been a quiet trickle, innocent and friendly.

The rainy season turned out to be a deluge, reminding him of the biblical account of Noah. They did not have an ark, but they were safely above the waters, high up on their wet and slippery hill. That February the rains came virtually every single day. The storms raged. Thunder and lightning punctuated the downpours. The storms were so powerful and continuous that Father Odilo was trapped and frustrated at the mission; he could not get out to do any more development for a whole month.

ASSESSING PROGRESS

Building is exciting, visible and measurable. An enormous amount was achieved in a short time. The people all helped and Father Odilo did the work alongside them. It was not easy, though, and the soil was terrible for their bricks.

"These bricks are rubbish," Brother Athanasius complained some years later. "Luckily you built your roofs with an overhang or else there would be nothing left when it rains!"

They sometimes sat in the evening and looked down over the Lukosi valley below, with the sun setting over the hills upstream. "Perhaps one day the people will understand and appreciate what we are doing. They will get their education, but they have all been involved in setting up the schools," Father Odilo mused aloud one evening, as they sat on the rocks overlooking the wide riverbed far below. "I don't believe in doing for them what they can do themselves."

"Quite right," Father Joseph responded, "and we are giving them some food and wages which they really need as well."

"There are some very clever men among them; I am most impressed with that Mutale. I think he is a brother of the chief, and he certainly knows how to keep the brick-making team working well."

They were happy and proud to report their activities the next time this was required. "My lord Bishop, despite all the shortages, we have established eight outschools within the last two years," Father Joseph reported on their behalf. "The money you gave us this year was spent before the winter, but we managed to supplement it with money from chickens and so on. We have also been delighted with Brother Basil Sofka. He has helped valiantly with his skill and labour. Many people helped willingly, but we still had to pay for some items like nails and wire etc., and some of the labour."

Making mud-bricks and carrying them to the little truck

Sabbath and Church Work

The routine of all priests includes the prescribed prayers of the Divine Office, the breviary and daily Holy Mass, with or without a congregation. Father Odilo also had a regular routine of teaching at the new outstations and mud-walled schools which had now been built, to take over from the open-air classrooms that they began with. When he was out in the bush, he would rig up a makeshift altar, and bring out his crucifix, chalice and vestments from his little case, and he would celebrate Holy Mass. His main task was also to bring the Gospel to these people. He had no doubt that he was doing this for their good, and the good of future generations.

Reaching a little village of straw-roofed, mud-walled huts, the dogs barked and children ran out to see him. He parked his bicycle against a tree and stood outside the boundary, from where he exchanged the prescribed greetings. He explained that he would be giving catechism lessons, and that all who would like to learn were encouraged to attend. Under the shade of a beautiful teak tree, several men and women came to listen.

He wondered, 'is it just curiosity, at this European? How much of my message will be received and welcomed?' The parable of the Sower reminded him that his task was simply to do what he could. 'Holy Spirit, I place my work in Your hands. Please help my words to reach these good people, and to find fertile ground.'

LANGUAGES AND CULTURE

There were almost no Europeans around, except for the few who lived in Wankie itself, so it was interesting to make contact whenever he met a European. One day he was on his way back from Mlambo School, saying good-bye to some children as he overtook them on their oxen and donkeys. He saw the turn-off to the road camp, and he had already become accustomed to pulling in and greeting the men who took care of the maintenance and occasional construction work along the way. The man in charge, a Mr Glendinning, greeted him warmly and they were soon sharing a cup of tea together, at the folding camp table.

He considered that his English was quite passable, although he was still trying to learn and improve. While he was there another European arrived, and was conversing away with Glendinning. But, try as he did, he could not understand much of what they were talking about. When the man left, he said, "I have to admit it; I could not make out more than a quarter of what that man was saying."

"Well you're lucky," Glendinning said. "Don't worry. Even I can't understand half of what that Scotsman says!"

Glendinning was quite a joker, and said, "you know the British are quite a muddle of different people; let me tell you about us."

"Go on," he answered, with an expectant smile.

"Well, Britain is really made up of four distinct nations."

"How is that?"

"Well, it's a bit like the tribes here, with their different cultures and languages—The Matabele, The Batonga, The Shona and so on."

Father Odilo nodded, and Glendinning went on, enjoying the telling, and his interested listener. "Well, first and foremost, we have the Scots, of course. Then you have the Irish and the Welsh, and the English," he explained.

"Oh, I see. Of course," he smiled.

"Anyway," he went on, "each of us is a totally different people. Take the Scots, now; they say the Scots will keep the Sabbath and anything else they can lay their hands on!"

The glint in his eyes helped Father Odilo catch on quite quickly. "Oh that's a funny thing," he laughed.

"Then you have the Irish," he grinned under his bushy eyebrows. Now the Irish will fight to the death for a cause, even if they never really know what it is all about."

When Father Odilo's chuckles settled he continued, "Now the Welsh are a specially fervent people. They pray on their knees, and also on their neighbours!"

He let the smiles settle before continuing, "But last of all, you have the English; they lay claim to being a self-made nation, and thus relieve God of a tremendous responsibility!"

Father Odilo roared with laughter and Glendinning was beaming happily. One joke often leads to another, and he could not resist asking, "Father, do you know what is the smallest joke book in the world?"

He pondered suspiciously for a while and then replied, "No".

"The German book of jokes!" he chortled. It took a bit longer before he saw a broad smile and Father Odilo's head nodded as if to say, 'well, that's probably a fair shot.'

He had learned his Zulu well, and so his grasp of iSindebele was good and the people were impressed and intrigued. He also came to understand the Tonga language enough to get his message across, and establish a good rapport with the people.

AFRICAN BELIEFS AND DIVINITY

His message was strange to many, but it also resonated with some of their deeper beliefs. Life after death was obvious to these people, and they had called upon their ancestors' intercession from time immemorial. Similarly, the great God, the 'Mlimo or uNkulunkulu, was acknowledged as the prime mover, behind and above all forces in the world. Good and evil spirits were part of their beliefs, although Father Odilo appeared to be explaining some new ones to them.

"God sent His only Son, Jesus Christ into this world, to speak to all of us. That is why I am here. I am doing as He commanded, when he said, 'go forth and teach all nations'."

He explained the divine mystery of Jesus' birth, and told them of his working life and miracles—these impressed them and they were quite eager to know more. A divine Son of God was not easy to explain, but these people had a more intuitive appreciation than many of his own people had.

He hardly had to reason at all, and simply explained how Jesus had revealed and declared Himself, thus incurring the wrath of those who decided that He was blaspheming. One old man shook his head, and asked why Jesus let Himself be killed. Jesus' unjust death was a hard subject, and also very difficult to reconcile with His divinity; he had to go over that several times, to convey that it was Jesus' own choice, made deliberately, out of God's great love for mankind. "He died to save us, you and me and all of us, and bring us to Heaven."

"But He could have just killed the Romans and been made King of the Jews," was the man's logical reaction.

"That would have been easy for Him, of course, but He loved us so much He chose to give His life like this."

There was great understanding among some of the people, but Father Odilo could not spend all his time explaining and preaching. He talked and worked with them and came to know them well.

He told them much more, about Jesus' resurrection and appearance after the crucifixion, which made it clear that He is God. He saw furrowed brows sometimes, but mostly there was the politeness of African listening. It was difficult to tell how much of the important message of the Gospels was being considered and accepted, but he trusted God and just did his best.

He found the people wonderful, and he could see how eager they were to please. This was often a problem, especially when they seemed to discern what he would like to hear and responded accordingly—even when he was asking about something specific and measurable, like distance. Clearly, this European on a bicycle did not want to be made unhappy by telling him that the Inyathi family's kraal was still a great distance away, for instance. It took some time before he came to realise that 'duzi' could be anything up to a day's walk away!

He soon realised that the assurances of its imminent proximity were not malicious fabrications, but born of a genuine liking and wish to make him happy. He learned not to accept the first answers to such questions, and developed a more probing technique for establishing things. (He found that such practical human psychology applied just as much to more sophisticated people as well, and first responses are seldom a good reflection of deeper truths.)

The teaching of reading and writing was clearly of interest, and exposure to news of the world at large had an awakening effect. The benefits to the people were becoming obvious. They were keen to learn, and could see that such learning was useful. Many years had already passed since the first Europeans had arrived, with their advantages of literacy and the many ideas that they had the ability to put to work for this country. Trains, cars, electricity, dams, piped water, roads, different buildings, administrative records, business accounting and systems had improved many things.

Now, they were still pondering this new system of beliefs, this religion, Christianity. A powerful message was clear—it was a religion of love and respect. Right and wrong were important distinctions to be made, as they did already, but there were some differences.

The approach to God was direct. One did not have to go through the ancestral spirits. Mary and the Saints would also help and intercede, and they did not need to rely only on their own personal ancestors. There was also more to Christianity than a way of improving material or earthly welfare. "Heaven is our true destination," Father Odilo taught, "but we must obey God and do what is right in order to get there." There was a distinction between heaven and hell, and life after death was not something that could be taken as the same for all—it could be very unpleasant or something wonderful, and for eternity.

Only persons who had taken instruction, understood the beliefs, had been baptised, been to Confession and had made their first Communion, could receive the host, the Body of Christ, at Holy Mass. At first this was a very small number, but it grew steadily, and so did the sincerity and devotion of these early Catholics.

THE ROMAN COLLAR

Bishop Arnoz used to make occasional visits to his missions. He was quite a severe man, with a strict sense of decorum and rigid views about appropriate conduct and dress. He absolutely insisted that his priests must wear their Roman collars at all times in public. Even though it used to become terribly hot around Lukosi, Father Odilo faithfully carried out his commands. He modified his attire slightly, though, by wearing a short sleeved shirt, collar and a waistcoat. He made sure it was also a wide, loose fitting collar, so there was some slight relief from a bit of air which was able to flow around his scorched and perspiring neck.

From Lukosi, he had to go over the Gwayi mountain areas, and cycle down to Binga via the Gwayi River, and Mlibizi. Some of the hills were quite high and steep. It was usually a ten to fourteen day trip, and he took his stretcher or hammock, as well as his Mass kit, food, clothing and so on. Although the cycling was hard and hot work, he always wore his "collar" as a public witness to the fact that he was working as a Catholic missionary priest.

He was cycling along the road one day, after the sun had already warmed away the cold morning. The hills were hot and dry, and he had exhausted his two canvas water bottles, when a car drove past him. Suddenly it braked and came to a stop, and out stepped Bishop Arnoz. Before Father Odilo even had a chance to greet him, the bishop rebuked him, "What are you wearing?"

"I am wearing my collar," replied Father Odilo.

"But where is your jacket and proper dress for a priest?" Bishop Arnoz insisted.

"My Lord, it is very hot."

"That is not good enough, Father Odilo. You must wear proper attire at all times."

"But my Lord, you are here in winter time, not in summer. In the heat, you would soon see how necessary it is to modify the code slightly." Shortly after, summer came, and sure enough, Bishop Arnoz did make a visit. He arrived at Saint Mary's Mission, drenched in perspiration, and in great discomfort. As soon as he entered their priests' house, he took off his jacket, and proceeded to say his breviary prayers.

Father Odilo could not resist. "Where is y our collar, my Lord?" he asked. The good bishop responded with a look of rebuke, as he still failed to see the funny side of it. 'He must come from the most stern, old school,' thought Father Odilo quietly to himself. 'If only his authority and discipline did not prevent him from enjoying the humour, he would surely be able to acknowledge the good sense of my reduced attire!'

A Honey-badger's Revenge

One day Father Odilo came to one of his outschools, Mlambo, and saw an animal hung up on a small tree. It was a honeybadger, but not the ordinary smaller black and white type. This was a big black one. The men of the area had just killed it, and although it was dead, he did not realise that its inner functions were still operating.

As he touched its tail, suddenly a wave of the most unimaginably foul stench hit his nose and he reeled backwards covering his mouth and nose. Needless to say, the Africans, standing round, had a terrific laugh at him, thinking it very stupid of him to do such a thing.

This type of honeybadger empties the contents of his special glands into the beehive, and the stench is so strong and so unbearable that the bees take flight and the badger is left with a good sweet meal of honey and honeycomb.

Rain and Insects

The rains came as they nearly always did. There were times when people almost gave up hope, but the rains came. Sometimes they were late, but there was always rain of some sort during the season, and what a relief those first rains were. The October heat scorched the last reserves out of the earth, and out of many people. "This is the time when we must be at our most tolerant of one another," warned Father Joseph.

After a downpour one day, he went across the wet patch of bare earth, and walked to the edge of the trees. The leaves on the trees were washed clean and glistened as the drops of rain continued to patter gently through them. There was a mist, like steam rising from the hot afternoon ground. It hung there and drifted gently, giving a strange atmosphere, like an after-glow, or some sort of after-taste.

All sorts of insects seemed to have sprung from nowhere, moving around on the wet soil and dried leaves. There were black tiktok beetles with their white legs, huge Matabele ants, tshongololos and flies.

The next day the white Mopani butterflies appeared like magic. They flew in unending waves, making short fluttering journeys from one Mopani tree to the next, and soon they were completely stripping them of their leaves. Then they would leave behind the amacimbi, their caterpillar stage, which the Africans collected and celebrated, just like Moses' manna from heaven. They fried or dried them, and ate them with great gusto, savouring this peculiar snack. "I don't think I can eat those," he declined a friendly offer.

"They are really just a form of processed Mopani leaves," Father Joseph said, but Father Odilo noticed that he, too, was not in a rush to savour this delicacy.

When he had the chance to use the main road, he was careful to cycle on the tarred strips of the road, avoiding the puddles of water that lay in between or on the side-shoulders. Straight after the rains, he would see all the ants scurrying about, and there was a huge variety of insects flying and fluttering across his path. Among the most fascinating were the brown or black *tshongololos*, slowly racing across the road with all their legs working in sets, in an orchestrated harmony.

One afternoon, he sat at his table after his mid-day readings and prayers, enjoying the smell of the freshly fallen rain. There was a long-bodied wasp at one of the windows, and he watched it fascinated. The stinger projecting from the rear body section was long and menacing. Its wings were black with an iridescent shine as the upper surfaces reflected the damp sunlight, when turned in just the right position.

He studied it further, and saw how its two feelers were striped orange and black, mirroring the large back legs. The lowest part of the legs were coloured orange, then the portion around the lower joint was black, until halfway up this middle leg section; from there it was orange up to the knee joint. From that joint the leg was black, like the rest of the body, and the two front pairs of legs. It was quite a fascinating insect, but all the same, one to steer well clear of.

A few days later, Father Odilo watched a tarantula spider crossing the open ground towards some rocks. Suddenly a blue wasp appeared. It saw the spider and attacked, trying to sting it. The spider stood up on its rear legs, and tried to fight back and catch or kill the wasp. However, the wasp came back like a Stuka bomber. The tarantula moved on, trying to get to the safety of the rocks. Before it could make it, though, the wasp managed to dive on it and inject a fierce sting.

The spider went into a state of paralysis within two seconds. Father Odilo kept watching, fascinated, as the wasp pulled it into the rocks, where it would lay its eggs in the warm body.

When he looked at it again the next day, it still lay there totally paralysed. Father Odilo knew that within a few days the eggs would hatch, and the young wasps had their food to grow on. (Another type of blue wasp, builds its clay nests on the rafters—with about three to four chambers into which they put caterpillars, in which they lay their eggs, so that when the young hatch they have food. If you destroy such a nest, the caterpillars come to life again after a few seconds of fresh air around them.)

MALARIA AND SOME BUSH EXPERIENCES

One hot Sunday afternoon, they went for a walk in the wide, sandy bed of the Lukosi River. Father Odilo's feet began to feel like lead weights, and he was uncharacteristically exhausted. He got back to the mission feeling very strained. The next day, he realised he had been struck with his first attack of malaria. His head ached so much that it felt as if it would burst. His temples were burning and aching in agony, and his body went into hot and cold sweats.

He often slept in the open, in the forests, and from time to time now he was felled by a bout of malaria. There was no other treatment, and he only had his quinine tablets to rely on. Although he used to take quinine, it did not really help to prevent malaria, and was a very tough treatment when you had actually contracted malaria. Sometimes, in his calculations to overcome malaria, he took two instead of one, and between the malaria and the quinine he really poisoned his system.

Malaria struck him many times, but he never allowed himself much rest and recovery time. Like most missionaries, the call to work was very strong, and he would soon return to duty, even though he was perspiring and aching all over.

On his trips to Luseche School, he used to go out for three or four days at a time, on his old bicycle. He had a very bad attack of malaria on one trip, and had to accept shelter in a hut. There was a dirty straw bed on which he slept off his fever, but the family cared for him and showed their love with their happy smiles, as they encouraged him through the malaria attack. His quinine tablets seemed to work their healing, but he was still sore and tired as he headed back to Lukosi.

During one bout of malaria, he just had to lie there for several days before he was fit enough to cycle back to Lukosi. One night, while he lay there, a hyena killed a full-grown cow, just nearby. "That is very unusual," Van Niekerk, the local hunter, told him later, "for a hyena to attack and kill such a large beast. If they get together, though, they are capable of hunting down a big animal, as a pack."

At another of his schools, on the Mbisha, he suffered the worst malaria attack he ever had. He was lying in a mud hut, with a temperature of one hundred and six degrees F, (41C), almost dying. However, a kind coloured farmer, Mr. van Wyk, came to his rescue and carted him on an ox-wagon to his nearby home where he was cared for while he sweated out the malaria attack in Mrs. van Wyk's bed!

The young priest cycled everywhere

He enjoyed sleeping under the stars when the weather permitted, or else a light canvas that he took with him to provide some form of roof. Late one night, he was suddenly awakened from a deep sleep by what sounded like the roar and growling of lions. It was like nothing he had ever heard before, an ancient, deep sad cry.

As he listened, somewhat terrified and puzzled by these sounds in the night, he realised the commotion came from cattle. They had wandered up the hill at night and smelled the blood of the slaughtered ox; an ox had been slaughtered the day before for meat supply for the villagers and staff of the school.

Their behaviour sounded like fury incarnate, that one of their own had been taken from them and cruelly executed by those dreadful humans. They made it clear that they were ready to charge anyone who would dare to disturb their mourning ceremony. But the sounds also implied deep sorrow and distress and inconsolability that one of them was 'no more'.

The bellowing and snorting and ghastly wailing was going right through his soul and marrow, and he wondered how deep the feelings and the pain of soul and body of animals could be at times

Ticks and Parasites

One day Father Odilo was cycling home from Milonga School, north of the Matetsi River. The sky was heavily overcast and ominous, and rainstorms were certainly pending. Mr. Muzamba Sibindi urged him not to proceed. "It is better that you stay and wait till after the storm." He was given a hut to sleep in, and he swept it carefully before settling down. The rain did come, and with a vengeance; he was glad he had been given this kind hospitality.

The next day, he got home and had a good bath, but he could not get some of the black dirt off himself. Even when he scrubbed very hard, there were specks of stubborn black dirt all around his waist and other parts of his body. He soon found out why; he was covered in tiny black "pepper ticks[v]". Like specks of dust, they get onto you fast, and within a few hours they burrow under the top layer of skin.

Brother Francis helped to tackle those on his back, and he thought he must be clear. Two days later, he met Father Antonio while on his bicycle on the Victoria Falls road. "I have never experienced anything like it. Those little so-and-so's got all over me and under my skin; they itch like crazy!"

Father Antonio asked, "They go for all the warm or moist spots and you only know where they are because of the itches. Have you looked in your navel?"

"No, I didn't think they would get in there. Now that you mention it, I have been itching there." There and then, he undid his shirt and checked, and sure enough there were lots of the tiny little parasites, quite comfortable in this choice spot.

There were also some ticks which have a septic bite, and he became infected before he realised that the sores were different from the inevitable bites and scratches of the bush. He suffered from tickbite fever for about two years, and used to get headaches and sweating fevers, sometimes similar to malaria attacks.

He also contracted bilharzia, but it was many years later before it was diagnosed and treated properly. He found he became unaccountably tired, and he was very angry with himself for not having the self-discipline to do what he felt he should be able to manage.

RANCHERS, HUNTERS AND LOCAL LEGENDS

He arrived at Dahlia, on the east bank of the Gwayi River one morning. He needed a few things from the simple supply store, and stepped up onto the veranda. Next door he could see two men talking to Mr. van Niekerk, at his small hotel. "Nobody tells me what the . . . . I can't do!" he was remonstrating loudly. "Verstaan julle?" he asked them if they understood in his native Afrikaans. It seemed as though these men did, but Father Odilo could not hear their responses.

He asked the storekeeper what was going on, and he explained how the Dett vlei was a protected area. "It is right there on Van Niekerk's boundary, and he just goes out and shoots the elephants as soon as they cross over into his lands." He looked up conspiratorially, and continued, "He just loves it! I don't think the tusks and skins even matter that much to him."

Father Odilo's face went red with anger, and he let out an uncharacteristic expletive, "the bastard!"

"Well, Father Odilo you must remember how massive the game culling operations are at the moment. The Native Commissioner's (NC) department have brought in hunters on contract to kill nearly all the game in the area."

"I know, but I think there must be a better way to roll back the tsetse fly. Are the authorities willing to destroy about a million animals to take away food from these flies?"

"Well, if it makes more land usable for the people, and for future farming, I say it will be worth it."

"Pha! I don't know. Anyway, do you have some more treated twine for thatching? I have run out again. And I need a new cooking pot, if we can afford it. How much will that be?"

He had just settled up and mounted his bicycle when he saw a truck pull in loaded high with horns and trophies. He returned Harry Bond's wave, but only out of ordinary politeness. Harry was one of the very men they had been talking about. He used to go out for four to six weeks of hunting operations or culling as it was called. Then he came back to Gwayi for resupply.

Meanwhile, he knew, the Tsetse Control Department was fencing off long straight boundaries. Sometimes, these were actually quite useful, as sand roads, although in dry weather, or in the heat of the day, they were almost impassable by bicycle or truck—the sand was loose and the wheels sank down and stuck, just as badly as if they were stuck in wet, black cotton soils. The Tonga did not keep cattle; only their goats and donkeys were able to resist the tsetse fly.

The reclaimed areas were later declared to be Native Land, and added to the Nkayi Native Reserve, which was already established. The Native Commissioner, Hugh Murray Fletcher,[vi] was presiding over a land reclamation project even bigger than the Dutch reclamation of the polders.

On a trip back to Bulawayo, Mr. Konson at Lupane asked, "Did you hear the story about Commander Combe's leg?"

"No, I was curious, but I have only met him once."

"Well, you know he has been a rancher and hunter in the area. So, one evening he is out on a hunt way over to the northwest and his gun-carrier, Chimwara, says to him, "Boss, you have never shown me how to shoot your rifle. I want to learn.""

"Most Europeans wouldn't teach their men to shoot with their hunting rifles, but old Combe showed him how to use his rifle. Would you believe it, but the very next day he was attacked and mauled by a lion. While the lion was shaking him around like an impala, his rifle was flung clear. That lion would certainly have killed him, but Chimwara picked up the rifle, and cocked it. The lion was thrashing Combe around, with his leg clamped in his jaws, and he looked down the sights trying to get a clear shot. Somehow he managed to pull the trigger and he shot the lion dead!"

"Now, there they were, deep in the middle of the bush, about twenty-five miles from the road. Combe was bleeding and he knew the wound would quickly be infected with the filth and germs that you get in a lion's mouth. He knew that his only chance of surviving was getting to the road and catching the bus, which travels once a week between Kazangula and Livingstone. A pretty slim chance, too! But this was his only chance, and his life depended on reaching it."

"They made up a stretcher of Mopani poles and leather strapping, and Combe ordered them to carry him. Now, Combe is quite a decent fellow, but the story is that he had his rifle in his hand and he made it abundantly clear, telling them all, "now you bloody well make sure you get me there on time. If anybody does not move fast enough, I will kill you." So his workers struggled and raced, and they actually managed to carry him the twenty-five miles, to reach the roadside and wait in the dark. He lay there in pain, not even knowing for sure if there was a bus due the next day. They moved under the shade of those huge teak trees as the sun got higher and higher, and eventually they heard the sound of a vehicle, making its way over that god-awful road. Oh, sorry Father, but you know what I mean—it was just dirt tracks."

"Well, the bus pulls up and stops. "What the hell?" asks the driver."

"Thank God!" Combe says to the bus driver, as he has almost passed out completely from pain and loss of blood. "Just get me to the hospital fast, or I will die for bloody sure!"

So the bus heaves and hauls its way on its route through the forest, and gets him there, still alive. They rush him inside and quick as a flash, the doctor knows that one leg has to be amputated. So, that's how it happened, but at least his life had been saved.

Mr. Konson paused, looking to see the effect the story had on his listener. Father Odilo had been entranced, visualising every part of the action, and now he looked up, as if there must be more."

"Oh yes," he continued. "You know what? He told me that he wants to settle down and buy a ranch somewhere around here, and he will call it Chimwara! By the way, what are you doing about all the Africans in the Lupane and Sebungwe area?"

"Nothing," he replied. "We are still not being allowed any sort of base there. It has not been proclaimed by some legal term, which would enable us to establish missions among them."

"Ah, well. Call in again on your next trip, Father. It's always a pleasure talking with you."

THE WAR CONTINUES

Bulawayo was a major RAF pilot training base, and the population of the town had swelled with the extra people involved as instructors or trainees. On his visits to town, he noticed the dashing young men in uniform, and saw the effect this had on the young ladies. There was something about bravery that inspired women. Perhaps there was also something about knowing that you risked your life which made men bolder with women as well. Certainly the social life of Bulawayo was busier than ever, and despite the distant war it was somehow a happy atmosphere.

One day the news came over the air that Germany had now invaded the Soviet Union, in a lightning attack. (Years later it was revealed how *einsatzgruppen* had gone in, and with help from the local communities, arrested the Jews, took them to the perimeters of the towns, and shot them, burying them in mass graves.) Far from focussing on his victories, Hitler was arrogantly taking on new enemies.

The war front was stretched over long distances and both sides kept reporting great victories. Casualties were very high, and the war effort built up until there had to be an all-or-nothing thrust.

The Cross overlooking the Lukosi River on
the route to Victoria Falls

CHAPTER 9

FORCED INTERLUDE

NIGHT VISITORS

'I am right in the middle of all this work, and now they want me to move and leave it!' thought Father Odilo. It seemed such a shame and quite a waste really. He was not happy, that's for sure! However, he had taken his vows and committed himself to God's work. 'I shall go with a willing spirit, and I know I shall do my best. That is what Our Lord would expect from me.'

Later that evening, after his prayers he opened his Bible, and again read from John's gospel. He fervently wanted to 'remain in Jesus' Love.' He was determined to 'keep His commandments and remain in His love.' He thought and prayed about it. It seemed that this was a directive to accept his move to town, and yet he was restless.

He flipped back to something that had disturbed him only yesterday. John's gospel about the vine and we, the branches, just do not fit! It seemed that he was actually just bearing so much fruit right now. He was surely not the 'branch that bears no fruit,' and which Jesus 'cuts away.' He prayed for guidance and affirmed his obedience again, but he went to bed with a heavy heart that night. It was a bitterly cold night, unusually so for so early in the winter, and the wind howled through the forest treetops. Eventually, he slept.

He woke up suddenly with a start. The darkness was pitch-black, as only an African night can be when the sky is clouded over thickly.

He had been dreaming something, but what was it? Had something disturbed him? Now, in spite of the cold, he could not snuggle up and get back to sleep. His mind was in a whirl of thoughts. He thought of work that had to be done, like the material he must get for the building and roofing. He had planned to visit three outschools tomorrow and to spend two nights out. He would be going with only his bicycle and some simple bedding. He understood their struggle, and he wondered if the people he was serving could feed him.

He got out of the warm bed, pulled on extra old clothes and lit the fire to make some coffee. Sitting at the rickety table, with his hands wrapped around the coffee mug, he wondered what he was being called to do. 'God, You know I have given my life to You. You have brought me through all sorts of troubles, and kept me going through Your grace and guidance. Why do You allow them to pull me away like this? Just when I am doing so much good for You! I can see how the people are responding. They have helped me to build these outschools, and they listen to Your words when I say Holy Mass or talk with them,' he conversed with his maker.

Just then he heard a loud crash in the forest nearby. He went to the window and looked out, but could see nothing at all. There was another sound, this time closer, more like a tree creaking. He instinctively checked his brow, to see if he was running a sweat again. He had only just recovered a week ago from the latest attack of malaria. "No, I am not in a fever," he told himself.

Then he heard a low rumbling sound, and he realised what it was; there must be a herd of elephants moving right through their Mission. He knew it was futile to think he could do anything about it. He recalled the account of the man in the DA's office who had tried to stop an elephant from stomping on his bicycle. The man had shouted and waved some branches at the big cow elephant, and she had taken offence. One would think it should be easy to out-run such a lumbering big pile of fat and skin—but he didn't. His remains were almost unrecognisable; he had been trampled upon and flung about so much that his remains were almost just pulp.

Father Odilo listened as the forest made noisy sounds, limbs were wrenched from the trees, and whole trees were being pushed over, just to get a few choice mouthfuls. Occasionally he heard the rumbling of their stomachs in the dark night; he knew this was an important communication mechanism of elephants, keeping in touch, and each of them with their own distinctive sound.

But their sounds would suddenly appear in a new place, popping up from nowhere, as they moved along with a ghostly silence. Their huge feet spread out gently and soundlessly with each footfall in the sand, two at a time. How long this continued he could not say, as he waited transfixed but fascinated. Soon they had all gone, as mysteriously as they had come. They had not threatened him, like a gang of bullies might have, but somehow he knew and felt their immensity and their power. They could do anything they wanted, and no puny little human would ever be a threat to them. Perhaps he would encounter them again, and they might not be so gentle.

Called Away

He thought again about how he had been recalled to the Cathedral. He was agitated. He was always obedient to his superiors, even though he hated the thought of going away. This was his 'somewhere' right now, but he knew he could be happy 'anywhere'.

He stirred the fire again and put the pot on to boil for a fresh cup of coffee. "Thank God for this fine coffee from Kenya," he thought. He was wide-awake now, and there was no chance of getting back to sleep. His Bible was on the table and he opened at the cloth tag where he was reading today. Again John quoted Jesus speaking to His apostles.

The first few lines made little impression, but then he read, 'if you do what I command you, I shall not call you servants any more, because a servant does not know his master's business.' Although the gospel went on to talk about going out and bearing fruit again, he came back to the line about doing 'what I command you.'

Now it seemed clearer. 'Lord, I want to follow Your commands. Forgive me for doubting who is in charge and also for wanting to follow my own wishes and desires,' he prayed. After a while he found a great peace came over him, and he sat there, almost in tears, thinking how much God had loved and guided him all the way through his life. Surely God had plans to use him, and he just had to accept and follow instructions in trust and faith.

It was not easy to explain this move to the Africans; the older men shook their heads, and uttered the clucking sound, which conveyed their amazement. To them it appeared as if Father Odilo was being treated as though he had done something wrong; in punishment, his bishop, his chief, had called him away.

By now, they had become quite used to his bossy ways, and the way he pushed them to get things done, much faster than anybody else ever had before. This energetic and determined man was a person in a hurry. Much as they sometimes thought he was over-doing it, they knew right away that they would miss him, and things must slow down without his constant pushing. Some, like Father Joseph, may have seen how he also needed a period of recovery from his constant bouts of malaria.

Saint Mary's Cathedral

He drove into the Cathedral grounds and parked the old Ford at the back. Father Andrew Baussenwein was there to greet him. "Ah, welcome, Odilo. I am so pleased to have you here, and there is so much to do," he soon revealed. "Thank you for your obedience and prompt arrival."

"Thank you, Father Andrew. I promise to do my best," said Father Odilo. "I must say, though, this call came at a very busy time for us also."

"Ja, Ja. That is understood," said Father Andrew. "However, we had to find a good man who can take the pressure, and you have been doing a splendid job in all we have seen. I tell you what; it won't be a bad thing to get away from all the malaria I hear you have been having."

They went through to the dining room and had coffee together. Then Father Odilo unpacked his belongings into his new room at the back of the Cathedral. It felt a bit like being in a small flat or attic, especially after his time at Lukosi. There was certainly no chance of encountering a herd of elephants at night, here in the middle of this bustling new town.

He soon set himself to work, asking for his duties and getting stuck in to all that was asked of him. He found there was plenty to do, and it was quite different from life at the mission. He spoke with people after Holy Mass, and attended the many society and committee meetings.

One thing he never did was to ignore the women; he always treated them with great respect and made them feel special. He had a genuine and obvious liking for women, and was a man who certainly noticed their beauty, but also had many of his own admirers.

"There is so much dignity in that lady," he told Father Andrew. "I must admit I envy the husband of such a woman; but more than that, I think her deportment and fine looks tell a great story."

He wanted to explain more about the artistic comparisons he drew; he had loved the statues in Germany, and held female beauty in great regard, as something wonderful for the eye to understand and behold. 'This is a personal reflection,' he told himself. 'It is hard to explain to anybody.' Such thoughts deepened his great love for and devotion to Our Lady. 'You are the only woman in my life. I shall venerate you always as Queen of my soul,' he promised in his prayers.

Ladies responded wonderfully to his presence, always supporting and empowering him with their appreciation for his sacrificing presence and encouragement in the work he was doing. The Catholic Women's League welcomed him at their meetings and when he went out to the bush later, it was they who were quick to find out what would help, and they managed to provide lots of important things to make a missionary's life more pleasant.

He had numerous calls to visit people who were sick or dying, and soon found he needed a routine rather than a reaction process for going to the hospital on the many occasions when he was called. Although his English was not that good, he managed very well, and he was soon a regular sight, striding solemnly and strongly through all the wards at the two hospitals. The Memorial Hospital was easy, as it was right near the Cathedral, but the Central Hospital, which later replaced it, was quite a trip, to go and visit the patients, on the other side of the racecourse.

Saint Mary's Cathedral was built by the Jesuits,
with large granite blocks – August 1903

Hospital Rounds

She watched demurely, but with great interest, as the young man strode firmly across the street. Her large wood-framed window gave her ample opportunity to take in the sights, while she was always ready to attend to the switchboard when it demanded her attention.

"Yes, this is the Memorial Hospital," she found herself saying mechanically. "Oh, of course Doctor Gibson; I shall put you through to Sister Robinson straight away."

She plugged in the extension, and then looked up; he was out of sight now, but he must have nearly reached her already; she blushed slightly. The extension was ringing, but nobody answered.

His footsteps struck the wooden passage floor, and he tapped politely but firmly on her office door. "Good morning," he said, in that accent which sent a little shiver through her. Was it his deeply masculine voice, which could not fail to arouse her interest, or did his Germanity click with the newspaper images of Nazi arrogance and militarism?

"Good morning, Father Odilo," she managed to sound businesslike. "Would you like to see the patient list?"

"Good morning, Miss Higgins," he responded and his eyes met hers, looking into her as if he knew something wonderful and exciting about her. She felt her face redden slightly, but controlled it well, confident that nobody but she herself could see that it had happened again.

"I have marked the Catholics as you requested," she went on. He was of average height, nearly a tall man, with a head of thick dark hair, slightly curling. She looked at his large strong hand as he took the list from her, and then their eyes met briefly. Undoubtedly, he was a handsome man, and she was aware that his brown eyes were attentive and full of life. His posture was that of an athlete, somebody who was ready for, and capable of action. His black cassock was perfectly clean and must have just come fresh from being laundered and pressed. The creases and seams were firm and straight, and she noticed how his broad belt sat level and flat around a trim waist. The clean white of his Roman collar accentuated his strong neck and jaw. He accepted the patient list from her with a smile, and began going through the names.

"Excuse me, Father," she suddenly remembered, "I must find Sister Robinson quickly. Please make yourself at home; I will be back in a minute." She brushed past him, through the wide doorway, and went daintily down the corridor, very aware of her womanhood; that was such an interesting man, and she was again thinking, 'if only he was not a priest'.

He checked through the neatly written list for new names, and saw one, a Mr. Welsh, in Ward Three. He noticed that Mr. Kelly was still there with his broken leg; it was a shame, he knew that he had hoped to get out yesterday. The phone gave him a slight start when it rang, but he let it ring; it was only a matter of four rings before Miss Higgins was at the door again.

After the call, she turned to him. "By the way, Father Odilo," she said, "Mrs. Mansford asked if you would see her. She is Anglican, but I know you don't mind that. She really needs somebody to pray with her, I think; she has no family here, and she does not seem to get on with her own priest. Could you call on her?"

"Of course," he responded instantly. "I spoke with her last week. She seems to have a serious chest condition, I think."

She listened to the steady and positive sound of his footfalls on the linoleum-covered corridor, and after a while she settled down to her routine tasks, mainly answering the phone, and directing people. A good hour must have passed before her attention was caught by those same footsteps, coming towards her now. Unconsciously, she sat up a bit straighter, and when he appeared at her door, she greeted him cheerily, "are you off now, Father Odilo?"

"Yes, thank you," he replied with an appreciative smile. She had long dark hair, and almond-brown eyes, and her dress fitted her well, clinging softly to a well-formed figure. He knew he was not immune to the charm of a pretty woman; in fact he knew he really liked women a great deal. They gave the whole world its charm and beauty, and their spiritual beauty showed so clearly in their eyes and demeanour. He knew deep down that it was only this; and he was confident that his commitment to a celibate life was solid and permanent.

"I had a good chat with Mrs. Mansford; thank you for guiding me. I shall keep her in my prayers, and told her that I shall offer up my Holy Mass for her this evening."

There was silence for a few moments, and then she asked, "is there anything else I can do for you, Father?"

"No, but you are always a pleasure to see. I shall be back tomorrow morning. Good-bye for now."

"Aufwiedersehen," she ventured with a very English accent. He smiled warmly, and with his own "aufwiedersehen," he was off down the steps and across the street, on his way back to the Cathedral. He could not help thinking of her, somehow. An attractive woman, she left a beautiful imprint on his mind. 'Thank God for women,' he mused. 'This would surely be a dull world if it could ever have existed without them.'

He kept up this routine of visiting the sick, and looked forward to it. Bishop Arnoz was happy to leave him on the roster as not all priests had the compassionate manner of this young newcomer. Some were too shy or brusque, and there were even those who simply did not like dealing with hospitals and sickness; they were also quick to encourage Father Odilo.

"I enjoy the sick calls," he told Father Elmar. "When people are ill, they are much more receptive to God and His messengers. I think I am able to help and encourage them in their difficulties."

"But how do you handle the families when you know the patient is not going to live?"

"Ah, that is much harder, but they need a priest more than ever at such times. I just hope the Holy Spirit guides me to bring comfort and consolation, not false hopes."

His pronunciation mistakes caused some laughter occasionally, and spurred him on to achieve a great command of the English language. There are some totally illogical and non-phonetic pronunciations to contend with in its large vocabulary, and once when he was visiting the ladies' ward he stopped at a bedside.

There was a huddle of about ten visitors gathered around the patient, but she saw him and called cheerfully, "hallo, how are you Father?"

He replied, "not too bad, but I am "cowing" a bit today."

"What is cowing?" she asked with great concern.

"You know, 'cowing'," he said, and tried to illustrate with a slight cough.

"Spell it, please, Father," she asked.

"C O U G H," he spelled the letters. "Cow, like 'plough'."

The bevy of ladies could not contain themselves and burst out chuckling and laughing, to his great embarrassment. One kind lady explained how in English this is spelt the same way, but pronounced quite differently, as 'coff'.

When he was back at the cathedral, he told Father Andrew he had been "cowing" in the ladies' ward and they all laughed at him. "Well, you are lucky you were not 'calving'", he replied and they both laughed heartily.

Patients and Patience

Although this was still at the height of the war, people did not seem to mind this German priest. He always dressed very smartly, with every detail correct and in place. Above all, his Roman collar gave him a distinction which was respected by nearly everyone, Catholic or not.

Despite the war, and his presence in this very British community, only once or twice did he feel he was being attacked, politically.

The horror of war, the cruelty of man and the great sins of pride were on parade for the whole world. Hitler seemed to be having it his way at this time. And yet, Father Odilo met mostly with courtesy, except from some whose disrespect typified some of the cause of war. One day a rude woman patient made some allusions to Germans, but he shrugged it off, knowing she was in some distress.

One morning Father Odilo was doing his rounds at the Old Memorial Hospital. He walked in and looked around at the male patients on the six beds in the ward. He had visited most of them many times already, but he could sense that one of them was not very happy with him; he was vaguely polite, but Father Odilo sensed his dislike.

As he walked on, the man accosted him, "where do you come from?"

Realizing the reason for his question, Father Odilo replied, "from the Cathedral across the street."

"You know full well what I mean," he retorted nastily. "You bloody Germans. Bloody Huns. We will fix you properly this time!" he added insultingly.

Father Odilo felt a sense of shock, but kept his composure. The man was a Scot, judging by his accent, and probably about sixty years of age. The other patients fidgeted a bit, but held their breath. Keeping his voice as calm as possible, he asked him, "Do you think that all Germans are bad? All bloody Huns."

The Scot shot back, "we shall show you. There'll be none of you bloody Huns left!"

Father Odilo now could not hold back any more; this was a man who needed some straight talking, so he said, "here I am, coming to visit you as a friend, and you attack me like that. If you were a gentleman and had any manners, your behaviour would be totally different." Then he added, "Besides, I can tell you one thing. I am a German, but I am a far sight better behaved than you are!"

He walked on leaving an open-mouthed patient staring and spluttering after him. One of the other patients, obviously very embarrassed at the man's behaviour, said, "Please don't take him too seriously, Father Odilo."

He walked out of the ward, shaking slightly, and had almost decided not to go back and visit these men next week. Anyway, he did visit them, and as miracles happen, the Scot greeted him with a very changed attitude.

All Bulawayans seemed to give him their co-operation and friendship, when things were so strained during those war years. He often saw the Scot in town later, and he used to get off his bicycle and go out of his way to greet Father Odilo very politely!

KEN AND MAUREEN

On another one of his normal visits he experienced another example of divine providence in his missionary life. The Norvalls' first child, their eldest son, Warwick, was seriously ill, and he visited him regularly and said his prayers with such reverence and feeling, that Mrs. Maureen Norvall felt compelled to tell her husband, Ken, "that Father Odilo has been fantastic. I think he has had the most effect in Warwick's recovery," she sang his praises. "Do you know, he comes in every morning and makes straight for Warwick's bedside? He speaks English very well, and is always so polite and yet very friendly."

Ken was watching children playing in the yard outside their farmhouse stoep. "What is his name again?" he asked.

The future Saint Luke's Mission Hospital at Kenmaur

"Father Odilo," she replied, "and he comes from Bavaria. He has told us a lot about the mountains, the forests, the eagles and the farm on which he grew up. Warwick loves his visits, and he cheers up and listens to the strange accent as well. We must think of a way to help him, to show our thanks."

It seemed to Ken that perhaps this man had a deeper effect than he cared for, on his beautiful young wife, but he quickly dismissed those thoughts. 'At least with those Catholics, the priests are sworn to strict good behaviour,' he assured himself.

There were much more important matters to think about at the moment. Hitler was at the peak of his frenzied assaults in Europe, and so much was happening which held the destiny of the world in its outcome. All the same, he made a point of taking Maureen out for an extra dinner at the Bulawayo Club each week for a while. 'Everybody would see clearly that Maureen was his wife alright,' were his unspoken thoughts.

The seeds were sown for what was to become St Luke's Mission Hospital, on land donated by Ken and Maureen Norvall.

The daily duties and observances already made life very full. There was Mass to be said, hospital and house visits, baptisms, confirmations, catechism classes at the Convent School, the government schools, and just being available to parishioners and even visitors from abroad. If he thought he was not being put to work as a productive branch of the vine, he soon realised that was a mistake.

There were also cultural compensations, which he had never dreamed of in the middle of Africa.

EXPERIENCING THE REFINED LIFE

Another side of Father Odilo, which he had thought had to be submerged, soon experienced a revival. In spite of the war, there were theatre productions and musical presentations. Bulawayo's Art Gallery regularly put on some fine displays of paintings and sculptures. He also made the odd visit to the fascinating world of the Matopos, and to the various water supply dams as they were constructed over the years, to the south of the city.

The music recitals, theatre, arts and painting appealed to the cultural instincts of a European, and a German in particular, and were important to a fully rounded being. "I would never have expected all these cultural activities in Africa," he confided to Father Andrew. "I actually feel guilty, enjoying these pleasures, though."

"Ah, that's natural enough," Father Andrew replied. "However, you should think of them as part of your duty. Firstly they help you to be closer to the people you are serving. But secondly, they all help to refresh and enliven your mind and spirit, all for the greater glory of God."

'What a happy bit of counsel,' thought Father Odilo. 'I would hate to have to deprive myself of this now. After all, we take care of the stomach and general fitness, but the eye and the ear must also have some satisfaction.' He had long ago come to an appreciation of his senses, as part of the whole man. Saint Thomas in his Summa Theologica had hit the nail on the head when he pointed out how sight and hearing were the superior two of the five faculties. Sight was clearly the noblest of the senses, with hearing next to it in excellence. Here he was able to enjoy and really appreciate both the visual arts and drama with musical accompaniments and orchestral performances.

Bulawayo's Theatres and Entertainments

Apart from the novelty of European contact, conversation and cultural experiences, he found he was thinking deeply of the comparisons between the European and African ways of thinking. The very contrast was enriching, and almost subconsciously, he was constantly deepening his understanding of people.

Occasional trips to the Matopos began with Catechism classes at Rhodes Estate Preparatory School. He enjoyed the grandeur of the tumbled granite landscape, and found he was able to take a few hikes and climbs to exercise the human strength in him. The hills were nothing like the Bavarian Alps, but they had a special atmosphere; he could pray and revive his spirits in the solitude and peace they offered.

The fifth anniversary of his ordination as a priest came, and he shared the celebration mass with two of his confréres. As he prayed and thanked God for His love and protection, he was reminded how much he had done in so short a time already. His dedication to his mission was renewed, and he felt strongly that he was following a wonderful vocation, a calling from his youth. He remembered the washing of the Apostles' feet, and how Jesus 'did not come to be served, but to serve.'

SPARED, BUT STUNG

Even in town, he had some close calls with nature's hazards, and on one occasion he was very lucky to be spared a most painful experience. Afterwards, it seemed quite unreal, when he thought about it. Somehow a scorpion, of medium size, had during the night got into his cassock without him noticing. In the morning, he had put on the cassock and the collar, and proceeded to celebrate Holy Mass. Afterwards he went to have his breakfast, and when he took the cassock and the collar off later, he could not believe his eyes!

A scorpion, with small claws and an ugly tail, was coiled up inside his collar, directly in position against the pit of his throat. 'Imagine him stinging me, during Holy Mass or during breakfast,' he shuddered. It was quite inert, but when he prodded it he got an instant reaction; its stinger sprung up poised to inject a lethal dose of venom into its victim. It was alive all right, and if it had been disturbed earlier it would certainly have stung him. His collar had obviously been a nice, warm spot for it.

But there were other 'stings', one of which he experienced on a bitterly cold winter visit when he called upon the Beretta family. Their little boy, Harry, had been looking through pictures in a book with his granny, and had noticed a man with a big red nose. "Do you know why his nose is red?" he asked.

"It is because he drinks a lot of wine and beer," replied his granny, unsympathetically.

Only a short while after, Father Odilo had just arrived, trussed up against the cold weather, and his nose was icy and red. With ingenuous bluntness, little Harry promptly asked, "Father, do you also drink a lot?"

A bit flustered himself, Father Odilo looked up to see Harry's lovely granny turning bright red with embarrassment!

Tricked by Thieves

There was a firm knock at the door one day, and he went to answer it. Although there is a step, he found he was looking up into the eyes of a big man. He came to the point straight away, "Good afternoon, Father. I have come to ask for help"

Father Odilo nodded knowingly. One of the biblical exhortations he believed in now was having 'the wisdom of a serpent but the gentleness of a dove.'

A few exchanges of names took place and he responded, "Well, how can I help?"

"Father, my wife has had an operation and is recuperating at the coast. On the way back to work, my car's 'diff' has packed in. I can have it repaired but am short of cash—I wasn't expecting this, you see."

"I see," he replied carefully. "What are you looking for?"

"Father, it is quite a lot, I am afraid. I need a loan of fifty pounds."

"Phew! That is a very big sum of money. What sort of security can you offer me?

"Paying back will be no problem, I assure you. I work for a big engineering company in Luanshya and will send the money back in about two weeks."

"I am afraid that is not good enough," Father Odilo answered.

The man could see now that Father Odilo was getting tired of him, and had become more suspicious. "Father I have a revolver. I can leave that with you. It has great sentimental value; I inherited it from my grandfather." Then he produced a revolver and offered it. "I would ask that you please return it by registered mail when you get the money."

Father Odilo could visualise the difficulties he would encounter, in going to the police and then parcelling and sending the revolver through the postal service. It would be a big nuisance. However, the man sounded so genuine that he began to give him the benefit of the doubt. In fact, he was completely taken in.

"Have you something else?" he asked.

"I could leave my passport."

And so it was arranged. The man signed for the money and left his passport behind. Father Odilo waited, but after nearly three weeks there was no sign of the repayment. So he wrote to him. Sure enough, a reply came back from the company that they had never heard of him there.

He opened the safe, and took out the passport. He looked through it carefully and saw that it was old and expired! He went to the police, the passport office and so forth, but all sorts of investigations led nowhere; that fifty pounds had to be kissed goodbye, with much embarrassment.

One of his seniors, Father Sixtus Impler, had many more such experiences. He was a short, happy man who just believed that he should be kind and helpful to everybody. "If they tell me lies, it's just not my business," he used to say, and he just chose to believe that all these people were honest.

He used to hold the keys to the dining room, and when beggars came, he would open his desk drawer, take out the key and go through to get something to give them from the larder. This routine became familiar to the returning beggars.

One morning Father Andrew came through to Father Odilo and asked, "what happened to the bread?"

"I have no idea," he replied. Let's see if it's in the fridge. They went through together and checked, only to find the fridge was empty as well. "That's strange. Who could have taken any food from us? This room is always locked." They went and checked the key; sure enough it was safely in the drawer. Then they went back to look around in the freshly painted dining room. There were handprints on the freshly painted walls. Somebody had come through the window, by removing the louvered glass panes.

They had stolen various things, and then put the key back in its place.

While they were investigating, Doctor Davis came through, from her little room at the back, and asked, "You are funny blokes! What were you doing at two o'clock this morning?"

"What do you mean?"

"Well, I saw the lights on; I supposed it was a sick call, or something. Then I saw the lights go on again at four a.m."

The thief had stolen, eaten, rested and then feasted again, helping himself to their beer supply also.

A NEW SEED IS OWN

Bulawayo had a community who co-operated in many things and one day Father Odilo accompanied Father Andrew to a meeting of the Christian Combined Churches. The Minister from the London Missionary Society pointed out, "One thing I believe we should be taking more note of is the Lupane district. The Africans in that area are not being served well by any of us." A seed was sown, and Father Odilo was a typical Mariannhiller who responded to a challenge; there was a lot of ground preparation needed before plans would germinate, though.

However, he asked the bishop to release him from his duties as assistant parish priest, so that he could undertake the missionary work that he saw as so desperately needed. Bishop Ignatius Arnoz called Father Odilo into his office a few days after that meeting.

"Good morning, Father Odilo," he welcomed him. He motioned for him to take a seat opposite him, across the wide desk, filled with folders and papers.

"Good morning, my lord," Father Odilo answered respectfully, as he prepared to sit. This was obviously not a social chat, and he hoped that his request was being granted; it was clear that there were new tasks and duties to be discussed. The rain was clamouring noisily on the metal roof sheets and gurgling and tumbling through the downpipes.

Flashes of lightning were followed by fierce cracks of thunder, and the Bishop had to raise his voice to be heard in the office.

"Well, Father Odilo, I am happy to grant your request. I hereby appoint you to be the Rector of the Shangani District."

A loud crack and rumble of thunder forced him to wait a moment, before he courteously responded, "thank you, my lord." He could feel how his blood was coursing with greater vigour with the award of this new challenge. This was to be the beginning of three years of missionary homelessness, as he tackled the unexpected frustrations and difficulties of official obstruction.

"I think it is wise to proceed with what we have been discussing. We should move to establish a new Mariannhill Mission territory in the area, and you are to be in charge," he continued. "You know this is a vast area, and none of our churches is reaching the people," he said, as Father Odilo nodded in assent.

He stood up and moved around the desk to a fresh wall map with a few pins in it. "We can see from this map that it is enormous. There are tens of thousands of people, and most of them know nothing of Jesus Christ," he continued seriously. "The territory officially encompasses the Shangani Reserve and Lupane Native area. You already know the area, and I think the region has an area of about four thousand square miles."

His analysis stated the known facts, and Father Odilo responded willingly, "I am honoured, my lord, and this is a great challenge." His thoughts were racing ahead now. He sensed that his pulse had quickened. He was always very aware of the veins in his neck, and they told him much about himself. Already he was visualising what lay ahead and picturing things in his mind.

He knew full well what would be involved in founding a new Mission, in a region as vast and wild and primitive as this. It would not just be a case of going out and building a little chapel somewhere and then coming back to report to the Bishop, 'your Lordship, the task is completed. The Mission is established.'

A bit disrespectfully, and probably influenced by Hilaire Belloc's[6] style of analysis and commentary, he thought on to himself; he considered the enormity of the task, and conjured up a vision of his

---

[6]   The Crisis of Civilisation, by Hillaire Belloc

victorious return, to ask the bishop, 'do you have any more Missions you want me to found? I have a few days to spare during which I shall not be particularly busy.'

'No!' he stopped himself. He certainly knew it wasn't quite as simple as that! Bishop Arnoz had been continuing, and was detailing some of the issues and work that he anticipated for him. While he was explaining this, Father Odilo's mind was soon racing ahead again.

He knew that the first step must be to carefully look over the region and select the best location for the Mission centre. That was very important, and it might take a little while. He needed to investigate options, and check them out on the ground. He must confirm where they would be most welcome, where the population centres are, and where the authorities would permit them to set up.

THE WAR CONCLUDED

From time to time, and to his great annoyance, people asked him, "and what is the Pope doing about all this?" referring to the terrible war, still raging. This was a vexing question, not really from people who expected an answer. Often this came from non-Catholics wanting to hurt the Church, but at other times it was from frustrated and unknowing Catholics themselves. He always kept his German dignity, while humbly responding as well as he was able.

It was hard to reply without revealing some anger and disappointment. Pope Pius XII had been placed in an impossible position. Fascism in Italy and Spain, Nazism in Germany and Communism in Russia were all evil forces, and the Church was caught in a vice, in Rome, and in the countries where war was being fought. Bishops, priests, and lay-people had been arrested and some of them had been brutally killed, for speaking out against Hitler.

Church diplomacy had proven powerless, and their most fervent prayers seemed to go unanswered. The Church had been attacked and deprived of rights that the concordat had guaranteed only recently, in what had soon turned out to be nothing more than a Nazi propaganda move. Hitler, in his totalitarianism, wanted full control of young minds, insisting that they be disallowed from taking part in religious activities when these clashed with the constant barrage of state functions arranged by the Nationalists. Anti-Semitic activity had stepped up from words of incitement and hatred, and progressed to open torture and even murder; every Jew was targeted, even right there in Rome.

It seemed as if things were becoming worse, but somehow prayers were being answered, and in totally unexpected ways. It actually took the insanity of Japan's bombing of Pearl Harbour to rouse the United States to take military action. Now the Allies, almost the whole world, had united to overcome Hitler and his ally, Mussolini, who was soon little more than a pawn in his hands. Gradually the far-flung German armies were pushed back.

Talk of a secret weapon was heard; the Germans were working on something, which would make them invincible. Niels Bohr, Rutherford, Albert Einstein and other scientists were also busy. The first anybody knew of what they were up to was the announcement and the pictures of the mushroom-shaped atomic bomb explosions that had lain waste the Japanese towns of Hiroshima and Nagasaki. The Emperor surrendered; the war in the East was nearly over.

Hitler's insanity knew no bounds and he remained defiant, but shaken. The army leaders were less certain now, and there were more and more Germans who wanted to surrender. On one sortie, Allied planes were looking out for the surrender signals, as they flew over Regensburg. The ultimatum had been given and they were ready to flatten the town with bombs. "Look, they are doing something there," the spotter shouted. In the square, the military were all over, and a platform was apparent. "They are not showing any signs of surrender," the captain said. "We have our orders, give the signal and make your pass. Make every bomb count."

"Wait!"

"What do you see?"

"Look, they are dragging that man out to the platform. I think they are going to hang him."

"The bastards!"

"Well, you know what that means?"

"Yes, you're right. There are some people still opposing Hitler."

"We must hold off. He was probably trying to offer the white flag," the spotter said. "I wonder who he is."

Another man said, "it reminds me of Sodom and Gomorrah. Do you remember how God said he would spare them if he found even ten just men?"

"OK, call off the bombing. Turn back from this town." And so Regensburg was spared as a result of what they saw and the pilots' reactions. The war was drawing to an end, with the scent of certain victory for the Allies.

Finally after the blitz on Berlin, and the rush of troops across nearly all the fronts, the German army surrendered at Rheims on 8th May 1945. The world breathed a sigh of relief. Allied troops reached the Concentration Camps, and Germans gasped in shock and shame as the horrors were exposed to the whole world. For many, it was too much to believe.

Years of propaganda and indoctrination made it easier to think that they were not the ones perpetrating crimes as barbaric as these; it could only be the enemy lying to them again. For other Germans, the revelation of what they had allowed to happen created a determination never to permit such manipulation ever again.

CHAPTER 10

TRAMPING ABOUT

TSETSE FLIES

Father Odilo's recently assigned new territory, in the west of Rhodesia, included huge areas, which had not yet been populated. But there had been an important reason why this land was unused, and that was soon changing. In recent years, much had happened in those areas, which were under the influence of tsetse flies. Dividing fences had been set up. Game had been killed, and a programme of spraying had been undertaken.

Father Joseph asked Maurice Kantor to explain what was going on, and how it would work. "Well, Father," he began his explanation, for he was a good rural storekeeper who liked to know what was happening, "the tsetse is the biggest curse in Africa. Huge parts of the continent are infected by tsetse flies. When the cattle are bitten, they soon die."

"What happens to them? How do they die?" asked Father Joseph.

"The flies seem to inject a poison into them. They have a strong sharply pointed mouth, and they bite right through the animals' hide. They bite humans too, and believe me, it's bloody sore! OOPS, sorry, Father."

"Don't worry, carry on; this is interesting, and I know all about it, because I have also been bitten once or twice. I usually swat them very quickly though!" he said.

"Well, the big problem is that Africans and cattle go together. If cattle can die from this, then the Africans will not go into those areas. Nor would I either; there is no point bringing your cattle or family there and seeing them die from this sickness."

"So who lives there?"

"Nobody. Well, there may be one or two, but they move around and hunt to survive. It is no place to have a family or live, though."

"So have they killed these flies now?"

"Not completely, but it's working. It took the arrival of the European for somebody to come up with a plan. They have tried lots of things, burning, chopping or clearing corridors, killing game that they thought was carrying it, and so on. Before now, there was no hope of any sort that this land could be turned to safe use."

"Just the other day I heard from one of my business contacts in Salisbury, that this land will soon be declared as "native" land. As soon as they give the 'all clear', Parliament will approve it for resettlement. It will be good for my store in Wankie, of course, but you Catholics should keep an eye out. I like what you are doing, and it helps the African people a lot."

Native Land to be Opened up

And so it eventually happened. The vast, unassigned areas of Lupane and Sebungwe districts were declared as "native land"; the process of opening up and settling people now began.

"The big difference between reclaiming this land and the Dutch polder reclamation, is that this area is so dry," said Father Joseph.

They were in Kantor's tin-roofed store, and he quickly chipped in, "I keep my finger on the pulse of what is happening around here. Believe me, this will have a big effect on your Lupane area. I am sure that the Africans will flock here soon. They will need schools, clinics, and there will be your chance to get in and help, right from the start. Perhaps you should talk to the P.C. about this."

He paused as he wiped the perspiration from his face. "You know, you definitely need to open a Mission Hospital," he said emphatically.

"We are struggling as it is, to find the money we need to develop schools and Father Odilo still needs somewhere as his own Mission base," Father Joseph complained to his friend.

"You know what? I am sure I can persuade my old friend, Schur to help. If you Catholics build a proper Mission, complete with a hospital and all, I think he will give you some money. He is very rich, and this is one of the places where he makes a lot of his money."

"What does he do?"

"He buys his hides from the Africans, here and in Botswana. Then he tans them and sells them to his shoe-making friends." Kantor smiled, as he added some background.

"Why would he help?" asked Father Odilo.

"Schur is a good sort, and this will help his business as well; he likes the Africans and gets on well with them. He comes from Lithuania, you know. Perhaps more than anybody, he knows how lucky he is to be away from all that trouble in Europe now."

He looked a bit sheepish realising he was in the company of these two Germans, priests or not; however, he carried on, "Hitler and his butchers have been killing so many of our people; thank God we are here and not anywhere within his bloody reach. OOPS, sorry, Father!"

"That's okay," they both assented at the same time.

He told Bishop Arnoz about these developments in the Nkayi area on one of his trips back to Bulawayo. "That is an interesting development, and could strengthen your case, to help a lot of the Africans in that area," he responded.

"Do you know how we can we find out more about it?" Father Odilo asked.

"Somebody else I know, Mr. Konson, might help," the bishop said. "You also know him; he is a storekeeper and cattle buyer at Lupane. I have sometimes stayed over in his guest house, when doing a trip to the northern missions."

Soon after, Father Odilo made a point of paying a visit to Konson and asked if he could go with him on one of his trips. As they drove along, Father Odilo acknowledged, "You certainly know what's happening around here. I can see you know exactly where most of the people live as well. For us to set up schools, that is important."

At the sale pens, people had brought in cattle that they wanted to convert into cash. The Native Commissioner stood off to one side, while Mr Wood and Mr Konson weighed up the animals visually, and after briefly haggling over prices, they came to agreement with the sellers on groups of cattle or individual beasts. Once the cash had been paid out, the people had begun to drift homeward in their different directions.

'That was not a very good sale today,' Konson said. 'I often wonder how they manage to keep cattle in these parts; you need huge areas for each animal to survive on this sort of veld.'

'What do they eat; There seems to be no grass?' he asked. His mind went back to the lush and thick green grazing in Germany, and the hay that they loaded up on the wagons and stored in their barns at home for winter feeding. It was thick and nourishing grass and the animals could not survive without this feed.

'They browse as well' he replied.

'What do you mean?' he asked. He had often been told to go and browse through the books, newspapers and notes in the library or the office, but he thought it wise to wait for an explanation before he mentioned that.

'There are some trees that they enjoy. Mopane leaves are quite good, but they seem to know what is most nourishing, and somehow when the grass is finished off they find enough to get by.'

'I see' he nodded wisely, storing another piece of information to remember and add to in the years ahead. After a few miles of weaving through the bush in the Ford truck, he came back to his main concern. 'What do you suggest I do to get approval for my mission, and the schools we want to build?'

"Well, what you should do is to get applications in to the Native Commissioner's office as soon as you can. I am sure the London Missionary Society hasn't shown any interest around here yet, but if they do that old P.C. will give them anything they want. You Catholics are a bit like us Jews, you know. You are sort of working outside the British government's little circle of immediate friends."

There were large numbers of Africans scattered through the Lupane area, and the needs were clear, but Church resources were very stretched, with not enough for major new developments. Although Father Odilo reported on his observations and findings, he still needed a suitable mission site, and simply had to do the best he could with his task of reaching and preaching to the people in the meantime.

THE PROPOSED NEW MISSION—INVESTIGATION AND APPLICATION

Spring's brief African season sent the message to the acacia and other trees, to shoot out buds and leaves, and flowers. Without apparent confirmation from anywhere, they obeyed in chorus. The bauhinia trees were in full bloom, and the much-vaunted jacaranda trees were just starting to come into leaf and display their purple covering of flowers.

When it came to getting on with it, the application actually took two full months. He already had a reasonable working knowledge of the area, but he had to check more carefully now. He spent those first two months mostly travelling, throughout that wild area, investigating the needs and possibilities of that part of Southern Rhodesia.

Finally, he located what he thought was a very suitable spot for a central Mission, in the Lupane area. He was now ready to take the next step, and to apply to Government for permission to go ahead. He prepared his letter, completed the required application documents, with supporting letters, maps, drawings, tables and evidence of needs and benefits. He put it all into a carefully prepared cardboard folder, headed 'Lupane District—Mission Development Proposals'. He enclosed it in a large white envelope, addressed to the Provincial Commissioner, and submitted it with the bishop's seal.

And then he waited, while continuing with his mission work. He waited and waited, and it took a full six months before he received a reply in the post. The envelope was headed, On His Majesty's Service, and he knew immediately where it came from. He also thought he knew what it said, 'Mission application approved.'

He went to his desk, and sat down eagerly. Opening the letter carefully, like somebody who was peeling a delicious fruit that he intended to savour, he withdrew the single folded sheet of paper. He opened it out. Then, to his utter dismay, he read that the request had been turned down!

The excuse used was that 'there was no scope for two missions in the area, particularly as the land was urgently needed for future alienation to Africans, especially at Lupane itself—the seat of the District Commissioner.' He read the letter again, and then tried to work out what was behind this rejection. At that time, although the Southern Rhodesian Government was predominantly Protestant and Anglican, it had generally been very co-operative with Catholic Missionaries. His proposal was nothing but beneficial, for the Africans as well as the authorities—the church was offering to do things that they should surely welcome with open arms! It made no sense.

Gathering his composure, he went to the bishop's office. He had seen him passing down the corridor earlier, and he knew this was a good time to see him. He knocked at his door. "Enter!"

"Good morning, my lord," he began. "I have received this letter from the PC. I am afraid he has refused our request."

"Incredible!" was the bishop's reaction. "What possible reason could he have?"

"He says it is because the land is set aside for alienation to the Africans."

"What on earth does that mean?" exploded Bishop Arnoz in uncharacteristic anger.

"He has not explained himself, but his tone is quite strong; he seems to be closing the door completely," replied Father Odilo.

After reading the short letter himself, the Bishop gathered his composure. Sitting back in his chair, he said, "Well, we must always be prepared to run into obstacles. This seems to me to be an official delaying tactic."

Father Odilo thought of the struggle that Abbott Pfanner, their own founder, had fought; he had tackled the Turkish and South African bureaucracies, determined to do what he believed God called their monks to do. That had been an inspiring story in the young history of their Order. The bishop sat pensively for a moment. Then Father Odilo responded, "I do not know what politics and other considerations are involved, but we shall have to find out what they want us to comply with, and then we must re-apply," he explained to the bishop.

When the brief meeting was over, he returned to his office. He prayed silently for a while, asking for guidance, but no answers seemed to come to him. He felt completely frustrated. 'What must I do now?' he asked himself. He had done so much already that he felt as if things were already under way. His disciplined approach to everything kicked in like a habit and he felt his resolve return. He liked the picturesque way that the Americans would put it, 'there is more than one way to skin a cat.'

There was no point storming across to the PC's office, as he knew that would only have an adverse effect. So he decided upon his next course of action. "We must pray hard, work with confidence, and have lots of patience," he said, when he discussed this setback with two of his fellow-priests the next day. No permission was needed to open up as many Outschools as possible in the district, and he decided that was to be his next course of action.

Confronting Official Obstruction

Father Odilo explained his plans and discussed the Outschools with Bishop Arnoz, who agreed with him. Now he was concerned by memories of the last time he was sent out, when he went to assist at Lukosi. "My lord, you know that I promise that I shall do my best. I shall obey you and do my best for Holy Mother Church."

Bishop Arnoz nodded slightly, but looked at Father Odilo in a way, which indicated that he should continue. He looked respectfully at his bishop, and almost apologising, he asked, "How much money will you be able to give me for this work to be done?" It had been very difficult at Lukosi, trying to squeeze every last halfpenny to make it go as far as possible.

"Well, I have to look carefully into our finances, but I think we will be able to give you one hundred pounds," he said with an air of some generosity. There was no doubting his sincerity, but Father Odilo had been around long enough to know that would hardly buy the doors and windows for what he had outlined. It would certainly not pay for the hundreds of other necessities, like cement, timber, nails, glass, or wages and food, and the cost of transporting supplies to site over those hundreds of miles of narrow strip roads.

"My lord, may I have a vanette?" he ventured bravely. "It is a long distance from Bulawayo, and the area I shall have to cover will be very great."

"I am afraid that will not be affordable," Bishop Arnoz answered. "You surely realize how we cannot spend money on luxuries when there are so many people in need of our help."

"But my lord, it is important that I be able to properly do the work; I am used to travelling around on my bicycle but it takes two or three days just to get as far as Lupane." He had a good idea of what lay ahead of him, and he realised that this moment was important to secure what he needed.

'Holy Spirit,' he prayed inwardly, 'please guide me to say the right things now, all for God's glory, and so that I can carry out the tasks which He can see for me.' Then he continued, "My lord, I am sure you must see that transport is essential for this undertaking."

Bishop Arnoz was a little taken aback. Most priests demurred quietly to him, except for one he recalled sharply who had virtually rebelled. That was certainly not in the spirit of a priestly vocation, and it had become clear later that he was not able to live the difficult life of a priest. However, he knew that this was not the problem with Father Odilo. He already knew that here was a dedicated man, with great energy and commitment.

"Of course, Father Odilo," he said. "You must know that I will not let you down on this matter. I want you to be based somewhere in Lupane, and you should be able to manage from there with a bicycle. Select one of the new ones on the veranda. You can also take two spare tyres and some tubes and patches."

Perhaps the quizzical expression on Father Odilo's young face called for more, so he added, "I will obviously pay for it to be checked and serviced regularly by Solly. He will make sure that it lasts well, and always gets you around safely."

Father Odilo stifled a rising cough, managing to control a reaction in his throat muscles. He had long ago learned when it is not wise to push a point. "My lord, I look forward to this work, and I shall begin immediately with preparations. I hope you will allow me to discuss the details further before I go," he concluded politely.

Despite his concerns about the lack of resources, Father Odilo's excitement climbed. He enjoyed getting on and doing things, and this was clearly an opportunity to do just that. He would be many miles from Bulawayo, and would be working closely with the African people, people to whom he had become very attached. He looked forward happily to bringing them the Gospel and teaching them whatever he could, and helping in any way that God directed him.

His audience with the bishop was soon ended, and he walked out with an extra spring in his step. He could proceed with his mission, and undoubtedly, he would give it his best!

As he walked from the bishop's office he passed two black bicycles parked against the wall. 'Useful', he thought, 'and I have travelled thousands of kilometres by bicycle already. But, Lupane area is a long, long way away. How can I even carry a single bag of nails, let alone doors, windows, cement and so on?'

He strode on further, and coming to the open side door to the cathedral, he walked in. Genuflecting at the door, he made the sign of the cross, and prayed, 'Blessed Jesus, thank you for everything in my life. Thank you for this new opportunity, and please strengthen me to serve You properly, for the good of all those poor African people whom Your word needs to reach.'

He paused to collect his thoughts, and found it was hard to be truly prayerful right now. There was so much to arrange, and he wanted to be ready to catch the afternoon bus, only three days away!

'Lord, please still my mind so that I may feel your presence. Guide my thoughts, and help me, as You always have. I will serve You faithfully, as I promised, and I only want to do the best I can. Make use of me, God, and give me Your grace and strength,' he prayed quietly.

His mind slowly settled, and he brought himself into God's presence, before the Blessed Sacrament. He knelt for quite some time, before he was stirred again. He thought about this move. Six years ago, he had taken his vows with great solemnity and determination, and he knew how essential it is for a priest to commit himself fully to the task given. He had been happy where he was now, but he would move on, and would never refuse to co-operate, knowing he would be happy wherever he went. That was a decision he consciously took and re-took.

After resting in prayer for a while longer, he made the sign of the cross, got up, and walked to the front door. He dipped his fingers in holy water, and again made the sign of the cross, before exiting into the bright sunlight.

'One thing for sure,' he suddenly realised, 'a bicycle just will not do! I have to convince the bishop to provide something more useful and suitable.'

As he turned the corner, he almost bumped into Father Andrew Baussenwein. He was soon telling him of this new posting, and the difficulty of working with a bicycle. "I think I can help you, Odilo," he volunteered. "Let me see what I can do; I may be able to manage to buy you a second-hand vanette." And sure enough, he did just that, for seventy pounds.

A few days later, Father Odilo was packed up, and he was ready to head North in his old half-ton Model 'B' Ford vanette! It was packed to the brim; he thought kindly of all those wonderful ladies in the Catholic Women's League who had helped so much.

He genuinely appreciated and respected the women of the parish, and they sensed how he was so at ease with them. They had taken quite a shine to this handsome, manly young Mariannhill priest. When he explained his needs, they had soon organised gifts and donations of all sorts of things. There was a black kettle to boil water over the fire, a little folding table and two chairs, sheets and blankets, food, clothes, books and all sorts of useful items.

BUILDING OUTSCHOOLS

His old Ford truck was soon prepared for prolonged 'warfare', not militarily, of course. He equipped it with a mattress, knowing it would be his travelling home and sleeping quarters for a long time. He also put into it all the building and carpentry tools he could get hold of, for building was to be his new profession for the tasks ahead. He had to put on a new set of tyres, as the tubes were beginning to protrude in the oddest places.

After Holy Mass, with the Cathedral driveway soaking wet from the fresh rains the night before, he left Bulawayo for his new 'home'. This was to be anywhere from one hundred to two hundred and fifty miles away. 'I certainly will not be cramped for space there,' he thought. 'Four thousand square miles is a lot of bush.'

In this big area Father Odilo concentrated his efforts on developing outschools. He soon opened nineteen schools within three years, as far as the Gomoza River, north of the Shangani River. These schools became the key, and enabled the Catholic Church to get established ahead of others like the LMS.

Except for occasional trips back to Bulawayo, he spent the next three years 'in the bush'. He lived like a vagabond and some of his confreres and friends cheerfully called him one in all earnestness, "welcome, Father Odilo," they would greet him, "are you still tramping about like a vagabond?"

"Oh yes," he would say, "but a very busy one."

The old Ford was his bedroom, his Church was God's great outdoors; his altar, upon which he daily offered the great sacrifice of Holy Mass, consisted of four sticks rammed into the ground, with an old plank over them. His companions were the Africans who lived out there, and the many wild animals of every description. His oratory and study was the Southern Rhodesian veldt and bush.

After careful consideration and discussions, he began to select suitable spots for outschools. At Luseche, he got his African helpers to start work. He explained what had to be done. He set tasks for them, once he had the necessary volunteers and paid workers lined up, each day. After the first few efforts at making Kimberley bricks out of the sandy soils, he realised that the results would not be very strong. There was simply no suitable material in most of the sandveld area. His solution was to use poles cut from the local trees to make an outline wall and to support the eaves poles upon which the roof poles were then supported.

Constructing the frame and roofing for a classroom

From morning until night, they made mud-bricks, fashioned poles, cut grass, measured out and dug foundations, erected pole walls and put up roofs. The walling was then mud-plastered or their bricks were used if remotely possible, at least to clad and protect the interior.

The great out-doors were the setting for his daily Masses

'This is hardly the sort of life I would recommend to those who have an allergy to hard and gruelling work and who much prefer to take things easy,' he wrote to a colleague one day. 'But it is, at the same time, though tough, an interesting and richly rewarding life. I really love what I am doing.'

It was sometimes a bit trying to work with the local people. Those who did not get to know, understand and love the Africans as he did, sometimes called them lazy and shiftless; but he preferred to describe them as 'easy-going by nature, and shunning responsibility'. With much patience and understanding, it was the greatest pleasure to be among them. They were always polite, cheerful, pleasant and, most of the time they were very co-operative and obliging.

He was a hard taskmaster though, expecting people to give almost as much effort as he did. There was a lot of pressure as well. If he did not complete his schools in time to open for the new term, he ran the risk of losing the territory. The PC and the Education Department were very strict, and their rules were inflexible in terms of enrolments, teachers, and commencements.

One day he came to check on progress at a new outschool. He had left Sibanda in charge and expected to see the walls filled in, as he had directed ten days before. The first thing he saw when he drove up, was that only a fraction of the infill had been done. His blood pressure rose; the veins on his neck were pulsing hard and his heart was pounding.

"What have you been doing for ten days?" he roared at Sibanda. "This was an easy task—it should be finished by now!"

His priestly authority suddenly meant nothing to Sibanda, who rushed at him with an axe held high, eyes blazing in anger. The other Africans watched trembling, but excited. The bush was quiet, and the late morning sun blazed down on the sweating figures. He was certainly not a coward, but he suddenly realised that a fight with this man would look wrong and could be very dangerous. He was also totally unarmed, and he would probably do himself more harm than good if he fought him. As the gap closed, and Sibanda's eyes glared into his soul, he got back in the cab, closed the door and drove off.

Later in the day, he returned. It took a few minutes to make peace, but he did. Stripping off his shirt, he worked side-by-side with Sibanda and the team of men until they nearly collapsed as the sun went down. The next day the people were there early. He had to attend to several sites but kept checking this one, and within three days, the classroom block was ready for the women. They finished off the floors with their cowdung and clay mixture, the practical and lasting surface of African flooring.

At the same time, there were also many people with obvious medical needs, and he did his best to help them. He dressed wounds, spliced broken limbs, issued aspirin for headaches and pains, and even extracted broken or rotting teeth.

COMFORT AMIDST NATURE'S STORMS

As rugged as this sort of outdoor life was, there were other rich compensations. 'What more could I ask than the beauty of this Rhodesian nature?' he would consider to himself. 'I get to see the sunrise and sunset, in unspoiled beauty; each one is more breathtakingly beautiful than the last. The shapes and colours of the clouds during the rainy seasons are truly marvellous.' He would watch as clouds almost formed up before his eyes, into those towering thunderheads, ready to disgorge their collection of water in the late afternoons.

He loved the colossal, awe-inspiring jungle forests. Walking through the forests, in the early morning or late afternoon, soon helped him forget any troubles, sorrows and anxieties. It inspired him and almost literally forced him to his knees, to adore God's infinite wisdom, power and love as revealed all about, in His nature.

Even getting stuck in the mud for hours, after a heavy rain, could be a pleasant experience. He had an eye for the surrounding beauty of the veldt, and for the cruel loveliness of sudden lightning and thunder, for the soothing charm of falling rain, for the thrilling roar and sweep of the suddenly swollen African rivers.

One night, three separate storms met in the narrow Lupane valley, through which he was travelling. With almost every fierce clap of thunder, his faithful old Ford shook and reverberated, and he huddled up inside it! He felt the power of the thunder and lightning and prayed, "Saint Thomas, you who knew the thunder and lightning so well, I do not have church to shelter in as you used to. If I am to continue doing God's work, I will surely be left unharmed, but please obtain protection for the people hereabouts. May they be spared the lightning strikes and saved from their fears." The storm continued through most of the night, and he was buffeted and drenched with the thunderous downpours. The ground around him was soon like a shallow lake, streaming with endless water.

In the same place, one winter night, he also felt extraordinarily cold, and could not pull enough blankets over himself to stop shivering. He worriedly thought it was another attack from his old enemy, the malaria fever. Next morning, after a sleepless night, he arose to offer Holy Mass on his outdoor altar when, before reaching the Offertory, his fingers and cheeks and even his lips, became so strangely stiff that he could scarcely move or even whisper the prayers. On looking around he noticed that all the trees and vegetation were black, and it was only then that he realised that during the night they had experienced one of the most severe frosts that had hit for many years.

The animals were everywhere in his 'little kingdom'. Saint Francis would probably have been more cautious with the elephants that he now regularly encountered at close range, and whose paths he often followed. Lions simply turned and slowly walked away from him, when he suddenly came upon them in a clearing.

He had to chase away a pack of wild dogs—African wolves—early one morning, when they tore a duiker buck to pieces, outside what he dubbed as 'his luxurious bedroom', or the 'Hotel Ford, 1933, Model B'. (He often wondered whether they were not, in reality, frightened away by the sight of his 'loud pyjamas'—in which he was attired at the time.)

One of the most blood-curdling sounds is made by the hyenas, which have a truly hellish cry that penetrates your very marrow. He admired leopards that he sometimes saw loping away in the distance. No animals ever attacked him, and he felt safe and secure. In his lighter moments, he sometimes wondered with a smile, 'is it my Guardian Angel—or is it simply a case of respect for my Roman collar?'

He saw all the beautiful and graceful wild animals of Rhodesia almost daily—the Eland, the Roan Antelope, the Reedbuck, the Duiker, the Steinbuck and dozens of others. Insects and reptiles were another story, and he had many experiences with snakes in the bush, under his bed and even in his bed.

Swimming the Shangani in Flood

The brown rivers were quite intimidating; and so different from the rivers in which he used to be able to swim freely in Bavaria; the lurking crocodiles certainly made many of them a big hazard. One day, he had to take the risk and defy these ugly and dangerous creatures. With four Africans he had, with great difficulty, crossed the rain-swollen Shangani River, to supervise the construction work at one of his new Outschools, Gomoza, ten miles beyond the Shangani. As he stood there deciding what he had to do, he had remembered that this was the same river that cost Alan Wilson and his brave comrades their lives fifty years ago in 1893. Now he was trapped.

That same night the very heavens seemed to open, pouring down still heavier torrential rains. By the time he got back to the Shangani River, at about noon the next day, it had risen another four to five feet. His African companions were not trained in swimming at all, and they feared both the rushing torrent and the crocodiles that they knew were there; they refused to even consider swimming back across the river.

'What am I to do now?' he asked himself. 'I could remain on the north bank, whilst my Ford is on the south bank. But, for how long?'

He knew from experience that the Shangani, once it is in flood, sometimes does not subside for weeks. 'Should I swim across?' he wondered.

Ordinarily that shouldn't be too difficult. After all, it is only five hundred yards wide—when it is in flood. As a young boy, he had often swum the Main River, a tributary of the Rhine, near his native hometown back in Germany. He used to do it several times back and forth without stopping, and that was certainly not a small river! Eventually he decided to try it.

As he prepared to jump in, he remembered the crocodiles. 'Should I take the chance? Is it not 'presumptuous' of me to run such a grave risk?' he pondered.

A voice seemed to say to him, 'have no fears. You are not doing it for sport, or bravado—but in the line of duty. So God will be with you.'

He tied his briefcase—which contained important and official papers—about his neck, waded into the gently swirling water at the edge, and then swam, swam, swam. It was tough going, but he made it, and crawled out of the water safely on the other side.

He looked back across the river and saw his assistants jumping up and down, and waving their arms in the air—a pantomime gesture of their happiness that he had made it safely. And then, as he stood there catching his breath, his heart sank at the sudden thought that his problem was far from solved.

He was now not much better off than he was before, because over there—on the other side of the river—there was still his Mass-kit, his wooden stretcher and blankets, his gramophone, and even his trousers and the rest of his clothing.

So he jumped in again, and made it successfully back and forth, carrying some of the things he had with him. And he did this a third time. And a fourth time too. This time, though, with his strength diminishing, the stretcher and blankets and clothing were getting heavier and heavier as they became more and more saturated.

One moment he was above the water, the next moment he was below . . . As he began to feel exhausted, his legs sank lower and lower in the water, and he had to struggle to rise for breath.

He began to worry now, and knew he was close to total exhaustion. Suddenly, he felt something brush against him, and he remembered the crocodiles. 'Oh God!' he prayed, 'surely You will not let me die now, just when I am trying to do my work for You in reaching all these people.' He had the temerity to challenge his Creator, but he hoped God had already seen his plight.

He felt the sensation again, but it was not something hard; he was being brushed by reeds waving in the flowing water. He lowered his feet some more, and was surprised when he felt sand below him, right in the middle of the river. He was able to stand, with his nose above the water, on a sandbar!

He caught his breath and then rested for a while. God's fatherly hands had once more held him up and kept him going. He swam the last distance with confident relief, and at last, he fell exhausted on the south bank—breathing a heartfelt prayer of thanksgiving to his Creator and God.

OFFICIAL OBSTRUCTIONISM

The struggles with officialdom continued. Objecting seemed to be a natural procedure for the civil servants anyway, but stopping this priest called for extra action on their part. Here was a German priest, in English, Anglican, territory, impudently proposing to set up a Catholic Mission.

Father Odilo saw it as his task to persevere and overcome these obstacles, for the sake of the flock. The quest for his mission site had a lot of similarity to the territorial conflicts which occur when eagles want to set up a new nest site, sometimes having to fight off other Eagles to secure a territory.

He knew how Abbott Francis had struggled and he took courage from the example of their founder. However, these obstacles seemed even tougher than those that their founder had encountered in Bosnia and Natal. Father Odilo remembered the accounts of the various summonses that the Abbot had received, to report to the pasha or his court, every time he commenced building or doing anything. He had eventually dug his heels in and insisted on a properly written summons, and declined the humiliation of the escorts, which they had delighted in providing, as they marched him off to argue his case. He had always avoided the pressure they used, to try and obtain baksheesh for all their approvals!

The Provincial Commissioner's Office and officialdom

Father Odilo wondered at the difference; 'some of these civil servants here have such a polite way of doing things. They can even appear to be helping, when all they are doing is avoiding a decision or blocking us.'

"My lord Bishop, I have tried time and again to meet with the Provincial Native Commissioner," he complained one day. He cannot prevent us opening schools, but he is completely opposed to another mission society coming into the area. He has already had our re-application for nearly six months now, and not even given us the courtesy of a reply!"

"What have you been doing in the meantime?"

"We have been building our outschools, and teaching catechism. The Africans need us. They are keen to learn and they are impeded by superstition and pagan beliefs," replied Father Odilo. "For us to establish a school, we are required to have a strict average attendance of twenty pupils. This means that at least thirty to forty students have to be enrolled. Any less, and there will not be enough to make up for absences, for many reasons. A second condition is that the spacing between schools has to be no less than exactly three miles, as well," he explained. "Of course this will remain a key factor in limiting us or other denominations from developing in the same areas."

One day, a further brown envelope, marked 'On His Majesty's Service', arrived at the Cathedral. The Bishop opened it and read the curt response from the Provincial Native Commissioner, "Your application to establish a mission in the Lupane district has been turned down."

Father Odilo fumed when he saw it. 'That man has been totally dishonest and mean with us Catholics. How could he again sit on our application for so long? He had no intention of allowing us to get a site, and has simply messed us around. What drives a man like him?'

"This looks quite hopeless, Odilo," the Bishop replied dejectedly. "I can't see how we can pursue this any longer. What is going on with your schools?"

"We have applied to the PC and the Education Department. The Education officer has harassed me over our mission base. I first claimed it was Lupane, but as we don't have a mission approved there yet, we have had to operate under Regina Mundi Mission. In fact, he even wanted me to close down our schools!"

"Can you keep on like this?"

"I can, as long as we persevere with our application. I do not know how this will end, but I just believe we must keep on," he responded, and that is what Father Odilo did, for nearly two and a half years!

THE EGGS THAT FLOATED

He experienced one of the saddest things in his life, one day. He had been in the bush for about six weeks, and was seriously short of everything, practically living on black tea and stale bread. One Sunday he was hopelessly stuck in the mud, knowing there was nothing practical he could do while the rains held out. An old African came to him, and generously presented twelve eggs. He was deeply touched and very, very grateful.

However, on closer inspection, the eggs looked rather shiny and he was afraid they might have been under the hen for a few days. So he decided to test them in a bucket of water, of which there was plenty! (You know that an egg is good if it stays down, but if it comes up it is bad.)

With a trembling heart and a hungry body, he put one after the other in the bucket and one after the other came up. He had not eaten properly for days now, and he almost despaired.

He kept going until eventually he came to number twelve, and that stayed down. He praised the Lord for giving him at least one good egg for his Sunday breakfast. So he got his kettle ready, and—when the water was boiling—he put egg number twelve in, with a grateful heart. After five minutes he took it out; his lips were by now smacking in anticipation of a lovely meal.

When he broke the shell, a tiny little perfectly-formed little chick fell out, with its poor little head dangling from side to side, and the little legs and tiny wings helplessly inert. He was so upset, he stroked it and hugged it and put it in the sun, but it was too late. He had boiled it for five minutes too long. That memory of this poor little creature often came back to him, in despair, for years and years afterwards!

Under the Marula Tree

On one of his trips, he was sitting on an anthill, under a beautiful big Marula tree. The trunk was so big that he could only reach halfway around with his arms, and the branches hung down from high up, casting a cool shade around him. A gentle wind stirred the leaves and punctuated his reading of the Divine Office. He looked at the bark for a while; it was peeled off in patches, smaller, but still a reminder of the lovely pine trees in Bavaria.

He could not get over how the psalms for that day, (morning prayers, week 4), had seemed as if they were written just for him, and just at that moment. Now, despite his anger at the obstruction, and even the hatred that he could sense, he was able to leave it to God, to bring about justice, and to deal with those who were deceiving him. He knew they had tried to do that. He was aware of the London Missionary Society's application for a site, which had even been ante-dated to make it appear as though they had applied before he had.

He had no bad feelings against the LMS, and he understood that they would have the sympathy of the P.C. That was natural enough. What angered him was the injustice in dealing with his own application. He was certainly the one who had applied first, and he had done all the work in analysing the district and presenting his case. 'How much of my information was passed on to them?' he wondered.

The appeal of Psalm 72, for justice, was simply not being heard—something he was to encounter many times in the years ahead. It was completely unfair, and his sense of right and wrong was deeply offended. 'Surely You know I am right,' he addressed his Creator. 'There are thousands of Africans here, who have never heard your Word. You have sent me from thousands of miles away, to be here and teach them. I can do what You commanded, and bring them to You; but why do you allow such petty officials to block my way?' The psalmist's complaint in his prayers for that day echoed his own and brought back the pain of his situation, and he realised how hard he 'strove to fathom this problem, too hard for my mind to understand . . . .'

He knew that he 'was always in Your presence, you were holding me by my right hand. You will guide me by Your counsel and so You will lead me to glory.' He felt a new breeze stirring and looked up at the leaves and branches above him. A small bird flitted across between the branches, and the sky shone blue beyond. A slight smell of something—he thought it was called formic acid—betrayed the presence of the roaming ants around him, but they left him alone, quite content with their more usual foraging.

Psalm 89 had been consoling, but now the canticle of Isaiah, (Is 42:10-16), filled his heart with great comfort and joy. '. . . . and I will lead the blind in ways they know not; in paths that they have not known I will guide them. I will turn the darkness before them into light, the rough places into level ground.'

TRAILBLAZING

Africans are astute and usually generous when they endow somebody with a nickname. Father Odilo found out that he had long ago earned the name umDabuli wesinanga, which means "the one who tears through the bush", a sort of high-speed trailblazer. The local

218

people could not believe that a European could move twenty to thirty miles through the bush in a day! He popped up all over the area, and did not need good roads or motor cars to get around.

The real purpose and thrust of all this mission work was religious and spiritual. Daily prayers and Holy Mass were the focus, and the teachers taught the basic curriculum, but added a lot of religious instruction and evangelising. However, it was certainly not a case of easy conversion or acceptance. Explaining this to Mr. Konson one day, he said, "Nobody is received into the church with less than three years of proper training and religious instruction. They usually have to go to the mission for final instruction and preparation to be received into the church. They are very devout and sincere."

"That is very tough; you must be limiting the numbers a lot, and how firmly do they stick to this?"

"I am sure you are right; we could baptise many more if it was just a quick thing. As it is though, I wonder what will happen as the younger ones grow up, and move to town. Will they fall away from practising their faith? There are so many material attractions and such allure in the town life-style," he said sadly.

Around this time, he chatted with the Assistant Native Commissioner, Noel Robertson. "I know Mr. Fletcher is sympathetic," he told him, and he sensed that they were both very helpful, but they kept suggesting that he should site a Mission further Northeast, near Jotsholo.

"I suppose that might be easier to secure approval," he concurred. "However, that is right on the fringe of the area where most of the people are living. We really need to set the Mission up in the middle, and be among them so that we can serve them best."

"And what if that is impossible, or is never approved?" Robertson asked.

"Noel," he explained, "we cannot give up. Normally we would have set up our Mission first, and then we would work out from there to open up schools and out-stations." He could speak frankly, but he paused to line up his thoughts carefully. "So far this has simply not been allowed." He paused, and stiffened his posture on the uncomfortable government-issue chair. "As it is, I have to work under the umbrella of Regina Mundi, which is very far away. In the meantime, we have not left the people without our help. We have established several schools already, not without some resistance and competition; it is almost a 'fight for schools', I think."

(In time, this strategy that was forced upon them was one of the factors that led to Our Lady of Fatima Mission having such a strong position in the region.)

As he continued building, he pressed on with great gusto, often pushing people around a lot to get the best from them. "Why are the men often so disinclined to do many of the tasks?" he asked Noel.

"It is traditional for the women to do much of what is considered as the menial work," he explained. "I think you already know how the men consider it to be more dignified for them to sit in the shade and direct or watch."

Be that as it may, Father Odilo was another sort of European. The men had a role to play, and he expected everybody to participate. Their families wanted schools, and they had come to realize that it was a good thing and improved their children's chances of getting work in Bulawayo, or even Wankie, if they could speak some English and read and write a bit. The Europeans had brought so many interesting things with them, many of the things that only money could buy.

"By the way," Noel said, "you do know how upset I become with all the trees you are using around here."

"Noel, you have seen how we struggled with trying to make those bricks. What else can I do? We simply have to build something reasonable, and I could never dream of bringing in bricks from Wankie or Bulawayo—I have no funds for that sort of thing."

"I know, and I understand. But, just please do it as carefully as you can. If it was somebody else I might have to be much firmer; at least, I can see that you make sure that you still preserve a good proportion of the trees wherever your people cut. The worst thing is to simply clear an area; these soils need the trees to hold everything together as well."

"Why do you not get builders from Bulawayo?" a visitor asked him one day, after Mass, as they sat in the shade of a tree, drinking tea at his old folding table.

"This way takes longer," admitted Father Odilo, "but I am convinced that it is wrong to simply hand things over for nothing. We pay the men something for their work, not a lot, but the main thing is the work gets done by all of us," emphasized Father Odilo. The priest and the people worked together to construct the classrooms, and it was not simply a case of the Church providing and paying for everything.

LEOPARD ENCOUNTER

In addition to his prayers and religious life, and outside his work and duties, life presented many new experiences. Some of them were very dangerous and could have ended his career quite early. At times like these his belief in Divine Providence was deepened even more. However, on one occasion, he also came close to ending the life of a person whom he respected a great deal—Noel Robertson.

He was on one of his mission trips, and decided he would stop at Lupane. The annual rains had started, and the land and trees were fresh once more. He crossed the low drift over the river and drove up the hill at Lupane. Turning in to the Native Commissioner's offices, he stopped and soon located Noel Robertson.

"Oh hallo, Father Odilo," he greeted him in a friendly manner. "I have just this morning been asked by an African man to shoot a colossal crocodile. He says they had it trapped on the Shabula River; you know the one, it's a small tributary of the Gwayi."

Father Odilo's instinct for novelty was aroused. "That will be interesting. When did this happen?" he asked.

"I was told that the crocodile had killed a calf yesterday," he said. "The man told me it came back for its prey at night, and had somehow been caught in a trap they set for it."

He could see that he was almost certain to have a companion for his follow-up and he went on, "it sounds a bit unusual to me. Apparently it managed to break the chain, which secured the trap and is now trying to escape. I think it must be impeded badly by the trap, though."

This definitely sounded intriguing. It also sounded like a most unusual crocodile, so Father Odilo was extremely curious. "Are you going to shoot it?" he asked.

"Probably. I think I had better get there and do what I can," replied Robertson. "I would hate it if anybody was hurt or killed, and I must say, I am keen to see what this is all about." Looking intently at Father Odilo, he asked, "would you like to come with me?"

"That sounds very interesting, I would love to come," he eagerly accepted.

"Let me see if George would like to join us," continued Robertson. Together, they strolled across to see George Raft, at his Lupane Store. "Count me in. This sounds most interesting," was his immediate reaction. "I would love to see this big crocodile wandering about out of water."

"I will take one of my rifles," said Robertson. He went back and chose from the three firearms in his office; he had no reason to think of taking more than one, with a crocodile, especially one trapped like that.

"It might be interesting to take a camera along," he suggested. "Have you got one?"

"Oh, Ja. I have a very good camera, and I will enjoy getting some snapshots of this prehistoric monster," Father Odilo quickly replied. They all climbed into the truck, and he jokingly remarked to Robertson, "before you shoot, I should like to take a few really exciting and unusual photographs."

First they proceeded along the Victoria Falls road for six miles and then turned north into the bush, following the small and dry Shabula vlei for about four miles. It was quite heavy going in places, as the district is very sandy, and the sun had already dried patches of it. Driving along, they discussed the African man's extraordinary report. "It is very unusual for a crocodile to kill away from a river. But what makes it even more intriguing was that it even returned for its prey at night. I have never heard of a crocodile doing that before."

"Oh well, this is such a strange part of the world," Father Odilo surmised. They were happily joking and laughing when the African man suddenly knocked on the cab of the truck, and said, "Here we are!"

They got out of the truck, expecting almost to step on the brute. Robertson looked around, and they all searched the ground to see this huge reptile. "Well, I can't see anything at all around here;" Robertson said in some surprise. There were not even any signs of it dragging itself. "Where is it, man?" he asked suspiciously.

The man simply pointed to the bush. "It went that way," he pointed into the bush. They walked in that direction for some distance but they still saw nothing.

Again Robertson asked, "Where is it? I can't see any sort of trail; surely it has to leave wide marks."

The man replied, "it has run away into the bush."

That was too much for Father Odilo. He knew enough iSindebele to be convinced that the man was exaggerating when he described it as having *balekile* (run away). "Good heavens man!" he exclaimed, "since when does a crocodile run, and why would it run away from the river to save its life in the bush?"

Understanding dawned and they could hardly believe their ears when they heard the answer. "Oh! It is not an ngwenya (crocodile), it is an ingwe (leopard)." They were quite taken aback by this revelation, but Father Odilo was even more thrilled. "Oh, if it's a leopard, then that is far more interesting than a crocodile!"

Gradually seven men appeared from the nearby kraals and gathered at the place. They had been expecting them. They had caught a glimpse of the leopard running away between the bushes some four hundred yards ahead.

"Obviously the thief didn't like the strange sound of motor-car, and our noisy voices. It seems he preferred an honourable flight to a doubtful fight!" This dangerous thought, unluckily, made the pursuing party rather careless.

They moved along as fast as they could, now easily following a spoor that had been made by the trap. After about six hundred yards one of the men suddenly signalled and said, "I saw him stop. He has gone behind those bushes!"

Robertson bent down and examined the spoor carefully. "It's close by all right. This spoor is very fresh, and the blood is still bright red."

They kept on its trail, and soon afterwards they heard a very angry and nasty growl. "Oh, good, he hasn't gotten away from us," said Father Odilo enthusiastically.

At that moment the leopard came out from behind the bush with a terrific roar. To their surprise it did not charge, but made for a big tree some thirty yards away, with them running after it, and keeping up quite well. Arriving there, it hesitated a second, giving them an angry look and uttering an infuriated snarl. Then without any start at all, it jumped fifteen feet straight up, embracing the tree and trying to get its claws into the bark.

At first it looked as though it might succeed, but it was badly hindered by the trap and it fell. One would have expected quite a heavy and clumsy fall, as the leopard was eight feet long and two-and-a-half feet high, yet they hardly heard a sound. Then, like a coiled spring, it immediately leapt again, trying his luck a second time. It failed again. After this attempt it shot off at great speed and then paused under a big, shady tree, about twenty yards away. It seemed to them that it showed a wary respect for this party of ten men!

All the time they had been closing the gap, but Robertson didn't get a decent opportunity to aim and fire. "I've got you now," he said at last. There stood his target under the tree, in all its beauty, elasticity, gracefulness, majesty—and fury. 'There is not another animal in creation as wily and strong,' he reminded himself. They were only about sixty yards away; Father Odilo was on the left of Robertson, George Raft was on his right, and the rest of the men were very well behind them!

THE PHOTOGRAPHER!

Just as he saw the rifle being raised by Robertson, Father Odilo asked, "please, don't shoot it yet! Allow me to go nearer so that I can take a better snapshot. I am too far at sixty yards." Although this was a silly request, Robertson graciously granted it to his priest friend.

He stood there ready to fire, though, just in case the leopard should make a charge. Father Odilo moved quickly up to about thirty yards, staying well out of the firing line. He was keenly watching the animal, which roared at him continuously. He could see the anger and pain deep in its flashing eyes, and the leopard beat the ground with its paws and its long, graceful dark-tipped tail.

It snarled and bared its long, yellow fangs at him. Its muscles tightened so that each and every one appeared clearly under its fine smooth skin. So impressive, artistic and wonderful was the sight, that Father Odilo simply could not take his eyes off it, wondering what was going on behind those malevolent yellow-green eyes.

Deep inside of himself, he regretted that they should, eventually, have to destroy this masterpiece of creation. He was so greatly impressed that fear was unknown to him at the time. Nor was there, in his opinion, any reason to be afraid. Although the leopard looked like fury incarnate, it did not appear to have any intention of coming for him just then. It actually seemed to be inviting him to come closer.

At this distance of thirty yards, Father Odilo considered it unwise to go any nearer. He stared the leopard in the eyes as he began to sight through his camera. No sooner, however, had the leopard noticed this, than it came for Father Odilo like a flash of lightning. It ran so fast and kept so low to the ground that the eye could hardly follow him. Whilst it had looked so fine a specimen under the tree, Father Odilo now saw only a great woollen ball streaking towards him—curled up in such a manner that it offered nothing much of a target.

Despite the danger, Father Odilo thought it great fun and an exciting experience, being convinced that it would be dead before it reached him; and, indeed, the shot fell immediately. He saw a cloud of dust come up and, in anticipated relief, imagined the leopard rolling on the ground, having been mortally hit. He could hardly believe his eyes when he realised that it was not down at all.

Luckily, however, it was not running any longer, but looking somewhat puzzled and bewildered instead, for the simple reason that the shot had come from another direction than it would have expected. Father Odilo waited for the second report, thinking that would finish it off. Sure enough, at that moment the rifle went off again. Then he saw the leopard taking up its charge anew.

Now he thought it time to run, realising, of course, that he could not save his life simply through fleeing. The distance was much too short for a human being to have a chance against a charging beast. However, he thought that—by so running—he would hold the distance between the leopard and himself for two or three seconds and thus enable Robertson to get a third shot in before the pursuer could attack. At the same time he hoped to get behind a heavy bush so that the leopard could not strike at him directly. He did not even consider climbing a tree, knowing only too well that he would be pulled down before reaching any height.

He had run some ten yards, without hearing the expected shot, or seeing a suitable bush, and Father Odilo began to wonder whether something had happened to the rifle. If that was the case—he calculated—he would be making a fatal mistake in running away, thus offering the leopard his unprotected back—something too horrible to think of.

He turned round, with nothing in his hands but his beloved Voigtlander camera, to face the beast and get a grip at him somehow. Horrified, he saw that the leopard was now making for Robertson, racing towards him like a champion greyhound. Feverishly he waited for the shot to fall, the distance between them becoming rapidly shorter.

Meanwhile, in order to gain more time for loading, Noel Robertson had retreated a couple of paces and, by so doing, had backed into a little tree. This turned out to be a providential move. As he watched, frozen in horror for the split seconds this took, he saw that the animal was only two yards from Noel. The next thing Father Odilo saw, was the leopard biting away at Noel's left arm, while he was still trying to get the jammed bullet into the weapon.

No sooner had he realised the terrible plight of his friend, than he ran with all his strength to pull the beast away from him. Whilst running towards them, he saw Robertson firmly erect, waving the rifle in his right hand. Against him was the leopard, standing six feet high, with the raised left arm of his victim between his jaws. It rested its left, trapped front paw on Noel's chest, and was striking at his back with its right paw, but luckily hitting into that little tree. Father Odilo was now only five to seven yards away. At the same time, George Raft approached from the other side and some of the men, who had earlier all run away, came at it from the far side.

The leopard could not claw Robertson, as both the trap and the small tree hampered it. It could see its enemies approaching from three sides now, and it let its victim go, running towards Father Odilo again. He expected it, of course, to attack immediately. To his astonishment it passed him, stopping some ten yards away.

There it stood—a terrifying sight! It was roaring and snarling and showing its terrible fangs, flames of fury and revenge shining forth from its blood-thirsty green eyes, but luckily delaying its charge by licking its aching paw, for a second. Using this precious moment, George Raft took the rifle, slipped the bullet in and fired. The leopard, roaring furiously, dropped its rump, trying still to get at them on its front legs, but failing to do so. George finished the beast off with two more shots, whilst Father Odilo attended to Robertson's dreadful-looking arm injuries.

They bundled Robertson into the vehicle and rushed back via Lupane to give the news to his wife, before proceeding to Bulawayo hospital. They all waited for the verdict, and the doctor pronounced, "He will be fine, it's a plain flesh bite, a bit ragged though. Anyhow we have disinfected the wound and stitched him up fine." Father Odilo heaved a huge sigh of relief.

Back at the Cathedral, two Redemptorist priests, Father Mark Flynn and Father Robert McHugh were visiting the Cathedral to give a mission to the parish.

"How is the poor man?" Father Mark asked.

"He is still recovering from anaesthetic, but the doctor says he will be fine," Father Odilo assured him.

Now Father Mark was not ugly, but he was not handsome; he tended to be a bit plumpish as well. On the other hand, Father Robert was a well-built, tall and slender man, and the two maintained a friendly rivalry as they gave their mission that evening.

They were a cheerful pair, and their lively banter enhanced the message they were giving to an appreciative congregation. "Now it is time for me to hand over to our own Wallace Beary!"[7] Father Mark said, having explained earlier that Father Robert was definitely not to be mistaken for the good-looking actor, Robert Taylor. The Cathedral was packed and they all laughed heartily, as they enjoyed this great pair of preachers. Despite a cheerful levity, they inspired their audience and helped to deepen their understanding and faith. Father Odilo wished he had more of their great talent, but accepted from one of the great epistles, that there are different gifts and different ways of serving the Lord.

At supper, Father Odilo described his exploits in detail. "Don't you think I was very brave?" he asked rhetorically.

There was a long pause, and everybody waited while Father Mark seemed to be thinking up an even better way of describing this heroism. Then he said, "No. It was idiotic!" While they recovered, he went on, "Thank God the poor man is going to be fine, though," he continued. "I suppose you will be able to laugh about it over a few beers soon enough."

---

[7] Beary was an actor well known for his ugly appearance.

The next day, when he went to visit, Father Odilo saw that Noel's eyes were rolling about, and he was recovering from an anaesthetic. He rushed to find a doctor, and located Doctor Richard Morris. Father Odilo asked him worriedly, "What happened? He was fine last night."

"I am afraid, that during the night, gas gangrene had set in, and it was all the way up to his neck." Doctor Morris explained. "We had to find a surgeon to operate immediately, and luckily Mr. Simpson was on call. It was a lengthy operation, but he seems to have cleaned out the gangrene."

"Where is he?"

"He is busy with another patient, in theatre."

Father Odilo was now most anxious and paced up and down the corridor, deep in thought, until the theatre doors opened. Mr. Simpson came out and Father Odilo asked, "How is he Doctor?"

"Well, I cannot promise, but I think we got the worst out, just in time, too. Keep him in your prayers. Heaven knows, he has come very close to death already, and he has some way to go still."

He had been told how the accident had happened, and now he addressed Father Odilo cuttingly, "If you ever want to take a photograph of a leopard again, please shoot him first, then take the bloody photograph!"

Prayers of compassion would have been natural and normal, but his deep feelings of guilt added a lot of extra pressure and urgency to Father Odilo's prayers over the next few days.

Noel was in hospital for three and a half months before he recovered. Apart from the anxiety caused to all, Father Odilo repeated a lesson to himself and others, many times after that, "Never give a wounded animal a chance. The risk you may be prepared to take for yourself can prove fatal to some other person, as I sadly experienced."

CHAPTER 11

PLANS FULFILLED

FATIMA MISSION, AT LAST

Meanwhile, after four refusals from the Government, his endeavours to establish a Mission in the Nkayi area were still in progress. After establishing fifteen outschools a new application had been sent to the Government—pointing out that the schools were already established and operating. Back came the answer—still "No!" With determination, he just went ahead and built more outschools, followed by another application. Thus as the number of schools grew, application after application went in to the officials.

Finally, in August 1947, the Government surrendered through the kind intercession of a Member of Parliament, Mr. Holmes, who was a friend of Bishop Arnoz. Evidently they realized that they would not have any peace from these missionaries until they gave them the land grant—and the official approval they were after.

A farm—Gwayi Settlement Farm, No 117—of two thousand acres—was 'leased' to the Church by the Government for ninety-nine years. They, of course, gladly accepted the offer—though it was not the ideal place. Pointing to the map, he showed the bishop, "it is right at the perimeter of the populated area, and that is nearly a hundred miles across. Anyway, we have waited so long, we can't do anything but accept the site."

"You're right; it has taken over two and a half years, of nothing but obstruction and stalling. If it hadn't been for Holmes, we would still be waiting," he added.

This enabled the Church to provide the essential Mission, serving as a nucleus and focus for the three key needs of the growing community of converts—education, medicine and religious instruction. It was this or nothing!

Father Odilo started by choosing what he thought would be the best site for building the mission. He chose a well-wooded area, slightly up from, and northeast of, the Gwayi riverbed. A little further to the south he scaled a lone basalt hill[8], just north of the road. It was not very high but was a good vantage point for surveying the land; from here he could see for a good ten miles in each direction along the Gwayi valley.

So, to get started, he built a small mud-brick house closer to the river, as somewhere to work from, deliberately not building it at the centre of the intended mission.

When Father Joseph visited him, the first thing he asked was, "why don't you build at the site you showed me?"

"If we build over there, I know that our temporary buildings will become the permanent ones; we will never replace them," he responded.

"Well, is that so bad?" he asked.

"Yes, my good father," Father Odilo replied. "You know how things are from Lukosi; you can't change things later, because there just is not enough money, and so many things are needed. We have a chance to plan here—it has taken so many years simply to get this site from government. We must definitely build a proper Mission and Hospital here, one that will last a long time."

Within a year they had built a little Mission centre. It had a house for the priests and a chapel, a convent, and a doctor's house. There was also a dispensary, a kitchen, storerooms, sheds, guestrooms and a day school. Fatima Mission was the name, which had been chosen—in honour of Our Lady of Fatima.

---

8   He had a cross erected here, dedicated on 13th October 1997, fifty years later.

A MYSTERY BENEFACTOR

'Forgive me, God, for my impertinence, but this work is all for You and the people You sent me to help and bring to You,' he had prayed. 'We are getting nowhere; the foundations are ready, the approvals are finally granted, thankfully; but at this rate it may be many years before we can begin functioning.' And, once again in his life, prayers were answered. Father Odilo never ceased to appreciate how God had brought help in a most amazing way, and from such unexpected sources.

A passing motorist had stopped in and seen the foundations. He had been a very genial man, and asked lots of questions about the mission, the area, and the new hospital. It was a short visit, though, and he was soon busily departing to complete his journey to the Victoria Falls. As he left, he shook hands and pressed an envelope into Father Odilo's hand, wishing him well. Father Odilo assumed it was a note or letter, and only opened it when the swirling dust of the man's car was already settling; in it he found a gift of twenty pounds! That had been more than enough to cover the next load of cement bags that he desperately needed to pay for; and he never knew who the mystery donor was!

HARRY SCHUR—A BIG BENEFACTOR

At the first opportunity, and those were not easy to come by, he approached Harry Schur, who had promised him a large donation towards the hospital; there were a few conditions but he accepted those. A few years before this, he had heard about the incident of the Grand Hotel. This was a classic hotel in Bulawayo, on Main Street, between Ninth and Tenth Avenues, and it had a very strict and formal colonial atmosphere.

Harry Schur was accustomed to patronising it whenever he arrived back from his cattle trading in Botswana or the Lupane bush. He usually went straight in to order dinner, still a bit dirty, and certainly very parched and famished. He used to sit himself down in a corner of the dining room. Sometimes, there were even some discreet screens that created a bit of privacy for him; he needed that, as he was not the neatest of eaters.

Now it happened that a haughty new manager had taken over running the hotel, and he caught sight of this man who looked as if he had come off the streets, or worse. With his head held high in the air, he hurriedly crossed the room, and standing with one arm on his broad hips, and circling the air with the other, he loudly demanded, "Excuse me. Just who do you think you are?"

All heads turned in Harry Schur's direction, and the manager sensed his own importance; clearly he had a duty on behalf of the distinguished gentlemen and ladies in the hotel. Harry Schur, however, was quite unruffled, and noisily finished what he was chewing, before he answered, in a thick Lithuanian accent, "I know exactly who I am—who the hell are you?"

"I am the new manager," he said, and puffed himself up bulkily, "and as long as I am in charge here, I shall not permit anybody in here who dresses and behaves like a hobo!"

The message seemed to be sinking in, and a few tense moments passed slowly by, before Harry responded, "well, if that's the case, I suppose I will have to make a few changes." He wiped his mouth broadly with the crumpled white table napkin, gulped down the remains of his cold beer and pushed his chair back. With a look of smug satisfaction, the manager stepped aside as Harry got up and stormed out angrily. One by one, the guests turned back to their own meals and companions, but there was a difficult stillness in the dining room.

The next day, shortly after the manager came on duty, he was required to be present in the lounge. Two men in suits were sitting back in the comfortable leather armchairs, and there was Harry Schur in an armchair as well, blowing smoke from a thick cigar, in close conversation with the owner. Schur picked up three sheets of paper from the card table, and stuffed them roughly into his jacket pocket, while the owner said, "I believe you two have met."

Before the manager had a chance to even guess at what this was all about, Harry Schur stood up and jabbed him firmly in the chest. "I am now the new owner of the Grand Hotel, and it is my very pleasant duty," he said, "to tell you that you are fired!" he exploded. "Now get the hell out of here, and don't ever come near me again!"

Well, Father Odilo had somehow earned Schur's respect, and this tough Jewish businessman had become the German missionary's biggest benefactor. Six thousand pounds was able to buy a lot of desperately needed building materials, and he knew that his generosity was not going to be wasted.

Furthermore, the Beit Trust, set up by another Jewish business magnate, matched the gift. His appeal to the Rhodesian State Lottery Fund was also successful and soon the Fatima Mission Hospital had what it needed to accelerate construction.

Father Odilo never forgot to include benefactors in his prayers, usually at the end of Holy Mass, but sometimes he made more mention of his gratitude, on occasions when this was befitting. It was their generosity that enabled missionaries like him to provide tangible help to thousands of people.

The Hospital

With the mission's funding reasonably assured, they pressed on with building Fatima Hospital. "A medical centre is almost an indispensable part of any central mission," it had been agreed with the bishop. Again it meant endless days and nights of hard work, struggle and worry. Bricks, sand and stones had to be carted great distances, and most of the building materials had to be transported from Bulawayo—one hundred and thirty six miles away. Watching over and worrying about finances, of course, was the ever present and heaviest burden. Accounting to, and dealing with, the donors was an ongoing difficulty as well.

After four years of working alone, in December 1948 the first member of staff arrived in the welcome person of the African Sister Paulina. Early the next year, in January 1949, Doctor Johanna F. Davis-Ziegler, a fully qualified Catholic lady physician and surgeon, arrived to help in the organisation of the new hospital, of which she was to be Medical Superintendent. In March of the same year Mariannhill's experienced builder, Brother Athanasius Sattich, arrived on the scene and began construction of the hospital. It was to be one hundred and thirty-five feet long by thirty-two feet wide.

While this was going on, Father Odilo again encountered van Niekerk slaughtering the game in the area. Early one morning, a vehicle arrived at Fatima Mission. Van Niekerk had shot three reedbucks, a male, a female and even their baby. "What are you doing, man?" Father Odilo protested boldly.

Van Niekerk responded, "What's your problem, Oom? There are more than enough of them. They are just vermin!"

Sadly, he turned his back, and burned off some of his anger and frustration in the building work that day and in the weeks after. 'Some people can never be changed,' he realised with profound sorrow.

And now the work went on steadily and securely. One could, of course, always do so much more if there was more finance. Father Odilo wondered, 'how often do Missionaries have sleepless nights, because they cannot carry on with their developments on account of lack of funds? How often have they not even enough money to pay for the food for their staff and patients?'

But there was the ever-present compensation of the beautiful examples of the grandeur of nature, and sometimes he saw again the most awe-inspiring spectacle in the entire world, the famous Victoria Falls, which are not too far North of Fatima Mission.

Several times, his morning and evening prayers included, 'Lord, I thank you for all those whose offerings and prayers, and help, directly or indirectly, have made the building of this Mission possible.'

The honey-guide's patient

There was much happening and he experienced some very interesting hospital cases. There is a certain bird called the Honey-Guide Bird, and there is a folk-story about its strange name. Many people confirmed the story, as told by one of the old men, "this bird wants to show you where you can find honey. Thus, when you are crossing his path, it will start twittering excitedly and unendingly, inviting you to follow it."

"Sometimes," he was told, "that can be quite a distance, but it will always take you where you can find honey—usually in trees, where bees or Mopani flies have their hives. However, if you do not leave some honey for it when you have taken the combs out, it will take revenge on you." Some time after hearing this folk-tale, they received a patient who seemed to be a confirmation of this.

One day, a man was brought to the hospital with very bad lacerations and bites on his body and, especially around his shoulders.

"What happened to you?" Father Odilo asked him as he lay there in some pain.

"Aaiiee!!" was all he could say that day.

The next day, when he was feeling a bit better, he told Father Odilo about his adventure. "I was walking with three dogs in the forest, looking for honey, or some buck that the dogs might be able to catch. Suddenly, the honey-guide bird appeared, calling excitedly and fluttering from tree to tree. At first, I did not want to follow, because I know that it may sometimes be an hour or much more before you reach the tree or hive."

"However, since the bird was so insistent, I decided to give it a try. After about twenty minutes, I suddenly saw a leopard standing under a bush and eating a duiker buck which it had killed. I realised the danger I was in, and turned to run as fast as I could. However, the leopard had already seen me, and it followed me with great rage and revenge. Naturally, the leopard was much faster, and soon caught up with me and jumped on my back," he explained.

"Then, something extraordinary happened," he went on to explain. "I am experienced in bush life and its dangers, and I bent rapidly forward. The leopard fell off my back, before it could bite through my neck," he said. He explained how he had the incredible presence of mind and undaunted courage to hit the animal with his small axe, on the head, stunning it for a moment. However, the leopard, being a tough and vicious enemy was ready in no time, for a further attack.

"At that moment my three dogs attacked it, taking on the leopard's fury, and giving me enough time to flee to safety. My old friends, those dogs I loved, never came back; they were surely killed, all three, by the infuriated animal; they had given their lives for me. It was because they loved their master."

THE GOAT-KILLER

In another one of his outlying stations, a leopard had killed a goat and dragged it into a ravine with thick bush. The owner was not prepared to let the thief get away with it. So he took his axe and a couple of dogs and followed the spoor. He was hardly gone a hundred yards or so when the leopard jumped upon him and ripped away at his left leg.

With the dogs attacking viciously, the predator decided to run rather than risk being mauled himself, and possibly being killed by the axe, as the man was still mobile. The owner was able to walk back to his kraal where tribal and customary medicines were applied to the bite. In fact he thought that after a few days he would be in order again.

However, he did not get better, but worse. Gas gangrene had set in. It was then that he realized he should go to Fatima hospital, which was only about ten miles away. On arrival, he looked comparatively well with bad injuries only on the leg. However, when Father Odilo touched his leg, it felt and sounded like air moving underneath the skin and between the muscles. This was caused by the poisonous gas, which had spread right through the badly bitten leg.

Dr Davis completed her examination, and then called him to one side, saying, "The gangrene is very advanced; there is only one slight possibility to save him. We have to amputate the leg!" There was nobody else who could assist her, and she asked him to do it for her.

He said, "Good Lord! I have never done anything like this. I won't be able to do it!"

But she replied, "Well, that's the only chance we have to possibly save him. If we don't amputate, he will probably die anyway. Come on, let's try, and give him that chance."

So he agreed, somewhat apprehensively.

She injected the wounded area, and got everything ready before passing him what looked like an ordinary little chrome hacksaw. There the man lay on the operating table and, after saying a little prayer to God to help him, Father Odilo put the saw on his leg. With a heavy heart, he began, but just as he started sawing, the poor man died.

Father Odilo prayed over him, feeling terribly sorry for him and the family. However, he added, 'thank you Lord, for sparing me from the dreadful experience of cutting off his leg.' Even so, he could still see blood all over the table and the theatre.

A RECOVERY GONE WRONG

Many more incidents occurred at the Fatima Hospital. Patients were attacked or mauled or badly injured by wild animals, and of course, there were ordinary cases of injuries, illnesses and tragedies as, for example when two wives of an African, in their jealousy, more or less chopped each other to pieces. 'The fury of a woman scorned,' he thought, 'is very real, especially when a man is involved with more than one woman!'

Another animal injury eventually resulted in the victim's death. "I think I can honestly say it was the saddest experience I ever had in my hospital work out there," Father Odilo said, as he told a friend, one day.

One morning a European farmer brought in an African who had, so he stated, been attacked and badly mauled by a 'lion'.

"What happened?" he asked the man, in iSindebele, as he was about to be discharged from hospital.

"It was late in the evening," he began. "I heard agitated bleats and cries of anxiety coming from my goat enclosure. Since wild dogs had been seen during the day, I presumed they had come back in the evening to get at the goats. So I left my hut where I had been with one of my wives. I walked towards the goat kraal and threw my spear, shouting and trying to chase the marauders away. I had hardly gone ten paces, when an animal jumped at me and threw me over. As I was lying on the ground I was convinced it was a lion."

"The attacker bit me all over the body," he said; Father Odilo could see the man was a fine example of courage and presence of mind. "I bit the animal in the ears and in the stomach and wherever I could sink my teeth in. Every time I did this, the 'lion' let me go for a moment. Eventually I managed to get up and make my way gradually to my hut, embracing the beast and biting it wherever I could. I told my wife to keep the door open—as I intended to get inside whilst giving the furious attacker a push."

"This I managed to do, and my wife and I held the door against the animal. It tried desperately to get inside to carry on its satanic work. However, we were able to hold out. When morning came, the animal had disappeared and we walked miles to get help from a European farmer." When he arrived at Fatima hospital they could hardly bear the sight of him; shreds of flesh were hanging down from his face, shoulders, body and legs.

Dr. Davis, who was visiting the Fatima Hospital said, "it is quite impossible to operate with the facilities we have available. I suggest you take this injured man to Bulawayo."

But the farmer had pleaded with them, "I really don't think this man would make it to Bulawayo. He will die on the way."

Dr. Davis then suggested, "Go and fetch Dr. Decker and Sister Raymunda from Saint Luke's Mission, where they have gone for the day." This he gladly did, and they operated on him for over three hours and saved his life. After three and a half months, he left Fatima—overjoyed and with deep gratitude. About three months later he came back telling the doctors that he had terrible pain all over his body—so much so that he was almost getting mad. The medical staff simply could not understand what had gone wrong.

A couple of days later, he began foaming out of the mouth and became so violent that they had to chain him to the bed to protect the other patients. Dr. Decker said, "There is only one thing he can have and which makes him behave like this; he must have rabies."

They discussed things with Dr. Davis who was based at Saint Luke's Mission, and got in contact with Bulawayo hospital asking them, please, to accept him for treatment. However, they refused, saying that the rabies had gone too far and nobody on earth could help him any more—only a miracle could save him.

Father Odilo tried to find out what had happened. A few weeks after the attack, he discovered that a rabid hyena had been destroyed and it was apparently it, and not a lion that had attacked the man that night. And indeed a few days later, he died in excruciating pain—after Father Odilo had prayed with him and over him, giving him all the spiritual help the Church could.

Right up to his very last moment he thought only of his wives and children, stuttering in indescribable pain, "my poor wives. My poor children. Who will look after them? What will happen to them? What will happen to them?" The sorrow and distress of the man, and his deep love for his family brought many tears to Father Odilo's eyes, as he stood by in helplessness.

He was a short, but stocky man, very muscular and hard working as his fine and well-trained body testified. Looking at his lifeless frame, Father Odilo thought, 'surely a pagan saint has just gone home to his Heavenly Father.'

Surviving a Not-so-dead Leopard

Elsewhere, a leopard had killed a calf—a very precious possession for an African. So the owner got a few friends together to hunt down the murderer with about a dozen dogs.

Eventually they located the leopard in dense bush. As the dogs were making for it, the leopard decided to climb a tree to save itself. Naturally, the African men threw stones and spears and so it decided to come down again and save itself by fleeing. However the dogs caught up with it and being so many they were able to hold it down—after it dispatched two or three to the other world! As the dogs were all over it, the men went up and stuck their spears into it until they were convinced it was dead. And indeed it did not move any more.

Then the owner said to the others, "well you can go home now whilst I am going to skin it since it was my calf it destroyed."

So they went and he set about to skin it. After two or three minutes, the leopard suddenly jumped up and set upon the unsuspecting man mauling him dreadfully. When the poor chap did not come back, another man went back to check on him. He too, was attacked by the enraged leopard, and their friends came back again, and found the first man half dead with the leopard now fully dead next to him. The second man had been badly mauled, but was able to walk.

They put the first man on a rough stretcher and carried him to Saint Luke's hospital. Dr. Davis immediately operated on him and saved his life, and he was able to leave the hospital after about two months. The second man was treated and stayed in hospital for the same period.

Man Against Baboon

Father Odilo had several direct experiences of his own with animals, especially leopards, lions, hyenas, jackals and so forth. In those days the Lupane area was very underdeveloped, and there were hardly any roads and certainly no decent bridges. The population was small and so there was an abundance of wild life—a fact which people can hardly comprehend nowadays.

When he started Fatima there were literally thousands of baboons in the area. If they got into the fields there was hardly a cob left afterwards—for they came in their hundreds. He shot quite a few, but he didn't like doing it, as they cry like babies if they are not killed outright. They were extremely cunning, but he had one advantage over them; his little house was next to the maize field and if they came to raid the fields when he was in the house they could not see him and so he got good shots at them.

The funniest—and at the same time the luckiest—shot he ever had—happened this way: He saw something dark in the maize field and presumed it was a baboon—so he aimed and shot, but nothing happened, which he thought was very peculiar. He was convinced there had been something there between the maize stalks!

He wondered, 'why no movement, why no commotion, why no running away?'

So he went there to have a look, and was surprised at what he saw! There was indeed a huge baboon, with a maize cob still in its hand and mouth, lying on its side! He had sent it off to a better world with a master shot through his neck while it was enjoying a stolen supper.

Unfortunately not all shots were as good, and one or the other baboon got away wounded. He sometimes tried to follow them into dense bush, but the fury of the animals was such that they would have torn him to pieces. Looking back he admitted that, on several occasions, he was extremely silly to follow them and invite danger to his life.

Baboons are very cunning, as the following story illustrates. He had advised his workers to locate the baboons' night-quarters, mostly in trees, so that they could go down to the river at night and shoot some whilst having their nocturnal rest. "Baboons will not remain on the ground at night for fear that they might be attacked by leopards," he had been assured.

Late one afternoon, his workers came and said they knew the tree in which the baboons were hiding. So they went down at night to the Gwayi River, with its lovely big trees, to teach them a lesson. They stopped under a huge tree and he was assured they were up there. They waited a couple of minutes, but did not hear a sound. So he whispered to the man next to him "Are you sure it's this tree?"

"Well" he said, "I must have been mistaken, I think it's the next one."

So they moved slowly and quietly a few metres ahead, but they had hardly gone ten paces when the whole troop dropped down to the ground from that tree behind him, and with incredible speed, disappeared into the darkness. As he turned to shoot, he got caught in a root, with the rifle going off with a big bang almost killing him. They did not get one single baboon, and he said, "I must certainly admire their cunning and timing."

KING OF THE BEASTS

Naturally, he had a few encounters with lions as well. One day his little old Ford broke down, and as he walked through the bush, he suddenly stood before two huge lions near a waterhole. They were apparently waiting for game. But when they saw him they turned and walked away and he had the temerity to walk after them to take a photograph, as they were too far away for his Voigtlander box camera.

He admired the footprints, which were colossal, but when the bush became very dense he thought it might become very dangerous and so he returned to the vanette. He was very upset that he didn't get a shot of these magnificent representatives of the cat family.

'Why did they turn?' he wondered. 'Perhaps they didn't like the Roman collar I was wearing and, maybe, my guardian angel made frightening gestures to them.'

One night he was sleeping in a hut and he heard heavy breathing and purring outside. Next morning, he saw the footprints of two lions all over the place. 'Imagine if I had a call of nature in the middle of the night, and the lions jumped upon me; that would be a rather undignified way of departing from this world!'

The most incredible experience he had with lions was in the Wankie National Park. He saw a pride of lions, twelve or fifteen of them, as they were trying to catch a buffalo. However, the buffalo herd of about two hundred, saw them in time and a phalanx of twelve bulls advanced towards them. The lions retreated and lay down, on the bank of a small dry riverbed. There they sat waiting for an opportunity to get at one in the course of time.

Eventually four huge buffalo bulls placed themselves opposite the lions, which were only about five metres from them, on the higher bank of the spruit. Four buffalo against fifteen lions! At times the lions would get up, flex their muscles and lie down again, the buffalo looking with contempt at them.

After a few minutes, one buffalo walked away, not even looking round. The lions repeated the same performance, flexing their muscles and twitching their tails. After another five minutes the second bull walked away, and then the third, leaving only one buffalo facing fifteen lions. In the end the last walked away, finding it unnecessary even to look back.

"Can you believe it?" he asked his dinner-table audience. "If I had not seen it myself I would not believe it; but, on reflection, I say the lions were very wise, for had they attacked the remaining buffalo, the whole herd would probably have charged them and horned them into mince meat. What an experience! I will tell you some other time how I behaved so foolishly in the Game Park, but right now it is better to leave you thinking well of me!"

WILD DOGS

He also walked into wild dogs several times. These are more correctly described as Cape Hunting dogs. The first time he encountered them, he was all alone. Suddenly he heard very funny sounds coming from within the high grass. As he got nearer, he saw figures jump up, which he recognised as wild dogs. However, after a quick look at him, they didn't think him worth eating and so they moved on for something better and more tasty.

On the other hand, his dear African friend, Makeke, was badly mauled when he tried to take a duiker, which had been killed by a big pack of wild dogs.

Father Odilo was quite upset when another friend of his, Hugh Miller, of Ndawana Store, shot a mother in milk on her way home to feed her puppies. He was sad and upset, especially as he liked the Millers, who were very good to him whenever he came their way or was camping near their store in the Shangani area.

There was another occasion on which he felt profoundly sorry for a mother wild dog. John Posselt, Hugh Miller and he, had been told that a litter of wild dog puppies was somewhere in the bush. So they got some labourers to dig them out. They usually use ant-bear holes in which to give birth, and nurse, their young. These ant-bear holes can be quite deep and long.

Anyhow they dug for about three hours and still had not reached the puppies, which they could all hear whimpering and moaning as they were by then very hungry. When evening was near they gave up digging, intending to come back next day to finish the job. By that time the hole they had dug was at least one and a half metre deep. They all bet that the mother would never jump in, or, if she should, in her mother's love, that she would never be able to come out again or free the puppies as they had put sticks and branches into the corridor leading to the lair, so they went to bed with full confidence in success next morning. They slept about one kilometre away at a kraal.

Coming back next day, they could not believe their eyes; the mother had jumped in, dug another corridor next to the blocked one and got the puppies. Furthermore, she must have worked the whole night to scratch enough soil into the deep hole to be able to jump out and take the puppies to safety. She put them into another ant-bear hole where they could hear them, but their admiration for that loving mother was so great that they decided not to interfere with her dear offspring again.

In those days the wild dogs were regarded as vermin and people were paid a pound per tail, presented to the DA's office as proof of killing. They certainly did a tremendous amount of damage, and indeed Father Odilo saw some dreadful things. One day, near Pongolo wild dogs messed up a herd of goats, killing one, tearing the udder from the second, wrenching a hind leg from a third, ripping an ear and half the head from yet another, and spilling the intestines of a fifth. "Why do they do that?" he asked.

"Because they tear pieces off as they run; they don't first kill and then eat like other predators," was the reply. "No, they just tear pieces out of the animal, eating whilst running. Eventually, of course, the victim will collapse and die."

CATCHING SNAKES

He also had some experiences with snakes. Indeed, he had quite a few! He caught snake specimens for Mr. Rea Smithers of the National Museum in Bulawayo, and found that he was ever so grateful. On one occasion, he had crossed the Shangani River, being on his way to Gomoza Primary School. Suddenly, his African guide jumped aside, horrified. He had almost stepped on a two metre banded cobra, which was lying on their footpath. He refused to go on, and so Father Odilo decided to kill it.

He cut down a sapling, and managed to get near enough to dispatch it, though it was rearing its head viciously and defiantly. He thought what a lovely specimen of a snake it was!

One afternoon he was pulling out weeds in the field when he picked up what he thought was a stick among the darnel. He quickly dropped it, though, when he realised he had just picked up a big puffadder!

One morning, a worker came and said there was a snake in the small shed. When they could not find it he assured Father Odilo that it was still there. "Well if it is still around then it can be in only one place, and that is that half metre of two-inch hose-pipe, which is lying on the floor," he thought. He took it into his hands and shook it, but there was no sign of a snake. He put his eyes to one end but could not see the daylight on the other side. So there was something inside, but he did not believe it was the snake.

Then he took a stick and poked it carefully into the hosepipe and felt there was something soft inside. He went with the snake, in the hosepipe, to his room, which had a cement floor and eventually managed to get it out. As the cement floor was very smooth the snake could not get a grip and so it could not move fast, tumbling from one side to the other, which enabled him to catch it by the tail and hold it up.

Though he had it by the very tip of the tail its head almost managed to reach his hand to bite him. Well, Mr. Rea-Smithers was very happy to get that catch, as he had no record of a rufus beaked snake in that part of the country.

One sunny day he gave his friend, Doug Francis, an insurance agent, a terrific fright. When he called at Fatima Mission, Father Odilo asked him to deliver a sack to the museum in Bulawayo. On getting to his car he asked, "What is in there?"

When he replied, "Oh, just half a dozen snakes," he almost jumped out of the window! But being a brave man he executed Father Odilo's wishes faithfully, for which he was very grateful to him.

One night, lying on his stretcher in a simple outschool, Matshiya, he heard a funny scratchy noise. He listened and listened again. When he was sure the sound came from under his bed, he got up, took his torch and had a look. Well, there was a metre long boomslang trying to creep into his bed.

One snake that he desisted from catching was over two metres long; it was a black mamba that came out of an ant-bear hole as he passed. He looked at it with great respect and it glanced at him with utter contempt and then slithered away, without effort, and at great speed. It probably thought to itself, 'let that chappie touch me, and see what will happen to him!'

In the same area, a young man was bitten at night by a black mamba and before Dr. Decker could do anything for him he was dead. The poison of this deadly snake is neuro-toxic and had quickly paralysed his respiratory system. He told her, "No! Black mambas are one snake I will not catch on principle!"

Once, he had just come back from a trip to Bulawayo, and was very tired as it had been a long drive in the lorry and the heat was sweltering. So he thought he would lie down for an hour on his simple bed in a tiny bedroom; it was no more than three metres by two metres, with only one small window for air and light.

As it was summer time he had only a white sheet on the bed. When he took it off, he saw something dark lying on the mattress. He did not look closely as he thought he had left his socks on the bed the day before. But before he could finish his thought, that 'something dark' slid under the pillow and he realised it was a snake. Luckily, it had not tried to bite him, which would have been easy, as his face was hardly twenty-five centimetres from it.

So, he went out and got two sticks to catch it. As he threw the pillow quickly off, the snake jumped out, fell on the floor and crept under his tiny wash table. He groped with his sticks and eventually was able to hold it down. As he did so, without being able to see it—the room was very dark—he felt a fine spray covering his face.

He just laughed about this and said, "You little so and so; I'll get you, just wait." With that, the snake spat straight in his mouth, and he experienced the very bitter and unpleasant taste of the poison. He ran quickly out to wash his mouth with fresh milk and then came back—a wiser and more careful man. He caught it without much difficulty—a spitting cobra about a metre and a half long.

He had a little house, of Kimberley bricks with a grass roof, built between some beautiful Mopani trees. One day, as he stood under them, two twig snakes, which had apparently been fighting with each other on the branches, suddenly fell down; right on his head, but before he could get hold of them, they slid away with great speed as they are very fast snakes. "No doubt they were as much surprised as I was, by this unexpected meeting," he told Brother Athanasius.

Father Odilo got used to catching snakes, and so in due course he got rather careless. Thus, one day, when he saw a small snake under a heap of stones he tried to get it with his finger into a cigarette box, but it managed to bite him on his left thumb. As it was a very small snake, only about ten centimetres long, he did not take much notice and carried on with his work.

At teatime, he told Dr. Decker that a snake had bitten him and she asked him to come immediately to the hospital for an injection. But he replied, "It was so small, I don't think that's necessary."

The doctor was very cross with him. "Well, do what you think best, but I really think you are being foolish."

He carried on working, and his thumb swelled more and more, and gradually two red lines crept up his arm and the lymph glands of his armpit began to swell and hurt. Eventually, he went back to Dr. Decker. "I think I need your help," he admitted sheepishly.

"You foolish, arrogant, idiot of a priest," she called him all sorts of names, which he knew he deserved. "The injection will not help much any more."

His thumb almost rotted away, so that the doctors wanted to amputate it. By then it smelled quite rotten. He suggested, "I think you must shelve the idea of an amputation, at least for a few more days. The stench cannot get worse anyhow."

And indeed, after three or four days it began to improve and after three weeks he was able to leave the hospital. It had been a burrowing adder!

Stinging Insects

He had a similar experience with an insect, although he never found out what it was. As he picked up a sack one day, he was stung and the sting must have hit a nerve. The sensation was terrifying; he felt the pain crawl from the tip of his left forefinger up the arm into his chest and round the heart. It was so severe that he almost fainted. He was afraid he might suffer heart failure. He quickly lay down, calling for the doctor, but before medical help came the pain eased off and he was almost immediately back to normal.

He also had several experiences with scorpions, and developed a cautious and sensible habit of checking his footwear each morning. A couple of times he was actually stung and suffered excruciating pain for several days.

Chapter 12

Drastic Changes

Why Empandeni?

"Father Odilo, I am sorry to do this to you," Father Andrew said, without any sign of remorse. "I know you are right in the middle of so much at Fatima and it is a difficult time to move you."

This had been a hastily arranged meeting. He had not been due for a visit until two weeks time, and somehow there was usually a quiet spell after Christmas in the life of the missions. The idea of moving now seemed a bit illogical and he wondered what it was all about.

Father Andrew had taken over the reins when the ageing Bishop, Ignatius Arnoz, had resigned the year before, and he was now still very much at the helm.

"Father Andrew, why do you wish to move me?" he asked, realising that he was possibly being a bit impertinent. It was not that he wanted to be disrespectful in any way—after all, this man was effectively the bishop, even if he had not been appointed as one. He had the authority, and he had certainly been shaking up the missions!

Father Andrew coughed and shifted on the rickety old chair. The others had gone off after lunch, and he had asked Father Odilo to remain with him. He took another sip of his dark coffee before answering.

"I don't want to go into details, but I have to do something about Empandeni," he said, rather brusquely.

Father Odilo was sitting straight-necked, with the alert look of an eagle. What was he going to hear? He needed more to go on; to just fly off from where he was so busy and needed, just did not make sense.

Perhaps the unspoken questions reached him, because he saw Father Andrew take another sip of coffee, before clearing his throat. "It has become necessary to shake up Empandeni—the people have been there far too long," he said. "I am moving you to replace Father Conrad Atzwanger. I need you to be the Rector."

Perhaps something had happened at Empandeni Mission, and he was clearly not saying what it was. His obedience restrained him from insisting on more answers, but his instincts cried out against this irrational move.

He wondered for a while if he himself had been found wanting in some way. Had he done something, which Father Andrew had considered wrong? He was a strict priest, and he knew that some of those under his authority at Fatima could find reason to complain about that. He had seen their reaction to his discipline, but he expected them to give of their best, and to do things properly.

A crazy thought came and went. 'Doctor Davis-Ziegler; could Father Andrew think there was something improper going on?' He dismissed the notion as ridiculous. 'No, I do not think the problem is here at Fatima. We have a good community. We live together like a good religious family. We celebrate daily Mass together, and all of us work tirelessly to look after the Africans in our care, and build up this new mission.'

As if relenting, Father Andrew's voice broke in, "you have been doing a good job here, Father Odilo; it is important that you take control and do the same at Empandeni. You will have a good team of colleagues, and Father Possenti Weggartner will continue as the Principal; he has lots of experience, and I know you will work well with him."

"When do you want me to move?" he asked, having calculated that he needed a good three months to hand over properly and ensure that the hospital construction was left in good hands. At least they had just built this little three-roomed house, and the primary school was operating. But, without the hospital building being finished, Doctor Davis was already agitated; any delays would aggravate that, and they could not afford to lose her.

The answer caused him to raise his eyebrows in an instinctive reaction that he could not conceal. "Next month?" he almost spluttered.

"Yes," Father Andrew replied, "that is when you are needed at Empandeni."

"Father Andrew, there is a lot to be done here," he explained respectfully. "We have been promised the funds by Harry Schur, matched by the Beit Trust." He knew Donald McIntyre fairly well, and his letter had arrived to confirm the donation only a few weeks before. "Brother Athanasius started the foundations ages ago. We simply must get on and finish this hospital."

The withering look from Father Andrew did not allow any further discussion. The decision had clearly been taken. Now, he knew he risked disobedience if he pushed any further. "More coffee, Father?" he offered.

"No thanks. I must do a brief tour and then drive back to the Cathedral," he answered peremptorily.

Obedience

As the dust hung in the still air, the Ford motor car reflected snatches of sunlight as it bounced its way from the mission and on to the twin ribbons of tarred strip road. "It is incredible," Doctor Davis blurted out. "I cannot understand it. And who is he to take these decisions anyway? Nobody has appointed him as the bishop!"

"You know that I am not happy to leave at this time," he said, "but I must obey. Besides there will be other missionaries taking over anyway, and things will soon be finished."

"We shall see," was her retort.

"Please excuse me," he said, as he made his way to his room. It was neat but full; it also served as a storeroom and office, and all that he had was neatly stacked in the confined space. At his table, he opened his prayer book, flipping through the pages. He soon came to a well-worn place and read the psalm.

Immediately his response was clarified. 'Here I am Lord . . . ', he answered in prayer.

EMPANDENI MISSION

Well, despite this acceptance, he was not happy, that's for sure. But he was obliged to obey. Now, he just had to get his attitude right and get on with it. In the next week, he was like a whirlwind. He gave himself no rest at all, as he planned the materials needed, explained how hard he wanted the bricks baked, and generally drilled the team of builders and workers.

'What a desolate place,' he first thought as he was driven into Empandeni, on a road that was so bumpy and dusty that it had a cheek to be even called a track! Hauled away from the fertile and active missions of the Lupane area, this was a real comedown. 'Still, it is all part of my duty, and God knows why I am sent here,' he soon pulled his thoughts back in obedience.

He greeted his colleagues cheerfully, and was pleased that he would be living with such a big group, many of them Germans.

The African people seemed friendly enough as they shook hands with him, but he noticed a difference in manner from what he was accustomed to. Some of the men seemed to completely avert their eyes, looking away from him. He knew this was often a sign of great respect, a cultural acknowledgement that the other person was too honoured for him to be looked in the eye. But this was different; he felt that these people were hiding their true feelings. 'What are they thinking?' he soon started to wonder, as this continued.

They were a large and happy community at Empandeni Mission, but naturally, he changed a few things. 'Wasn't that one of the main reasons that he had been sent—to shake things up a little bit?'

The early morning call to prayer was soon more strictly enforced, and they prayed in community. "I know you consider private prayer just as good,' he explained to one of the Sisters who voiced her discomfort at the change.

"However, we must improve our community life; I have noticed a tendency for some people to avoid one another's company, and that is not how Jesus taught His apostles to live." Soon everybody attended daily mass and then joined in together for breakfast.

The hired teachers were encouraged to join in; most of them were Catholics, and willingly joined in. Father Possenti ran the school, and his cheerful discipline was well received. But even there, Father Odilo insisted on cleaner classrooms, and soon the books were being stacked with greater care.

By now, Father Odilo had developed an interrogation technique of his own for catechism lessons. Those children who had not learned their responses were called up to the front of the class, and a light twisting of an ear was used to focus their attention. It seemed to work well, and an improvement in learning was soon apparent; his routine of class visits assured the teachers of a disciplinary example, which most considered very useful in the crowded classrooms.

The Big Reshuffle

Soon after he arrived at Empandeni Mission, the phone rang, and he had received the news, "Bishop Arnoz has died." He was dumbstruck; he knew the retired bishop had been ill, but he was far from being frail and elderly, or ready to die. He still lived at the Cathedral, and had recently gone for treatment, but that had been a normal enough thing; besides, there were good hospital and professional people about to care for most things.

"What happened?" they asked him.

"It seems he must have picked up malaria when he visited his old friend, Monsignor Flynn, a Capuchin, at Livingstone. It flared up when he was back in Bulawayo. In fact, he had only been back for three days." He paused sadly for a few moments, and then added, "Somehow, he left it a bit long and the doctor did not diagnose it."

"That's ridiculous! Any doctor should have picked that up," said Brother Korbinian angrily.

"I suppose they should have reacted sooner. After all it is the rainy season, and Livingstone is a known malaria area." added Brother Ceslaus.

"Well, somehow it was too late," explained Father Odilo. "It quickly developed into a high fever and he died from cerebral malaria."

There was a lot of sadness that this could happen, but nothing could be done about it. "When is the funeral?" asked Father Possenti quietly, and the mood changed.

"I shall hear later today, but it will certainly be at the Cathedral. However, I understand he is to be buried here at Empandeni."

The next morning, as the 'go-away' birds fluttered clumsily in the foliage outside his room, he washed, shaved and dressed, and went outside for a walk. He wanted the peace of the bush, as he prayed a rosary for the bishop. He walked down the dusty road, with the early morning sunshine breaking through the Mopani and thorn trees. The air was still and the green leaves hung brightly open and waiting for the warmth of the day.

His fingers pressed the beads as he counted the Hail Mary's, and his mind wandered from time to time from the Sorrowful Mysteries he had chosen to pray. Jesus' suffering made anything we ever had to experience seem so small and insignificant; and yet, he knew he could offer up his sorrow for the death of a colleague and superior. His own acceptance of the cross of dutiful obedience was lighter when he accepted and offered it up as well.

Another pair of 'go-away birds' flew off, without their usual warning call, as he walked into the bush towards an anthill. Under the *wag 'n bietjie,* (wait-a-bit), tree, he nearly slipped and fell as his feet went gliding over the hard round balls of those uMphafa seeds. He looked back towards the Mission, and realised he soon needed to start back to be in time to say Holy Mass for them. The trees were smaller and more sparse than those in the Lupane area, mostly Mopani trees, but they made him recall the walking and cycling that he had grown accustomed to there. As he finished the rosary, he offered a prayer for the work and the people of Fatima, wondering how the building was getting on.

THE MISSION SCHOOL

Empandeni is the oldest mission in the province. The Jesuit missionary, Father Prestage, had initiated the mission, patiently, and eventually had secured permission from King Lobengula, even before the King granted mineral concessions to Cecil John Rhodes. Soon after, the Company had granted them a large tract of land, and they had farmed it and developed the schools. Empandeni Mission had begun in the dry and harsh bush, well south of the future railway line from Cape Town, via Mafeking and Bechuanaland, (later Botswana).

Twenty years earlier, the Mariannhillers had taken over the mission, in an unhappy exchange of territory, when the Jesuits insisted that the order's Natal and Zulu origins equipped them better to work with the Matabele. The Notre Dame Sisters ran the nearby out-school for Coloureds, Embakwe. Father Urban Staudacher was the second Rector, and the first motorised Mariannhiller, with his 2-ton lorry. When he left in 1942, Bishop Arnoz commended him for having 'urbanised' Embakwe! The Precious Blood Sisters had taken over the school at Empandeni; it soon grew until it was changed to a secondary school and they also developed a teacher training college.

Father Possenti Weggartner had endured a period of internment in Canada, as he had been studying in England at the outbreak of the war. Upon his release, he was re-assigned here, as the Diocesan Education Officer and he was made the designated principal, in charge of various mission schools.

Teachers were not always easy to obtain, and some came from as far away as Salisbury. Father Konrad Atzwanger had set a great example in building and development with all that he had done at the schools and missions.

One morning, when Father Odilo arrived at the office, a sturdily built young teacher of medium height, brushed past him, without the courtesies that are normal in African society. He wondered what was different about him; something caught his attention as he watched him swinging his long arms in a soldierly manner, striding along the dusty pathway.

'Oh well. The school is Father Possenti's domain,' he thought to himself, knowing that he did not have much to do with the teachers, and also having only been there a very short time since his arrival.

Something was wrong though, and he sensed an angry atmosphere as he glanced again at the retreating figure. This man was particularly dark, and what struck him the most was the way his large head was set in a haughty and defiant manner. When he entered the office, Father Odilo asked Father Possenti, "what's the matter with that fellow?"

"Oh, nothing much. Robert was just muttering something about his birthday. I must say, I have never really figured him out," he continued. "I had to tell him that you want everybody at the funeral service." Father Odilo was silent, piecing his impressions together.

Father Possenti continued, "He's a bright fellow, brought up by the Jesuits and did some teaching at Kutama. I think he is off to Fort Hare; he's quite well qualified, but a bit too political for me. I believe his mother is a very devout and saintly woman, but he doesn't seem to like my authority."

"Oh well, you can't please everybody. I need to talk to you about the children's places at the service. Let's go and have a look at the church and the area around it," he said, and they went off together to confirm the funeral arrangements.

THE BISHOP'S FUNERAL

Bishop Chichester came down from Salisbury to conduct the funeral service, as Father Andrew was too distraught to compose himself for this sad occasion; he just could not believe that his bishop had died so soon, and so needlessly. "Father Odilo," he had said, "I need your help. Please drive in early on Saturday, and take over as Master of Ceremonies for me. I just cannot manage."

"Of course, Father Andrew," he replied with deference and understanding.

Bishop Ignatius Arnoz had served the missions diligently for many years, and everybody knew him well. He had been a firm leader and worked tirelessly. Even after his retirement, he had always been there; Father Andrew relied on him heavily, and it had been re-assuring to know this support was there. Father Odilo remembered how he had eventually been able to use his influence to break the impasse over a Mission site for Fatima Mission.

There were several bishops on the altar, from around the country, as well as from South Africa. His mind wandered during the sad service, and he heard that things were not going well at Fatima. The same old P.C. had been obstinate enough with the Mariannhillers, but the Spanish Missionaries were treated even worse, it seemed. The British bureaucrats of Rhodesia could not help thinking about General Franco, the Spanish dictator, even though these Spaniards were here as Catholic missionaries, and had nothing to do with General Franco!

The priests themselves were very good and zealous people, although he himself remembered how difficult it had been to get Father Rubio to agree to his own way of doing things. Perhaps he had been a bit too insistent himself—he knew he was inclined to be a bit too forceful for some people's liking. A smile crossed his face, as he remembered how Father Possenti had analysed the situation.

"Ah, the Spanish," he had said, "they are wonderful Catholics; but they are so cocky!" His face creased in a broad smile. "Do you know they are absolutely convinced that when they get to heaven, the language spoken there is sure to be Spanish!"

RE-ASSIGNED, AFTER 100 DAYS

Before the end of the first school term, Father Andrew came on one of his routine visits to the missions. They went for a brief walking tour of the mission grounds, before Father Andrew said, "Let's get ourselves a cup of coffee."

Dusting his feet on the small woven grass mat, he carefully mounted the small step into the dining hall. They continued to make small talk over coffee and biscuits for a while. "You have been doing a good job here," Father Andrew permitted himself, by way of passing a compliment.

"Thank you, Father," Father Odilo replied.

"Can we go to the office for a chat?" he asked, as he promptly led the way to the priests' house.

As soon as they had settled in the wooden armchairs, he coughed and began to speak. "Things have not been going fast enough with Fatima, I'm afraid."

This was not news to Father Odilo—the grapevine had already told him that the hospital project had stalled completely. It even looked as if the funds might be withdrawn because of this.

"Our Spanish colleagues are having second thoughts about their ability to look after Fatima, with such a big hospital. I know they are having a hard time in government circles; the old Spanish-English conflicts are not over."

Father Odilo admired them as great fellows, these three Spanish priests. He knew how zealous and good these men were; they lived very closely with the people, and had been quick to learn their customs and language.

"That Father James seems too casual to me," said Father Andrew.

"Well, we are none of us perfect," Father Odilo replied defensively, "and Father Prieto is a great man as well. I know we have enough difficulty dealing with the bureaucrats; I just think it is a bit harder for them right now."

Father Andrew seemed to pause to consider this, and the silence started to become uncomfortable.

"How is Dr. Davis?" Father Odilo asked.

"She is well, but she is getting impatient," Father Andrew replied. "I am also a bit worried that she will lose motivation the way things are going."

"The new hospital is vital," Father Odilo said spiritedly. His strong interest was difficult to conceal, and he leaned forward on his chair, as he continued, "There are thousands of Africans needing help, and they have to go all the way to Bulawayo, or Wankie to get it. The money has been arranged; the building is started; and we even have a doctor. It simply has to be pushed and completed!"

Father Andrew moved about a bit, to make himself more comfortable on the hard wooden chair, before revealing his solution. "I believe you will be more useful back at Fatima; I know you have only been here for about three months now, but I intend moving you again." He stopped and looked at Father Odilo momentarily, before glancing away.

Father Odilo felt like getting up and doing a happy little jig, but he kept his composure. Somehow, he felt wonderfully vindicated. Moving him to Empandeni had never made sense to him. He had done his best, and he knew he had been useful; but the hospital could have been well on its way to completion by now.

He had come to understand a bit more of Father Andrew's technique now. There had certainly been a lot of discussion at Empandeni, in this large community, some of whom were quite outspoken in their ideas. Fatima and the Lupane area had become quite synonymous with Father Odilo. 'If only they could see that it is all for God,' he thought, when he guessed what was on some people's minds. 'I don't think I am doing anything for myself—I certainly do not look for praise and thanks, although a little bit helps, now and again.'

At the time when he had done his planning, he had established that in an area of nearly four thousand square miles, there was a population of over fifty thousand Africans. There were no schools or hospitals within reach of them. Furthermore, and right at the top of his priorities, they had not heard about Jesus Christ. Their chance of being saved and brought to heaven depended upon missionaries, and so little had yet been done.

Father Andrew surprised him again, when this time he said, "And what is more, I want you to be there next weekend; that gives you a good ten days to hand over here, to your old friend, Father Josef Ebert."

"I will be pleased to obey," he agreed with carefully restrained joy. He wasted no time in telling his colleagues, and especially Father Elmar Schmid, over at Embakwe.

The sun was descending, but it was still so hot that the rain puddles everywhere were adding to the clammy air, and his shirt was drenched with dark perspiration as he stood waving farewell. Storm clouds were building up again, assembling into those giant water-laden clouds, with dark bases and tall white tops. It would soon be pouring with rain again, scouring the earth from among the stunted trees and bushes, and making parts of the gravel road impassable. He hoped Father Andrew would not get stuck, and would arrive safely at the strip road, which ran alongside the rail line, from Plumtree back to Bulawayo.

Looking east, to where it had been raining earlier, he took in the beauty of a broken rainbow. It was a good sign, he was sure, and he thanked God for his re-posting to Fatima.

When he chatted with his colleagues at supper, there was much jollity. Father Possenti had done a quick calculation and he announced, "at last, Napoleon's hundred days are over, and he will leave us!" There was good-natured laughter from everyone, and Father Odilo was beaming with delight.

"I have enjoyed being with you all immensely, and I will miss you," he said. "However, you all know that I have felt frustrated and anxious about Fatima; I cannot wait to get back and invite you soon to the opening of the new hospital."

There were cheers of genuine appreciation, and a happy mood prevailed in the few days of packing and leaving. The Ford truck was loaded with his few effects and various parcels and files which he had to deliver to the Cathedral en route. He had delivered a most encouraging sermon at Holy Mass, and given everyone his solemn and sincere blessing; now he waved fondly to his friends as his light dust-trail billowed and blew in the morning wind.

He reached the strip road, and was soon happily on his way northeast back to Bulawayo, with the sun now high overhead. Coming to Figtree, his mind went back to his arrival by train—the railway line ran alongside him to the left; part of Rhodes' ambition to link the Cape to Cairo for the British Empire. He remembered reading somewhere that the contractor, George Pauling had laid the last four hundred miles of that line from Mafeking to Bulawayo in only four hundred days. As he drove alongside the line, he realised just how fast that had been—and to sustain that pace for over a year; those were men after his own heart. Now it was time for him to get busy again!

He also thought about his friend, Father Elmar Schmid who had been there from 1948 to 1960 and had really loved this mission. He had travelled up with him when they had come to Rhodesia together on this railway line. They were parting company again, leaving him behind where he was planning to build a large dam to relieve the constant water crisis.

When he had settled back in Fatima, he soon found out there was a lot still to be done. He had to revive his old building teams, and get the brick-making operations going much faster. Despite his generosity, Harry Schur was not an easy man to deal with. Every purchase had to be accounted for in detail, and he released payment item by item—this was not a case of him simply saying, "here's my gift of three thousand pounds; go and use it well."

This was an amazing man, though, and Father Odilo admired his grit and the drive, which had made him so successful. He was a Lithuanian Jew, who had made his way by hard work and the clever use of life's opportunities. He was so unpretentious in the way he dressed, that many people thought he was poor. The story of the Grand Hotel was a lovely anecdote and he thought how true to character it was. Despite his financial success, there just had to be something much more to the man.

FATIMA HOSPITAL OPENING

The work went with great gusto, and the driving force was this young German priest, a man with a determined vision. Walls were built up to eaves height, and plastered. Timbers were laid and firmly wired in around the eaves. Roof trusses were made on site, from Canadian pine planks; as they were erected, they were tied back and braced and the brandering was nailed on.

In the evening, with the insistent buzz of the mosquitoes in his ears, he climbed the little hillock and looked down on the long, low roof structure. He was delighted, and it reminded him of some sort of skeleton. He remembered a prophetic passage that he liked, 'send forth your spirit and they shall be created, and thou shalt renew the face of the earth.' He could imagine life being breathed into this building and he was sure that many lives would be helped and saved under this roof, with God's spiritual blessing and the practical 'flesh' on the bones of their dream, their mission.

By the middle of the year, the new Fatima Hospital was ready, and after Easter the following year, it was dedicated at its official opening in 1951. Like the actual process of building, the opening was anticipated and planned well, and became a very special occasion. It was most gratifying to see how the invitations were accepted, and several hundred people arrived to show their support and encouragement, at the opening ceremonies. Archbishop Lucas, the Apostolic Delegate, even came up from Pretoria, and many priests and sisters came from all over the country.

Many dignitaries were present, officials of the Southern Rhodesia Government, His Excellency, Governor Kennedy, many European friends, plus Chiefs Mabikwa and Gumede and a vast gathering of Africans. The Minister of Health, Mr. Winter, was there. The Secretary for Health, Dr. Richard Morris, was there; he was a fine man whom Father Odilo had come to know quite well from the time when he was at the General Hospital in Bulawayo. "Good to see you again, Richard; so good of you to come," he greeted him warmly.

"I would not have missed this for anything," he replied. "Well done; you have done a great job here. This is going to be a tremendous hospital, and I am sure your mission will prosper for the benefit of us all."

The Medical Treasurer, Mr. Powyss-Jones, was delighted to witness this achievement, very conscious also of the great fiscal savings. "If you only knew how tightly our finances are stretched," he said, "it would give you a better idea of how much we appreciate your Church's work, Father Odilo." He thanked the Catholic Church, the benefactors who made this possible, and especially the man whom he commended as the driving force who made sure the vision became a reality. "Badly needed as this hospital is, it might have never come about within the limits of our tax revenue and with government purse strings pulled so tight in these difficult times."

The local community had experienced the benefits of the limited help that had already been possible. Many smiling faces showed off brilliant white teeth, and mothers carried cheerful little children. Elderly African men and women had been rescued from the danger of malaria and other illnesses, which may otherwise have ended their lives.

Chief Mabikwa[vii] and Chief Gumede had been very enthusiastic, and had both put their full weight and support firmly behind this missionary—'he who charged through the bush', and appeared out of nowhere in the most remote parts of their districts, often on foot, or his black and chrome bicycle. They had their own retinues with them, and the large crowd of local Africans swelled and murmured happily in the forest clearing, among the Gwayi teak trees, a low dust playing about their legs, and the air buzzing with happy Ndebele voices.

Serious speeches of congratulations and good wishes were followed by a special dedication service, and its prayers and singing. The women rose up together and danced, some of them only scantily clad, but all with great dignity and decorum. They swayed to the rhythm of Africa, their voices and bodies in perfect harmony. The rhythm of Africans was natural; it seemed as if it had been born in them. Even the little children, those that could stand anyway, stood and moved with the drums and the singing. Their little hands moved gracefully and with a childish simplicity, and Father Odilo thought to himself, 'these are such good people. Thank you God, for giving me the chance to help them and to bring them closer to you.'

As they danced past, in time to the music, close to the veranda and the seated guests, he watched their beautiful, serene faces; and the way the young girls averted their eyes modestly. One of the schoolgirls looked up and saw he had recognised her. She smiled at him, respectfully, and the brilliant flash of white teeth contrasted beautifully against her dark skin. Her tightly curled black hair covered her head neatly; it was so truly practical, and the epitome of Africa's people.

He saw a mother holding her little daughter in her arms, and the girl was using her hands to make the same graceful movements which the other girls and women were using. The older girl next to them had a baby on her hips; their mother was probably dancing. Another group of mothers had their children strapped onto their backs with cloth. It was the perfect way to carry a child; the child was pressed lovingly to its mother, in an intimate closeness, and she could still carry on with her duties and move about with her child always present and easy to care for.

One of the babies started to get restless, and began whimpering slightly. He saw the mother stretch her hand behind her, and gently pat its little bottom to soothe it. She moved her body up and down, rocking the baby, and it was soon pacified and sleeping again. The patience and love of these mothers truly touched him. They were really good women; how happily they were able to relate to Our Lady, the mother of Our Lord.

A little while later he saw the same mother swing the baby off her back, around to the front, and without any feeling of self-consciousness, she was feeding the infant. Everything a child needed was right there. The mother looked serene and fulfilled, and he guessed there must be a great feeling of really being needed and loved by her baby, as it sucked happily at her breast.

He saw a little girl walk nearby with her mother. She must have just fallen and grazed her forearm in the last week or so, and the skin from underneath was a pink contrast against her own shining brown skin.

Some of the African women wore dresses, and a few even had hats for the occasion. Some of the African men wore suits, but many of them were unclothed above the waist. The little children mostly had something tied around their middle, and sat or walked about entirely naturally. When they needed to, the children unashamedly fingered their nostrils; even the adults did the same, unfettered by the European custom of blowing into cloths.

Meanwhile, it had taken a long time to find somebody to be the new bishop of Bulawayo. Father Odilo was one of those who were considered, but he asked not to be given this honour and its duties. He preferred to be among the people, doing what he did best. He was especially delighted when he heard the news, "Father Adolph Schmitt has been chosen to become our Bishop. He will soon arrive from the USA."

Father Odilo wondered if Bishop Schmitt had responded like their own founder, Abbot Francis, who had seen the reluctance of his colleagues to go to Africa, and he had stood up to answer, "if nobody else goes, I will go!"

THE IMPOSSIBLE SPEAR

One night, some years later, Dr. Decker, who had meanwhile moved to nearby Saint Paul's Hospital, Shangani, was called to attend to a man who had a spear in his head. "How did this happen?" she asked. The men with him explained, "We were at a beer drink, and another man started quarrelling with him. During the argument, the second man took his spear and rammed it into his head just missing the eye."

When Dr. Decker and Brother Conrad got there in the very early hours of the morning, after a terrible drive over impossible roads, they were flabbergasted and did not know what to do, as it was impossible to extract the spear.

After some deliberation they put him on the back of the vanette and Brother Conrad held the spear as carefully as he possibly could, resting it on his shoulders to avoid the worst shocks and vibrations resulting from the bad road. When they arrived at the Mission hospital, after hours of anxiety, they cut the long shaft of the spear off with a saw, leaving only a small piece sticking out of the head of the poor victim. When morning dawned, they carefully transported him to Mpilo Hospital, Bulawayo, over a hundred and fifty miles away. With the grace of God, they arrived safely, with no further damage done to the sore head of the poor man.

X-rays were taken immediately which showed that no essential damage had been done, as the spear had missed both brain and eye by a fraction of an inch. The spear was skilfully removed and the man was very lucky to be alive.

ELEPHANT

Elephant, the most magnificent of all the African animals, had been a constant feature of the area over the years. Father Odilo was chased many times by them, and luckily always got away. But on one occasion, he was in grave danger, as a huge bull came straight for his little Ford. It came with unusually fast speed and with its trunk against its body (and when they do that they mean real business; in other words it was not just a mock-attack.). How he got away he didn't know.

Elephant are the most magnificent animals in the world

On another occasion it was even more dangerous; not for him, but for Dr. Decker and the other occupants of their car. This was in the Wankie National Park. The Apostolic Delegate, Monsignor Damiano, paid them a visit at Fatima Hospital and in recognition for their hospitality, he took them to the Game Park. He, Dr. Decker, Dr. Davis and Sister Ann, and one or two more of the staff went in the Delegate's car, whilst Father Possenti, and Father Odilo travelled in a small pick-up.

Dr. Decker realized that Father Possenti and Father Odilo had not seen a small herd of elephant standing under a tree, as the two of them had moved ahead, following with their eyes the graceful leaps of two duikers. She knocked on the door of her car trying to attract their attention, but they were too far away already to hear it.

However, the knocking on the door upset the leading bull elephant, and it became quite incensed, running straight up to their car. The car had stalled just at that moment—and the enormous bull elephant put its trunk on the car, trying to put its head through the windows. These were luckily closed, but it sniffed up and down all over the vehicle.

The occupants thought their last hour had come. By God's grace and the urgent intervention of their guardian angels the elephant left after about five minutes. Naturally, their hearts were still doing record beats half an hour later.

Once, he was sleeping at Gomoza School, beyond the Shangani, when some elephants came and rubbed themselves against the wall of the small building. The clay was falling out of the pole and mud wall, and he was very worried that the building might collapse upon him at any moment.

The funniest encounter with elephants, however, happened to him many years later, at the Main Camp of the Wankie National Park. As he drove to his lodge at night, his companion, Geoff Archer, and his nephew, Max and his wife Clementa, saw what they thought were tarpaulins swinging from a tree. What they saw were in fact the huge flapping ears of an elephant that had wandered into the main camp to eat his favourite pods off the camelthorn trees. "I still can't understand how I managed to avoid hitting him," he confessed.

The animals in the Park were quite curious;
a giraffe inspecting the Ford

PART THREE

Father Odilo went on leave to Germany and returned to a new era of his life, and a country racked by successive changes. He continued in service, and his mature years continued to yield a great harvest for his missionary order.

"Ecce Venio"

"Ich bin bereit"

"Behold, I come"

CHAPTER 13

HALF-TIME

A NEW SHEPHERD

Bishop Adolph Schmitt pondered long and hard. Since the time he had arrived from America to serve again in Southern Rhodesia, there had been a lot of changes both in the country and the Church. What had not changed was the enormous amount, which needed to be done, and he was responsible for ministering to a huge territory, with so few priests. He viewed this as a great challenge and humbly accepted that he had been chosen for this important task.

The map on his wall showed his parishes, missions, hospitals and schools. He stood looking at the map one morning after the early weekday Holy Mass, and said to himself, 'the map does not show me the people, the priests, sisters and other helpers. Who are they, and how are they coping?'

As a man of action, he had soon arranged meetings with those who were in or close to town and then he set out to pay individual visits to all those who were far away. His presence was an instant and strong re-assurance; the clergy all recognised that a new shepherd with a clear and wise outlook was in their midst.

Father Odilo was especially pleased, as were those who had met the bishop before, mostly at Wurzburg, where many of them had studied. "My Lord Bishop, it is a pleasure to see you again," he welcomed him warmly. After a few reminiscences and the usual social chit-chat, they discussed the mission needs and work, and then Bishop Schmitt asked, "How is your health, Odilo?"

"I am fine," he gave his assurance. "I am coping well, although not quite as well as I used to manage."

"And why is that?"

"I seem to have a few minor illnesses." The bishop waited, and it was clear that he should continue. "Well, I have had malaria quite a few times; this has had a bit of an effect on me," he said.

"Well, you know what? I have been watching you while we have been meeting. You are far from well." He paused, and studied Father Odilo's reaction. He saw his eyes look down, and his shoulders settle, as he adjusted his position in his seat.

However, he responded, "it is nothing serious, my Lord. I am just getting over a mild bout of fever, and will soon be fully fit and strong again."

"Have you seen a doctor lately?"

"Yes, I saw Dr. Shee a few months ago. He is a wonderful doctor, and he checked me over thoroughly."

"And what did he say?"

"He said I have been affected by malaria and he has also been treating me for bilharzia. You know it is quite common here, and makes one feel a bit drowsy. Of course, like all doctors, he said I should rest a bit, but I think he knew that was not very practical." Seeing the bishop's questioning gaze, he continued, "but I have been resting, you know. I must admit that I have been taking an afternoon nap on a Saturday, just for an hour or so; but it has helped."

"Well, I want you to go and see Dr. Shee again. And then you are to come and report to me, before you drive back out to Fatima Mission. Is that clear?"

"Yes, my lord."

"And, by the way, I am appointing Father Heribald to assist you at Saint Luke's. I know you will approve of him and enjoy his company." He stood up to signal that the interview had ended, and came around his desk to shake Father Odilo's hand. "We need to look after good priests like you. God bless," he added warmly.

Father Odilo set off from the Cathedral, on his walk to Dr. Shee's rooms, down the gently sloping Ninth Avenue pavements, with the sun still low in the sky. The parking bays were lined with Jacaranda trees and a few Flamboyant trees. It was the end of winter, and the trees that were sprouting new leaves would soon begin flowering. A stiff wind was gusting, and blowing the fine little leaves about on the concrete pavement. He looked at the time on the City Hall clock, and noticed that the Union Jack flag was fluttering noisily as he walked past the shop-front windows of Haddon and Sly.

He felt a few of his aches as he walked, and offered them up to God; these were his own little crosses, but so small compared to the sufferings Our Lord has borne for us. He had always been a strong and athletic man, so he did not feel out of breath for very long after he sat and waited for a few minutes before being admitted. "Come through, Father Odilo," the smiling young lady said, as she led the way and handed a folder over to the doctor.

"Hallo, Father Odilo," he was welcomed cheerfully. "I don't see much of you here, so what can I do for you?"

"I would like a general check-up," he asked. "Bishop Schmitt insisted, although I think I know what the problems are, and I am coping fine."

"Well, what are the problems, then?" asked Dr. Shee with a respectful smile. He knew Father Odilo, as he knew many of the other priests and sisters. This was not a man who admitted to being laid low. If he was sick, he might admit that, but he never let it stop him from doing his work, saying Mass daily, visiting his schools, giving catechism classes and visiting people in hospital.

"I think the malaria has not left me completely," he began. I have occasional bouts of sweats and chills; I suppose these are just typical malaria fevers, but I take my quinine and I am soon back in action. I sometimes get a bit frustrated at the way I quickly become exhausted. I just do not really feel myself," he admitted.

Dr. Shee cast a professional scrutiny over him, as he continued with a few general questions. He could see how recurrent bouts of malaria had worn him down and debilitated him.

"Do you swim in the pools or rivers?" Dr. Shee asked.

"Of course."

"I want to check you for bilharzia,' the doctor told him. "It is almost inevitable, and most of those small rivers and stagnant pools are infected. People urinate near the streams, and it is passed on until nearly everybody gets it."

After a few more examinations, he said, "well, get dressed now, and I want you to come and see me again on Tuesday, please."

Sure enough, bilharzia was finally diagnosed, and he was given a series of intra- muscular injections. He asked the administering sister, "What is the name of this medicine?"

She refused to tell him what the name was. Upon further pressure, she said, "Salvarzan. I feel terribly embarrassed as it is also used to treat syphilis."

Father Odilo replied, "What is that?" and had a good laugh!

Bilharzia had taken a heavy toll and what he really needed was a good long rest; but how could a priest ever get that, especially now?

On his next visit, he obeyed orders as he was told, "well, take off your shirt, and hop up there for me to examine you." Doctor Shee closed the folder on his desk, and came across to the examination table; he rubbed the stethoscope on his white jacket to take off some of the chill and began listening to Father Odilo's chest.

"Breathe in."

"Fine. A deep breath now," and so it went for a good few minutes. He breathed in and out and coughed obediently, and went "aaah!" on command, as Dr. Shee looked down his throat. "I need samples to send away for testing. Do you think you can pass some urine for me? Nip into the toilet over there and use the little bottle with your name on it; you will see it on the shelf."

Then he drew a sample of blood and went on to check his pulse and blood pressure. Finally he hooked him up with little suckers and electric wires to check his heart on his latest bit of equipment, an ECG machine.

"You are not the only one who has been seeing me quite a bit lately," he said. "I have had a few of you priests in to see me, on Bishop Schmitt's orders. I will confer with your doctor, Bernard Pepper, but I want you to come back to me on Friday. I will have all your test results, and then we can discuss things," he said as he dismissed Father Odilo, with a friendly invitation, "it would also be great if you can make it to dinner with me and my family on Friday night. Can you manage?"

"Thank you, Jimmy. That will be a pleasure, but I have to call somewhere first. Will seven-thirty be all right?" he asked.

"Absolutely fine, Father. I look forward to seeing you then. If it's all right with you, I think I'll ask Bernard to come as well. I know we can enjoy a good social evening together."

"Thank you," he smiled, "and please, give my love to Kitty and all your lovely little family."

THE DOCTOR PRIEST

What was discussed behind the scenes he never knew, but Father Odilo was surprised a few weeks later to be told that he was being sent home on leave. Much had happened since that life-changing meeting with his bishop, but now it had all been arranged. Permission to go on home leave was a new dispensation that Pope Pius XII had insisted upon, for the hard-working missionaries of the Catholic Church, most of whom had accepted that they would not see their homes or families again.

In a follow up visit, Dr. Bernard Pepper said, "you are a tough fellow, Father Odilo. However, you are far from well," he paused and smiled. "You really should have been resting up long ago, to get over your illnesses. Anyway, in spite of your ailments, you should manage fine on the trip. Heaven knows, I think you are long overdue a holiday and some rest. When did you last get home?"

Father Odilo coughed politely, and said, "Bernard, it has now been sixteen years since I left Germany. I have never been back home. When I left, I said goodbye to my family and did not expect to come home." Looking over Bernard's head, he noticed thick white clouds building up for some afternoon rain, and continued thoughtfully, "that was really what being a missionary priest was all about."

"Well, thank God that's been changed now," Bernard replied. "I can't think of any reason to deny a priest, or anybody, the right to see his family and home again."

"It's a big change, but I must say that I am looking forward to getting home for a while," Father Odilo said. "A lot of things have changed, though. One of my greatest sorrows is that I could not see my mother before she died. I would have loved to see her one last time." There was moisture in his eyes when he looked up and continued, "Do you know, they found a little parcel of coins under her pillow; she had kept them there, and was saving them for me. It came to about ten marks."

Bernard noticed how his neck tightened with emotion, and he looked away shyly. "I am sure she loved you, and was deeply proud of you," Bernard responded. "You can be sure that God is taking good care of her now, and she is looking down on you from heaven with great love and pride."

Father Odilo knew that was true, but it was good to have a friend to talk with right now. He explained, "My mother had to save those small coins at a time when there was no money for essentials. They were suffering so badly, all squeezed into a single house, with extra refugees as well; and food was hard to buy, even if you had the money." After a while, Bernard discreetly ended the reverie, saying, "well, put your shirt on again and come sit down over here."

He retired behind his desk, and proceeded to scribble copious notes on his patient's record card. Looking up again, he said, "I suspect the malaria is still your main problem; I cannot understand why we can't get rid of it properly. You will have to take another course of this medication. I am giving you a fresh prescription. Now, don't let the fevers build up again before getting attention—if you have another bout of fevers and headaches, please promise me you will see a doctor straight away. Tell him you have had numerous bouts of malaria, and get him to check and treat you for it. Will you do that, Father Odilo?"

"Of course, Bernard," he answered him. "One thing I have done all my life, is to take care of this," he gestured, "the only body God gave me to get on with His tasks!" He spoke with a warm smile on his face, and a characteristic inclination of his head and movement of his right hand. "Thank you for checking me so well, and please pass on my love to Elizabeth and your beautiful little girls—Jennifer and Judy, I think."

"Quite right—how do you remember peoples' names the way you do? Oh well, take care, and God bless."

Royal Visit and Centenary Celebrations

Before his departure, he enjoyed the splendour and dignity of the Royal visit, followed some years later by the Queen's return to celebrate the Centenary of Cecil John Rhodes' birth, in the small English town of Bishops-Stortford. His dreams were based on an overpowering belief that the best gift he could bring to Africa was the civilising and developing influence of his motherland, Britain.

A festive mood gave a cheerful atmosphere to the whole of Bulawayo. The town was being spruced up as it had never been before.

Metcalfe Square, in front of the railway station was also being turned into a drill square and was to be the venue where the Queen Mother would acknowledge the achievements of the loyal and patriotic subject, whose dreams and ambitions had led to so much development of this land of opportunity.

Along the way Rhodes had also amassed wealth second to almost none in the whole world; when he died he left behind a business empire and a will which encompassed the noblest generosity the world had seen. His will would continue to educate and assist people for centuries to come, some of them leading figures from around the English-speaking world. He had a known heart condition and although he never married he led a very active social life. Driven by powerful ambitions, he was passionate in pursuing what he considered urgent and noble objectives, devoted to Britain and its far-flung colonial empire.

"I can see what he achieved, and it was enormous," Father Odilo said to a businessman involved in organising the Royal Visit. "However, I think his life was totally dominated by earthly ambitions."

"Well, his ambitions have left our country and the whole of Africa much better off," he replied. "I wonder if is appreciated by everyone, though," he mused.

Father Odilo was quiet; he thought of the rich advice of his faith, to "deal wisely with the things of this world, but love the things of heaven."

'How did Rhodes stand up to that test?' he wondered; still, he could not fail to admire him for his energy and achievements. He died at a relatively young age, having known that he had less time than most men.

The new Centenary Park was being developed on Selborne Avenue, with beautifully laid out gardens and low stone walls.

The pomp and ceremony was fantastic and appealed to his German heart. The speeches were uplifting, encouraging and full of praise for the people of Rhodesia. Later in the year, the Queen signed the order establishing the Federation of Rhodesia and Nyasaland, a partnership of three countries united under the British flag and their common objectives. Mr. Godfrey Huggins, later knighted, resigned formally as the Prime Minister of Southern Rhodesia, to become the first Federal Prime Minister. Mr Garfield Todd was sworn in as the new Prime Minister of Southern Rhodesia. Great ideas were discussed and the vision for the country was vibrant and full of optimism.

FLYING OVER AFRICA

A few days later, a friendly crowd was seeing him off from the Bulawayo Airport, just outside town. He looked back at the crowd on the lawns, and waved to his friends, all calling out to him, "bye-bye! God bless! Come home safely. Aufwiedersehen! Love to your family. Keep safe. Bye. God bless! We love you. Bye. Come back soon . . ."

The whole gathering seemed to know him and treat him as if he was a member of their own family, and this send-off reminded him of the emotions he had felt when he was on that first train journey, when he was assigned from Bulawayo to Wankie.

He felt elated and loved. 'I have a much bigger family than a married man ever could,' he thought to himself. He concealed his emotion with long experience, and with a quick swallow he stood there elegantly in his black priest's cassock and white Roman collar. He waved fondly at them all, and blew kisses to the sisters and ladies, some of whom he could see were unashamedly in tears.

Setting his shoulders, he strode manfully to the four-engined Constellation plane with South African Airways written boldly on its side. At the top of the mobile staircase, he turned and waved again, before ducking his head and disappearing into the plane.

He greeted the other passengers as he made his way to his seat near the rear of the plane. He found that he knew quite a few of them. As he sat down, his companion introduced himself, and they exchanged small talk while the engines were tested one by one. The feathering of the propellers must have made him look alarmed, and he was asked, "Is this your first flight?"

"Yes, it is," he admitted.

"Nothing to worry about. These are the safest planes the world has ever seen, and this airline takes their safety very seriously."

"That's good," he said. "How long does it take to reach to the Victoria Falls?"

"Once we're airborne, I reckon it will take a couple of hours. We don't land on the Southern Rhodesian side, though. The airport is in Livingstone."

"I know the route on the ground very well," Father Odilo told him. "The best I can do is about six or seven hours, and that's only since the new tarred sections of road have been completed. It used to take a lot longer."

Conversation died down as the plane began to taxi, making its way to the approach pad. He noticed an orange windsock flapping gently in the breeze, and he could see the buildings of town nearby, as he looked out from the window seat. There was talk of moving the airport, and he wondered why that was necessary. This airport had seen good service, especially when it had been an RAF training field not so long ago.

The plane lurched slightly as it heaved itself into the air, and the engine sound changed. He suddenly felt queasy, and wondered if it was the malaria flaring up again. His companion looked at him, and said, "There's a packet in the pouch in front of you. Here, get it out just in case. OK?"

He looked out of the round window, and watched the ground speeding away beneath them. He could see their shadow, and was intrigued as he saw it dashing over the bushveld below, changing shape to fill up the land and trees as it went; it seemed to have a life of its own.

After gaining height, the plane began to level off and the engines were throttled back further. A steady humming reverberated through the plane and soon became background noise as his ears grew accustomed to it. His ears were blocked and flying made him feel quite uncomfortable. "Hold your nose and blow gently; like this," the air hostess told him. It helped a bit.

Despite the noise, the passengers chatted and got to know one another, while the busy stewardesses were constantly attending to them and offering drinks, snacks, pillows, tablets and re-assuring those who were obviously ill at ease.

From high up in the sky they saw the "smoke that thunders", and soon had a dramatic view of the fantastic tumbling sheet of water that is the Victoria Falls. The plane banked and circled to give them all a chance to look from their window side, and then landed quite smoothly, at Livingstone Airport.

The next day, something called the auto-pilot was found to be faulty; this was not a good start for him! They had to wait another day before continuing the journey. From Livingstone, they flew north until eventually, they flew over and around the huge Kilimanjaro Mountain, the highest free-standing mountain in the world, and the tallest point in Africa. The landing in Nairobi was a bumpy one and they were pleased to be able to get out, stretch their legs, and head to town for their two-day stopover in Kenya.

From Nairobi, they flew to Khartoum, in the Sudan. There it was unbearably hot, even in the middle of night, and they were pleased it was only a one-day stop.

After taking off from Khartoum the desert soon appeared below them, and the Nile was regularly in sight. They came to the Mediterranean and flew across a sea, occasionally dotted with islands, until they landed in Athens. It was a short flight from there to Naples.

Visiting Friends in Italy

This was his first visit to Italy, and he was met by a friend, Count Gerardo di Bugnano. "Father Odilo," he pumped his hand with vigorous Italian enthusiasm. "How lovely to see you again. Come, give me your bags, and I take you to our family home here in Naples. It is called the Palazzo Donn' Anna."

He met Gerardo's mother there, Marchesa di Bugnano-Colonna. It was in fact her generosity that had made this trip possible.

When he had been settled in, the conversation worked around to Rhodesia. "Gerardo, you still have your farm near the Matetsi? When are you coming out to visit again?"

"Father Odilo, I am not sure, my good friend. Things have changed, and I must deal with our affairs here in Italy. How is Tony Combe?"

"I don't see him much, but his wife has returned to England. It would not surprise me if he does the same."

There was so much to reminisce about, and so much to see, and his hosts were fantastic. He was driven all over southern Italy, to Amalfi and

Pompeii. There he climbed the famous volcanic mountain, Vesuvius. At the museum, there were the 'suddenly-dead' people, whose bodies had been interred in its ashes. Many had suffocated and died while still at their daily work; at a baker's oven, or even in their bath. Marinella, Gerardo's mother, was a fine-looking woman. He admired her nobility; she was truly aristocratic, in body and soul. She was also deeply pious and kind, and had brought up such a wonderful family.

She went with him to show him Caserta and many other castles and palaces. "There is such a great sense of history here," he said at Paestum, a fascinating temple in southern Italy, dating back to Greek rule. "The history of Africa is so new by comparison; at least the records are so recent, and there is so little to show for the centuries without recorded civilisation."

In Naples, he went to see the relics of Saint Gennaro, an early martyr. "His dried blood liquefies each year on the first of September," he was told. "It is a great miracle, and there is no other possible explanation."

One day Gerardo said, "I must take you to see Raimondo's museum. He was an alchemist, and you will see some of his secret anatomy experiments." Father Odilo soon saw what he meant. Veins had been injected with metallic fluid, and the flesh was then boiled away until it left behind solidified veins, arteries and organs. "He had to do this in an underground cellar, because it was illegal research. He would have been hanged if they caught him!"

At other places, he stood transfixed by the beauty of the art. An amazing marble statue of Jesus in the tomb was so lifelike that you could actually see tears in his eyes, right under the veil of carved marble!

Gerardo and Principe Don Carlo Colonna took him to Firenze. Savanarola, a Franciscan monk, was burnt on the stake there, after he had preached against the pope of the time, who had been morally bad. They showed him where he was publicly burnt in the square. The cathedral was magnificent, all clad in exquisite marble. It is such a beautiful sight," he marvelled. They drove out to Fiesole, a beautiful Benedictine monastery, up on the hill, about three kilometres out of Firenze.

"It is amazing what the Benedictines achieved," marvelled Don Carlo. "The whole agricultural industry owes its existence to them. They were the ones who prepared lands, and introduced large-scale scientific farming."

THE FAITH IN THE ANCIENT CITY

Another highlight was Rome. Words could not describe how he felt when he entered Saint Peter's Church. The grandeur and beauty was one thing, but he could truly feel the presence of God in a special way. All around him, he was encouraged by the prayerful reverence of the worshippers, who flocked there from all over Italy and the whole world. He was privileged to be granted an audience with Pope Pius XII[viii], and he arrived early and waited outside his rooms, with a few other people who were due to see him.

The Pope greeted him by name as he walked towards him, and he felt greatly honoured, although he knew that a secretary must prepare the appointments and brief the Pope. He could imagine how much this man had endured and suffered, but he had the dignity of a person accustomed to dealing with people from all levels. His handshake was firm but conveyed great love and kindness, and he was deeply touched by a feeling of holy warmth when he received the parting handshake and blessing.

He told an Italian priest at supper, one night, how moved he was, and the priest then told him about how the Rabbi of Rome had converted to Catholicism. "He was Rabbi Israel Zolli; we all knew him quite well in the city, of course, although he had been Rabbi at Padua for some time before coming here. I heard that he changed his name from Zoller to Zolli at that time. Anyway, he worked closely with the Church in our efforts to save as many Jews as we could."

Father Odilo was intrigued, and he had to listen quite carefully as the priest's English was pronounced with a strong Italian accent. "What really brought him to the Church, though?" he asked, knowing it could not have been the good deeds alone.

"He asked lots of questions. He was a scholar, you see. In the end, I think it was the Pope's example that softened him, so that he was able to ask and get the answers he needed."

"When he converted he adopted the Christian name, Eugenio[ix], so that must tell you how much he thought of the Pope. Of course, he came under a lot of criticism from his own people, but I hear he is writing a book about Jesus as the Nazarene; he has noticed how that term did not come up anywhere in the Bible." The priest said he had some papers, and Father Odilo looked at them later. One of the articles described how, in an emotional address, he had said, "you, Pope Pius, have shown us all the greatest example in doing so much to save the lives of Jews here in Italy. My studies have led me to believe with all my heart that Jesus Christ is our Messiah, as promised by the Prophets and as awaited by us, God's Chosen People . . . ."

He returned the papers the next day, saying, "thank you; that was wonderful; such a pity more people do not know these things."

A parishioner, Barbera Hore, had given him her aunt's address, so he visited her; her name was even Roma! She took him to see Tivoli, and the Villa Farnese, with its unique gardens and statues. He was a guest that anybody loves to show around, as his appreciation was obvious and sincere.

From Rome, he travelled by train to Switzerland, staying a few days at the Mariannhill House in Brieg, from where he travelled around and enjoyed the magnificent mountain scenery. The people were very kind and welcoming and he loved the lake and the perfectly clean village. He climbed the snow-covered mountains and revelled in the beauty and fresh mountain air. Finally, he was on the last stage of his journey home.

BACK HOME, FOR THE FIRST TIME, IN GERMANY

"What is home now?" he asked himself. "My mother died before I could see her again. My father is living with my brother, Josef, at his parish in Leuchtenberg. My brothers and sisters are all over the place. It could have been so different, coming home to Arberg, to our old family Gasthaus and farm. All that has changed now."

After all these years away from home, far away in Africa, he was not sure what to expect. The journey itself had been such a long one, with a lot of stops along the way; he had felt revived by Italy and his friends there. The stay in Switzerland had been short. Compared with his sea journey, sixteen years ago, this had been a short trip, though. And now, finally, the train was arriving in Germany, and it really was a wonderful feeling. Despite everything, this was his homeland, and it had a look and feel that touched some deep yearning in his soul.

"Welcome home, Father Odilo," said the young immigration official, as he looked through his passport.

"Thank you," Father Odilo replied in the German dialect that he could again speak. He knew his pronunciation was as good as ever, but he wondered if this young man thought he was very foreign now. He looked the fellow over curiously. He was neat enough, to be sure, and he was definitely from Bavaria, because he had responded well to Father Odilo's initial "Gruss Gott!" However, there was something so different about him, that he was puzzled.

Of course, this official could only have been a child during the war years. He wore his uniform, but almost apologetically, and as if he was not sitting up straight. Then it hit him, and he asked himself, 'what has happened to that old German Pride of bearing?'

The man was very officious and insisted on looking through his hand luggage as well as opening his two suitcases. He asked strange and irrelevant questions, like, "have you brought anything illegal into Germany? Drugs? Pornographic literature? Anything like that?"

"Of course not, man!" snapped Father Odilo, becoming quite impatient with this stupidity.

"Sorry, Father. I am only doing my duty," he apologised.

He first went to see his father and brother, Josef. From there he travelled out and returned frequently. Father Josef was delighted to have his brother visiting. Josef held his younger brother in the highest regard, and admitted, "You know, Otto, I wish I had the courage you had to become a missionary."

"You have done just as much here," Father Odilo re-assured him.

"No, no. That is not true. You are being falsely modest. I have been kept informed of what you have done; and all the others with you, as well. It is fantastic."

As they drove to his parish house, Father Josef warned him, "you will see how much father has aged, I am afraid. He is still pretty sharp mentally, but since mother died he has gone down fast."

"Well, I expected something like that. We all knew how close those two were; it was impossible to think of one without the other really."

When he saw his father in the living room, he realized what Josef had meant. His father was bent over with age, and so thin; he looked almost like somebody from one of those dreadful pictures of the concentration camps. But, as his son greeted him, his eyes lit up and he seemed to become animated again. "Oh, oh . . ." was all he could say for a while. "Oh, oh . . . it is you, Otto."

Father Odilo's eyes brimmed with tears, and he could not say anything at first. "Hallo father. It's so good to see you again." He shook hands warmly, easing his own grip to suit his father's now, and put his arms around his father. He could only guess what this dear man had been through. The war; the move from Arberg; taking shelter with his son; his wife's death; tragedies in the family; humiliation and suffering beyond anybody's wildest expectations.

On his first evening there, Father Josef brought out the little parcel of coins that his mother had saved for him. "Mother was saving this for you, as I told you in the letter," he said, as he handed over the wrapped bundle. Father Odilo opened it with tears welling up in his eyes. He could see her so clearly, and he felt keenly how much she loved him and had hoped to see him before she died. Each little coin had been a huge sacrifice. Even a single Pfennig was a big amount when they had almost nothing; she had squirreled them away, and hid them under her pillow.

"It must have been so hard for her, and the family," he said at last. "You were all in so much need; it must have taken a lot of resolve to keep this little saving going . . ." He could not put into words what his heart felt, and he broke off. Josef looked away, allowing Odilo the privacy of his grief. She was gone, surely to heaven, he knew, and he had to accept that now. This act of motherly devotion and love brought home to him how sorely he missed having seen her all these years.

He enjoyed Leuchtenberg and somehow people socialised differently from Arberg. Their social occasions and celebrations had an extra dimension. Josef explained, "They have developed very strong social traditions and these help them to keep their identity. That has become so much more important, especially nowadays, after all we Germans have suffered."

HOME-TOWN WELCOME

Josef presented him with the keys to a Volkswagen. "This is yours, Otto. Father wanted you to have your own transport and so he managed to buy this Volkswagen. He said it was to be for you when you come on holiday." Josef noticed the moisture in his eyes, and added, "Father can't believe that you have been away for sixteen years in Africa."

The car was perfect, and he used it to drive from one place to the next, pretty well independently. He made a trip to Arberg, and pulled up outside their old family Gasthaus. His brother, Max, greeted him warmly and ushered him inside. He looked out at their Linden tree; it had grown so huge now. "I remember when that was just a sapling," he said. How long ago it had been, when he had sheltered behind the water trough? The iron frame that he was forbidden to climb or pull on had then supported the tree.

"It is a beautiful tree," Max agreed fondly. "I think Linden trees keep on growing forever."

After an exchange of news, Max asked about some of his travels and his impressions. Wherever he had been his eyes were treated to great and interesting sights. "Max, one of the things I have appreciated the most is the beautiful architecture here. Of course, I suppose I see the contrast with rustic grass-roofed and mud-walled buildings in Rhodesia."

"We probably take it all for granted."

"Yes, I am sure. Coming back like this, though, it is a reminder of the centuries of refinement and culture to which we have been exposed in Germany. There is so much still to be done back in Africa, and I even feel guilty that I am not there doing something right now."

"Have you ever seen the altar at Durach?"

"No, tell me about it, Otto."

"I saw it last week. It has been carved from the trunk of a single Linden tree. It is incredible—to think it all comes from one single tree. There is a crucifix plus the whole altar, all out of the same tree trunk. Quite fantastic!"

Arberg welcomed him home and honoured him as one of its heroes. He was there in time to attend their fire brigade celebrations, and he celebrated Holy Mass with them. From there he joined in the cavalcade to the tented party, which tried to revive and keep the old spirit of this ancient town.

THE DECKER FAMILY

He was introduced to Rosie Decker, a cousin of Dr. Johanna Decker, who was now working at Fatima Mission. "Dr. Davis has been delighted to have Dr. Decker's help," he explained, and he gave her news of her cousin and all the work being done on the mission. She had soon confirmed her own interest, especially now, with this personal feed-back; the idea of helping on a Rhodesian mission appealed to her very strongly. She was not a doctor, but she spoke about her own desire to do something useful.

"We have not had much success with our appeals for sisters to run the secondary school; perhaps you would be willing to help us there."

He answered many of her questions and encouraged her to think about things carefully before making a decision. It was not long at all after his return that she decided and arrangements were made for her to come out and help.

He travelled all over Germany in his Volkswagen, and visited numerous Mariannhill Houses, in southern, middle and northern Germany. Alt-oetting, for instance, was a place from which special help came for decades afterwards. Despite the war damage, a lot had survived or been rebuilt already. Wherever he stopped, he found there were lovely churches to visit and pray in.

He visited their Congregation headquarters in Wurzburg, and his confreres were keen to hear how things were going. They were equally willing to tell him what was happening there, and within the Order. He had the chance to visit some of the famous places like the Residenz, Marienburg, the Chapel and other landmarks from his young student days.

The wood carver, Riemenschneider, had made a solid altar of wood, but years later woodworms began to attack it from behind. The curators had injected chemicals into it and saved this masterpiece.

There were famous paintings by Gruenewald, and he enjoyed reading some of the famous poets, like Walther von der Vogelweide and Friedrich Schiller.

History, Art, Culture and Monuments

He spent lots of time in Munich. There was much to see and do there, and he really enjoyed being in the mountains. The priest who hosted him reminded him about the Watzmann Range, and how the hills had been named after the King and Queen and their five children.

When he arrived in Karlsruhe he immediately thought how well the city had been laid out.

He visited Mainz, at the confluence of the Main and Rhine. Among other things, this was the home of Gutenberg, the inventor of the printing press.

In Aachen, he recalled that this was where Charlemagne had resided.

The town of Marburg has a beautiful university, but he noticed how more and more of the Catholic churches were Lutheran churches now.

One of the most fascinating cities was Nuremberg, made even more famous or notorious by the trials and sentencing of numerous Nazi leaders. Many of the churches had been rebuilt, down to the last detail, and in such a short time. They had used old photos and drawings to reconstruct everything as accurately as possible. It had been an old mediaeval city, with a great wealth of art and history. The treasures and art had been stored away and preserved during the war, so much had been saved.

In the German Museum, he looked at the first globe of the world, by Boeheim.

When he was in Bamberg, he stood fascinated by the statue of a German knight. It reminded him of the Crusaders, and their desperation to liberate the Holy Land and Jerusalem. He had enjoyed his history studies, and had also seen that wars are never that simple, and there are always two sides. The victor usually writes the history, though, and it is almost inevitable that the foe is painted as a terrible villain, and the winners as heroes. The Arab rulers, however, had brought marvellous architecture, astronomy, algebra, medical science and many other benefits while they subjugated almost the whole of the old Roman Empire.

He drove past and visited some of the famous monasteries, like the Wieskirche, near Munich, and the Ettal Monastery and Weltenburg, built by the Benedictines a long time ago. Each princedom had prided itself on its treasures, architecture and art and these monasteries remained as a solid testimony to the past. In the beautiful churches, so much faith was depicted in the art. There were priceless paintings and detailed carvings in wood and stone. Everything spoke of the dedication and faith of their forefathers.

His interest in history, and a feeling of patriotism towards his homeland, steered him to Valhalla, built like a Greek temple, overlooking the Danube near Regensburg. King Ludwig I built it when the Germans defeated the French. It is a museum in honour of distinguished Germans down through the centuries, featuring people like Bismarck, Goethe and so on. That passion for monumental construction left such a great legacy behind, and people like Ludwig II later built many palaces; Linderhof, Neu Schwanstein and others.

Not far from Arberg, he went to see the stone and earth wall with turrets, (Limes[x]), built by the Romans to defend themselves from the middle German tribes; they had been considered too wild and fierce to rule. Augustus had lost a whole legion there. It runs about five hundred kilometres from Frankfurt to Kehlheim.

The Befreihingshalle (Hall of liberation) is a round structure on top of the hill. It was also built by Ludwig I, adorned with the 'angels of victory' after the battle when he defeated Napoleon. All his battles are recorded there, and all the German tribes were represented there on the cupola, except the Bavarians, even though King Ludwig was from Bavaria, because they were considered to be more pro-French in those days.

RECONSTRUCTION

He was deeply impressed with the rebuilding of Germany, despite initial resistance from people like Morgenthau. It made him think of the passage, 'vengeance is mine, says the Lord.' Marshall had stepped in and told Eisenhower that allowing Germany to crumble was the best way to hand Europe over to Communism! The Marshall Plan had followed, and American funding had fast-tracked German recovery.

Wurzburg, for instance, had been severely bombed with incendiaries, and most of the wooden construction had been burned, leaving only shells of stone structures, like a ghost town. But here it was now well on its way to being repaired and restored.

In Nuremberg, the people had worked three eight-hour shifts, day and night; they were very hard working, and the rebuilding had been completed in a fantastically short time. This was an eloquent demonstration that "nothing bad lasts forever', and he was very impressed and proud of the strong German will to survive!

"One of our problems is that recovery has come too quickly," his brother, Josef said one evening. "Prosperity has been attained too early for people to appreciate it, and there are all sorts of unrealistic expectations and attitudes that mix people up."

Many of the villages and smaller towns had not been destroyed. As he drove through them, they looked as beautiful as before. He was inspired, and he was constantly reminded of the beauty of his home country, after having left and returned like this.

The more typical mediaeval towns had been circular and walled with turrets for defence, like Rothenburg, where life had been preserved as it was about five hundred years before. There was a display of large beer mugs that held about two litres, called "Liesels". The mayor of Rothenburg had been challenged to a drinking feat or have his town sacked; he had finished all the contents in one go without stopping but collapsed and died in saving the town from this challenge.

When he went to Austria, his memories of horse-riding were stirred, and he accepted an invitation to see the famous Lipizzan horse displays. He could understand some of the skill and training that was required to make these beautiful horses leap in the air and pose. He always managed to find the right people when he wanted more information, and one of the handlers told him, "These are the greatest horses in the world. They were first introduced from Spain, but they have been bred with selected horses from Morocco, and some of the finest Arabian stud. They can all be traced back to their six original sires." With his usual interest in detail, Father Odilo probed and learned more about a breed whose detailed history goes back to 1700.

Again, with his love for knowledge, history and information, he was reminded of how the Turks were said to have been on the very brink of taking Vienna. What would Europe have been like today, if that had happened? It was the Polish King, Jan III Sobieski, who had repulsed them, and the date of that historic victory was inscribed here, 11th September 1683[xi]. Father Odilo knew from his history studies how a strong Bavarian force had lent their might to this historic relief of Vienna.

BENEFACTORS

This home leave trip was not just a holiday, however. The needs of Africa, and his own conscience would not allow that. Although he was travelling, he spent much of his time preaching and collecting. He was perspiring all the time and was not at all well. He was still suffering from the effects of being eaten up with malaria during this trip. He still had bilharzia, but did not realise that, and he only discovered that when he was back in Rhodesia. He had a projector and slides, which he took with him in his Volkswagen. When he stopped he would preach, with a slide show. He used to give about three sermons at each stop plus a show in the evening. People could see that he had endured a lot and this made a deep impression on all who saw and met him.

Although Fatima Mission had been started it still desperately needed more money. Germany itself was very poor at this time, but the people were most generous, giving what they could. Old women, often very poor, would still come and give him two marks, apologising that they could not offer more. Others gave or sent what they could, and he always remembered to pray for and give thanks for his benefactors.

THE WEEGER FAMILY

All his family were still alive, except for his mother. Josef was the parish priest in the small town of Leuchtenberg, near the Czechoslovakian border. He lived in an ordinary parish house; just after the war, he had somehow accommodated about twenty refugees, together with his own father and mother. It had been terribly congested, but no worse than many other homes and buildings throughout Germany. By now these difficulties had eased, and Josef was alone with only his father, and Maria, the housekeeper, to look after them. From time to time, during Odilo's stay, he was able to return and spend a week or so at home with Josef and his father.

His sister Maria's husband, Max Prinzing, was especially helpful. He worked in a provincial dairy processing plant and he knew all the priests in the area. Their own poverty was still severe, and a collecting missionary was not always welcome, but somehow Max smoothed the way for him.

He went to see his sister, Rosa, in Regensburg. Her husband had been an army officer, and the war and its aftermath had brought deep turmoil to their lives. He thanked God that he had been spared, and there was so much to talk about; he could feel how much his own life had taken a different path. He sympathised with her aches and pains, and wondered why the doctors had been unable to ease the pains she complained of in her stomach. He offered many prayers with her and for her, asking God to 'give her peace, and true health of mind and body.'

The long days of a European summer were something he had forgotten, being out in Africa for so long. One day, he woke up and sprung out of bed and dressed hurriedly in his cassock. He thought he had over-slept, and wondered where everybody was when he rushed to go outside that morning. As he opened the door and looked out, he saw the church tower; there was a clock on its face, and it was only three a.m.! He managed to go back to his bed and enjoyed a good lie-in. He happily allowed them to tease him about this for weeks afterwards.

He managed to meet several old friends and teachers. When he saw Fritz Neuwinger, he realised how much he had aged, but he still saw in him the same dedication and inspiration he had received as a young student. He met this man's young nephew, and told him, "Your uncle taught me so much. I will be in his debt all my life."

The time soon drew to an end and the six months seemed as if it had just begun, when it was time to leave. It had been sixteen years, although he would have been allowed leave after ten years; somehow that had just not happened, with things being so busy.

At the end of his trip, he handed the Volkswagen over to the monastery at Wurzburg. They had been involved with the car arrangement, and ended up paying half of its price, as well as helping with some of the expenses, like insurance; they had insured him heavily! This was a most welcome gift for them, though, and all the more so as there was no damage at all to the car! It was a good car for the monastery, and a very good deal for them. It was very kind of Mr. Weeger, and they ran it for many years afterwards.

FLIGHT BACK TO AFRICA

In some ways the trip ended all too soon; he was happy to be with family and friends and he felt re-affirmed, remembering well the vision of missionary life and the purpose of it all. Much as he appreciated home, his life had changed forever and he was a totally different man now. His real purpose in life was to give himself in serving the people in Rhodesia, especially the poor and needy. He looked around and appreciated the industrialisation and the cultural heritage of Europe, but he was happy to wave good-bye as he boarded his plane from Frankfurt.

He arrived back in Bulawayo revitalised. He could not wait to be back at his mission, or wherever he was assigned. Soon, he was back at Fatima Mission, feeling a tinge of guilt at having had a spell away from his work. He plunged in with even greater gusto than before and was able to do so much as his health was much improved.

The new Secondary School was soon opened, in 1954, with three wonderful Dominican sisters from Salisbury.

SAINT MARY'S CATHEDRAL

Father Andrew Baussenwein was elected Secretary General of the Mariannhill Missionary Society, and was transferred to their headquarters in Rome. Father Odilo was given three months to finish his building and other work, and was appointed to the Cathedral towards the end of the year, in 1957. He soon settled down to his new duties as the administrator and pastor of Saint Mary's Cathedral.

This beautiful church was made of solid granite stones, with the cement joints neatly raised and pointed by the masons who built it about half a century earlier. Its high vaulted roof was panelled with dark timber, and the copper sheeting on the outside had long since lost its shine and settled to a dark grey that would endure well into the future.

"I find that I miss the challenge of mission work," he confided to his bishop. "Out there you know you have to do so much yourself, and I must admit I enjoy the pioneering spirit."

"Oh well, Odilo, there is a lot that needs to be done here as well. I am sure you can apply yourself with equal vigour in Bulawayo as well."

"Sure, sure." They paused to sip the hot coffee, a comfortable stillness between them.

"You have been a good missionary," the bishop praised him. He was not a man who flattered and cajoled, and Father Odilo accepted the compliment graciously.

The Parish and People

People are what a priest's life is all about, and a good priest does an amazing amount of work in serving his parish. As parish priest, Father Odilo had many duties and there was never a truly peaceful and quiet day in his week.

He leafed through the second edition[xii] of 'The Saint Mary's Messenger', the fairly new parish newsletter, from earlier in the year. It summed those priestly 'labours' up well, and passed a few other comments that he liked for their descriptiveness:

1. at least two hours each day, saying Mass and devotions such as the Office and meditation visit Hospitals for minimum of one hour
2. visit the jails
3. visit over 45 schools every week to give religious instruction
4. hold at least two Catechism classes per week at the Presbytery
5. giving instruction in over 22 cases of mixed marriages
6. giving instruction to over 30 converts
7. examinations in First Communion, instruction at two Dominican Convents and Christian Brothers College
8. January—over 40 Baptisms, 15 marriages, 5 funerals and Extreme Unctions
9. Spend a considerable amount of time giving advice to people who come with problems
10. Attend the meetings of the 10 Parish Societies
11. Hear innumerable Confessions each week

'The priests are aided in their work by two small decrepit motor cars and one fairly creditable one . . . . Social calls are limited by the above pressures . . . .'

'Finally, the Parish Priest, who administers the Parish, has more problems to solve, more decisions to make, more reports to compile, more personal contacts to fit in, than the Managing Director of any company in Bulawayo.'

The August edition explained the new reduced Eucharistic fast. It was still required that those wishing to receive Holy Communion must abstain for three hours from food or alcohol. Non-alcoholic drinks were now permitted up to one hour before communion.

He soon took on the task of editing this monthly newsletter, and had to wrestle with the age-old problems of printing costs and timings. He received a very high donation of about ten pounds in May, but the person who gave it asked that it should remain an anonymous gift.

When Pope Pius XII died, shortly after Father Odilo's forty-sixth birthday, it was a time of great sadness, and many people were moved, recognising just how much this great man had done and tried to do. Father Odilo was very touched when the Rabbi of the Bulawayo Hebrew Community, Reverend Wolfe Yesorsky wrote a letter to Bishop Schmitt, passing on his condolences, and so he reprinted it in the Messenger.

Father Odilo became more and more active in religious education at the schools in Bulawayo, and many boys and girls from those times recall his teaching, as well as his quite strict teaching methods. He also took a keen interest in the histories of the various missions and parishes, and encouraged Father Adalbert Balling, CMM, in the work he did compiling and keeping records.

CHAPTER 14

NEW WORLD ON FIRE

CONSTRUCTION AND DEPRESSION

The largest dam project in the whole world was initiated when the decision was taken to build Kariba Dam[xiii] and harness the energy and water of the mighty Zambesi River. Things moved quickly and efficiently, and the main contracts were awarded within a little over a year. The road down into the valley was completed in record time, aided by an unusual approach to alignment and survey; in order to accelerate things, it was agreed to utilise ancient elephant migration routes—and it worked.

Specially appointed contractors and their men soon descended on the Zambesi valley and built a town that would accommodate many thousand people during construction. At the same time, the main contractors strung a temporary cable bridge and a Blondin cable system over the river, and soon began building the large diversion tunnel and the coffer dams, undeterred by the initial floods of their first rainy season.

The diversion tunnel was ready, and a fleet of heavy dump trucks was marshalled, to complete the final cut-off of river flow. Rock was tipped, and tipped and tipped. Bulldozers spread it and made way for the next dumpers. Gradually, but with great determination, and even greater urgency than the pyramid builders must have had, the builders watched the gap being closing down. The water racing through the gap in the temporary rockfill dam was flowing faster and faster, and the levels began to rise.

The design charts were re-checked, and the flow rates were compared. They were on target. A huge tower of rocks was quickly built up, aligned with the gap. On signal, an explosive charge was set off at its base sending a cloud of dust and rock into the air. With a thundering roar, the onlookers saw the rock tower collapse and fall. It fell towards the last gap in the Zambesi, and flung its sudden pile of rock across the breach. The splash drew a gasp from the crowd and the spray of water concealed everything. When it settled, the engineers and the whole workforce let out a loud cheer, "Yes, Yes! We've done it!"

At the discharge end of the diversion tunnel there was a rush of wind, and suddenly a solid wave of water rushed through, and disgorged back into the Zambesi, well below the new dam site. The flow grew and then settled to a steady roar; it was as if the whole Zambesi was being forced through a giant wormhole!

The river swirled and backed up. It rose. Water was still coming through on the downstream side of the rock wall, but nothing like the flow before. Dumpers and bulldozers worked bravely in the valley bottom, and the rock barrier held. Gradually, the leaks were sealed, and the diversion took all the flow. The news reached every corner of Rhodesia, and people were suddenly awe-struck. This was now a reality, and the world's biggest man-made lake was beginning to fill up.

The Zambesi River put up incredible resistance to being sealed off by this dam at Kariba. As if in conspiracy with Nyaminyami and the legendary river gods of the Tonga people, the heavens had opened and the flood levels rose and rose as the helpless contractors watched the concrete walls of their cofferdam and waited. The flow was just too much; the works were soon deluged, on 22nd February 1958 and the Zambesi resumed its old course. Some of the Batonga people were strengthened in their resolve not to leave the valley, and old men nodded wisely and scorned the educated young tribal leaders who had accepted the inevitable.

But these contractors were tough and determined men; as soon as they could get closer, these engineers and builders came straight back, and construction soon resumed. The next season was even worse, and the floods overtopped the cofferdams again, and took away the road-bridge as well. Within six months the new dam was closed and the lake started to fill up on 2nd December 1958, while they carried on building the dam wall, two thousand four hundred and twenty feet long when finished.

The Italian engineer, Dr. Bergamasco said, "The Zambesi is the worst river in the world. I have worked on rivers in all parts of the world, but the Zambesi is the worst and fiercest of them all." When completed, however, the enormous £80 million hydroelectric project was finished at below the original estimated cost.

The Dam at Kariba formed the world's largest man-made lake in the world

The new lake was to be nearly two hundred miles long, with a surface of two thousand square miles, making it the largest man-made lake in the world. Much of the valley floor had been cleared using giant chains and huge rolling balls dragged by powerful bulldozers. As the dam filled the animals moved to higher ground but many became trapped on shrinking islands.

Dedicated and brave men like Rupert Fothergill rescued huge numbers in what came to be called Operation Noah, but they could not save them all. The villagers in Binga experienced the strange phenomenon of a tide of rats and other rodents rising out of the valley; they took nearly three months to settle down, eating anything they could find, while they settled themselves in new homes.

There was a great spirit of courage and optimism in this period and in Bulawayo, the Agricultural Showgrounds were established next to the Bulawayo Golf Club. In 1961, the Rhodesian International Trade Fair was inaugurated there and a tall concrete spire was being built, and had already become the subject of much discussion. It was chosen to be the emblem of the new showgrounds.

Back in Bulawayo, Father Odilo was very pleased that his colleague, Father Elmar Schmid was appointed as regional superior of the Mariannhill Order. This gentle giant of a man had overseen construction of the lovely new parish church of Christ the King in Hillside. Its tower was topped with a tall cross, which could be seen all the way from town along the Matopos Road.

THE WINDS OF CHANGE

Africa would never be the same. Macmillan's surrender to calls for change marked the beginning of British withdrawal, and the collapse of the mightiest empire that the world had ever seen. Their proud claim, that the sun never set on the Union Jack, was replaced by apologetic speeches and fumbling political expedients to abdicate power to hastily accepted African lobbyists.

It began in the Western bulge of Africa, and soon progressed to the Federation. The original rationale behind the Federation had been optimisation and strength in unity. In reality, the benefits had not been fairly shared. Although the whole economy was soon working well, it was mainly for the benefit of the capital, Salisbury.

The outbreak of the Congo uprisings on 10th July 1960, with crazy people like Alice Lenshina, seemed to confirm the civilised world's worst fears about Africa. People who were more prejudiced made comments like, "You can take a savage out of the jungle, but you can't take the jungle out of a savage".

On the Federation's borders, bloodthirsty, drunken mobs ran wild, women were raped, children were killed, and property was being looted and destroyed. The will to control and restore order had already evaporated. Chaos loomed, and a pall of doubt spread like a dark cloud, from North to South. The revolts spread all over the vast territory of the Congo. Hundreds of refugees fled across the border to nearby Northern Rhodesia, and most of them made a dash for Southern Rhodesia, or even South Africa. Kitwe soon became a vast refugee camp.

The course of African history was changing, and the managed peace of colonial governments was soon passing away north of Southern Rhodesia. It was not long before the country was becoming part of the crumbling British Empire's problems. Internally, as with much of the outside world, recession was taking its toll, and steadily growing worse.

A TELEVISION CAREER

Television had soon become enshrined in homes around the world. It was already well established in Europe and America. No longer would people huddle around a wireless with thermionic valves glowing like little lights, nor even the modern transistorised radios. Now, they could look at pictures while they heard the announcers, or the actors. Rhodesia was soon propelled into it by popular demand, while South Africa waited several more years, (perhaps rightly so), fearful of the effects television might have on its supposedly puritan population.

Of course, TV was set up in Salisbury first, and it took many more months before Father Odilo and his colleagues were able to watch a television screen. It was soon seen that this was an important medium of communication, and the Church was quick to receive invitations to be on some of the panel discussion shows.

A programme was established with inter-faith dialogue and Father Odilo was selected as one of the church panellists. His solemn, friendly bearing and his handsome presence soon made him a firm favourite with people of all faiths. He seemed to have the ability to say things in a non-offensive manner, but he never wavered from the Church's teaching positions on the issues that were debated. Soon he was able to hand over the media matters to his young assistant priest from the USA, Father Mark Lucasinsky.

Father Odilo also joined a religious committee that worked with other denominations. There were several issues about which their opinions were divided, and one of the most contentious was the newly fashionable 'birth control'. Most other churches had welcomed the pill and other options as an apparent boon to family planning, thinking it would be especially good for poor people around the world. However, the Catholic Church stood firm in opposition, especially to the many ways that newly conceived lives could be terminated during early pregnancy. Another issue was self-control in an age that was becoming increasingly hedonistic.

"Life begins at conception, not at birth," Dr. Pepper confirmed without hesitation. Father Odilo enjoyed his company and was able to discourse with him on other medical-biological issues, such as the ethics of caring for all life.

His own ministry of visiting the sick continued to grow and he found great consolation in helping the sick, and even seeing their dignity and faith as people approached the biggest test of all, their death.

Bishop Schmitt and Changes in the Church

There were also big changes going on in the Catholic Church. Bishop Adolph Schmitt had brought his own influence to bear on the Bulawayo diocese and their Mariannhill Missions, and in 1960 Father Elmar Schmid was elected as a popular Regional Superior for Rhodesia.

The English Mass was introduced as well. Catholics had grown up all over the world, used to the same, universal Holy Mass, always celebrated in Latin. The new Pope was soon at the centre of a great controversy when it was decided that Mass should be celebrated in English, or for that matter in the different languages of each country. Even some of the priests found this hard to accept, and many older parishioners complained to Father Odilo, "This is no longer a Catholic Mass. We are becoming more and more like Anglicans."

Modifications soon had to be made to the altars, as priests were encouraged to celebrate Mass facing the people. "That was how Our Lord instituted Communion and the Mass, facing and being part of the Church he founded," Bishop Schmitt explained to them. It took a bit of getting used to, but Father Odilo soon found it to be a big improvement.

Further Treatment

Father Odilo had continued to battle with fatigue and bilharzia had remained in him for at least ten years before he was cured of it. After the first treatment over two years, with intravenous injections, Dr. Shee admitted, "well, the Salvarzan hasn't killed the bugs; they still show up on our tests. I will have to start you on a course of Fuadin; it is a kind of blitz cure, but should do the trick."

He was given these enormous capsules, and Father Odilo battled to swallow them. After taking the course, he went back for tests some months later. "Bad news, Father Odilo," Dr. Jimmy Shee said. "You still have bilharzia. I am not sure what we can use next. You certainly have allowed this to get its hooks well into you."

"Well, Jimmy, do whatever you need to do. I really do want to get my strength and energy back to what I am used to," he answered.

"I know you have so much to do, but I would prefer to hospitalise you for treatment."

"Can you do it any other way?"

"Well, there is one more treatment which works for ninety percent of stubborn cases. I am going to give you another course of intramuscular injections, and hope this will knock the bilharzia bug dead, without killing you, of course!"

"Will that do it?"

"I am pretty confident it will work. I would rather try that before resorting to Triostem. If it does not work, though, we have no choice. You will need to be hospitalised for a different course of intravenous injections, and you could be in Mater Dei Hospital for about three weeks.

Two months later, he was back, and Dr. Jimmy Shee said, "You are a mess still. I am afraid the injections were not strong enough. It's hospital for you, and I am booking you in right now."

He had a course of two injections per week, and had to endure being in hospital, as a patient and this time he was not a visitor!

SILVER JUBILEE

The year after his fiftieth birthday, Father Odilo celebrated the twenty-fifth anniversary of his ordination, together with Father Elmar Schmid, at the Cathedral. Bishop Schmitt spoke highly of them and their other classmates who had done so much for the people of Rhodesia, and the Church. Their dedication and sincerity impressed everybody, and they had many good friends wishing them well and thanking them for all they had done.

It was time to go home on leave, and Father Odilo managed to spend time with his brother, Father Joseph, and to see his older brother, Max, before he died two years later. His own health was better this time as well. Although he still collected money for the missions, he was now more of a pastor to the people he spent time with in Germany—even friends and family.

Their needs and troubles were real enough, but the people in Bulawayo were facing far more immediate challenges and difficulties. He was soon glad to board the plane and fly back to what had now become his home, and where he knew he was most needed. He had been appointed as the Vicar-General, and now had added responsibilities, as well as the opportunity to spend time with more of his confreres.

CRUMBLING EMPIRE

The collapse of the Federation was now almost inevitable. A conference was convened and took place at Victoria Falls on 29th June 1963. As if to emphasise the troubles in the region, disturbing tremors were felt in parts of Rhodesia where nobody could recall that happening before. (The Batonga people in the Zambesi valley had attributed the much older rumbles and minor earthquakes to a great underground snake moving about.) The superstitious had a field day, while the pessimists predicted that there would be a failure of the Kariba dam wall. Engineering reports soon confirmed that the tremors had been anticipated, as the earth's crust adjusted to the changed loads on it, and were well within the severity for which the huge concrete arch structure had been designed. Although the concerns died down, they were revived regularly in the years that followed, as exciting news stories in the local press.

Political Developments with long Ripples for the Future

Political dissent was building up, and soon the name Joshua Nkomo was being repeatedly heard. Feelings about him differed widely depending upon people's political perspective. His trade unionist tirades and township riots were zealously suppressed, and attempts at rebellion were halted with emergency mobilisations and strict police action.

Nkomo's Zimbabwe African People's Union soon suffered from its own turmoil when Reverend Ndabaningi Sithole broke away to form the Zimbabwe African Nationalist Union. However, the movement he had set in motion was to strengthen and become a critical influence in enforcing change in the country.

The promises made by the British leaders before the Victoria Falls conference were not kept. Self-government was still being withheld, and a series of leadership changes and personality clashes led to a confrontation. Ian Smith emerged to be selected as Prime Minister of Rhodesia. He had served gallantly in the War, and had inherited some great qualities and strengths of character, combined with the stubbornness of a man who worked the land as a farmer near Selukwe.

Ian Smith had been elected on 13th April 1964 to succeed Winston Field and his prime task was to secure independence from Britain. It was soon clear to him and others that Britain was not honouring its promises to grant self-government and independence, at least until it had brought about changes in the make-up of the franchise and the government. With civil strife flaring up, he voiced his determination that Nationalists would not come to power in his time.

The sort of diplomacy that he was called upon to exhibit was too much for him, or for his colleagues. After failed negotiations with the locally derided Harold Wilson, things had gone too far.

On Thursday 11th November 1965, early in the rainy season, and after much deliberation, these men took unilateral action and simply declared for themselves that Rhodesia would henceforth be independent of Britain. Their Unilateral Declaration of Independence, UDI as it became commonly known, had been inspired partly by the action of their American predecessors, and it extolled noble ideas that were soon readily espoused by the young and frustrated white population.

These people were not the civil-servant-British, typical of many of their colonies; they were permanent settlers who had sunk their lives and best efforts into the country. Rhodesia was their home and they believed in it with a passion.

The sparring nations were too polarised for successful talks, and stung pride evoked an immediate British response, with trade sanctions, rhetoric and a withdrawal of many sorts of help and involvement. The people rallied to their new flag, and cockily proceeded to circumvent the sanctions, further developing a sophisticated industrial sector, which proudly claimed it could make almost anything that the country needed. Diversification and the imposed needs created many opportunities, and the business community responded vigorously to fill the gaps.

Opposing voices were silenced, including those from within the Catholic Church. People who sided with Britain's stance were isolated and quite a few left the country permanently. Newspapers were soon subject to severe censorship, and articles they were about to publish were often summarily disallowed, so that newspapers were printed with large blank spaces, denoting the censored omissions. On some days, nearly half the front page had been blanked out.

CATECHISM IN BULAWAYO

Some of his colleagues passed on, each leaving their own particular memory, and a sense of loss tinged the Masses said in the knowledge of their almost certain welcome in heaven. The ever-trusting and kindly priest from the Cathedral, Father Sixtus Impler died on 19th September 1967, shortly before Father Odilo celebrated his own thirty years as a priest. Father Joseph Kamerlechner died and was buried in Bulawayo the following year, and he recalled his first assignment at Saint Patrick's Mission, and how he had been encouraged in his determination to get out into the bush, the harsh and wild Africa, and help in the mission territories where these older priests had already started working.

Father Odilo visited most of the schools to give the Catholic children their religious instruction. Standing in front of the class, he was determined that they should learn and know all that he could compress into the short lesson time that he was allocated. One of his enforcement or inducement techniques was to offer a sixpence to the child who answered first or got most of the answers right. As part of his 'stick and carrot' philosophy he used to tweak the occasional ear of a boy who stubbornly failed to give the required responses.

Some children appeared more obstinate than others did, and one day a young Italian boy was misbehaving, so he called him up to the front of the classroom. "You know the punishment," he said, swinging his wooden ruler ominously. "Bend," he ordered, and then gave him two sharp hits on the behind. The boy didn't flinch. And he certainly showed no sign of reaction or remorse.

"Alright young fellow, I can see that you are not in the least bit sorry for what you have been doing. Bend again!"

A few more cracks with the ruler had no visible effect. Now, it seemed the boy's defiance called for more action, and he asked, "Have you had enough?"

"No, carry on," came the cheeky reply. He held his neck and bent him over the table for a few more 'dawks'. He soon realised that he had gone far enough, still without a reaction. Something in his own mind clicked and he remembered his own defiance and the painful consequences as a child in a similar situation.

Well, the young boy went home after school and kicked up a big fuss with his parents, about his painful tail end. That afternoon, Father Odilo was approached by a very angry mother, who may still never have forgiven him after all these years.

Perhaps because of his own recollections of being the victim of an undeserved beating at school, he apologised to the mother, and later admitted to the bishop, "I took it too far with that young fellow, that was a big mistake on my part."

Another mother took exception when he beat her son, but he grew up to become a good Catholic parishioner, and bore no resentment or malice towards the sometimes-severe teacher.

KILLER BUS ON THE OLD GWANDA ROAD

The next year was a year in Father Odilo's life filled with great and long-lasting changes. Just before he was due to go for his second ever home leave, on a trip to Germany, he received a phone call. It was Peter Cavill, who said, "I have bad news, Father."

"What has happened?" he asked.

"Bernard Pepper[9] has been killed."

Father Odilo slumped in shock and sadness, before asking, "What happened?"

"We don't have all the details yet, and I am just letting you know what I have heard because I know he is a great friend of yours," Peter explained.

"Well, tell me what you know," he said impatient with sadness.

"Doctor Pepper was driving back home from their farm to Bulawayo, with Elizabeth and Judy. They were all three killed in an impact with an oncoming bus. The ambulance has taken them to Central Hospital."

Father Odilo immediately got in his car, and drove to the hospital, to pray and administer the last rites. The sisters on duty were in a state of shock themselves and were very upset, but they soon allowed him into the morgue. What he saw was devastating.

Bernard was such a fine man, and he looked at his body lying next to his beautiful wife and his lovely young daughter. Bernard had really been the church's own family doctor, always there for the priests and religious. He was their friend in a special way and most of them had been tended by him at one time or another.

His body was a mess; his face was lacerated and damaged almost beyond recognition. His ears and eyes and mouth and his whole body was still covered with traces of white mealie meal, which had burst from its packets. His one arm was so broken and mangled that it did not even seem to be part of him now. He heard one of the sisters saying, "I don't know how God can allow such a thing to happen!"

He drove past the race-course in deep sadness, like an automaton, hardly aware of the traffic and pedestrians. Back at the Cathedral, an hour or so later, the bishop gave him more details. Apparently, they had been heading north on the dusty and winding road, when they came

---

9   Sunday 15th March 1970

face to face with one bus carelessly overtaking another. There was no time, or space, to move before they collided head-on. Their Land Rover was no match or protection against the impact, and all three were killed instantly on the spot.

"This has been the worst accident I can think of. There was just nothing I could think of when one of the sisters asked 'how can God allow this?' His voice quavered slightly and he paused to settle his emotions.

The bishop waited patiently, admitting, "I can well understand—it is a terrible thing. Many times I have seen how God seems to take the very best to Himself."

"Not only was he a parishioner, but he was a real friend," Father Odilo explained through moist eyes. "I admired him so much, and his lovely family."

"You knew them more than I do, but I think it will be best if I say a few words on Thursday. You will surely struggle too much," he said. "Do you feel like telling me a bit more about Bernard?"

"I will make some notes for you, my lord, but he was a great man. He was the perfect, real family doctor. I know how highly he was respected by everyone in Bulawayo. We called him the doctor priest. He was just as effective as any priest, in his work as a doctor, and also in counselling families."

Father Odilo concelebrated at the funeral and the requiem mass, which Bishop Adolph Schmitt celebrated for the Pepper family on the Thursday afternoon. Saint Mary's Cathedral and all of the grounds were filled, with an overflowing congregation of two thousand people. He was known and loved by so many people, from all races and religions. There were hundreds of schoolchildren as well. They came from the Convent, Townsend, Eveline, Founders, Christian Brothers College, Milton and most other schools.

It was amazing how many knew and had become friendly with the lovely girl, Judy. Suddenly she was much more than an acquaintance or school-friend. Each young person who had met her felt the sudden loss, and perhaps experienced the fear and loneliness of bereavement. She was a beautiful person, and in a flash she had been killed. There were very few dry eyes to be seen anywhere, and Father Odilo looked at the proud young sportsmen who were so confused and embarrassed, as their necks stiffened or they adjusted their shoulders suddenly. He caught at his own tensing throat and managed to fight back near-tears.

The eulogy was read to a silent congregation, and told a little bit about Bernard and the Pepper Family. He had studied medicine at St. Mary's Hospital under Professor Alexander Fleming, at the time when Fleming was working on his discovery of penicillin. He wished to become a naval surgeon during the war, but the authorities kept him in London, in the Emergency Medical Service, until he was commissioned and posted to West Africa. He later practised in Johannesburg, and then went to Ndola with the Anglo-American Corporation, before coming to settle in Bulawayo, as a partner in the practice of Mr. Standish-White. He spent the rest of his professional career in Bulawayo, where he built up a good practice, and where he was well known for his social and charitable work.

A strong contingent of the Bulawayo Catenian[10] Association were there to honour their founder. He had been their first President and later took over as secretary, although he was a very busy man. Father Odilo had to fight back his own emotions when one of his stalwart parishioners, France Slaven, shook hands with him and said, "he was such a wonderful man, but also a very humble man."

Elizabeth Pepper was herself descended from a historic family, whose grand-father had been a friend of Mzilikazi, whom he used to visit in the nearby kraal of Mhlahlandlela[11]; he had even spent a few months there, in the royal kraal. By a tragic co-incidence, this was only

---

[10]   The Catenian Association is an organisation of Catholic business and professional men, which avoids party politics and whose objects are mainly social, but also to foster goodwill between all sections and sects of the community. Their aims are:

   To foster brotherly love among the members

   To develop social bonds among the members and their families

   To advance the interests of members and their dependants by individual or collective action

   To advance the interests of young Catholics and to assist them in the choice or pursuit of a career

   To establish, maintain and administer benevolent funds

[11]   iSindebele for 'hacking through', after Mzilikazi's mfecane and long journey from Tshaka's kingdom in Natal

a few kilometres from the spot where his granddaughter was to perish over a hundred years later.

"Judy was a beautiful seventeen-year-old girl at the time she died. She was bright and vivacious, full of fun, and a keen sportsgirl. She was popular as deputy head girl of the Dominican Convent High School in Bulawayo, and was active and community minded. Her death has been a great shock and sad loss to her many young friends."

There was only one survivor, the sister, Jennifer, who had not been in the car. Bernard's brothers were there, Father Francis Pepper and Professor David Pepper, as well as Elizabeth's brother and sister.

APPOINTED AS PROVINCIAL SUPERIOR

While he was in Germany on home leave in 1970, he was appointed as the Mariannhill Provincial Superior. His colleague, Father Elmar Schmitt, who had developed the new parish of Christ the King in Hillside, was appointed as Bishop of Mariannhill. Now, he suddenly had to present his report in Rome, having had almost no chance for preparation and with very little data and information at his fingertips.

He had been actively looking after his missions and hospital, and was becoming comfortable in his work. Now he was required to move again, and he would happily have stayed where he was. However, the vow of obedience had to be combined with a spirit of willing endeavour, and this was how Father Odilo accepted the position. He was unhappy to move, but he moved happily anyway. He took on the task and soon he was working tirelessly for his fellow priests, brothers and sisters, and the communities, which they all served.

Back in Bulawayo, Father Odilo was regularly interviewed on radio, and had become a spokesman for the church. One of his young parishioner families, Norris and Maureen Baker, had a son, Jonathan, who used to attend Mass from the "crying room" as the baby and toddler room, next to the altar, was called.

His mother used to shush him, saying, "Shh! Listen. Jesus is speaking," meaning of course that God was talking to the congregation, through the scriptures and the prayers invoked by the priest, Father Odilo. One day, hearing a combined churches service being broadcast from Saint John's Anglican Cathedral, he suddenly said, "Mommy, come quick. Jesus is speaking!" At first, Maureen was baffled until she realised the connection with Father Odilo's voice over the radio.

PASTORAL LIFE

Parish duties included attendance at several meetings, and one of his favourite groups was the Catholic Women's League. Perhaps this was because they were always such admirers of him. For his own part, he had a deep respect for the women of the community, protected by his vows of celibacy, but nonetheless he often caught himself admiring one fine-looking lady or another. He was often aware of the sacrifice he had chosen to make for God, and found that Our Lady was a wonderful comfort at such times. Her own dedication and purity strengthened him in his prayers and thoughts.

One evening, though, the meeting became very contentious, with lots of womanly wrangling and argument, some of it about the men in their lives.

When he addressed the ladies at the end, he professed, "I thank God that I am a priest. As I am not married, I don't have to go home and sleep with the person I am angry with." He politely said goodnight, and left behind a group of very shocked ladies. The next meeting was characterised by unusually courteous exchanges and ended half an hour earlier.

DEDICATION

There were some disappointments along the way, and one of the most difficult was seeing a fellow-priest giving up his vocation. "The difference between us and other Christian pastors, is that we make a full and total commitment, and it is for life."

The bishop responded sadly, "yes, but we are all human, and some will not be able to keep their promises, as has just happened."

He thought of the gospel acclamation of the day, "The Lord is Compassion and Love, slow to anger and rich in mercy", but it did not make it much easier for him. 'I am also very human,' he mused. 'How can I aspire to be like God?'

He could not help explaining, "I just find it upsets me when a man does not keep his promises. I know very well that our vows are difficult, and we fail sometimes. But we promised in the most solemn way."

He knew that nothing could change what had happened, though. He could only look at his own life, not those of others who seemed to have let their confrères down. When he thought about it later, he put it all down to that prized value, consistency, or dedication.

One evening after a dinner with his friends, Roy and Sheila, he put it in words. "Dedication is the key. I agree that the priesthood is far from easy. But you know, we have so much extra grace and help from God. A priest has to make a full and total commitment to his vocation. I remember one of my professors telling us that a half-committed person will never be able to do all that will be expected of us as priests."

Sheila nodded in understanding, and Roy was pensive again, as he went on, "of course, all of this is only possible with God's help, as you two know so well yourselves."

THE WANKIE DISASTER—AN UNDERGROUND EXPLOSION, 6ᵀᴴ JUNE 1972

Just before his sixtieth birthday, there was terrible news about an underground explosion at Wankie Colliery. "The details are still being checked," Eric Marshall told him. "It looks very, very serious, though; I think there are about five hundred men trapped underground."

There had been a cave-in of Number Two shaft, and three men were already known to have been killed. The records were quickly checked and it was soon confirmed that four hundred and twenty sixty men were trapped underground. Father Odilo knew some of them personally, and he offered his prayers throughout the night.

The methane gas, of which these regions were a still-undeveloped reservoir, impeded rescue, and the mine was in an extremely dangerous state. As the days dragged on hope was gradually lost; all rescue efforts had failed to get to the men and they had no way out. "I am afraid that the gases are certain to have overcome them all by now," one of the engineers told him. "We have no way of even ventilating the area, and too much time has passed."

The agonising decision was taken some time later. With great sadness, the reality was accepted and the shaft was sealed, becoming the victims' tomb.

GRIEVANCES AND GUERRILLAS

There was a growing under-current of political dissent. As has occurred throughout the course of history, people began to see two groupings—those who had and those who did not have. Communist influences and teachings were readily on hand to ignite and fan these flames. Building upon the partial reality of social injustices, a whole edifice of developmental history was soon being targeted, with what later became an Orwellian farce of tragic magnitude.

When problems became apparent, people spoke about it, and many of the urban parishioners were from the more fortunate group. A headmaster argued, "The national income is finite, but we are expected to provide free services across an impossible base."

Most of the opposition came from the ranks of the 'working classes', but some churchmen and others spoke out strongly in condemning government inaction or skewed policies.

The forces that drive people to cling to their possessions and their positions are the same things that blind them to all reason. The insistent shouts of the slogan-makers are equally blinding, but the passions they stir on both sides are the fuel for conflagration. Rhodesia was a juicy target, and the 'prince of this world' was soon happily at work fanning up division and hatred. In later years, the continued effects of envy and covetousness would be seen, but for now there were enough grains of truth for the world's war-mongers to build on, and with skilful exaggeration, to fan into an awful and cruel conflict.

It was hard for priests to deal with the differing groups in the community, each of whom had a case for their own position. When a person became emotional and responded in an unchristian manner, Father Odilo reminded himself, 'that person is one of God's beloved children, even if the devil seems to be stirring up such anger and hatred. It is not the person, but the devil who is our enemy.'

"We demand higher wages," or "look at the way they live, from our sweat and blood," and "down with imperialism", were some of the cries. "We want free schooling. We want free medical treatment." Anger was growing.

A police officer in the parish argued, "Jesus, Himself, said, "The poor will always be with us." Looking Father Odilo in the eye, as if to wrest his agreement, he continued, "how can we be expected to raise the living standards of everybody? These people are making demands that are quite impossible!"

The Church was faced with a difficult task. Jesus had not actually set about toppling the oppressive rule of the Romans, and the people had turned away. The miracle worker could not be the awaited Messiah, they thought. He even preached against the wrongs in the temple and their own leadership. Now, it seemed to Father Odilo, a similar picture is repeating itself right here. As a priest his main concern was for the spiritual life of his flock, but he could clearly see the crosses that they were given to bear.

In his peace-making role, he often had to contend with people's emotional outpourings. 'I truly understand what he is saying,' Father Odilo thought, 'but how do I get him to see the other side?'

There were times when priests could not condemn those who were more fortunate, but the pressure from those who had so little was growing stronger. People involved with the missions came to sense this quicker than the town parishes, which were sheltered in their urban affluence, and surrounded by the infrastructure, which the European community was convinced they had introduced to this country.

The difference in education standards and facilities between the Europeans and Africans was obvious to all. Ian Edmeades argued, "Nobody disputes that. However, you have to ask where the money is coming from. Then you must decide how it is to be spent. He who pays the most is entitled to expect the greatest benefits." As the Town Clerk of Bulawayo, he was respected as a man of sound vision; his city was well-kept and ran well, but Father Odilo had a strong feeling that he did not hear all the voices, some of which were muttering more and more in the townships.

"Consider our hospitals and schools for example. It is human nature for people to be envious. Look at Milton School, for example. It is one of the best government schools you could attend in the world, but it costs almost nothing for those who can attend. Even a well-run township school does not compare in terms of teaching, facilities, sport and other amenities." The reality of a black-white divide was not put into words, but they understood what was going on; the real taxpayers were white. The towns were of their making, and most Africans lived in the 'tribal trust lands'.

One of the parish's lawyers, Frank Walsh, was firm and made his point forcefully, "that is simply a case of where the taxes come from; the Europeans pay nearly all the rates and taxes, and so they are entitled to call the shots. It is not a case of black or white at all."

The evening would have continued with this gathering of men re-assuring one another of their position, but Father Odilo asked, "are you sure you are doing all you can to help, say for the people you employ?"

"We all pay well above the minimum wages, I am sure. I certainly provide housing and rations for my own workers, and I am sure you do, Eric. And you, Frank. And you, Larry. What more can we do?"

"You are on the committee at Christian Brothers College; how many other races are there?"

"Not many, I admit. But we are already breaking the law, I think. Certainly government schools have been set aside for Coloureds, like Founders, and it is a very good school. The schools in the townships are practically free as well, and some of them are already going right up to 'O' and 'A' levels."

"We pay high fees to send our children to the Catholic schools. We could just as easily send them to Hamilton, Milton, Townsend, Eveline, and Gifford and so on, and for a very small fee. After all, it is our tax money that pays for those schools and teachers."

"Yes, but you do it for a good reason. You know that your children are being given a good Catholic base at our schools," Father Odilo reminded them. "We don't get the same government assistance, so the costs are higher, but I am sure you know it is worth it."

Dinner-table discussions grew more and more political, and the newspapers took positions against the more outspoken critics.

To add to the troubles, terrorist activity, as it was called, broke out in the country. The guerrillas were trained in Russia and China, and used the neighbouring territories to stage their incursions and attacks. Kenneth Kaunda and other rulers lent their support and provided bases.

Even their troops assisted, and Zambian soldiers openly stood in armed opposition on the other side of the Zambesi.

The 'Frontline' was drawn, and Rhodesia was its first target. On 17th May 1973 some Canadian tourists at the Victoria Falls took a walk within sight of these troops, and were shot at, and two of the girls were killed in the gorge downstream of the Victoria Falls. The Zambians defended their right to kill like this, adding to the growing resentment and anger, which was polarising countries.

Conflicts soon grew from isolated bombings and other acts of terrorism, to training recruits and manning major bases for incursions from neighbouring countries. "They are being supported and supplied by China and Russia," a parishioner explained. "It is clearly a fight against communism, but nobody wants to help us, except the South Africans, I suppose."

"What about the things they are complaining about?" asked Father Kevin. "It is the black people who are suffering through all of this."

"That may be; at least they should be given the opportunities and training to advance more," Don replied. "However, we have limited resources, and right now we are having to waste even these fighting terrorism."

At Midnight Mass, Wallis, one of the young wives, fainted during the service. Afterwards, revived by tea, they were chatting about what was going on. "All our men are away at this time; it makes us nervous, and I think lots of people are quite strung up."

"Do you know, I couldn't find a single condolence card at Kingstons or Philpott and Collins today," Allison said.

There were more and more deaths of people that Father Odilo knew. Sometimes, they were even parishioners, and it was very hard to comfort people like the Kirtons when their son, Tom, was killed in action. These funerals were so unnecessary. "I don't understand what has gotten into people; we have good relationships at work, in the schools and on the street. What is this fighting really all about?"

One of the ugliest incidents of the war was the rocketing of two Air Rhodesia Viscounts, and the ruthless murder of the downed passengers. This added to the publicity and propaganda of hatred that was being generated against enemy leaders like Nkomo.

Of course, many priests, sisters and brothers were also in great danger throughout those war years, and Father Odilo worried and prayed for them all constantly.

Some Mariannhillers were also lost to their community through resignation; his young assistant, Father Robert Borland, was laicized after five years as a priest, and Brother Felix Ndovorwi resigned.

CHAPTER 15

A SERVANT OF THE CROSS

SERVING MARIANNHILL AND CHRIST THE KING

The biggest turning point had occurred while he was in Germany and, in his absence, he had been appointed Provincial[xiv] of the Mariannhill order. This was a serious obligation, although it was a great honour as well. Few men would ever wish to take this task upon themselves. His friend, Father Elmar, had done a great job and was now being transferred to the Mariannhill motherhouse in Natal. Father Odilo, on leave in Germany, suddenly had to report at the Chapter, which was held in Rome, and had not been at all prepared for this task.

On his return, he settled in at Christ the King parish; it was quite new, and the Mariannhillers were rightly proud of their congregation and parishioners. The Catholics in the area had collected and contributed a large part of the costs. This was a relatively prosperous parish, with many people who had their own businesses, or ran large companies, or worked as doctors, lawyers, architects, accountants and other professionals. They used to gather for Holy Mass in the old Hillside Scout Hall, near the Hillside shops. They had all been delighted when Father Elmar had celebrated the first Mass in the new church, the cross on its tower visible along the tar road, heading out from town to the Matopos.

The foundations had been laid and the Church hall was getting along quite well when Father Odilo arrived to take over. This had to be completed, and opened, and Father Elmar was invited to be there for the official opening; after all most of this had been his brain-child, or at least he was the priest who brought it this far.

Christ the King Church, in Hillside, Bulawayo

The Provincial Chapter was held at the parish on 6th September 1971, and it was a purposeful and inspiring assembly of the Mariannhill Missionaries from all over the huge southern African province. A lot of laughter and cheerful banter was mixed with reporting, planning and encouragement.

He shared the bitter disappointment of the local sporting community when their highly talented athletes, from a small but tenacious country, suffered at the hands of the politics of the world and were sent back from his homeland, Germany, barred from competing in the Olympic Games at Munich.

Perhaps they were spared being close to the fate suffered by the team from Israel. A gang of terrorists attacked them, and took thirteen Israelis hostage. The fierce rescue shootout killed five terrorists, but resulted in the deaths of eleven Israelis and one West German policeman.

The Second Vatican Council in Rome had also resulted in many changes in Church administration and rituals, and Father Odilo convened the necessary additional chapters to discuss reforms and implement these.

There were soon lots of changes. In 1974 Bishop Henry Karlen, CMM came from Umtata, to take over the running of the diocese and Father Kevin O'Doherty arrived to help. "I think I owe my vocation to Bishop Schmitt," he told Father Odilo. He went on to explain how, when he was a young, tough, footballer, he had become disgusted by some of the foul language and locker-room nonsense. He was troubled and searching for a purpose in his life, and one day he was waiting in a car when the priest came and spoke with him. He ended up suggesting, "Why don't you become a priest?" It was Bishop Schmitt and that was the start of his calling.

Father Guntram, from the class after him at Wurzburg, returned to Germany and the following year Father Martin Schupp was appointed Vicar-General.

Around Father Odilo's sixty-fifth birthday, in October 1977, a popular Bulawayo-born secular priest, Father Chris Gardiner, took up a transfer to the USA, much to the sadness of many people.

Hospital Visits

Perhaps it was all too much pressure, or perhaps it was from the effects of years of mission work and the illnesses, but he ended up in hospital himself for an operation. Now he was the patient again, and the Franciscan Sisters of the Divine Motherhood gave him devoted care and had a wonderful chance to make a motherly fuss of one of their favourite priests.

On one of his frequent visits to Mater Dei Hospital, Father Odilo met an elderly Colonel with whom he spoke. He was a very disciplined and proper gentleman, but their conversation moved the Colonel to shed some tears. He was mortified and embarrassed, and on the next visit, sought to explain how he should not have cried or broken down in that way. He had been drilled all his life not to show any emotions, and he apologised for this lapse of self-control. "So what," said Father

Odilo. "Good Lord, man, Jesus Himself cried; why on earth should you feel ashamed?"

Hospital visits

One day, a lady whom he visited was about to go in for an operation, and he began to pray with her. "By the way," he asked, "what is the operation you are having?"

She immediately rebuffed him with, "mind your own business!"

Another young woman impressed Father Odilo with her deep faith. Although she was not a Catholic, and had lost her husband in an accident, she had a beautiful faith in this time of grief, and simply said with assurance, "I know the Lord will help me."

Father Odilo managed to be there to hold the hand of one of his typical patients, Doreen Sullivan, as he did for so many other women, as they went in for an operation at Mater Dei Hospital. He said a prayer with her when she went in to the theatre and she always remembered how he gripped her hand so firmly, with the strength of a man who can support and balance his body perfectly in gymnastics, and fight an opponent to the floor in a challenge. Those same hands also conveyed warmth, comfort and love, and passed on God's blessing when most needed.

When she came round later, he was there at her bedside again, ready to comfort and pray with her. There are so many people, Catholics and non-Catholics alike, who have found his prayers and comfort to be a rich help in their times of doubt and worry.

Many years later, Diane told the story of her father being visited in hospital. Over a period of time he told her that he had decided to convert and become Jewish. She was not perturbed, but wondered what had brought about this decision, so she asked her father.

"Oh", he replied, "I have been so impressed by the Rabbi who visits and prays with me each day."

"What's his name, dad", she asked.

"Rabbi Odilo, of course", he said.

TEASING PEOPLE

Father Odilo could not resist it one day, on his visits. "Do you have any idea what you told me when you were coming round from your anaesthetic?"

A worried look crossed this lady's brow, and she asked, "What Father?"

"Oh, you said far too much; I could tape your words and pass on the names of all your old boyfriends to your husband!"

"Oh, Father, you wouldn't" she pleaded.

He looked at her compassionately, this lovely mother of four children, who had suffered so much. "Of course not," he relented. "You didn't say anything intelligible at all; you were just moaning and mumbling for quite a while."

"Why do you tease me like that?"

His face creased into a smile, and he said, "Because you are such a lovely person. I just could not resist it. I also know you well enough, that I would never harm you."

"You are full of mischief, but what would I ever do without you in my life," she answered. "You have always been there, when we were married; when each of our children was born; when we had that terrible accident; when my mother died. I could go on and on. Thank you, Father. You have been a wonderful priest and friend to us all."

Neville Turner was a non-Catholic who used to come to the parish quite often with his wife, Nikki. He came round one day from an operation and found Father Odilo there. "What's happened?" he asked in a hushed voice.

"Nothing to worry about. Your operation went well, and I was just sitting here saying a little prayer for you as you came round."

"Thank God, I got such a fright, I thought I must have been dying, seeing you at my bedside!

Chapter 16

Cain and Abel

The Hitch-hiker

It was early morning, and the rising sun was casting dappled patterns as it shone through the roadside trees. Father Odilo headed out on the road past State House and Northlea School. At this time of day there was still not very much traffic, although there were always a few people standing hopefully with their thumbs out-stretched, mostly trying to get a lift the other way, into town.

He drove past the small dam next to the old stone castle on the left. The eccentric old Mr. Redrup, a member of the local Meikles dynasty, had even equipped it with suits of armour and all sorts of similar oddments. He thought of him with concern, and wondered how the old man was keeping. As he came up towards the Victoria Falls Road garage, he saw there was a youngish European man hitch-hiking. It was not always wise to give lifts, sometimes for safety, but sometimes also to avoid conversation with strangers when you wanted a bit of peaceful thinking and praying time.

This morning, he felt sorry for the man, and pulled over to offer him a lift. Normally a hitchhiker would run up, open the door and get in with effusive gratitude. This fellow was different. He walked carefully all the way around the car. He was looking in through all the windows, and seemed very snooty or quite strange.

Eventually, he said, "I will come," as if he was doing a great favour in accompanying Father Odilo.

In the meantime, the delay and his attitude were annoying Father Odilo. He was starting to think a few uncharitable thoughts, like, 'why should I bother?' or, 'what a cheeky fellow . . . .'

The hiker opened the passenger door, and got into the front of the car. They exchanged 'good mornings' and the usual social exchanges and drove on. After a while, Cyril explained that he came from Ireland, and he had been warned to be very careful about taking any lifts in Rhodesia, for fear of his life.

"I come from Belfast, and we have a lot of trouble back in the home country," he continued to explain. "My cousin was caught by a bomb in our pub a few years ago, and he has been badly maimed. I can't help sympathise with Sinn Fein's anti-British sentiments, but terrorism is never right."

"Well, I have never understood your troubles in Ireland," admitted Father Odilo. They travelled on in silence for a while, on the well-kept tarred road, crossing a few small rivers, and climbing through a short stretch of gentle winding hills.

A convoy of police vehicles came towards them and flashed past, doing a good one hundred and twenty kilometres per hour or so. The men wore military camouflage, and sat on the back of the vehicles, with rifles facing out, looking quite alert. "What's going on?" he asked.

"There was a small group of terr's in the area yesterday, and they must have been out following up."

"Who are they, what are these terr's?" he asked.

"That's a slang name for terrorists. That is what the army calls them. They are local Africans. They have gone to be trained in Russia and China," he explained. The road took a wide turn, and they were soon bumping up and down. "Bumpy patch here." The Mopani trees on either side were like short bushes, with a few which had survived the regular chopping for poles and firewood. He continued, "They are trying to intimidate and frighten everyone, so that they can take over the country," said Father Odilo.

"Why? Have they got a cause?" he asked.

"I don't believe it's them really. There are others behind them," he mused. "Of course, there are always things which people can pick on. It is true that the Europeans do not want to be over-run, or give up what they have developed. So, the government is afraid to give everyone the vote. Right now, there are almost no African people who are entitled to vote; you have to be a rate-payer or own a business or farm or things like that," he explained.

"Does that matter to them?" asked the hiker.

"I don't think it is a big issue; but there are a few, mainly trade unionists, who want things to change now. One of their leaders is a man called Joshua Nkomo, and there are a growing number of more political Africans."

They startled a pair of hornbills, as they drove up to them on the road. "Must be something there they were eating," Father Odilo commented. "Things have changed, I think. Quite a few Africans are being stirred up now, and they think they are being deprived of something," he answered.

"Well, I guess they are. I know we have resented the British in Ireland for ages now, and perhaps they have a case," he provoked. He sat still for a bit, and Father Odilo was quiet as he concentrated on the road, always alert for animals that could come out suddenly on, or across, the road.

They had given each other things to think about, and drove on in silence, as men are able to do on a long journey. The trees became taller and denser, and it was a bright sunny day. The road was cleared on either side, up to the fence, but there were large trees in the road reserve; it gave the road a unique atmosphere, something between a park and wild bush.

After a while, the hiker broke the silence. "You know, I wonder how useful it is to vote really. Perhaps the most important question is—have they got jobs?"

"Good point; there are definitely not enough jobs for everybody. Most Africans are not very well off," Father Odilo replied. "They live quite simply; they make a modest living from their crops, and a few cattle and goats. Look at that little village." He glanced to the right as they came up and sped past. "Can you see the huts?"

"Yes, and there are quite a few people milling about."

"Well, that kraal will have a family with a lot of 'extended family' members living there as well. You can see they have ploughed their fields, and I think they have planted their maize seeds already."

"Is that their staple food?"

"Yes. You fellows eat a lot of potatoes in Ireland; well here it is maize. They grind it themselves by hand, or else buy it already ground from town. It is a good basic food, and they add rape[xv] and pumpkins, with a bit of meat sometimes."

"Those people we passed along the road all looked quite healthy and happy; they waved at you, I noticed, just like people do back home."

"Ah, sure. The people here are good people. They are generally honest and decent, and they work well enough when they have the right management. It is only when they have bad ideas drummed into them that things go wrong."

"Like what?"

"Well, the communists tell them that if they take the Europeans' things they can be rich and successful as well. Things like trucks, tractors, equipment, and even their houses and land."

"There don't seem to be any Europeans around here. Where are they?"

"You will see further along. We will come to European farmlands. You can see straight away. There are farms with planted trees and orchards, bigger herds of cattle, and much larger fields, which are being worked. They are also well fenced to keep their animals in, and others out."

"Who owns this land, then?"

"It is called Tribal Trust land, and is owned by the government really. It has been set aside for the Africans. Nobody else may own it, and the Africans have a tribal system of ownership and inheritance."

They journeyed on in silence, until Cyril broke in on Father Odilo's thoughts. "I am busy reading this book, "Path of Blood". Have you read it?"

"No, what is it about?"

"It is about the Zulu nation, and the Matabele who came here under Mzilikazi, eventually. They certainly were a fierce lot, and he describes their scorched earth path along the way."

"That was what they called the mfecane." Fr Odilo commented, pronouncing the "c" with a click behind his front teeth.

"How do you say that?" asked his hiker.

"Mfecane," repeated Father Odilo, again making a clicking sound, which drew a puzzled look from the man beside him.

"I have heard a few of their pronunciations, but I can't get it." I know that English people think we have some odd ways of saying things, especially in Gaelic, but this Zulu is so different."

"It is easy when you learn it, but I agree, it takes a bit of getting used to. Just place your tongue behind your top teeth. Now, pull it down sharply, like you are doing a noise to express disapproval of something."

"c, c," went the sounds, and slowly but surely, he was able to pronounce the word very well.

"There are lots of words like this, and with other click sounds as well," explained Father Odilo. "I have often made a wrong pronunciation, and it can get you in all sorts of difficulties. Mind you, I've done that with English as well."

He told the story of how he had mispronounced "cough" as "cow", and several other incidents, as they continued their journey in the sort of friendly conversation which men can easily get into. The kilometres passed by as they drove through the teak forests of Matabeleland, and soon it was near the end of Father Odilo's trip.

"By the way, that sounds an interesting book you were reading. Who is it by?"

"Peter Becker. He seems to know his subject well, and I enjoy his style of writing. He gives an excellent account of the rise and fighting of the Zulu nation. As you say, that mfecane was Mzilikazi's path of death and conquest, on his way to settle near Bulawayo."

"I spent quite some time in Natal, at our Missionary Headquarters, and I met many Zulus; in fact that was where I learned their language. I developed a great respect for these people, not that I did not already have it, as a priest, you know. It is simply that when you can understand people more, you see things through their eyes. I have learned that we can't just change things instantly, even when we are sure we know better."

When he was being dropped off, he said, "I really enjoyed meeting you, and thank you very much for the lift. I think you will enjoy this book." and he gave it to Father Odilo.

VISITING THE MISSIONS

As Provincial Superior, Father Odilo had to travel a great deal and visit his many scattered confrères regularly. He would leave their Provincial House, at Christ the King, early in the morning, and he enjoyed his ride. Most of the time he was alone, as there were very few people whom he could take away from their busy tasks.

He remembered how Bishop Arnoz had made his tours, and caught him out with his collar off. He also remembered the way he had cycled among his out-stations, and the roads that they had to use in those days. A lot had changed; there had been huge improvements.

The missions were the mainstay of the country's rural education and health-care, and most of the people they served deeply appreciated what was being done for them.

"What is happening in Rhodesia?" he was asked one day at Saint Luke's Mission. "Why can't we put a stop to this terrorism and lawlessness?

"Things seem to be getting worse. There has been an increase in terrorist acts each month." Despite controlled newspapers and broadcasts which did not reveal much about what was happening, missionaries and people living out of town got to hear about things pretty quickly. He was speaking to those who already knew.

"The locals are scared of everybody now; and the army and police can't be everywhere," he pondered aloud. "Still, I am certain you are all desperately needed by the people; I hope they respect that always," he said to Dr. Davis.

After tea, he drove on for a while on the beautiful forest road towards the Victoria Falls. A little way further along, he turned off to the left, and headed along the sandy dirt road to Fatima Mission. The sun was high in the sky, but the shadows were thick under the forest trees. It was a familiar route, and he had driven and even cycled it many times in the past. He was greeted warmly by so many of the people as he drove in dustily.

"Good morning," he greeted his colleagues. "How are things going with you?"

"Fine, all is fine," was the stock answer. Then after a while, they sat down to lunch and the conversation came more to the point. "We are quite worried really. There have been a lot of incidents around our area. Will this terrorism ever be stopped?"

"It is certainly getting worse, but still, nothing lasts forever. Keep hopeful and put your trust in the Lord," he encouraged.

"What I don't understand is how they get people to support them. They beat them up, abduct them, rape the women, talk a whole load of rubbish, and still expect the people to feed, hide and support them."

"Which they do."

The hopelessness of things was discussed on many visits and with many different clergy. Most were strongly against the viciousness and cruelty, although after a while, it started to seem that they must have some cause; they certainly kept up a steady stream of new infiltrations and attacks, and must be well-supplied with arms and equipment.

THE RHODESIAN WAR

Things in the bush were definitely hotting up now. It was not long before it was considered dangerous even to go out to the nearby Matopos Hills. There had been a few incidents and attacks, and it was a vast area to control or patrol. Inevitably, it came under curfew rules, just before and for a while after Independence. However, these restrictions were not enough to dissuade Father Odilo from making his regular trips and climbs.

There was also a determination in him, to suppress anything that might seem like cowardice. He was not going to be deterred by the dangers; God had brought him safe thus far, through many dangers already. "I place myself in Your hands," he prayed while he also recalled his own schooling in the classics which had imbued him with attitudes, such as those of Boethius' Muse quoting from the Iliad:

'If first you rid yourself of hope and fear
You have disarmed the tyrant's wrath:
But whosoever quakes in fear or hope,
Drifting or losing mastery,
Has cast away his shield, has left his place,
And binds the chain with which he will be bound.'

As a missionary, he also felt confident that the good work he was doing must speak for itself. The acts of terror being reported across the country were increasing, and some of them were quite diabolical. Innocent villagers were the greatest sufferers, and he sympathised with their plight. These good, simple people just wanted to get on with their lives, earning a living as well as they could, and seeing their children grow up, happy that they were being better educated than they were themselves.

At the same time European families saw their sons conscripted to do National Service. There was a period of basic training before deployment to resist and track down these terrorists, as they were called. The stories of what was happening in the operational areas were increasingly disturbing, and these boys had to contend with landmines and ambushes. Some told him about terrorist atrocities that they had been called out to, and overnight they became men, torn out of the safe city world they had grown up in, and now burning with a fierce passion to capture and even kill these callous murderers. Once again, communism was fuelling the strife, supplying the weapons and training, and fanning flames of envy and hatred.

Father Odilo had a way of caring for and enhancing his inner peace. He appreciated a solitude and closeness to God, which the granite hills and struggling trees of the Matopos gave him. He continued to drive out to visit the Rhodes Estate Preparatory School, and give religious instruction there. After that he would head off to climb and walk in the Matopos.

One day he climbed up Imadzi, a high, bare granite hill whose lower slopes are heavily and thickly wooded. There is a well-known old MOTH[xvi] shrine at the base of the hill. This is far from a gentle climb, and as he was climbing, on all fours using his hands to grip and haul himself up the slope, with his eyes to the rock face, he suddenly heard a voice, "what are you doing here?" He knew straightaway that this was not a Moses experience. He looked up, and there, partly hidden under a shady bush, he saw a soldier in camouflage uniform!

"I am going for a climb," he replied.

"Don't you know these hills are out of bounds?" the young white soldier asked rhetorically.

"I am getting my exercise," Father Odilo responded.

After a few more exchanges, the soldier moved off, saying, "Remember to obey the rules in future."

"Okay," he replied cheekily. "I will see you next week!"

As winter gave way to summer in 1976, there were frantic efforts to achieve a peaceful settlement of the Rhodesian situation. Henry

Kissinger, trying to apply his Middle East negotiating techniques, made several proposals and for a while it looked as if the impasse might be broken but that was not to be. The war intensified, with a huge rise in deaths.

BISHOP AND MISSIONARIES AMBUSHED AND MARTYRED

The rains had come, and it was always a pleasant relief. It was as if the sky had been wiped clean again, clearing away all the haze and dust from countless veldt fires. The air smelt fresh and pregnant with moisture, and everything was green again. There were little puddles on the ground along the sides of the road, and the sky began to fill up with those beautiful anvil-shaped storm clouds.

In the midst of the tensions, they felt some relief, as they drove along the corrugated dirt road, through the enveloping forests of Matabeleland. The light-barked trees were now in flower, and the mauve colours showed up well against their heavy green foliage. Occasionally, they passed trees that had been felled, and some of the trees had ring markings around their stems, indicating that they had been approved for felling by the Forestry Commission.

The congregation had appreciated the Mass at Regina Mundi Mission on Sunday 5th September 1976, but there had been a few less people than usual. It was the end of the term of course, and the army had been chasing small groups of terrorists in the area. Of course, that was not really their worry; as missionaries they knew they were not seen as targets, and their work for the people obviously spoke for itself.

Bishop Adolph Schmitt was driving the car, although he may have felt more comfortable if the younger man with him had been qualified to drive. He knew that he was slowing down since turning seventy, early the year before; but still he was alert and in full control. They were on their way to Saint Luke's Mission, to visit Brother Konrad Russer, who was receiving medical help there.

Father Possenti Weggartner, his junior by a good six years, was sitting next to him. The two Precious Blood Sisters, Frances Berkhout and Ermenfried Knauer, accompanied them. They all enjoyed one another's company, and it was always good to meet with their confrères at the other missions. The road surface had not been graded for a while, but did not carry much traffic so the car was not feeling the corrugations too badly.

They were driving around a bend, with the shadows of the trees falling over the road, when Bishop Schmitt noticed something unusual ahead. His neck tensed slightly, as he peered ahead, trying to see what it was. It was probably an animal; this was a wild part of the country, and they often encountered kudu, occasional cattle, or even the odd elephant from time to time.

As he got closer, he began to slow down. "What is that on the road?" asked Sister Ermenfried from behind.

"Looks like a branch fallen down," he suggested, as he slowed some more.

"That's unusual," Father Possenti said, "I suppose we will have to stop and move it."

As they came to a halt, it was clear that the road had been deliberately blocked with a few felled branches. "I can see a rock in the middle of that," said Sister Frances. "We'd better be careful; perhaps it's a trap."

Bishop Schmitt looked carefully, but could see that there was no way to go around it, as the road was narrow and the trees made sure there was no by-pass. He stopped the car, and said, "Well, we'd better move it and carry on."

There was nobody around, and they had not passed anybody at all since about five kilometres from the mission. So out they all got, and prepared to clear the route.

Suddenly, a man stepped out from among the trees, right into the middle of the road. He was wearing a red balaclava over his face, and full dark green camouflage uniform. "Hands up, or I shoot you!" he barked. They obeyed reflexively, and he walked closer, pointing his AK47 rifle at them menacingly.

"Who are you? What do you want with us?" the Bishop demanded.

"Shut up," he replied. "I ask the questions. Put your hands up, properly, and move together over there," he gestured with his rifle.

"I want money," he demanded.

"But we are missionaries. We don't have money," explained the Bishop reasonably.

"Of course you do," he shot back. "Show me your wallets, or I will kill you!"

"We are missionaries," pleaded Sister Ermenfried. "We really don't have money. Perhaps if you come with us to the mission, we have a little bit there. We can help with that."

"We come from Regina Mundi," Father Possenti started to explain.

"I don't care about that. All missionaries are servants of the capitalist pigs. You are enemies of the people."

'O Lord,' wondered the Bishop, 'how can that be true?' Decades of service flashed through his mind, and he knew how much wonderful and dedicated work the Mariannhill Missionaries had been doing for all these people.

Sister Frances now piped up, "Please, let us go. We have nothing. We do no harm to anybody. Just let us go on our way."

"Silence!" he shouted harshly. "All missionaries are enemies of the people. If you have no money, I must kill you."

With that, he let rip with a senseless hail of automatic gunfire, at point blank range, straight into the Bishop. They heard the dull thud of the bullets entering his flesh, and blood splashed all over the place. He slumped to the ground, and Sister Frances dived over to try and rescue him. The terrorist let rip again with a fresh hail of automatic fire, mowing down Father Possenti in an instant. The anguish was still on his face from what he had just seen happen to his Bishop, and the sisters saw him flung to one side like a stuffed doll.

Sister Ermenfried watched in horror, dumb-struck and paralysed. Suddenly she prayed, silently, but desperately; it was instantaneous prayer, and she appealed for protection from evil:

> "Holy Michael, Archangel, defend us in the day of battle; be our safeguard against the wickedness and snares of the devil. May God rebuke him we humbly pray; and do thou, Prince of the Heavenly Hosts, by the power of God, thrust down to hell Satan and all evil spirits who wander through the world seeking the ruin of souls."

As if in answer, she just knew that she had to act. Without thinking, she dived to the ground, and got under the car. She just managed to put her head behind the left rear wheel, and listened apprehensively, with all her senses, as suddenly the terrorist fired a round of bullets at

Sister Frances. She heard herself crying out, and almost felt the rounds thudding as they punctured her soft flesh.

There was a brief moment of silent horror, and then shots came flying in her own direction; she was cringing as she felt the shattering crunch as a single round ripped into her shin. 'This is it,' she thought, and was fully prepared to join the others and meet her Creator. She waited for another hail of bullets, which must surely follow. But nothing came, and then she thought she heard the man moving off, into the forest.

'What stopped him?' she wondered, in a complete daze. Her emotions were a complete jumble. She felt relief, horror, anguish, great sadness, helplessness and gratitude to God. Gingerly, she looked out from under the car. She could see the Bishop's body, and next to him the lifeless bodies of her other two friends. You don't need to wonder sometimes if a person is dead; they were absolutely still, with not the least signs of life, lying in overlapping pools of blood.

The smell of the rifle still hung in the air, and there was not a sound from the forest. Not a bird stirred, and even the endless cicadas had been silenced.

'Perhaps this is just a terrible dream,' she hoped, wishing the scene away. Seconds flashed by, and she knew it was all too real; she just lay there, not even thinking any more about how long she was there. After a while, the ground transmitted a familiar rumble to her. It was a car, and it was coming from the direction of the far-off main road.

She snapped into action; this was a chance that could not be lost, and she knew she needed help urgently if she was to have a chance of surviving. "Help," she cried out feebly, looking up as the car slowed down apprehensively. It was a coloured family, and as they stopped, she thought she recognised them.

"What has happened, sister?" the man asked, as he instantly recognised the missionaries. "It is me, Sister, Mr. West, from Lupane." While he spoke, his wife ran over to check the others. She went from one to the other. Although she felt each one for any sign for a pulse, their bodies were so ripped open by the gunshots that she held almost no hope. The horror of the sight emblazoned itself on her mind, and she shuddered as she turned to her husband. "Jimmy, they are dead," she cried out. She realized with a stunned sense of the impossible that these good people had been well and truly slaughtered, but no reason came to mind.

"How can God can allow such a thing to happen?" he asked, not expecting any answer.

They carefully dragged Sister Ermenfried out from under the car, and eased her into their own car. "Don't worry, sister," Jimmy feigned confidence; "we shall have you safe and sorted out in no time." Then, driving at great speed, he headed back along the way from which they had just come, to the Mission Hospital, Saint Luke's.

When they arrived at the hospital they found Dr. Davis in the men's ward. She was stunned and quickly organised cleaning and dressings for Sister Ermenfried. It seemed like seconds to the others, but it felt like hours to her, before she was able to get into her own car and head off down the road. As she moved, she was still ordering, "Give her some more sugar water for the shock, and prepare to take her to Bulawayo. She has lost a lot of blood; we don't want to lose her also."

The trees seemed menacing, their brooding shadows spreading deep into the forest. She didn't care now if they gunned her down. Nothing was going to stop her. She looked up at the clouds hanging low and dark in the sky, adding to the gloomy atmosphere. She managed to offer up some broken prayers, mainly to still her own racing thoughts. 'What is happening? How can the terrorists do such a thing? When have we missionaries ever done them any harm? It is senseless, senseless completely. Mad people are running wild . . . .' Bishop Schmitt's face flashed before her eyes time and again, always full of encouragement, he was a man who gave such loving support; even his corrections were like those of a loving father.

She slid around the sandy bend, righting the vehicle with an experienced turn of the wheel. There they were, lying in the road; inert shapes that she knew immediately were those of her beloved colleagues. She felt the urge to cry out, to scream something, but her throat was dry, and nothing could relieve the anguish she felt with every fibre of her being.

Coming to a halt, she took in the scene at a glance. Cold-blooded murder had been committed; no resistance was offered, or probably possible. Their bodies were ripped apart by multiple gunshot wounds. The brutality and horror of it were unbelievable. She did not want to believe it, either, but, slowly she composed herself again.

Death and blood were no strangers to her as a doctor, but this was something else! 'Where is the sense in it? Who have they ever harmed?' Images of the horror during Nazism came to her mind. She thought of them now, seeing them as God's beloved creatures; humans, made in His image and likeness, precious in His eyes—but treated like this! 'What madness has been invited into the country?'

Dr. Davis moved silently from one to the other, hopefully checking each body, remembering each missionary and friend. While she was still feeling Sister Frances for a pulse, a Land Rover arrived on the scene. Within minutes, army and police were all over the scene, combing the area for tracks to follow, and she heard a young white officer sending a stick off in hot pursuit. "Find the bastards that did this!" he yelled, "and make it fast; it'll be f* * *g night-time in a few minutes."

The sandy soil was firm on the road, with plenty of signs to work from and they had soon established that this was the work of a single gunman. Where the signs showed in the forest, they could make out the direction that this man had run off in. They fanned out into a sweep line and went swiftly but gingerly through the trees, keeping in visual contact with one another, all the time sweeping the trees with their eyes, FN rifles poised and ready for action.

The teak forests are thick, and the floor was covered with leaves, enough to conceal a whole group of tracks. Even a highly experienced tracker gets thrown by the jumble of conflicting evidence. Soon the tracks faded and they had to radio back to say they were no longer sure they were on his tail.

"Just keep moving in the direction he was last running. I don't care if you have to walk all the way to f* * *g Botswana; just stay searching!" the lieutenant barked back. "The blues are on their way, so keep in touch. Over and out."[xvii]

Dr. Davis did not get to hear if they found anything that night, but she had greater things on her mind. There were some bad people around, and she was sure she had seen some of them herself.

You knew your own people, the good ones. They were friendly and appreciative. As she drove out on her trips to her clinics, they waved as she passed. The waves were friendly, with a greeting and meeting of the eyes. But lately the people were troubled, and she could see that in their bearing.

There were some strangers round about now. They were not just people who were visiting from town; that was life in Rhodesia and happened all the time. These people she had noticed were different. They didn't return her wave; in fact she had felt something like hatred coming from them, she who attended selflessly to anybody in need. 'What is happening?' she asked God, while she kept busy with her ever-increasing duties. 'Please protect us from all evil.'

Only a short while later, on 7th February 1977, they received news of the massacre of seven missionaries at Saint Paul's, a Jesuit Mission at Musami, in Mashonaland. It shocked everybody, but especially the religious and missionary community. "What is this crazy behaviour?" Dr. Davis asked Father Odilo, as they sat together after lunch at Saint Luke's.

"I cannot understand it," he admitted. "These people are determined to do anything. They don't seem to care who they kill or hurt. If you are white you are a target, even if you are a missionary."

They chatted as close friends for quite a while, interrupted often by nurses and others coming for orders or asking permission for the many things they needed at a busy mission hospital. "I saw Dr. Decker this morning, and I warned her to be careful as well; these terrorists are moving around still. Please keep your gates locked, especially at night, and try to have somebody with you, one of the male staff, to keep an eye out for you."

"Yes, I will do what I can," she demurred unconvincingly.

A little while later, Father Odilo closed the door of his car to get on his way. "Be careful," he urged them all again, and he wanted to add words like, "I love you all deeply." Speaking like this was not something that he did, so the words stayed in his heart and thoughts. What he did was to silently pray and ask for Our Lady's special protection over them all, as he headed out on the sad and lonely track back to the Bulawayo road.

Deep in thought, he thought back over the Requiem Mass, seeing it again in his mind. It had been a sad and solemn occasion, with the Cathedral packed to overflowing. Many dignitaries and civic officials were present, and so many of the clergy that he had not realized how the

Church had grown since he arrived in Rhodesia, nearly forty years ago. Saint Mary's Cathedral had just celebrated its Feast Day, the feast of the Immaculate Conception. He thought of Our Lady, and her humble acceptance, when she said, "Be it done unto me according to Thy will."

That was a motto these missionaries understood and accepted; he felt relief, sure in the knowledge they had found their place in heaven.

BUILDER GUNNED DOWN AS HE SAVES MISSIONARIES

The ring of the phone seemed ominous, and he sensed that something serious had happened. "All right, slow down and tell me again. Tell me carefully. How did it happen?" he asked Brother Konrad. It took quite a bit of patience to calm him down and to understand how he saw it.

'He is so agitated; I must talk to one of the others to get a clearer picture,' Father Odilo realised. Later, after he had said some prayers with them, he sat down with an equally shaken Father Alois, and then interviewed the sisters.

This last attack, on 6th August 1977, had been a lucky escape, although they were all frightened and deeply saddened at the killing of Mr. Rudolf Kogler. He was an Austrian, who worked as a builder in Bulawayo; he often helped the missions, and the German priests knew him well and were always pleased when he came to work on their buildings, as he was doing now at Regina Mundi.

It was Transfiguration Day, and Father Alois had said Mass as usual for the sisters and the rest of the community. Father Odilo remembered vividly the day's readings, from the Book of Daniel; they were a source of special comfort. They must have all been listening hopefully as the Gospel relayed God's message about Jesus, "this is my son, the Beloved . . . . listen to him."

Later in the afternoon, trouble had come. Six armed men pitched up and walked into the beautiful circular church, while the sisters were gathering for Father Alois to hear confessions. The men had lined up Father Alois, Brother Konrad, the Sisters and others, against the wall, quite plainly intending to shoot them.

Rudi Kogler walked across the yard without realising what was happening. He was seized, beaten up and put in the line as well. He still had a revolver concealed on him, and as the leader was aiming at him and pulling his trigger, Rudi managed to get a shot off, killing the man with a shot to the chest. He himself was killed with a bullet through his neck, at that same moment. In the pandemonium, the others managed to run off. 'Thank God for his dear life; he had certainly saved many lives as he gave up his own.'

WOMEN MISSIONARIES KILLED

Saint Paul's Mission, in Lupane, was surrounded by troubles and the situation and these tensions had grown steadily since the beginning of the year. There were also a large number of reported incidents in the area, sightings, robberies, feedings and intimidation or even attacks on villagers.

The police required that Dr. Johanna Decker should report and give details on some of her cases. They had no phone at the hospital, and communications were a problem. The police persuaded her to accept an Agric-Alert radio, which connected them to the Lupane Police station. "At least, we can warn you of trouble," the young European officer explained, "and if you need help, we can get to you quickly."

After Bishop Schmitt's murder, the situation became more tense. A curfew was imposed, and nobody was allowed to move about between six p.m. and six a.m.

Sister Damiana had been working at the mission hospital for many years and she was confident that the people in the area were quite friendly to them as usual. However, they all began to notice some strangers who were watchful, and some even came into the premises. Once, she saw three young men in the hospital dispensary at about midnight. They caught sight of her as she came down the corridor and quickly disappeared.

The curfew was even more strictly imposed; the police told them they were not even allowed to move fifty metres from their houses, or they risked being shot.

Dr. Decker was warned by the police not to travel into certain areas, where she had clinics. She ignored this advice; she still travelled to the Dandanda area, where the police did not even go anymore! However, she came back; and said, "The people are very friendly to us still, and there are lots and lots of sick people who need our attention." She brought the more serious cases back to the hospital with her for treatment.

Sister Damiana had come across more young men in the past few weeks, whom she did not recognise, and could not identify. They were not at all friendly, and did not wave as the other people did. It was a bitterly cold winter now, and the situation had become even more serious. There were robberies and beatings, by well-armed guerrillas at the shops and kraals nearby.

The situation became even more serious. One evening, they sat over supper and discussed what they should do. "The danger has increased, and we are sure to be attacked," said Father Heribald.

"I think we all see that, and yet we just hope and pray that God will protect us," said Dr. Decker. "After all, we are simply here to help the people. We are not taking sides, even when we see how the guerrillas behave. Look how we stitched up that man last weekend and sent him safely on his way."

That night they again discussed what to do, but concurred, "It is our duty to stay and help, as missionaries. There is no question of vacating our mission station," Dr. Decker said. "I shall never leave this mission."

Sister Ferdinanda was the newest sister to join their ranks, having been working in South Africa. She had volunteered to help, when the appeal was made. They were extremely short-staffed and it was a great relief to have her help. She knew the seriousness of the situation as well.

One cold morning, the nurses found a note, attached to the fence of their houses.

The note said, "To the nurses. I feel sorry for you. If you want life, go back to your houses. The one we will find, it's the end of her. So tell the people to go back to their homes as well. For we are coming soon. We are near. Boys of the earth."

Dr. Decker discussed this letter with the missionaries and also with the hospital staff. Sister Damiana had an icy feeling about it. She watched Dr. Decker carrying on, as if she was in a dream, performing her duties tirelessly and bravely, pretending that she was not afraid. She thought to herself, 'She knows somehow that death may be imminent to her.'

This was reinforced as Dr. Decker often mentioned the letter to her, and asked Sister Damiana, "What do you think? You have been working here for over five years now. Are they going to attack us, even though we are missionaries, helping the people?"

"That letter was intended to upset us; I think they just want us to pack up and go," she said one day.

Not far away, the attack had just been made on Regina Mundi and Rudi Kogler had been killed.

They went to Holy Mass together on the morning of Tuesday 9ᵗʰ August 1977, something Dr. Decker never missed, unless as a result of a hospital emergency. On the way she asked about the threats, and Sister Damiana replied, "doctor, none of the staff have ever asked to go away, or to go for leave; they have not even complained of having problems, for which they just want a few days to go away. I personally have the feeling that, if it is really so dangerous, they would have done so. I think we should be safe."

Dr. Decker said, "Yes, I will stay. I know the people need our help. It is your day off, today. What are you going to do?"

"I have to do my house work. I have also promised Brother Matthias that I will sew the curtains for the end house."

"Oh, yes, that is where he wants us to put up the mobile team from the diocese."

"It seems that they are preparing for more troubles. They want to teach the people how to continue with services if a priest is not available."

Sister Damiana went off to her room, to get on with her housework, and the curtains.

After noon prayers, they went in for lunch, but Dr. Decker and Brother Matthias were late. After lunch, they went back to their duties, Brother Matthias heading back to work in the fields. Dr. Decker checked in on the Agric-Alert radio. There were reports of some incidents in the area, but she had nothing to report herself. She returned to the hospital with Sister Ferdinanda.

A short while later Brother Matthias came to see Sister Damiana and check on the curtains. "It is two o'clock, sister, are they ready?" he asked.

"I am sorry. I am having problems with my sewing machine, and they are not quite ready yet. I expect to fit them at about two thirty p.m.," she assured him.

"Ja, Ja," he acceded, and went off back to his work in the fields.

Just as she was finishing off the curtains, she heard a single shot very close by. She froze, and then moved carefully to look through her window. There she saw Sister Ferdinanda about twenty metres away, walking with her hands up, ahead of two men in camouflage. They were pointing AK rifles at her. Then she heard a whole salvo of high-pitched AK shots. She turned to the African woman who was helping her and asked, "Are these the boys?".

There was no reply, and her helper simply ran out of the house! Sister Damiana expected that they would come in and look for her. She waited in fearful apprehension, but nothing happened. After two or three minutes, she ran out. At the back gate of the hospital, just opposite her house, she found Dr. Decker lying on the ground. She had been shot directly in the heart; there was no sign of life, and she must have died immediately.

Rushing on along the fence, she found Sister Ferdinanda lying at the other entrance to Dr. Decker's house. She had about seven shots in her body, and she must have died immediately as well.

She ran to the maternity department, and asked, "what has happened?". There was total panic; patients were leaving in panic, even those who had just been operated on.

Outside, she found Sister Mary Tasisi coming from the church, with a teacher lady with whom she had been discussing problems. After hurried explanations she went back into her own little house. She was anxious about Father Heribald and Brother Matthias, but there were no reports of anything else having happened.

She reported to the police on the Agric-Alert radio, and said, "They have been here and have shot Dr. Decker and Sister Ferdinanda."

The radio suddenly went dead. She didn't know then, but the police were disconnecting anybody else who might be listening, and then a police voice came back asking for more details. "How many were they? What time did it happen?"

She answered and the questions kept coming until there really was not much more that she knew, so she simply could not give any more information.

Shortly after, Brother Matthias arrived on a bicycle. He had heard the shots and was walking back from the fields to investigate, when he had been warned by one of the workers that Dr. Decker had been shot. Then he heard more shots. He assumed Sister Damiana was also shot, having only seen her some thirty minutes before.

The worker had offered him his bicycle, and he told her, "I grabbed the bicycle and cycled off to make my escape. Then I thought better of it, and I decided to come back and see if I could help[12]. I climbed over the fence at the corner of the teacher's house, and the headmaster's wife told me that it was not even one minute ago that the terrorists had climbed that exact place and disappeared into the bush."

Meanwhile, the police had called back on the radio and instructed them not to touch the bodies or the scene of the killings. They waited a long, long time.

In the meantime, they found out that Father Heribald had gone out by lorry into the bush, to deliver a roof for one of the outschools. One of the Catechists came up to her. "Give me the key to a car, and I will drive out and look for him."

"No, it is too risky. The terrorists are probably still close by and they will simply ambush and kill you, for nothing."

As the sun was low in the West, eventually, the Lupane police arrived, from forty-five kilometres away. They came in camouflage, leaving their vehicles outside. Sister Damiana went out when she heard vehicles, and found men in uniform advancing from tree to tree. When they saw Dr. Decker's body, they asked, "What information can you give us, sister?"

"I cannot tell you much," she explained and went on to give a detailed account of what little she knew had happened. The bodies were only covered with a sheet, but had been left on the spot where they were killed.

From the distance, a whining hum approached, and suddenly two Alouette helicopters arrived, beating the air, and circling menacingly. One landed on the road, but the other stayed hovering about above. The soldiers leapt out, and fanned out quickly, scouring the ground for ammunition, booby traps and anything suspicious. Then, just as quickly,

---

[12] About six years later, he was to experience torture and murder himself, at Embakwe Mission.

they were gone again. The police took statements from them, and then allowed them to wrap the bodies of their dear dead. "Stay here, sisters," they ordered, and Brother Matthias and a Catechist were allowed to help carrying one of the police coffins to the helicopter.

Meanwhile, the nurses and others came back from the bush, and the policeman in charge advised, "Stay together in one house for the night. You are much safer, and can look after each other. They may come back, but I think they will have gone now, especially with the army on their tails like that!" They all prayed the rosary, and then Sister Damiana went to look after the patients, as none of the staff dared to go. "We are scared, we fear the soldiers even," they admitted with eyes filled with tears. Night settled, and they only managed snatches of sleep.

Early in the morning, Sister Damiana paid all the staff their full month's salaries. "You may go, but be ready for us to call you back as soon as we know what is to be done," she explained. There had still been no communications until Dr. Davis came through on the Agric-Alert. She asked them, "please just pack up all Dr. Decker's things, plus important hospital equipment." People streamed in from the surrounding villages to collect their patients, and the hospital was soon emptied.

Father Heribald came back on the same day. On his way back, he had crossed the Shangani River that day, close to the mission, and had come across patients fleeing towards him. They told him, "Father, you cannot go back! They have been and they have shot the doctor".

He crossed back over the Shangani and travelled along the other side, until he reached Saint Luke's Mission. From there he had made his way back. "We must stay put. This is a mission; surely there can be no more trouble."

Father Odilo was devastated. "These terrorists have struck again, but what makes them do this?" he asked knowing there was no sensible answer. His colleagues knew how fond he was of Dr. Decker. "I remember how she volunteered to come out here. Things were nice and peaceful in Germany, and she gave it all up to help the Africans. Look at what she gets. Nobody even had the guts to help her!"

"Come, Odilo, let's go back to the house for some tea," one of them said. He went calmly, deep in thought, and his whole body seemed to sag and droop in an uncharacteristic way. He had to meet with the survivors, and he did his best to console them. But who would be able to console him?

That night, when he was alone, he prayed, 'oh, God, help me to understand your will.' He knew they were safely in heaven, but the shock and the loss were terrible.

In the end, they all followed orders at the mission, and packed up everything that they could. They could not find any keys for the doors, as they never used to lock them. There had been no need and they trusted everybody.

Bishop Henry Karlen presided at the funeral service and requiem mass, assisted by Father Odilo. He preached the sermon, and spoke on behalf of the Mariannhill Missionaries, as their Provincial Superior. He was too overcome to cope with it all, and he handed over some of the funeral duties to his colleagues. He battled like never before to control his emotions, and had to pause frequently to compose himself. (He was a quiet-spoken man, but he spoke out bravely against injustices during these years of struggle—and there were excesses on both sides.)

In his sadness, Father Odilo asked himself, 'what ever made us leave Germany, and come here? What was the purpose? How can I justify persuading Dr. Decker to come and help? As for me, I could have become a secular priest and served God, where we would have been appreciated! Why did I come here?'

The church was packed, and the congregation was numbed with sadness and anger. He looked into their midst, and saw their faith, and their needs. 'All things work for good, for those who love the Lord,' he reminded himself. 'They died serving God; they are martyrs, and are surely in heaven looking down on us right now. That is where I want to be one day; nothing else in my life matters.'

He thought of these good friends and colleagues, killed senselessly; they had come to help the people of Africa, as he had. Their whole purpose was to live with compassion and helpfulness, and now this is done to them. What sort of a world was this?

Although he heard the words being said, his mind would not focus any longer. He saw each of them as if they stood there before him. Now he remembered especially, Dr. Decker. She used to chide him when he got angry; she had even given him a birthday composition of her own, where she ranked his anger by the words he had used, calling her 'Hannchen', 'Mother', 'Doctor', 'Deckerin', rising to 'Doctor Decker', 'madam' and ending with 'Rindvieh!'

He smiled to himself, knowing how closely she had understood him, and how she allowed him to say things like this to her. It was a special friendship they had shared. Now, he looked over the coffins, and he thought of her. Gone from this earth; brutally killed. Such a gentle, hard-working doctor, who had done nothing but work for and love all the people in her care, without judging them.

'How can I understand or explain what has been happening here?' he asked himself. 'God, You have brought me through all sorts of dangers and tough situations, but what has it all been for?' he prayed and risked speaking out against his Creator. 'I could have stayed and served You well as a secular priest. Now I would have had a stable parish, and been close to my remaining family and friends . . . .' No. The answer was even clearer now. 'These people need God in their lives, perhaps more than we ever realised.'

There was great purpose in their calling, his and all his fellow-religious. Their compassion and willingness to do God's will brought them here in obedience to His call, to 'go forth and teach all nations.' He had come to bring them the word of God, to educate them, to bring them modern health care and the dignity, understanding and uplifting which pagan Africa had lacked. It was still sorely needed.

The thought of these callous murders tore at his feelings, and his anger began to rise again. The surest way he could stop it was by praying again that prayer of Our Lord's, "Father forgive them, for they know not what they are doing."

Shortly after, in 1979, Father Joseph Ebert died, and he thought back on how much they had done together at Lukosi. These losses saddened him, but he cherished happy memories of these good people. He sorely missed this good man, who had been a good mentor to him, and had allowed him to get on with so much. "He was one of those people who come into your life," he told Father Elmar, "you know, a bit like a father really."

MURDERS AT EMBAKWE

Not long after this Father Odilo answered the phone early one morning. A call at such a time did not bode well, and he answered apprehensively, "yes, Father Odilo, here?"

"Good morning Odilo." It was the bishop. He stiffened. "There has been an attack at Embakwe. It is bad news; they killed Peter and Andreas."

"Oh my God! This is terrible," he shot out. "What happened?"

"I don't have all the details, but Antoon Janssen has told me how they gunned those two down on the porch of the house. He and Engelmar chased the killer off. Engelmar fired shots to scare them."

"Thank God. They could all have been killed."

"I am calling in those two brothers. There are twelve sisters, and I want them safely back here today."

The mission was looted, and when the missionaries went back, they found that everything that could be moved had been taken; even the doors and windows had been stripped away.

One over-ambitious villager had even carted away a huge wooden wardrobe. However, it was too big to fit in his hut; undeterred, he placed it in a new position and built a new hut around and over it. When the police finally began to round up the stolen property, he had to demolish his hut to release the stolen cupboard.

Father Odilo and Father Johannes shared several discussions over this terrible event, and the looting that had followed. It shook their missionary commitment deeply, but they affirmed one another and never gave up on the people they had chosen to come and expend their lives in serving[xviii].

Change of Government

The African Methodist Bishop, Abel Muzorewa, was soon publicised meeting with the fighters and lobbying for them. His picture often appeared in the paper, toting an AK47 rifle, much to the horror of some of the clergy. "How can he do that, as a man of God?" asked one of the elderly priests.

"I don't like it, but he is certainly a lot better than some of the other candidates," answered Father Odilo. In fact he was soon considered the most likely candidate for succession in a new form of shared government, which the white community was coming to accept as inevitable. Supervised elections were held and Zimbabwe Rhodesia was ushered in for a short while. It was not acceptable to 'the powers that want to be' and its leadership were considered puppets by a lot of people.

The message got through to England and Lord Soames was appointed to head a British delegation that was tasked with bringing an end to British involvement and handing over power to African rule. Elections were held for the first time ever on universal suffrage, and voting was considered high; there seemed to be at least two potential winners. In the end, Independence was announced with Robert Mugabe shown as having the highest vote tally. There was a stunned reaction at first as the news burst out on Monday afternoon that he had won! Lord Soames quickly made a statement and then General Walls called for calm; Robert Mugabe said some brief and seemingly sincere words of re-assurance, "let us join together, let us show respect for the winners and the losers."

The results were officially announced on Tuesday morning, and all over the country there were workers and employers, soldiers and villagers, housewives and school-children all over the country, listening to radios or watching on TV. His supporters were jubilant but for many this was the unbelievable nightmare fulfilled, and resignations and emigration arrangements were being furiously implemented.

At 8.00pm 'Comrade Robert G. Mugabe' was introduced as the elected Prime Minister, on a television broadcast. He diplomatically assured the losers that there would be no victimisation, and that 'we want to assure a place for everyone in this country.' He spoke of a broad coalition, including whites and his main rival, Joshua Nkomo. He addressed himself to each of the various communities and categories of people, assuring businesses that there would be no sweeping nationalisation, white civil servants that their jobs and pensions would be guaranteed, and farmers and home-owners that their property rights would be respected. 'Let us forgive and forget, let us join hands in a new amity,' he enunciated.

His promises worked for most people, people who loved their country and now wanted to accept the possibilities he held out in this transformed political landscape. The 'jewel of Africa' had come under new management.

The civil service and the army and police accepted their duties to a new government, and the guerrillas in Matabeleland came together in hastily constructed assembly areas and camps and from there they were demobilised. Saint Paul's in Lupane district was swarming with about fifteen hundred former combatants, who came in and surrendered their weapons. The security around them was tight, and an atmosphere of deep suspicion pervaded everything.

Some were brought into camps in Bulawayo, and there were some fierce conflicts between the two main rivals, ZANLA and ZIPRA. One morning, the residents of Bulawayo awoke to explosions and gunfire in their midst, both in the exclusive Kumalo suburb, and in the 'high density areas'. A pitched battle was being fought in Entumbane. War had broken out, and people stayed at home for the first time ever. "This is independence?" a parishioner fumed and worried Father Odilo. "The war is right here in town now; for the first time ever!"

After a while, outmanoeuvred again, Joshua Nkomo accepted Robert Mugabe's promises and the factions merged to share in the power. Dissident forces continued to operate, and these were also helped in a few instances, by some renegade Rhodesians, with assistance from South Africa. That government had no wish to see a Black government on its borders, and many did not yet believe that Black rule could work.

At the missions and in most places, there seemed to be an attitude of goodwill and co-operation, despite the pressure in certain quarters to take control of everything. "The people of Zimbabwe are wonderful," Father Odilo was saying. "Just look at their patience and forgiveness. We can all learn a great deal from them."

On one of his visiting trips, he said Holy Mass, at Saint Luke's and settled down to breakfast. "What will become of our work?" he was asked.

"From what I see, this is a vital hospital. You serve a huge area, and you are desperately needed," he re-assured Dr. Davis.

PRIEST SHOT DEAD THROUGH WINDOW[13]

"This is Sister Editha. Can you hear me?" she called through the crackling phone line.

"Who is it?" he asked.

"This is Regina Mundi Mission, Sister Editha, can you hear me?"

"Yes, sister, what is it?" Father Odilo answered.

"Father Odilo, something very bad has happened. They have killed Father Edmar.

"This is terrible, sister. Are you and the others all right?"

"Yes, they have gone, but they killed him. We couldn't help him."

"Of course; that's understandable. You can do nothing with these fellows!"

When he met with her later, Sister Editha explained what had happened. There was a knock at the door to the priests' house, and he had opened up to two men; it seemed this was a robbery attempt, so he resisted. A scuffle ensued, and one of them had somehow got hold of the iron bar, which he kept behind his door.

Father Edmar wrestled it back off him, and overcame the men, who quickly ran off. He was badly wounded and his head was bleeding. He wrapped a towel, soaked with cold water around his head. He thought of the other people in his care, considering himself as their protector.

He had phoned the sisters in their house and told them he had a bleeding head, and the men had run off, but he was sure they would be back.

He wouldn't let us come over to his house and help," Sister Editha explained.

"Quite right," Father Odilo commented.

"Suddenly we heard a shot, and then all was quiet. After a long wait, we went over, and entered the house. There was a lot of blood in the corridor, and when we reached his room, we found Father Edmar dead."

There was no way to describe how he felt at this killing on 25th April 1981 and at other incidents where priests and sisters were senselessly martyred, or simply killed by terrible people. Whatever the grievances

---

[13]   25th April 1981

of the blacks might have been, these people were certainly not behaving in a way that Jesus would have condoned! The term 'terrorist' obviously had its propaganda value to the Rhodesian security forces, but when one looked at the maiming and raping of innocent villagers, and these murders their bullying and thuggish tactics seemed to fit that name quite well.

On many occasions, terrorists or dissidents also visited Dr. Davis at Saint Luke's Mission Hospital and Dr. M. Eder at Brunapeg Mission Hospital. They were constantly endangered and threatened, as were many others. These were the only two bush hospitals in the country, which were kept open and operating during these war years.

Saint Luke's has survived to this day and is the mainstay of medical care in the whole of Matabeleland North, thanks to the Catholic Church and many benefactors and amazing volunteers, especially the Sharlaz family. Although government provides some assistance it would not be providing a fraction of the much-needed care in the area if it were not for this mission.

CHAPTER 17

THE BLESSINGS OF CROSSES

HARDSHIPS AND SADNESS

"It just does not seem fair," the mother was complaining. "Our sons are being killed and wounded, and for what?"

Her husband, ever on the attack, was quick to silence her, growling, "we all know that it has to be done. Look what happened in Germany when Hitler was given control; or Russia, or China. We can't let that happen here."

At times like these it was not easy to put the other issues across. The war was growing in intensity, and families were hurting from the worry and casualties. Businesses were suffering from the lost man-hours. The Church was often caught in the middle, especially the mission institutions and the people who only wanted to do the very best they could for the poor and suffering.

At times Father Odilo had to console parishioners, and the example of Jesus and His cross, humbly borne, was often in his mind. Suffering was not always bad for people, and he greatly admired some of them, especially the women. They were the ones who had to cope with the realities of life, the homes without their men-folk, the wounded, the upset wives and children and many tasks that they would not normally have taken on—so-called 'men's work'.

When he conducted the Stations of the Cross, Simon of Cyrene, an African, was a great example, too. He had certainly never asked to be given a share in carrying Jesus' cross. And yet, how privileged he turned out to be, and with what growing awareness he must have sensed the innocence and even the divinity of the bleeding and humiliated man he was helping.

Outspoken Voices

"Father, I cannot understand why the church allows a man like that to get away with what he is saying," a parishioner tackled him. That morning the Chronicle had slammed Bishop Donal Lamont for his outspoken views, and Father Odilo had thought with sadness, "if only he would say more about the good things, which have been done. Then his message would be more palatable."

"Well, you must remember that everybody has the right to express their own views. These are not an official church pronouncement," he said.

"But look at what he is saying. He is out to destroy the European community here. I agree with Mark Partridge; the church should not meddle in politics," the man pleaded his case.

Of course, it was not easy being a Catholic at a time when government officials were stirring up anti-Catholic sentiment, for whatever their reasons. He remembered how it had been in Germany before their departure. Father Odilo felt this man's anger and hurt, and yet he did not want to condemn a Bishop for what he was reported as saying. "I believe he may have gone too far myself, but some of what he says is true, you know. We all need to show more consideration and respect for one another, European and African, I mean."

"Oh, Father, surely you are not taking sides with him!" the man countered.

"No, but things are seldom a simple case of right or wrong when it comes to political opinions. For instance, Bishop Lamont should, in my opinion, have given a more balanced picture by acknowledging some of the good things that the government has done for the benefit of the rural people. There are many new dams, lots of good new gravel roads, schools and so on."

This sort of conversation could go nowhere, and Father Odilo wisely recalled the reading of the day. "Ask yourself what Jesus Christ would expect of us if He was walking in our midst today."

"That's a tough one," the man admitted, and promptly stopped his tirade.

ECCE VENIO

Meanwhile parish life had continued, and the Parish Council of Christ the King, under Peter Cavill's chairmanship, had instituted an 'outreach' programme, to improve contact with and to include more of its parishioners in the life of the parish. At a special Mass in 1978, Father Odilo was amazed at, and deeply moved by, the selection of 'Here I am Lord' as one of the hymns. He was also very gratified at the building of the grotto to Our Lady that was built near the parish house.

When he held up his chalice at the Consecration, he was reminded of how he had responded to that call forty years before. His family had presented him with the silver chalice, and engraved on it in large letters were the Latin words, 'Ecce Venio', (behold, I am coming to you) and 'Hic Sum', in smaller writing, (here I am). This was most powerful coincidence, or again God's gentle hand at work to strengthen one of His priests.

THE CROSS FROM ST PATRICK'S

When Father Odilo had been the assistant priest at Saint Patrick's Mission, he had often prayed before the most gruesome crucifix, which had then hung above the altar

"Do you know," he had told Father Joseph one day, "I feel as if Jesus' eyes are staring right at me when I pray before the cross."

He had often prayed and been deeply moved by the sight and reality of what Jesus had suffered. He, God, the Word, the Messiah, had allowed himself to be tortured and flayed, so that his bones were exposed, and his flesh was torn and shredded. He had accepted human form to show us His love, and to somehow reach us, His stubborn people.

Now, many years later, that cross had been considered to clash with the new church when it had been built. (On 29ᵗʰ May 1977 Bishop Henry Karlen had blessed the new church at St Patrick's' Mission.)

"I think it would have been better to risk the clash with the architecture," he said. "It makes people think about Christ more; they see how He really suffered."

But Father Marino had it changed and so it had been replaced and the cross and figure were then stored in the basement, covered by a tarpaulin. It was not too long after that Father Odilo saw the opportunity to have it moved to Christ the King, the Mariannhill House for the diocese.

"I am sorry, Odilo," the bishop had said, "I don't think the cross should go to your parish. It may be needed somewhere else later on."

"Well, my Lord," he countered, "that may never happen." He was very fond of this cross, and it had meant so much to him in his first posting to a mission. He was not a man to give up easily, as his record certainly showed. "Would you prefer that it stay under a canvas in the basement at Saint Patrick's? There is nowhere else for it that I know of, and it is such a waste. Besides, three fingers have already been broken off, and it will only get worse, you know."

The bishop relented, and he had it placed upright at the back of the church, for parishioners to look upon the cross that he remembered so fondly. Many parishioners were shocked. "It is far too gruesome," they said. One person said, "I cannot accept Jesus like that; it puts me right off coming to church!"

"Surely you must realise that this was what Our Lord's death was like," he tried to explain. "It was certainly not a happy scene. He had been scourged nearly to death, and then brutally nailed to the cross. That cross shows you what the crucifixion was really like."

Some time later, his parish council decided to put up a memorial, and Leon Bufe, an architect at Christ the King parish, proposed a glass enclosure. It was soon erected, in the car park, near the priests' house; the occasion used was Father Odilo's Jubilee, his fiftieth anniversary of ordination as a priest. He was very happy to see this salvaged cross safely restored and preserved

THE CROSS ON MOUNT INUNGU

Mount Inungu is the highest hill on the boundary of the Matopos National Park, rising steeply for nearly three hundred metres, from the Maleme valley. It has been at the centre of early African history, when the Bushman lived there and left their painted records of hunting achievements and other occasions, still clearly visible in many of the caves and overhanging rock faces.

King Lobengula's Mbiza regiment later used the area as one of its strongholds, and there are caves with clay grain bins, still well preserved to this day. It is prominent on the old wagon-trail that passes by on its East side; in a sense this route came all the way from Cape Town with recently established towns and stops along the way. One of those stops was Friar's store, just north of Inungu, where the wagon trail snaked through a narrow gap in the hills before proceeding up the Maleme Valley. Fortified caves and grain-bins remain as evidence of those times. Since then, Inungu has been climbed by thousands of people to enjoy the beautiful view and the feeling of closeness to God, which one cannot fail to attain when surrounded by such magnificence and rugged grandeur.

The burly and inspiring Father Renk, at St Andrew's parish, had organised the Legion of Mary in Bulawayo, and Colin Tuson and other junior members helped him erect the first cross on Mount Inungu in 1964. That cross was eighteen feet high, made of wood, wedged into a rock crevice, and packed firmly with broken rock. This cross suffered many vicissitudes—the base was not strong enough to hold it and, after a series of storms, it toppled over. Father Elmar Mayr, another Bavarian with a great love for the mountains and shrines in Germany, organised the Youth Club of Saint Mary's Cathedral, to re-erect it. Exposed to the harsh elements, the cross later fell over for the second time, when the wood began to deteriorate.

Father Odilo could not allow this, and he persuaded a group of young and older parishioners, like Tom Murphy, Charles McGregor and Brother Horan, to go out with him to climb up and repair and re-erect it. They clad it with aluminium sheeting, and secured it with stay wires to resist the strong prevailing winds on the mountain top. It stood well and shone its reflected image over the Matopos Hills for some time, although vandals repeatedly cut the wires and even pushed it over. Each time this happened it was fixed up again by Ken Low, Charles McGregor and other parishioners.

Father Odilo had a special feeling for this cross-site and was very concerned about its permanence. He bided his time, until one day he took the opportunity of putting a team together to undertake the work. Perhaps the guidance he needed only came in God's own mysterious way, when it was appropriate. He first spoke to Angelo Stipinovich who contacted two young engineering colleagues and met with Father Odilo. He asked them, "Do you think you can construct and erect a permanent cross? We need something which will not be blown over by the wind or damaged by vandals."

He took them up Mount Inungu one day to look at the damage that vandals had done to the old wooden cross. "We could put on stronger stay wires and re-clad the cross," was one suggestion. But soon there were suggestions of a new and more substantial monument. "We can construct it using the rock and sand here. All we need to bring up is cement, reinforcing and water."

The three men put their heads together a few times and compared the possibilities. In the end, it was decided to fabricate a steel frame and clad it with aluminium sheeting, because it appeared relatively easier to transport segments and assemble them on top of the hill. There was a lengthy time scale for these discussions, but Father Odilo kept up a consistent but subtle pressure, which finally led to action.

The cross was designed by John and checked by Peter. It was to be six hundred millimetres square in cross section and would stand ten metres high with six metre wide arms. When Father Odilo visited the factory and saw the fabrication that was being done, he said, "the proportion looks incorrect somehow, now that it is laid out it here."

"You are right," Angelo commented. "When it is up high on the mountain, the stem will not be seen in full."

"I think it could do with another twelve hundred millimetres onto its length," Peter suggested. Cephus Mhuri and Freddie Van Hese soon modified it, and they all became very keen to help erect it.

The steel segments were pre-spliced and joined and the aluminium was drilled to fit, and carefully marked for riveting on in position. By the time the erection weekend was decided on, their memories of Inungu hill itself had become very weak. At Father Odilo's seventieth birthday celebration in the Church Hall, on 14th October 1982, they announced, "we are ready to erect the cross next weekend."

"This is fantastic news for me," Father Odilo acknowledged. "I look forward to being able to look upon a new cross from Rhodes' Grave, one that will be clearly visible to everybody who comes to appreciate the spiritual beauty of the Matopos."

The work party set off for Inungu on Saturday morning in a variety of vehicles, with a Leyland Comet truck loaded with all of the cross components. They were quite confident that, with enough manual effort everything could be taken to the top that day, or at the latest midday Sunday. They had even taken the erection tools with them, and hoped to get most of the steel erected. At the foot of the mountain, they were met by Mr John Tendele Moyo, the owner of the farm. He had twelve more helpers whom he had managed to arrange to help, at Father Odilo's request.

A bush road and eagle pair flying overhead

The helpers started carrying steel fairly enthusiastically. Meanwhile, an advance party, with the three young engineers, headed up the hill to drill the anchor holes necessary for the base plate of the cross. An ideal, "Providential" spot was found, with good all-round visibility and, more important, a flat surface. Angelo had brought a petrol-operated rock-drill and this natural hollow on the crest of the hill had an amazingly flat bottom. It was almost as if it was created for the cross' foundation.

Unfortunately, further down the hill, very little progress was made, as there was insufficient experienced labour to handle the heavier sections of the cross which, therefore, remained at the base of the hill. The helpers ploughed through thick undergrowth as well as they could, but that weekend they only got the steel to the bottom of the steeper ascent. It was only then that they began to realise how daunting the climb would be.

On Sunday, a vastly reduced labour force completed the drilling of the holes, and epoxy-grouted the anchor-bolts in position, ready for the base plate. The base plate itself was moved to an intermediate point on the route up, at the start of the heavy up-hill section. That first weekend was quite disappointing in terms of progress, although they were able to identify some obvious shortcomings, such as the need for bush clearing. "We also need some big wheels to help roll the big sections," somebody proposed. And, we need a set of rails, so that we can get across the crevices and irregularities."

On the second weekend, 23rd / 24th October 1982, Phineas came along with a group of more experienced men to take over from the volunteer labour.

Ken Low led a small gang to clear the bush along a suitable route, all the way to the top of the mountain. Meanwhile, the new, robust and highly motivated gang moved all the cross elements to the same point where the base plate had been moved the previous Sunday. This point, which was about halfway along the total route to the top, was just below the steep uphill section, and was an ideal intermediate base camp for lunch and a rest.

Once all the components had been moved to this site, a concerted effort was made to get the base plate to the top. The base plate was an extremely awkward item to handle. It was square and bulky, weighing nearly a quarter of a tonne. It took much winching, sweating, muttering, (swearing was not allowed), and plenty of "close shaves", but eventually they got it to the top just after noon that Sunday.

It was a sultry and hot October, and they were all dehydrated, but it had rained and they were fortunate to find some pools of water on the high granite mountain. All this time, Father Odilo, like a true mountaineer, was regularly seen going up easily, as if he were walking on flat ground.

"It was a great morale booster, getting the base plate to the top," Peter commented to Father Odilo. "It proves that the whole project is not impossible. By comparison with the base plate, the rest will be easy."

On the third weekend, after the excellent progress of the previous weekend, the four major remaining elements of the cross almost flew up. The longest piece, the main upright section of the cross, was taken up first, and, ironically, its great length, (approximately six metres), made it easier to get it over the awkward spots on the route.

Once that was on the top, the main piece was spliced onto the base plate, in a horizontal position. The combined weight of these two pieces was well over half a tonne, but it was felt that it would be easier to erect them as a linked pair, rather than individually. The two cross-arms and the head-piece soon arrived at the summit as well.

On the fourth Saturday, John, Peter, Freddie, Tim, and two other friends of theirs, plus a small number of helpers, had a highly successful day—the heavy carrying work was over, and the end was in sight. On Sunday, the erection started. A light pole was erected, adjacent to the bolts sticking out of the rock, and braced at the top by three guy ropes. Using a winch, and via a pulley fixed at the top of the pole, the base and main section were lifted into a vertical position and dropped neatly onto the base bolts. After that, it was easy. Then the gym-pole was lashed onto the section already erected, and the top piece was winched up and bolted on. Finally, the two side arms were winched up and bolted on.

They had all the steel erected within four hours, except that they had to leave off the levelling up operation as the base plate was catching on the rock on one side of the hole. "That was amazing," John said to Peter, just after midday. "It also looks very impressive. Let's drive around to World's View[14], and see how it looks from there."

It was a tremendously imposing sight. "It's great. We can see it clearly from here, even without the aluminium."

After that, they drove back to Christ the King Church, and caught up with Father Odilo just before the four p.m. Mass, to give him the good news. "I am delighted, and a bit surprised," he said. I thought you had another weekend of hauling ahead of you."

---

[14] Locally World's View, Rhodes Grave, is known as Malindidzimu Hill—the dwelling place of the Spirits.

At last the task was achieved, at least to the extent that Father Odilo could breathe a sigh of relief. "The rest will follow with greater certainty now."

On the next Saturday, Father Odilo celebrated Holy Mass at the bottom of the hill for the working party, and Freddie and his friends went up and started the sheeting operation.

While most of the people were employed bringing the sheets up, a small advance party quickly repainted the scratched frame of the cross before cladding it. On the Sunday they worked until midday; then Father Odilo celebrated Mass at the base of the mountain, for them and their families and friends. That afternoon, while they continued to fix the sheets, the handiwork was viewed by those who had been at Mass.

A few of the top sheets were fixed but an early afternoon electric storm sent them scurrying to the bottom, to avoid the risk of being struck by lightning.

The cladding operation turned out to be harder than expected, and during the following week, people went out during the week as well as the next weekend, to complete the riveting of the cladding, and concreting over the base.

The Cross on Mount Inungu

Finally, on the Sunday before Christmas, Mass was said at the foot of the cross, and Father Odilo said, "What a wonderful achievement, and all for the glory of God. I hope that seeing this cross, visitors to the area will be prompted to become better Christians."

Of course, there were detractors. "I don't like to be reminded of religion when I go out to the Matopos," one tour operator complained. A teacher criticised the Cross, claiming it defaced Nature, and others added their complaints.

These voices reached Father Odilo, and he was quick to put things in perspective, as he told the teacher, "If you think like that, you would have to pull down every bridge, dam, cottage, building etc if it was not natural! Besides, look at the Corcavador in Rio de Janeiro, and climb anywhere in the Alps and mountains of Europe as a tourist or a local. The cross is a wonderful reminder of Christ, and his love for every one of us, whether you be a believer or not."

Holy Mass was celebrated there on the next Africa Day, 25th May 1983. The people who made the climb were deeply impressed and resolved to repeat this the next year. One day, Charles Langlois said to Father Odilo, "something is missing at Mt Inungu."

He was perturbed, and wondered if the precious Cross had been damaged. "What is it?" he asked calmly.

"You cannot have the Cross there without having the fourteen stations on the way up," Charles replied with his usual calm logic.

He had to admit that this was an oversight, but it was good to be reminded by a parishioner like Charles, quietly living his faith, a man of great dedication to God. "I am ashamed of myself," he replied with a smile. "How can it be that you need to tell me this? I should have thought of that myself!" They enjoyed a laugh together, the sort men who know and respect one another can share so happily.

"Well, I will organise some crosses," he continued, "if that is okay with you."

"Of course, that will be great Charles. You might talk to Norman as well; I am sure he will be keen, and I will come out with you to choose the places to put them."

It was a short while later when they made the ascent together, picking appropriate spots for each of the fourteen stages chosen to commemorate

Christ's last walk, up Mount Calvary. The last Station, Jesus is Laid in the Tomb, fitted in perfectly with a large lightning damaged fig tree which had endured the summit for centuries perhaps.

Some years later, at his seven-thirty a.m. Mass on Sunday 27th June 1999, Father Odilo gave a report in his homily of how this cross came to be erected, and how people's questions might be answered when they ask, "what is that cross for on Mount Inungu?"

"First and foremost the cross is a sign of God's great love for everybody," he said. "The death of Jesus on the cross was meant for all mankind, and this visible sign, the cross, reminds us of His suffering, death and resurrection. He endured the most awful pain and humiliation to show how much God loves us and wants us to enjoy eternal happiness because we hear and obey His word."

The Mountain has been home to a resident pair of Black Eagles, nesting on the steep eastern cliff face, below the cross. They have hatched and reared a chick most years, and they divide the hill and share it with another pair on a nest site further to the northwest. These eagles soar and glide along the thermals on Mount Inungu, watching for and selecting dassies as their prey.

There are also snake eagles and, not far away, the Fish Eagles at Maleme Dam.

Mount Inungu with its Cross

CHAPTER 18

NEAR DISILLUSION
UMCOLI NGUMONI[15]

EMBAKWE VENDETTAS

He had served four terms as Provincial Superior, and had good reason to hope that the troubles were over. However, terrible things were still happening, and once again in the Embakwe area . . .

Brother Matthias had been hard at work around the mission, fixing up after the damage and looting when Brothers Peter and Andreas had been killed. He had restored locks and doors that had been vandalised, replaced windowpanes, re-laid pipes, and done a host of other tasks on his meticulous lists. One of his most appreciated achievements was the repair and re-commissioning of the swimming pool, especially now in the hottest time of the year.

He used to get up to tricks, and was a great joker; he was a good unifying influence. He had a cigarette lighter, which he would offer unsuspecting visitors. As he prepared to strike a flame, all eyes were riveted, waiting to see what happened. Just as the visitor flicked the lighter, he got an almighty shock, and the lighter would be flung from his recoiling hand; it gave off quite a powerful electric shock. The audience would be in stitches!

---

[15] A proverb of ingratitude. The person who provides the feast often finds himself thought of as a bad person

Under Father Elmar Schmid, they had built a large dam at Embakwe and Brother Matthias had been mending the fence, to keep cattle from trampling the earth wall of the dam that they had built. An element of local troublemakers had stirred this up into an issue. They made out that he was preventing people from accessing prime grazing—even as though they had some right to just graze on other peoples' land! The people then became determined to graze their cattle on the dam wall, although this is a practice that leads to surface degradation and jeopardises the dam structure; he knew he needed to protect the earthfill.

The readings for that Sunday were far more apt than anybody could realise, and the first reading, from the second book of Wisdom, said, 'the godless say to themselves, "let us lie in wait for the virtuous man . . . condemn him to a shameful death . . ."[16]

Then Psalm 53 seemed to predict this senseless and cruel murder, ". . . ruthless men seek my life . . . I will sacrifice to you with willing heart . . ."

James wrote an Epistle extolling peacemakers. "Wherever you find jealousy and ambition, you find disharmony, and wicked things of every kind being done; . . . You want something and you haven't got it; so you are prepared to kill . . . . you have prayed for something to indulge your desires."[17]

In the Gospel reading, Our Lord predicted that He would be killed and would rise again after three days.[18] Here was death and evil at work, contrasted with peacemakers, and God's great sacrifice and gentle offering for us.

All these messages were recounted, at Mass, in the midst of a community torn with bitter rivalry, handed down from so far back that nobody could honestly explain it. One group felt that the mission did not have the right to its lands. The missionaries handed over a huge tract of the mission lands to the state, and now somebody wanted it all.

What they saw was a dam, right in their midst, in a parched and seasonal land. The object of their avarice was plain for all to see.

---

[16] Wisdom: 12:17-20.

[17] James 3: 16-4:3

[18] Mark 9: 30-37,

Another group, across the river, at Dukwe, saw the Embakwe people getting a benefit, and they argued that they should participate. Rivalries went back to the times of King Lobengula, who had consigned here many of those he least trusted, and some of their offspring kept the feuds going.

Missionaries had brought them Christ and education and selfless example. But, they wanted something and they had not got it. They were prepared to kill . . . at least; they were willing to bring in killers who would help them do it.

"Surely he knows I am back from Germany. Why has he not come to see me? He is the chairman of the parish council, and there are things we need to arrange for Sunday," Father Johannes said.

"Well, there was a little problem, while you were away. You know we employed his son as a lorry-driver. His name is Russia. Well, Brother Matthias found him totally insubordinate and dismissed him a few days ago."

"Oh yes. That would make him angry, I am sure."

Father Johannes noticed how some of the teachers and workers seemed to be averting their eyes more than they had for a long while. He had taught them to adopt the European custom of looking at people when you speak to them, and that worked for a while. Their custom is to look away and show deference by avoiding eye contact. 'What were their eyes showing, or not showing now?' he wondered. He decided he would have to go all the way to Dukwe himself, to see him.

When Father Johannes arrived at the house, nobody came out. 'That's strange,' he thought. 'He could see me coming from a long way off, surely."

Father Johannes called him in greeting from the fence, but he would not come out of the house[19]. Going in, after a respectful enough wait, he found him there. He appeared nervous, and avoided looking at him. "Did you see the boys?" he asked Father Johannes.

"What boys? What are you talking about?"

---

[19]   Right at the time of this visit, Brother Matthias was being bludgeoned and speared to death by his own workers, although admittedly they were being forced to do it at gunpoint.

"Aha, there are many houses," he muttered unintelligibly. Then he pointed out the window, and said, "There they are, look." Sure enough, about a kilometre away, a group of eight men, some clearly armed with AK rifles, were crossing one of the fence boundaries some distance from them.

Back at the mission, nobody had worried yet, as Brother Matthias was intending to finish his fencing of the dam wall that day. Later, after nightfall, they began to worry. Brother Horan was took a truck and drove to the dam wall. He was back within half an hour. "Terrible, terrible," was all he could say for a while, and his expression told them that something awful had happened. The truck was still burning he said, but he could not find Brother Matthias, nor any of the workers.

The neighbouring farmer was called, and he alerted the army. They arrived in the dark of the night, but could not do much. Early the next morning, helicopters and dogs were brought in, and they soon tracked down the body.

There he lay, forced deep into an anthill, and speared and bayoneted to death. The ground around him had been clawed as he lay dying there, a cruel and vicious death, at the hands of evil men. None of the workers were to be found, and when they re-appeared some days later, they said nothing. Later, it emerged that they had killed him; but they had been forced to do it at gunpoint. First, he had been paralysed with hammer blows to his spine. Then he was dragged and carried away, so as not to alert anybody with gunshots.

Then the vengeful and evil final killing took place. It was a cowardly murder of 'the virtuous man', just what those readings had spoken of. Brother Horan also learned later from the workers co-opted into assisting the killers, that they had intended to tie rocks around Brother Matthias's neck and throw his body into the dam, but the sound of the approaching truck had disturbed those plans.

This man, who was protecting the dam wall from cattle damage, who had done so much to rebuild, preserve and develop, serving happily, but firmly expecting normal obedience between an employer and his workers, had strongly disapproved of indolence and dishonesty. There were some obstinate people who were not yet ready for such ordinary, decent conduct.

BROTHER DIES TO SAVE PRIEST[xix]

Several years later, at the end of the rainy season, there was a spirit of celebration at Empandeni Mission. (This mission, founded in June 1887, was the first Catholic Mission in the country, and a great celebration was held to commemorate its Centenary on 27th June 1987.)

President Robert Mugabe had declared an amnesty for all dissidents and political criminals. 'At last, we can settle down. Matabeleland will boom now, I'm sure,' Father Johannes had thought that afternoon.

A short while before, on Saint Patrick's Day, one of the Africans had seen a long, black snake cross the grounds and disappear into a crack in the wall foundations. Brother Danny Horan had joined in, and together, they dug to where they had it cornered, carefully standing by with a steel bar, ready to strike if it came out suddenly.

They managed to kill the snake, and holding it out, Brother Horan said, "Well, look at that, man. I have never, ever seen such a big black mamba. Thank God, we killed him," he proclaimed. It was quite a co-incidence that this was done on Saint Patrick's Day, as well—he is renowned for having chased all the snakes away from Ireland. They had killed this snake, but had they done away with the evil that this snake seemed to have symbolised? No.

"I guess we can forget about the warning note those children brought yesterday," Brother Kilian said. They all murmured their assent, optimistic at the overdue changes.

Sister Editha Schultheiss, CPS, a seasoned and hard-working missionary, was Rector of the School. She had a beautiful face and when she smiled it lit up with real joy. When she was serious, as she was now, her face conveyed a calm serenity. She confided to old Brother Erasmus, "There is something not right around here. I have seen people whom I do not know, and they don't wave or act in a friendly manner towards me. In fact, I feel as if their eyes are boring into me with hatred."

In true missionary spirit, he responded, but not from his heart, "they are good people, Editha. I think there is so much confusion, that's all. The dissidents are definitely telling them bad things and they are scared to disagree." Deep down, he was also worried. That note was a serious warning, and there was something most strange about the manner in which people were behaving. Even people on the mission appeared furtive.

The very next evening, a group of dissidents came. The five local men were led by a man called Gayigusu[xx], who had just come from committing a series of wide ranging crimes in Gwanda and elsewhere. He came that day, via nearby Botswana, and met up with this group. "We are sick of that school and these missionaries. They refuse to let us graze cattle, and they do not listen to our orders to shut down the school and mission."

"Come with me," he commanded. "I don't sit around talking like you women!" And off they went, as the sun was settling into the dusty western sky. Leading them along, he knocked on the door of the teachers' house. Nobody answered, despite the loud music he heard.

He did not want to stand around, looking stupid. They pounced on a teacher as he stepped out of one of the rooms, bare-foot and ready to settle down for the night. "Where are the Makiwas? Where is the person in charge?" he asked.

"The priest's house, over there," he told them in great fear and trembling.

"Come, show us." Off they went again, walking carefully, in the dark. When they reached the priests' rooms, they were blocked. Because of the problems, they had installed security gates at the house, and these were kept locked.

The group forced their captive to knock and he asked the priest, Father Luke Mlilo, "open the door, it is me." This he innocently did, and suddenly four gunmen rushed in, past him. They were now past all the gates and security. They got hold of Brother Kilian, Father Johannes and Brother Erasmus, and were lining them all up to shoot them.

They ordered young Father Luke to tie their hands. Despite his nervousness, he was quick thinking enough to leave the end of the rope in Brother Killian's hand, in such a way that he could loosen his bonds. He signalled silently by touch what he had done.

"This is the end for sure," thought Father Johannes. He was backed up against a door, and he reached for the handle and eased it open, preparing to make an escape. But the movement caught a dissident's eye, and he yelled, "hey, stop!" Viciously grabbing him, he hauled him inside, and pushed his head down onto the desk.

Gayigusu, the leader of the dissidents, stood there with an air of fierce, almost drugged arrogance, holding a sharp axe, with an old timber branch as a handle. He pushed it at Luke and ordered him, "take this and kill that white swine, or I will shoot you!" Young Father Luke was scared out of his wits, and it was quite clear that this ugly man fully intended to do what he said. Whether it was fear or bravery, he stood in shocked silence and refused!

"Get out of the way, you snivelling white man's servant," he yelled, and grabbed the axe from him.

Gayigusu then hoisted the axe up high and brought it down with a bone-splintering crunch, right into Father Johannes skull.

Just as it hit home, Brother Killian jumped at him, deflecting his arm, so that the blow angled off slightly, cutting into Johannes shoulder as well. In the struggle and confusion, he wrestled the axe off Gayigusu and struck back at him, opening a wound on his arm. "You bastard!" he yelled, and the other dissident came to his aid, quickly, shooting Brother Killian dead. While this was happening, Father Luke seized the opportunity and leaped out through the window.

Brother Erasmus, in a dazed state, made it to the convent, and told the sisters what the shots were about. They phoned the bishop and made an urgent appeal for help. Father Johannes was eventually taken to Bulawayo in an ambulance, and he survived miraculously. After convalescing in Germany, he courageously returned.

The campaign against dissidents and pseudo-dissidents, was even more sinister, though. President Mugabe, with North Korean troops, had a cruel Brigade trained up and then he deployed them against the people of Matabeleland. Widespread intimidation, torture, rape and killings were applied to subdue his old opponents, the last likely resistance to his gang's ambitions for totalitarian rule. His former ally, but chief rival for authority, Joshua Nkomo, had been silenced and rendered powerless, and yet he must have been painfully aware of what was happening to his people. The Matabele people themselves watched helplessly, a nation who had subjugated the more populous Shona tribes until the British established a more benign rule, themselves unaware of the future consequences for this proud and dignified nation.

CHAPTER 19

LE CHAIM!
SIKHONA!

NOBODY SAID LIFE WOULD BE EASY

There were puddles everywhere, and the trees dripped with glistening diamonds of water. He drove with his window open, savouring the smell of the clean wet air; 'you cannot appreciate rain as much as this anywhere else in the world,' he thought.

At the side of the road, this year's grasses stood tall and strong. The taller grass stems stood upright, much more stiffly, while the short grasses were drooping low, burdened down by their wealth of captured water and their soaking seed heads. This made him think again about the fallen paper-bark tree he had been looking at last week, just outside a cave, nestled in a kopje in the Matopos. It was a healthy looking tree, but it had been blown over in the storms. The rains had been excellent, and it had grown well—too well. Its top branches had overshot the protective rocks that shielded it from the high winds that came up the valley sometimes. Now, rich with well-watered leaves, and proudly growing to new heights, it had been unable to resist the trials of life.

Just like so many people he knew; their fondness for wealth and possessions made them gather and store. And yet, when a tragedy befell them, like the death of a spouse, some of them were not prepared. Their roots were shallow, their faith was weak, and they sunk into depression and confusion. There were others who had very little, had withstood much hardship, and whom one might be tempted to pity. But it was they who had the ability to cope; they had the faith and trust in God which saw them through everything, smiling and cheerful. In many ways Job had been like that, a sort of strong tree, buffeted and bowed down, but never letting go of his faith in God, rooted in it, and always reaching upwards, praising and thanking God.

THE PAPAL VISIT TO BULAWAYO[20]

"This is a wonderful occasion for us, here in Matabeleland," Bishop Henry Karlen was telling his clergy. "Thank you all for your co-operation in making preparations. How are the details coming for Holy Mass at Ascot?"

"My Lord, things are going well. We have had the grounds cordoned off into parish areas, and the Catenians are well on the way with erecting the podium and altar. The police have given us full co-operation and the routes are well mapped out and traffic will be carefully controlled to avoid any disruptions."

"What time does the plane arrive from Harare?"

"I believe it arrives at nine a.m. but we shall receive a confirmed itinerary later today. The Pope has requested that you meet briefly with him before he drives to Ascot in the Popemobile. As you know, Holy Mass is set to commence at ten-thirty a.m. We are going to be punctual; this is not 'Africa time'."

Apart from a few inevitable little flaps, the arrangements for the visit worked perfectly. At the Ascot Racecourse grounds, the crowds had begun to arrive early in the morning, to secure their places and to make sure that all were in place in good time. There was an excited atmosphere of holy expectancy and hope. News and TV coverage had increased the anticipation, after yesterday's Holy Mass, which the Pope had said in Harare. Borrowdale racecourse had been packed with an unprecedented crowd, and his words made a deep impression on the Catholic, and other, Christians in Zimbabwe.

---

[20] Pope John Paul II visited Harare and Bulawayo from 10th to 13th Sep 1988

At Ascot racecourse, the wind was blowing the yellow fabric draping on the enormous raised altar, and the crowds were singing hymns and praying as they waited in their respective parish areas, with a long wide corridor down the centre and around the sides.

Along the road from the airport, the Popemobile drove through streets lined with people anxious to see this holy man. At last, as he drove into the grounds, the crowd strained and clamoured to see him and to be seen. As he greeted the people, he made the sign of the cross. The Pope was smiling warmly, and while he blessed people, in his left hand he held the staff with a bent crucifix, and the figure of Jesus, with knees bent far, and head hanging low.

Pope John Paul II made a special visit to Bulawayo

Father Odilo was seated where he could watch this cavalcade, and he remembered how a previous Pope, Pius XII, had shaken his hand many years ago in Rome. He had followed Karol Wojtyla's life as Pope, and had been deeply moved to know that another person with such manly qualities had been elevated to the papacy. Here was a man who had been a great boxer and athlete in his younger days, a man of strength and courage, perhaps much like Peter, the first Pope. This was a pope after Odilo's heart and he felt a reverent spirit of gratitude to God.

Father Odilo thought how right it was that this leader of the Catholic Church should have come from a country like Poland, emerging from the suffering and human torment of a country so cruelly wronged by Nazi Germany, and then pillaged and brought to its knees by communist Russia. This Pope had lived with poverty, hardship and the anguish of people under a tyrannous rule. (Jesus had also walked with His fellow-Jews under strict Roman rule nearly two thousand years before.) With his charismatic outreaches, he was a good ambassador for Catholicism, not only to Catholics all over the world, but to the whole of humanity.

The Pope was well informed[xxi] about all the pain and suffering which Zimbabwe had been experiencing, and he acknowledged the service and dedication of missionaries, saying "it was God's truth and love which inspired Father Goncalo da Silviera to come to the Zambesi Valley in fifteen hundred and sixty, and in the following year to lay down his life in order to plant in this land the first seeds of the Christian faith."

In encouraging the missionaries who had been 'moving hearts to accept the saving message of the Gospel', he went on and mentioned "the heroic witness of those who have given their lives in the service of the Gospel. I am thinking in particular of those who have been killed in the past fifteen years, including Bishop Adolph Schmitt, a number of your priests and religious and many of your laity."

He had addressed other groups of lay people and youth and then met with diplomats, on Sunday evening, when he affirmed their special role, and told them, "Each one of you is at the service of your country's interests. But the very nature of your profession and your personal experience of other countries and cultures make you aware of the wider picture, the solidarity of the whole human race, which expresses an irreversible process of interdependence making the well-being of each part depend on the well-being of the whole. In this we share a common challenge: we must be builders of international peace, servants of the common good, promoters of understanding and dialogue everywhere."

He had spoken to them about the problems of Africa—hunger, poverty, disease, illiteracy, drought and famine, refugees and displaced persons. He had reminded them of the theme of his visit, "Human rights: the dignity of the human person," and stressed that diplomats had the opportunity and great responsibilities to "do everything possible to promote the true well-being of the human family, and that you will serve the cause of peace and human dignity with all the force of your intelligence and good will."

Now, he was being welcomed in Bulawayo, with great joy, by Bishop Henry Karlen, 'as a pilgrim to Matabeleland.' (This good and sincere bishop had been appointed, to come up from Umtata in Natal, after his predecessor was viciously martyred. Bishop Karlen had to contend with great troubles of a spiritual, religious and worldly nature. He was appointed Archbishop and when he retired he chose to stay in his archdiocese, assisting and praying constantly in his own special chapel in Kumalo, until he died in 2012.)

Bishop Karlen acknowledged the unifying presence of the Holy Father, "because you, as the successor of Peter, the Supreme Shepherd and sign of unity, are personally in our midst." Bishop Karlen was now reminding the Pope how, "the people of Matabeleland have suffered much during the liberation war, and after the war in many ways of violence and of drought . . . The blood of ten missionary Martyrs of the diocese of Bulawayo (amongst them my predecessor, Bishop Adolph Schmitt) and the blood of five missionaries from the diocese of Gweru has flowed into the soil of this area since nineteen seventy six. May this blood bear abundant fruit." After a few more words, he handed over his flock to the Vicar of Rome and of the whole world.

With great dignity, the Pope stepped forward, and the crowd was hushed. This was an unprecedented gathering of people of all races and cultures, united in their faith, and listening with their eyes and hearts as much as with their ears. Pope John Paul's measured voice came over the speakers as he blessed the congregation, with the priests before him, and those with him on the raised altar. Throughout the inspiring Mass, his prayerful reverence was evident in a most uplifting way. The whole congregation was audibly and visibly moved in an especially emotional and spiritual way.

Pope John-Paul quoted a verse, which Father Odilo knew by heart and remembered from his first days of training, "All authority in heaven and on earth has been given to me. Go, therefore, make disciples of all the nations: baptise them in the name of the father and of the Son, and of the Holy Spirit, and teach them to observe all the commands I gave you. And know that I am with you always; yes, to the end of time[21]."

His thoughts flew back to Bavaria, and he felt as if he was sitting again in the beautiful baroque church, being sent off on his permanent departure to the missions in Africa. That was the day he had left Arberg and his family, and followed his call.

It was as if the Holy Father was talking directly to him alone, and he was moved emotionally, in a way he had to conceal from his confreres and the huge crowd listening attentively. "I assure you, dear brothers and sisters in Christ, that it is a great joy for me to be here among you, to witness at first hand the marvellous works that Divine Providence is accomplishing in this land, and to celebrate together with you these Sacred Mysteries," he continued.

'How can he know this so well?' wondered Father Odilo to himself, deeply touched as this theme came up yet again in his life as a Mariannhill Missionary.

The Pope praised the work which was being done, and prayed for the success of the evangelisation efforts in Zimbabwe. However, he also said "we think immediately of the great suffering caused by war. It is only eight years since your struggle for national independence was brought to an end. Even after that, many people in Matabeleland did not find true peace. How the civilian population continued to suffer from guerrilla warfare and other forms of violence! As recently as April of this year Brother Killian Knoerl of this diocese was a victim of such violence."

He urged that there should be "no more training for war[22]. Yes, 'no more training for war'. But there will be training for peace and development, and especially training in the truth."

He spoke about the threats to family life, such as "sexual immorality and irregular unions as well as economic insecurity and inadequate housing."

He called for evangelisers, and for all who accept the word to bear witness to it and proclaim it in turn. He reminded the gathering of

---

[21]   Mt 28:18-20

[22]   Is 2:4

Paul's letter to the Romans[23], ". . . they will not hear of him unless they get a preacher, and they will not get a preacher unless one is sent."

Father Odilo listened intently, and these words rang in his ears, 'here we are, and here we have been,' he was still thinking, when the Pope concluded with the plea in Matthew's Gospel[24], that he 'send labourers to his harvest'. The Pope's voice had a special quality to it, as it rang out over the whole race-course, conveying his sincere love for the people gathered before him, "To his harvest! For this harvest is indeed rich!"

Later, the Pope met with priests and religious at Saint Mary's, the Cathedral of the Immaculate Conception, using the words of St Paul[25], "I am so proud of you . . . . I am filled with consolation and my joy is overflowing."

He took note of the beautiful west window over the altar, whose stained glass images depict "the Immaculate Conception and scenes from the life of the Mother of God . . .", and he ended his encouraging address, again remembering Bishop Adolph Schmitt and others who had lost their lives, and urging them to "press forward amid the persecutions of the world and the consolations of God, announcing the Cross and resurrection of the Lord until he comes[xxii]. I entrust you all to Our Lady, Queen of Peace, whose shrine nearby is a reminder that true peace comes as a gift from the heart of our loving God. May the peace of Christ be with you all!"

At the Anglican Cathedral

The Pope went to the Anglican Cathedral for an ecumenical prayer service, and after a welcome by Bishop Naledi, he delivered a discourse on "longing for harmony and friendship with others . . . In fact the desire for unity among Christians has been gaining momentum in a significant way in the course of this century, and especially since the calling of the second Vatican Council by my predecessor, Pope John XXIII."

---

[23] Rom 10: 14-15
[24] Mt: 9:38
[25] 2 Cor 7:4

He spoke of the potential for growth in unity and said, "Above all, we must never lose confidence in what the Spirit of God can accomplish in our own day. For, as the Angel Gabriel said to the Virgin Mary, "nothing is impossible with God[26]". Let our hearts then be alive with faith and always steadfast in hope. And may the praise of God be always on our lips: "Glorify the Lord with me. Together let us praise his name[27]. Amen."

HEART TROUBLES

For some time now, Father Odilo had been feeling discomfort and suffered from weak spells. He was not going to be much good to his continued vocation if he did not attend to this, so finally he made an appointment with his old friend and physician, a Jewish doctor, Mike Gelman. "I am afraid your heart is giving trouble," he explained. "You are at a good age now, so that is to be expected."

"Tell me what this means, Mike," Father Odilo asked, a bit more truculent than usual.

"Well, you are suffering from arrhythmia. That means your heart goes out of step sometimes, sort of misses a few beats. It could carry on like this indefinitely or it could just stop for too long and then you die unless you have immediate medical attention."

After a quiet pause, he continued. "There are alternatives, but most are prohibitively expensive and risky at your age, I must add. Heart transplants have been successful, as you know, ever since Doctor Chris Barnard's first one in Groote Schuur[xxiii]."

He looked his old friend in the eyes, and knew that he was saddened at the prospect of dying; he did not seem afraid of death, but he just had so much vitality and zest for life. He thought of their walks together in the Matopos Hills, and knew how fit he was—he easily out-paced many people who were half his age.

"There is another operation which can work well, a pacemaker. I am sure you know of these; they have been around for some time."

"Will that work?" Father Odilo asked hopefully.

---

[26]   Luke 1:37

[27]   Psalm 33(34): 4

"I am sure it will. However, there is no guarantee as to how long it will last." After some more medical explanation and a bit of social chatter, Father Odilo left the rooms; he ignored the liftman's invitation to take a ride down and walked the two flights of stairs to the ground floor. He had a lot to think and pray about, and faithful old Joshua, the housekeeper, was worried when he saw him so quiet and pensive.

When he prayed the psalm and canticle in that Saturday's Psalter there was new meaning yet again:

> "It is good to give thanks to the Lord
> to make music to your name, O Most High,
> to proclaim your love in the morning
> and your truth in the watches of the night,
> on the ten-stringed lyre and the lute,
> with the murmuring sound of the harp.
>
> Your deeds, O Lord, have made me glad;
> for the work of your hands I shout with joy.
> O Lord, how great are your works!
> How deep are your designs!
> The foolish man cannot know this
> and the fool cannot understand.
>
> Though the wicked spring up like grass
> and all who do evil thrive,
> they are doomed to be eternally destroyed.
> But you, Lord, are eternally on high.
> See how your enemies perish;
> all doers of evil are scattered.
>
> To me you give the wild ox's strength;
> you anoint me with the purest oil.
> My eyes looked in triumph on my foes;
> my ears heard gladly of their fall.
> The just will flourish like the palm tree
> and grow like a Lebanon cedar.

Planted in the house of the Lord,
they will flourish in the courts of our God,
still bearing fruit when they are old,
still full of sap, still green,
to proclaim that the Lord is just.
In Him, my rock, there is no wrong."

The antiphon said, simply but lovingly, "I will give you a new heart, and put a new spirit in you."

He was stunned at first, before he let this seemingly personal and timely message sink in. 'What a good God, You are,' he prayed in thanks and praise. 'You are always there to comfort and guide me.' The readings and prayers, early on this Saturday morning, had been overpowering in their message. 'I will keep going with all my powers as long as you allow me,' he promised God again.

And so, he went to the Milpark Hospital in Johannesburg, where Doctor Obel 'burned out' the node in his heart's upper chamber, and attached the barbed electric wire, to take over giving the necessary impulses. Now he had to become accustomed to this amazing little modification to his human body.

The visitors used to stream in and he loved it, being ever-willing to greet and chat with them, even when he was feeling over-taxed. He had been promised release by the surgeon, but when he had not come in, he asked one of the other specialists about it. "Oh, you are fine now," he assured him. "You may check out, and I shall clear it with Doctor Obel."

He got dressed and packed up his things, and some time later, he was driven to the Victory Park parish house, next door to the famous 'lemon-squeezer' church, to rest for a few days. That night, a disconnection of one of the embedded wires caused some concern, but he made it through a 'touch-and-go' night, and had to report back for re-attachment of the probe.

After a period of model behaviour a phone-call came and the specialist caught him when he was going to answer it away from his bedside. "Where do you think you are going?" he raised his voice angrily, and went on to give him a very public dressing down.

"The sister assured me it was alright," Father Odilo tried to explain, but he stormed off. He understood the man's good intentions, but later, when he took the good man to task for his public anger, he simply reacted by walking off in silence.

Father Odilo was soon walking and climbing with renewed confidence and vigour. With very little fuss, he simply got on with his life again, as if a new heart had been given him, in order that he could carry on with his mission.

A COUNTRY DRIVE

He still drove his own car, a gift from his brother, Father Josef, and he was fiercely independent as ever. There was very little traffic, in the mid-morning, and driving is a good time to think and pray; he always felt close to God on this journey. There was a bus smoking its way along ahead of him, and he drew close to overtake it. Something made him wait; he watched for a while as the grass was gently blown into a waving pattern, bowing low and rising back up. There was still the odd flutter, an irregularity to remind us that nature is in charge, and has its own way. As the bus rounded the bend, it swung out, overtaking a stalled truck, which had not moved off the road while it affected repairs.

At Inungu, he drove over the bumpy little concrete drift, lowered by river scouring, and passed the hidden pump-house under the thick Umphafa trees. He noticed a solitary stork on a high rock, above the little watering pan, when he drove up to the house. It had been a long time since he watched the storks gathering in the fields near his childhood home. In the distance he could see the resident pair of Black Eagles. They were soaring effortlessly above Mbejane, the hill that was shaped like a rhinoceros' head, enjoying the rising heat of the sun's warmth.

He had so many memories, which he stored up and cherished in his soul. He remembered back to his childhood, wondering what made those storks head off, thousands of kilometres away, each year, and return the next. What made them go to the ends of the earth, and what guided their path unfailingly?

And here he was. He was at that end of the earth. One of the last storks was soon to take to the high winds and fly all the way back to his homeland. A solitary and gentle wind rustled the leaves and he felt it caressing him as he walked slowly to shelter under a large and prickly Umphafa tree.

WARM-HEARTED FATHER KEVIN

His colleague at Christ the King was the big man from Detroit, Father Kevin O'Doherty. Few people knew much of his upbringing and childhood. His father used to make cement blocks and the sons helped out. To carry a sack of cement is a reasonable task for a man, and that was how the sack was designed. The boys soon managed two sacks as they grew older and stronger, pushing themselves, until they were strong enough to manage three sacks of cement at a time! They were a formidable family of boys on the football field. Now, this gentle giant was one of the most peaceful and spiritual of priests, but a man who understood men like few ever could.

As they concelebrated the Midnight Mass that Christmas, the church was packed. He looked over to where the crib had been beautifully made, with the little carved figures, which had been given to him from Germany. Father Kevin's masses were always a bit longer than his, and he was content with that himself, although he worried about some parishioners' reactions. He sat deep in thought as Father Kevin gave the sermon.

'What a good man,' he thought to himself. 'God has blessed me so much in my life. I have had the privilege of working with many wonderful people, and Kevin is certainly a man of God.'

He could not suppress a little smile as he thought of the fridge at their house, though. Parishioners had plied them with Christmas cakes, puddings, hams and chickens, and he was sure that Kevin would be keen to get there later. That would not be until after he had gone well over the ten minute homily, something that he kept to with typical German discipline. "After that your congregation is not paying attention," had been his dean's caution in final year.

Later, as they joined together in raising the host at the offertory, he could almost feel his colleague's soul, as they uttered the sacred words together. 'We are so different, but God has used us both in wonderful ways.' He gave Doreen and Larry extra smiles and pat on their hands, as he gave them Holy Communion. He remembered their Mass, to celebrate their Golden Wedding anniversary, just two days before. 'I have so many people to thank God for,' he thought, and when he went to bed he was exhausted but filled with a deep sense of satisfaction.

He was up early as usual, to say the seven-thirty a.m. Holy Mass. This was a wonderful season, and although he was feeling stiff and a bit more weary than usual, he felt his strength grow as Mass progressed. "Our Blessed Mother is with us, right now, just as she was two thousand years ago," he said as he delivered his sermon.

"Just look at her, see her in the crib, with little baby Jesus. Thank her, for she said "yes" to the archangel. Our Lady accepted the Holy Spirit, and truly became the mother of God. Think of those shepherds, when they heard the angels singing and were guided to the stable. They must have had great faith, as they knelt down and worshipped baby Jesus. They knew that the greatest event in history had occurred, and this little baby was to be their king and saviour."

He stood outside after mass, and greeted every person as they slowly filed out after mass. He knew them all, especially those who had been parishioners of his for forty years or more. For everyone, he had a firm handshake or a kiss on the cheeks, or even the lips for a few of the ladies whom he loved so dearly.

They were all trying, and he knew how some struggled and failed; but he could see some of what he knew God saw in each of us. As a priest, he was passing on that love in a special way, and he enjoyed sharing this love and warmth. He often thought, 'the gift of priesthood is like being a parent to a huge family. The name "father" has been wisely chosen.' He had given up that precious privilege of having his own children, yet he had so many who called him "father", and whom he loved and cared about, as all true fathers do.

NEW PRIESTS

"Vocations to the priesthood are on the rise," Father Martin Schupp observed to his colleague, one day.

"That is wonderful, and the new seminary will soon be in full swing," Father Odilo replied.

"I always feel disappointed when some of them leave, though, even after being ordained," he continued. "I don't really know why that happens."

"Ah sure, it is because it is so easy nowadays," mused Father Odilo. "I am sure most of the postulants are good and sincere people, but I don't think we make it 'hard enough' for them, during training. That is important to test if they have a true vocation." In his many years of priesthood he had often seen and thought about these losses. "There is a lot of prestige here in becoming a priest, not to mention getting the education and training, at a time when unemployment is very high."

"Yes, Father Odilo, but we can't be doubters. We must accept that they are all sincere, and then discern what is best over a period of time."

"You remind me of Father Sixtus," he said. "You remember how well known he was for trusting everybody and thinking the best of them all. Well, he was let down many times, because of that."

"That is very different, Odilo," Father Martin said. "Times have also changed a lot. You know, I was talking to one of your parishioners the other day. He told me about two books he had just been reading. I think one was 'Half-Time', and the other was about ending your life still strong. Well, he said these were written by a Baptist, and one of the topics was about the failure rate in their seminarians."

"Well, what does he say?"

"It was very interesting. One of the professors had told him that only ten percent of them would stay the course, through life. That means ninety percent fail, or drop out for some reason. It seems like too high a percentage to me."

"I also cannot believe that they have such a big problem. I am sure we don't have more than a ten per cent drop-out rate, if that," Father Odilo said.

"Well, he also quoted the example of Billy Graham and his colleagues. Apparently there were two men of the same era who were just as dynamic as Billy Graham, packing tents and theatres with followers wherever they went. And you know what? One died a drunk, after leaving the church altogether, and the other committed suicide. Only Billy Graham stayed on track."

"Well, those high pressure preaching routines probably put too much strain on them."

"Well, there was something else. He told me this author kept a tally of his own classmates, and then looked back over it after many years. He crossed off those who had fallen by the wayside. And there he saw it, and was amazed to find that only about ten per cent had stuck it out—his own classmates."

Father Christoff came in to the lounge and poured a cup of tea, after greeting them. "Am I interrupting?" he asked.

"Not at all," they said. "Join us."

The three of them had a good chat, and Father Christoff assured them. "I am very pleased with all our candidates. Do you know, I can foresee the time when we shall be sending missionaries from Africa to re-convert people in Europe and America!"

"You are right. I have seen that already, in Germany. Some parishes no longer even have a priest. The young people are only interested in their wealth, television, sexual diversions and all sorts of pleasures and entertainment. God is hardly even mentioned, now that they are all so well off."

OTHER FAITHS

"Coming back to that book and all these new 'bible churches'. They seem to have skipped out nearly two thousand years of Christianity and simply started their own movements."

"Yes, but they are good people. Many of us can learn a lot from them. But they are just missing so much."

"And when you look at our own parishes, many Catholics don't seem to have much appreciation of their faith. How can they be so indifferent, knowing that they truly receive Our Lord in the Blessed Sacrament?"

"That's true; many are weak, and that is how these other groups lure them away."

"These churches push hard for conversions, and many of our Catholics succumb. Perhaps they go because they like the way the minister preaches, or perhaps he gives advice that they can easily accept. Like their easier ideas on divorce, birth control, and even abortion. The services have a lot of good entertainment, so children enjoy that and the social side of it."

"If only we could bring that into our parishes a bit more. I don't mean the advice about marriage and sex, which they get. Perhaps something that makes it more enjoyable for the youth, for instance. We have everything, really, but it is often not appreciated."

Just then, in walked Father John. "This looks like an interesting discussion," he noted, as he pulled up a chair and joined them. "What are you talking about?"

"Now, here's a man who reads and studies a lot. You have been reading up on ecumenical activity in Zimbabwe and elsewhere. How should we approach other Christians?"

He hesitated, and deferred to these more experienced priests, but answered, "Firstly, with great respect and love, I think. But, why do you ask that out of the blue?"

"We were just chatting about the way a lot of other faiths attract and interest their followers, and even lure them away from Catholicism."

"Oh, that subject," he said, seeming a bit put off.

"Yes, it's important," said Father Odilo.

"I know your views on that, I think, Father Odilo," he replied. "You and Noel Scott and Graham Shaw in Hillside all get on very well."

"That is true," he replied. "We respect one another, and are always friendly and considerate of each other. If one of Noel's patients is sick, at Mater Dei, I have no hesitation in doing what I have always done; I just go in and visit. I always ask if they would like to say a little prayer, and most times they are quite happy to do so."

"How does Noel Scott feel about that?"

"I think he does the same, quite often. You know, a lot of our parishioners went to the Alpha course, which the Anglicans gave in Hillside and Riverside, and they said it was great."

"Well, that may be okay with Anglicans and Protestants, but what about others who also call themselves Christian?"

"Ah, now you are talking different issues. Firstly, we should decide who are Christians? To follow Christ, we must believe what He said and understand the true meanings; there are so many modern distortions going around; I can only wonder who is behind that. As Christians we believe that Jesus is God; and we also believe in the Holy Trinity. We all believe that Jesus died and rose from the dead. So, at least we have these beliefs in common. There are other things that have led to the different breakaways in history, but I like the idea of calling these other Christians 'our separated brethren', as distinct from Catholic Christians. I think that is how we should view them."

"Well. That can apply to many churches, calling themselves Christian, but are they all Christian? What about JW's for instance?"

At that moment, the phone rang, and by the time Father Martin had answered and been called off urgently, the group broke up. "That was a good chat," Father Christoff observed. "We should talk more about how we interact with other beliefs."

PILGRIMAGE TO EMPANDENI

The day began with clear skies, although there was a touch of milkiness in the dull blue sky. It was not a good sign. The last few days had been scorching hot, and it was already several days since the last break in the dry weather. That had been worth the wait, though, with a huge storm filling the night sky with lightning and thunder for a few hours, and the next day the rain gauges showed that around seventy millimetres of rain had drenched Bulawayo and its surrounds.

The ordination of two new priests and two new brothers was to take place at Empandeni, and Father Odilo drove off with seven parishioners in his Kombi. As he got onto the main road for the hundred kilometres to Plumtree, he said, "Charles, I think we need a rosary. You lead it; we should say the glorious mysteries." After that the ladies sang and then chatted happily while he discussed a few of his concerns for the parish as he drove.

At Plumtree's main intersection, with the railway line on the right, he turned the corner, stopped and handed over the controls to Ben. It was a bumpy ride from there on, and the gravel road was typical of the lack of government spending in Matabeleland. "Gee, Ben, we were fine with Father Odilo driving. Can't you stop shaking us all over the place?" one of the passengers quipped cheerfully.

Near the mission, the road had a series of mounds on the road where the culverts had been built to relieve flow in the flat terrain; the road simply rose over these in mounds for which Ben had to slow right down each time.

The church was made of carved stones of grey granite, and outside stood a lovely set of statues—a crucifix, with Our Lady and Saint John beneath it. Inside the church, on the left side, stood a statue of a missionary with a young brown boy at his side. It portrayed the calling, which had urged these Germans to serve as missionaries in far-off Africa.

It was a boiling hot day, and the open-air service was sure to last until lunchtime. It was almost entirely in iSindebele, so some of the white guests from town parishes or elsewhere missed quite a bit of what was said. But there was no mistaking the happy and prayerful singing and the loving welcome which the forty-odd priests extended to their new colleagues.

After their vows were repeated in public, Archbishop Pius Ncube ordained them. The three Archbishops and all the priests laid hands on them and stood facing them in a circle with their right hands upraised, praying for the Holy Spirit to come upon these new priests and brothers and stay with them in their ministry.

Something made Father Odilo think about how he had celebrated some thirty thousand[xxiv] Holy Masses over the years. Today's ordinations brought back vivid images of his own ordination; he thought about it more, now that he had served sixty years as a priest.

The young girls began the service with their singing and dancing. They moved and rolled their hands gracefully to the rhythm of the music, and looked about demurely, revealing white eyes as they looked aside, or the brilliant white of their smiles against their brown skins. Even the toddlers and babies had the rhythm. The women came in, with some elderly ladies bringing up the rear, still active and supple. Two toothless ladies sat nearby, swaying to the music and ululating loudly but tunefully.

Those of the men who could afford it, wore suits; others came in overhauls, or shirts with trousers and shoes that were in a wide variety of condition. The women wore their best dresses, some of them in skirts and blouses, and many of them were wearing hats. Several women wore printed cotton cloths, which they wrapped around their dresses or skirts; as they arrived, they spread the cloths on the soil and sat themselves or their children on them. Afterwards, they picked them up, dusted them off and wrapped them around themselves again.

The singers had practised their introduction well, and danced up the aisle singing their greeting, 'Bayethe", in wonderful African rhythm. Led by the more mature ladies, the young girls followed shyly, making graceful arm and hand movements in time with one another, as their bodies swayed to the music.

The children were amazing. Little toddlers sat or moved about a bit, but their mothers and sisters kept them quietly there from around ten o'clock to after two p.m. One mother had her baby secured on her back with a white towel, patterned with brightly painted pink and blue birds with happy yellow beaks. Late in the service it started to whimper, sucking its hand; she sorted it out by patting its bottom with her hand behind her back. She moved her body up and down in a gentle rhythm, and the baby was soon asleep again. At meal-time, the mothers unwrapped little parcels with sadza and other food for their children and themselves.

Some little girls were dressed in perfect little white communion or christening dresses. Their dark colouring made a magnificent contrast, and they were very careful not to dirty these beautiful dresses. Far out at these mission stations, it seemed the dresses must have come as gifts from Europe, or perhaps from Bulawayo, once they had fulfilled their uses, and the children had long outgrown their little treasured collection.

There were only a few white people among the largely black congregation; some of them were friends visiting the priests and brothers who were concelebrating, and others were parishioners who had driven from Bulawayo or Plumtree area.

A few wispy clouds had formed high in the sky, and occasional shadows flitted across as they passed before the noon sun. A young man dressed as a Matabele warrior appeared after the service. He chanted praises and thanks to the priests, the early missionaries and the parents of the candidates. The crowd applauded him enthusiastically, although he made a few political comments, which drew a mixed reception.

JUBILATION AND HOLY MASSES

Father Odilo concelebrated the Easter Masses with his colleague Father Kevin. The Church was packed and the choir had been revived by Onneke Born to sing some of the rich repertoire of old church hymns, and the Latin chants and songs. His regular walking friend, Onneke, played the organ with gusto and directed the singers at the same time. 'God has been so good to me,' he thought appreciatively during the service.

At the consecration, his solemn words obeyed the command of Jesus at the Last Supper, and he knew, as he had in nearly twenty six thousand masses before, that he was God's faithful instrument. 'I am nothing,' he reflected, 'only Your servant. I have no power of my own; only what You confer upon me as your dutiful priest. Thank You, God, for the many years, and the wonderful people You have given me.'

Although he was physically exhausted, as any other eighty-eight year old man well might be allowed to be, he was spiritually renewed in a special way, as always at Easter. 'Next week, I shall have been a priest for sixty three years,' he realised. 'I must go and climb Mount Inungu again!'

A GREAT TREE FALLS

As he was about to leave the parish one week-day morning, one of his parishioners drove in to the church carpark. 'What prompted John to come here?' he wondered.

"Where are you going, Father?" he asked.

"I am on my way to the Nkomo family, for Mass," he answered. "You know about the memorial service, I think?"

"Oh, yes; it was announced on Sunday. Well, may I come with? Perhaps I can join you as an extra representative for our Parish."

"Of course," he said, happy to have the company today. "Come on, then. We must not be late."

"Okay. Let's go in my car then." In his arms, Father Odilo had all the items that he needed, so this time he did not raise any objections to the younger man's suggestion. He was still intrigued by this unexpected arrival, in the middle of a week-day morning.

"Do you know where the house is, in Aberdeen Road?" he asked.

"I think I know it. It's quite near where we used to live, just off the Esigodini Road, near Fortune's Gate Road."

"That's right. I'll show you how to get to it, though," he said as the pickup truck turned right into Cecil Avenue. "I think you remember how I said that Johanna Nkomo is a good woman; do you?"

"Yes, Father. Why was that though?" he asked. He knew his mother somehow related well to her at Mass, but it seemed it was more because they were both short, but strong people.

"Well, she was the first president of the Saint Anne's movement, at Empandeni, you know. I have known her for a very long time. She has always been very strong in her faith, in spite of everything." John seemed to him to be a little unconvinced, but he said nothing further.

There were armed police and army guards on the road, as they approached the house. The Mercedes ahead of them was waved through the entrance gate, but the guards were exchanging signals about them already, and it was clear they would be stopped. "Let me do the talking," Father Odilo insisted.

"Let's just park outside anyway," John said, as he drove on, past the entrance, and then angled the truck into the dry grass at the side of the road.

"Good idea; we can get away sooner without disturbing everybody."

"Yebo, Baba," he commenced the exchange of greetings, as they approached the gateway on foot. The initially suspicious looks had started to fade already, as these two white men drew closer. His Roman collar and obvious priesthood were factors, as was his older age, something still traditionally respected. The policeman gave them directions, and they walked up the long driveway towards a modest single-storey house, with a white tent pitched to the right of the driveway circle.

A large number of Anna's were already seated at several of the rows of white plastic armchairs in the tent. Their brown and white uniforms were topped off with distinctive hats, and they looked like a group of nuns.

Misses Nkomo sat to the left of the big man, who was seated on a cushion, on a high-backed wooden armchair, just to the left of the long altar table. They made their way towards seats, but were ushered closer to the front. As they made their way, many people came forward to greet Father Odilo, and he singled out several people, introducing John to them. He knew most of them by name, and many other personal particulars, but occasionally, he asked for more information.

"Oh, John, meet Misses Midzi." They shook hands in the African way, and soon moved on.

"John, I would like you to meet Mister Dube," he paused, as they were about to sit down. After a few moments, he said, "come with me. I think we should first greet the uMdala." He went up and respectfully shook hands with Joshua Nkomo, greeting him with great warmth. There was a happy and smiling exchange, as they stood near his seat.

One of the Nkomo brothers came and greeted them, and then a daughter and other members of the family came and spoke to them briefly.

John looked surprised when he told him, "one of the main purposes of this Mass is to receive him into the Church."

Father Christoff had begun the opening prayers, so there was no chance for further explanations. Shortly after that, everybody's attention was directed to a five hundred-gram jam tin that was on the left end of the altar. A match was lit, but it soon went out in the wind. After two more attempts, the match had been shielded and kept alight until the papers in the tin were aflame. He clearly knew more than a few casual snippets, and as the papers burned away, Father Odilo whispered, "that is his written confession. It's a bit unusual, but he especially asked that he be allowed to make his confession in this way."

The Mass was a very moving service, and the big man was also confirmed, with the holy oils. During all the proceedings he stayed seated, and his attentive wife gently and respectfully dabbed at his tear-streaked face with a large white cloth. This was a very different face of the man whom people were accustomed to seeing at public meetings.

He was also clearly in some pain and discomfort[xxv]; the big man, a strong leader, who had been outmanoeuvred by his supposed ally, looked sad as well. His cherished dreams had not been fulfilled, and the means he had sometimes used to attain them were now part of his confession. He had once spoken for so many of the Matabele people, and it was undoubtedly their impetus that had turned the tide of the war against the Rhodesian forces. Leader of a proud race, with a history of courage, but also cruelty, he symbolised the defeat and humiliation that somebody had managed to impose; the revenge of those he thought were allies-in-arms had been the last thing he had expected.

Now the tears were freely dripping from his eyes, but he held himself with the dignity of a man who has long been accustomed to a position of leadership. It was clear throughout the service that he was experiencing many deep and emotional thoughts.

After the consecration, Father Christoff reverently received communion, and then left the other priest to walk to the front with hosts for the congregation, while he took the communion wine and hosts to Joshua Nkomo. The congregation watched as he received the

Body and Blood of Christ, and the Anna's broke into their communion song.

Only a few obviously non-religious people could be seen unaffected. Glancing to his right, Father Odilo noticed that John's eyes were moist with feeling; he could only guess at some of them. Here was a young white Zimbabwean, who had seen and experienced a lot during the war years; he wondered if he was able to forgive, as God does.

Forgiveness is a complex thing, he knew, and he thought about it for a while. It is not a case of ignoring the wrongs, for that gives evil the right to persist. Long ago he had learned, from many human encounters and many confessions and counsellings, that wrong-doings could never be made right; however, nursing bitterness and angry resentment were behind more distress and illness than any other cause, even alcoholic addiction.

Forgiving a person did not ever mean allowing oneself to be trampled by him, but it was a brave and powerful act of love, a human gesture, uniquely capable of breaking the cycle of violence and retaliation. Pope John-Paul II had visited his attacker, Agca, in the prison cell, not to have him released, but to forgive him in a personal and loving way. Here they were witnessing God's forgiveness, something possible for every person, no matter how he may have strayed, right up until he breathed his last. Visiting sick and dying people had shown him this grace time and again.

After Communion, the congregation was invited to come up and welcome Joshua Nkomo into the Church. Father Odilo greeted him and welcomed him in fluent iSindebele; then he listened as John said, "welcome Mister Nkomo, and congratulations."

As the last hymn was being sung, he suggested, "I think we should leave now, before the food and celebrations."

"Fine, Father," John said. "You just lead the way."

As they drove back to Christ the King church, John said, "do you know, Father, that was quite a co-incidence today, and I am glad I was there." With a bit of emotion in his voice, he went on, "I was really amazed, and I found that I could forgive him; you know, I felt as if I was standing in for the white community, somehow. He has certainly done a lot of bad things, but you could see that he was genuinely making his peace with God. I never thought I would see something like that."

"God is always ready to forgive us, any of us. All he wants from us is that we have a truly humble spirit, and that we really are sorry for our wrong-doings."

"Yes. All the same, I certainly had many misgivings and bad recollections about the things he has said and done."

"Yes, of course. But this just goes to prove that God's love and forgiveness is there for all of us." He gave a kindly pat on the fore-arm, and added, "You, too, you know."

"Yes."

"Now, Johanna's prayers were answered today. I must say, I had not thought it likely, but she is a woman of great faith, and God always listens to the prayers of a mother. He was a Seventh Day Adventist for most of his life, so that was a big matter for him as well."

When he had said goodbye in the carpark, he walked over to the glass-fronted shrine, with the terrible statue of Jesus in agony on the Cross, the one he had rescued from Saint Patrick's Mission. 'Lord, you are a funny fellow,' he prayed with reverent familiarity. 'I didn't know why John was here, but it was you again!'

A PILGRIM CLIMB UP MOUNT INUNGU

With three workers, he headed out privately one morning. He did not want to be fettered by a social group for this occasion, as he wanted the time and solitude to climb and pray at his own pace. It was a beautiful morning, and he left two men cutting the grass to prepare for the crowd which comes out to attend Holy Mass at the summit on Africa Day each year, to pray for peace and goodwill and the many needs of Zimbabwe and the rest of Africa.

Slowly, but surely, he made his way. 'Eile mit Weile', he thought to himself in German. He paused at each of the fourteen Stations of the Cross, which mark the way; he was pleased to see them all intact again, thanks to Norman Scott, no doubt.

It was a hard climb for him, though; he would soon be eighty-nine years old. His pulse was fine; his breathing was a bit short now, but slowly, slowly, he just kept putting one foot ahead of the other. He took care as he pulled himself up and over the rocks. His hands had the strength of a gymnast still, and he swung himself around the small tree trunk, above a sheer drop of a few metres, landing his feet firmly back onto the ascending trail.

The soil was dry already, but the trees were still in full leaf. There were lots of birds chirping and hopping all over, and there was plenty for them to eat. As he prayed quietly, an emerald-spotted dove called out sadly in the distance. Something startled a few francolins, and they crashed and screeched their way through the undergrowth in their mad escape. Ants were plodding along across the path in a busy convoy, colliding with empty-handed colleagues on the return path.

He put his finger down in their path to test them. He got a brief flicker of being noticed, but then they all just moved on and around his finger. Their awareness of him was as limited as his own awareness of God; "except that God managed to get through to us, in a way that I can not speak to the ants."

He thought of Jesus comforting the women of Jerusalem, and finished his prayers at the eighth station. This was His task, and He was coming right into our midst, in human form, to get through to us in the most unforgettable manner. It was as the prophets had foretold, and Father Odilo could feel close to his Lord, praying the Calvary stations as he trudged up the hill. He had trod this particular path before, and many others like it. Each time, he felt a sense of wonder and gratitude, and also deep sadness.

Cresting the hill, past the stretch where a steel wire rope assists climbers, he paused to look across towards Rhodes' grave, among the giant pebbles on the bare granite dwala. He was the man whom legend claims "stopped the fighting of the bulls", right here in the Matopos. He ended a war of resistance, not unlike Zimbabwe's recent struggle in some ways; late in the last century, it had been waged fiercely among these very hills, but neither side could ever have won it.

So much development and civilisation followed. Zimbabwe still had the chance to be the "Jewel of Africa", as Nyerere had put it so well; just as Germany had flourished again, once the legacy of Hitler was over.

Gradually he made his way across the upper back of the porcupine, and came to the cross. He loved this cross. Eleven metres of aluminium clad steel shining in the sunlight, in the heart of this beautiful scenery. He chuckled to himself as he remembered how he had cajoled his three young engineers into taking on this task. He had to admit he had felt defeated for a while, when the first weekend of climbing and carrying its parts had made so little headway. They had all had second thoughts then, and been brought down to earth and humbled by Mount Inungu. But they did it—even if it had taken many weeks.

After a rest, he set out his altar on a rock, and said Holy Mass. He offered his thanks and his prayers to God, like Abraham on the mountain top, with the ram which God had provided.

As he climbed out onto the steep rock face above the ancient lightning-struck fig tree, a shadow moved swiftly below him. Quickly looking up, he caught sight of a black eagle, flying the hill in search of dassies for breakfast. "Or was it greeting me?" he wondered.

A second shadow passed along the rock below him, and he was above the other eagle. He looked down on the clearly defined white Vee on its back, the primary feathers, like delicate fingers feeling the air, as it glided by moving its head to check the rocks and crevasses for dassies.

He stopped and sat on a rock for a while. Looking out to the West, he could see their nest; a pile of sticks was nestled onto the East face of a rocky promontory which looked like a small version of Rio de Janeiro's famous "sugar-loaf mountain'.

They had not bred last year; nobody knew why, after so many years of regularly launching a new fledgling into the Matopos skies. Something had upset them, or their food supply was too threatened. John had told him they had been putting new sticks on the nest—a good sign. These amazing birds, giants of the sky; 'they have the same gentleness in the air as the elephants padding through the sand-forests. There is such elegance and art in God's creation.' He knew that his climb was doubly blessed now.

As far as the eye could see, the Matopos hills were a jumble of ancient granite—bare onion-skin dwalas, decorated with giant balancing rocks; cracked and balancing castle-rock formations. There were caves and crevasses everywhere; fig trees, like these two magnificent specimens on the top of Inungu, clinging to, and capturing life in whatever way it came at them.

In the valley below, the Maleme and Mamlongwe rivers still had brown, shallow water sluggishly seeping towards the full dam downstream. Some Brahmin cattle were browsing and grazing like ants below, and the cottage below Mbejane hill could only just be seen as it hid among the giant boulders, and stayed out of sight from Rhodes grave.

"May Almighty God bless and protect this place. May he bless our parish, our city and our whole country."

Prayers for the People

A month or so later, with a slow winter and the total solar eclipse in the offing, he was successfully warding off a spell of flu. On the Tuesday morning, he walked through the empty carpark from the parish house to the church. A young man, barefoot, but with long trousers and a well-worn jersey, watched from where he had sheltered for the night, as Father Odilo paused at the base of the crucifix within its glass enclosure. So many thoughts were together in sequence in his mind, as he beheld his Lord and Saviour, and he could feel God's love for him and those he served. He made the sign of the cross again, and walked on, with the cloudless dawn sky lighting up now.

He entered the church with great reverence, making the sign of the cross with the holy water at the entrance, and genuflecting slowly. He was thinking of Gene Vickerey whose funeral he was to conduct later. He wondered who would be at this early winter mass today. He knew many of their difficulties, and felt the depth of their hope and faith.

There were parents who prayed for their children and the healing of family conflicts. There were teachers and hospital workers, and businessmen with heavy burdens. There were those who prayed fervently for their own healing and the healing of their loved ones. He knew many of these things, and he looked forward to saying Holy Mass for them; he knew how much Our Lord cares and gives of Himself in the Holy Eucharist.

He was struck anew by a deep feeling of gratitude to God. 'Thank you, heavenly father for the wonderful gift of my priesthood. Words cannot express my humility and thankfulness. I am nothing, but You have consecrated me to do your bidding. You empower me like the apostles of old, to bless and sanctify the bread and wine, following the example of your priest Melchizedek, your servant Abraham, our saviour, Jesus, and your Popes, bishops and priests down through the ages.'

In the sacristy, he vested hurriedly, for somehow he was late this morning. As he went out to begin Holy Mass, his eyes took in the small but faithful congregation, and he offered a silent blessing upon them all. After genuflecting, he went up the steps and kissed the altar, looking up at the large crucifix, with the crowned figure outstretched depicting Christ's kingship over all. Descending with slow dignity, he genuflected again, feeling a tiredness, which he knew he had to resist. He walked across to the lectern, and bent down to switch on the lights.

The Lectionary was shut, and he opened it at the red string/cord. No, today was Tuesday, and it had not been set up; he turned the pages and found the Tuesday. Looking at the people, he greeted them warmly, "Good morning everybody."

"Good morning, father," they responded.

"Lovely to see you here." He began the opening prayers and when the time came for the readings, Sheila was on her way. This mother who had cared so lovingly for an afflicted boy-child who had died early, many years ago now, was his regular reader. Two of their three grown up daughters sat in the pew now.

Sheila began the reading, and seemed to hesitate a bit; then she continued, "Abram was a very rich man, with livestock, silver and gold ..." There was more shuffling through the pages as some parishioners who had daily missals leafed through their missals. She went on to read how Lot had settled in the plain of the Jordan, and Abram set up an altar to the Lord, at the Oak of Mamre.

Psalm 14 would have special significance for a businessman locked in a wrangle with his brother. 'How will that end?' he wondered. That was a tough teaching about not wronging your brother or casting a slur, nor accepting interest on a loan. 'If only he can grasp the principal, and understand what God is really saying,' he prayed silently. 'God does not expect you to give up seeking a just solution.' He thought about the anguish that parents experience when their children are in conflict.

Father Odilo returned the bow as Sheila respectfully bowed and went back to her place in the front right pew. He introduced the gospel and made the three signs of the cross, as he prayed inwardly, "May the Holy Spirit be in my mind, on my lips and in my heart."

Matthew recorded Our Lord's admonitions about casting pearls before swine, but more importantly, "so always treat others as you would like them to treat you; that is the meaning of the Law and the Prophets."

He offered prayers for the intentions of the sick and deceased, "for our beloved country, and that our leaders may return to lawfulness," for benefactors, and for the church and clergy, and for the petitions of the people at Mass.

He was aware of his solemn responsibility and power, as he continued with a humble dignity. At Holy Communion, he gave out the sacred hosts, and as he reached a man whom he knew needed so much of God's grace, he chose a quadrant of the large, priestly host and gave it to him with a brief look into his eyes that spoke his prayers and love for him. As he consumed the fragments and cleaned the chalice, he looked out lovingly over them all, heads bowed in prayer, knowing that Jesus was within them in the unique and mysterious way which He promised, and which Catholic Christians are especially blessed with.

"Where are the others?" he wondered. Out of such a large parish, only a small number made it to Holy Mass during the week. He had long since accepted that it was not possible for many of them, with morning tasks and work, and transport problems; but these people showed it can be done. "If they only truly knew what rich blessing Our Lord brings in coming to them at Holy Communion, surely nobody would want to miss such a great gift" he thought for probably the thousandth time.

Outside the entrance, Sheila admitted, "those were the wrong readings. The book was opened there, but I couldn't understand why it was different to what I had just read earlier."

"Oh well, that explains why I couldn't find my place," John replied. "Still, perhaps that was meant to be."

THE 'PRINCE OF THIS WORLD' RUNS FREELY

New York[28] woke up to a day that would change the whole world. The incredible terrorist attacks and the massacre of defenceless civilians was the action of fanatics, determined to fan warfare and hatred, justifying this in their minds by the most devious torture of truth and love. Father Kevin spoke about the devil, as the one who creates division, 'Los Diablos'.

THE TEST OF ALL TESTS

He had driven down with Father Kevin to join the other priests on a retreat at Embakwe Mission, and it was an inspiring and uplifting time. He forgot his daily tablets one morning, and left after breakfast to go to his room and fetch them. "I will see you in the hall," he said, and moved quite fast, so as not to miss anything.

On his way back, he walked over a low step and as his foot landed on the grass mat, the mat slipped on the smooth cement floor. Father Odilo came crashing down onto his right hip, hitting his right elbow and his shoulder, and when he looked at his foot, it almost made him laugh; it was displaced at an angle of forty-five degrees from where he expected it to be.

Father Kevin and some of the other priests came to his aid. "Oh I'm alright," he said, trying to stand up. But he simply couldn't put any

---

[28]   11th September 2001

weight on that leg. Soon the agonising bone-deep pain kicked in, and he realised that he must have given himself a serious injury.

"I think we should get you back to Bulawayo this morning," Father Kevin proposed, but he wouldn't hear of it.

"Just help me to my room. I shall rest up a while, and then I shall join you later."

A whole two days went by before he admitted that things were not right! "It's not getting any better. I hate taking those pain-killers, but I think I need to see a doctor soon."

An ambulance was called from town, and eventually it arrived and drove him to Plumtree and then back to Bulawayo's Mater Dei Hospital, where x-rays were taken. The image of the joint was not clear, but there was a pronounced line across the hip joint. There was a bit of concern as Doctor Ncube was away. "He is one of the best orthopaedic surgeons around; people come from South Africa and the UK even, for him to operate here," Sister Jamieson was telling one of the visitors. "He is especially well-known as an expert in hip replacement surgery."

Colin Tuson, a Bulawayo-born orthopaedic specialist was contacted in Carltonville, and he even tentatively arranged to fly up from South Africa if needed. The specialist from Bulawayo Central Hospital reviewed his case, and special arrangements were made to admit him to Mater Dei, where he was not yet registered. It was an emergency, and it soon became clear that the hip had been broken right off the end of the femur.

A lot of time had already been lost, and so action was decided, and he confirmed that he had the necessary prosthesis. He operated successfully and performed a partial replacement of his broken hip, with a titanium ball and peg, with a fancy sounding name. Father Odilo insisted on being given the severed hip ball, which he kept in preserving fluid, to show his many squeamish visitors.

"Don't go in there," was an often repeated warning. "He will insist on showing you his relics!"

With his usual assurance, Father Odilo was up and walking on crutches within four days. He pressed the physiotherapists to speed up his recovery, as he had so much to do, and was sure they were being overly cautious when they said, "you should rest much more, and do not put weight on the leg for the first two weeks at least."

His confidence soon began to suffer, as he developed severe and continuous pains, and some infections had to be treated. In addition muscle or tendon strains seemed to be slowing down his recovery. One night, in a disturbed and uncomfortable sleep, he thought about their big old horse, at the old family farm, in Arberg; it had been tired and arthritic, and took ages to loosen up, before he could harness it or get it to move normally.

'Now this is my own time in life to be stiff with pain,' he thought. It was truly a great test of humility and a time to face up to his own normal human frailty. It also seemed to strike at one of his greatest pleasures; walking and climbing had always enabled him to enjoy nature's special beauty.

He remained outwardly cheerful all the time and several times when he complained, he did so with a special reverence. "He is a funny bloke," he would say, pointing heavenwards. "He is quick to smite, but slow to heal!" All the same, he accepted this test with humility and a sense of humour, and realised it was really only a small suffering to share with all that Jesus had endured to show His love for humankind.

REVISION

"You really need to get that joint seen to," he was told by several people, like Sister Gemma, and even Mike Gelman, his physician. Stubbornly, he refused, although he knew that he had been offered a trip to Johannesburg by car, if necessary.

'I will leave it to John,' he decided. 'If he is able to take me down I will go; but there is no rush.' He told them, "I can endure a little suffering. The doctor assured me that the operation was perfect, and this is just part of the healing. Still, I don't like these antibiotics; they upset my appetite and make me feel ill."

After several months of worsening pain, with Brother Alois doing his best with some of his oils and remedies, he explained, "when I get up, I have to stand still for a whole minute or more. There is a sharp pain like an electric shock. But once that has settled, I can get moving."

When John asked Sister Gemma for advice, she said, "he really must go and have it seen to. If you can get him to do that, it will be the best day of work you have ever done!"

There was even a slight clicking noise, and one day he relented, "I think I should go and have it checked. I know that you mentioned a friend of Colin Tuson's, whom he recommended, and I would like you to arrange for an appointment"

He was checked by his doctor, and given a referral letter to take with. His friend and physician, Mike Gelman urged him to have fresh x-rays taken, and they were ready the morning that he flew to Johannesburg. He was met and taken to the Victory Park parish, the famous 'lemon-squeezer' shaped church.

The next day, he called on the heart specialist first. Mister Dalby was a very kind and considerate specialist, 'a good Anglican,' he told John. He checked his pacemaker and did a live heart-scan and all the routine tests, declaring him 'very fit, and quite able to handle another operation if that is necessary.'

At the Kenridge Hospital, Mister Scheepers looked at the x-rays and immediately saw that the prosthesis had become loosened. "This type of prosthesis used to be quite common. However, it is totally unsatisfactory for anybody who is active; it is intended for ninety-year olds who are very limited in their movements. Clearly this would not work for you."

Unfortunately, he was not able to schedule him for surgery until two weeks later. "That is fine for patients here in Johannesburg," John said, "but can't you get a colleague to fit him in tomorrow or as soon as possible."

He kindly referred him to a young but very capable colleague, Doctor Bhutt, who examined him carefully that afternoon, and scheduled him for a complete revision and full hip replacement.

Two weeks later, he had flown back and was obediently walking with two crutches and staying put at the Mariannhill House, in Queens Park, where he had a room at the end of the corridor, and everything was pretty well on one level. He graduated to a single crutch for the next six weeks and by his ninetieth birthday he was walking with a stick, after he had patiently followed instructions and allowed the operation to heal well.

After inflicting a detailed account of his travails on the congregation that loved him so much, he said, "a little bit of suffering is good for you." At the early Sunday Mass, one day, he added, "It helps you appreciate the good health you normally have and reminds us about what is important in life".

Just then, a teenage boy, Desmond went into an epileptic fit, and was tossing about as his body was racked with one of his frequent seizures.

It was as though he was there to demonstrate exactly what Father Odilo was saying. He stopped and asked the congregation to join him in special prayers, and then continued, "As I was saying, there are people all around you who have some cross to bear." He gestured to him, saying, "little Desmond has had this problem for many years now, and he is a wonderful example to me and to his family; his faith is so strong, and he deals with his affliction in such a mature manner. I am certain God is with him in a very special way, and he will be richly rewarded for his suffering."

He went on, "there are some foolish people who say things against God when suffering comes their way, or whose faith evaporates. Others make out that suffering is a punishment from God. I think it is quite the opposite; it is a special blessing, a caress from God. And do you know why I say that? It is because He always provides the grace and strength we ask for, to enable us to cope with it." He held up his hip part, and said, "So I say, 'thanks be to God'—for the little suffering He has given me!"

PROPAGANDA AND THE JUDICIARY

The newspapers soon became quite unreadable, especially the state media. The Truth that Pope John Paul II had called for was being tortured out of existence, and the degree of propaganda brought back chilling reminders of the Nazi era. The expression, 'a culture of impunity' was being heard more and more, and seemed most apt, even more so for those who ought to have been stewards of the common good.

He had corresponded with, and tried to urge, his friend, Chief Justice Anthony Gubbay, to hold firm in his position, for the good of the country, but the pressure was impossible and he had eventually been coerced into acceding to a resignation, with words almost bullied into his mouth. There appeared to be no room for impartiality, for the rule of law, and certainly not for any criticism.

After a very dubious election, the stunned people of Zimbabwe wondered if there were any limits to the arrogance to which they had been subjected. Perhaps ancient African power had always been abused like this; the education and development of the past century was now a big stumbling block to a determined caucus, who planned to hold onto power and keep looting, no matter what.

Farms were viciously targeted, both as loot, but also as the seat of a large portion of the people, reliant on and generally appreciative of the benefits of the large and successful commercial agricultural sector. These prize farms, developed over generations, with the investment in energy and capital that alone could make land productive on such a scale, seemed apt rewards for these self-appointed rulers and those who underpinned them by any means they deemed necessary.

A hastily cobbled together plan was put into effect, delivering mobile squads of so-called 'war veterans' and a band of fiercely loyal 'youth' to each of the farms that had been selected. Harassment failed to provoke the expected armed backlash, and several people said things like, "the farmers are absolute saints, the way they have resisted the provocation." Father Odilo agreed quietly with a parishioner who added, "They are fantastic people, with so much courage and wisdom."

The illegal attempts at acquisition soon found the culprits called up before the judges, whose obvious duty was to uphold the principals and tenets of the law, and even the country's own constitution that was being deliberately defied.

An irate ruling group refused to be halted and the cry 'aluta continua' was clearly being misinterpreted as 'let the looting continue'. Some true benefits, like education, had been visible, but twenty-two years of wealth transfer and job creation for selected appointees, in huge and excessive numbers had siphoned off a huge chunk of the productive sector's efforts. Now, the farms were to be next. The whole legal system was a blocking mechanism to such plundering and so it had to be 'overhauled'. A few unexpected obstacles appeared, in the form of judges stronger than their age would have seemed to make possible.

The Chief Justice was an eventual victory, but the newly appointed Minister of Justice still wanted even more absolute control. Another judge held out until he died, and Justice Fergus Blackie bravely and justly convicted the Minister of 'contempt of court' when he repeatedly refused to appear in court, as summonsed. The Minister's revenge was diabolically plotted and a few months after his retirement, at four o'clock on a Friday morning, Judge Blackie was hauled out of his bed and taken into custody for the weekend.

Denied medication, food and bedding, he persevered with the dignity that Father Odilo knew him for, and he was eventually released on bail. To try and damage his exceptional integrity, the propaganda machine set to work with one of the biggest lies it had ever tried. Remembering the adage of propaganda, 'the bigger the lie, the more likely it will be believed', the judge was ludicrously accused of having an affair with the woman whose conviction he had rightly overturned!

A large part of the international community had eventually condemned the pre-election violence and the questionable result, but the rulers scoffed at it with the confidence of mass control, and their strategic abuse of might. The advantage of criminality is that conscience is no obstacle to wrongdoing. A few slaps on the hand were no worry for those who had extracted so much wealth from the country, and feasted on the corruption that some of the rest of the world had actually fostered for their own short-term profiteering, anyway. Mysteriously, neighbouring countries and their leaders seemed to turn a blind eye to all the revelations and exposures of the blatant electoral fraud.

The war in the Congo was used as a wonderful opportunity to loot again; this time it was like hiring out the soldiers of the country, so that some of the officers and politicians, and all manner of other 'schemers', including some white collaborators like Rautenbach and Bredenkamp, could reward themselves with sophisticated plunder. As time went on, more and more rumours and information leaks were openly spoken about, and the lies and denials by the official press had to become louder and more heated. The tragedy of such misinformation, and the hatred and division that it generates, is a legacy that will take a long time to heal.

Many educated and professional Zimbabweans of all races were becoming more and more expatriated from their home country, but it was the very earnings of this diaspora, Zimbabweans abroad, that propped up the populace at home, despite the collapse of the currency, and inflation which rose to levels not seen since Germany's economic collapse. Per capita income had dropped in twenty years to less than a tenth of what it had been when the 'Jewel of Africa' was put into the hands of new rulers, by a tired British and South African axis. This was only the beginning of the slide, but who would have expected it to get worse?

The 'new rich' had quickly amassed fortunes, but much of their money arose through 'unearned income', so-called affirmative action, corruption, theft and the general scheming and patronage that had grown to be an accepted style, partly condoned and called 'wheeling and dealing'. These families and individuals were the 'Afro-mafia' of the country; totally and inextricably mingled with the essential political power; they were desperate that this should never be relinquished, especially as new ways were emerging in the world for bringing exploitative and political crime to trial.

Priests and laity were instant targets if they became involved in any form of public objection to the party's rule. Father Kevin and ten others were arrested and held in cramped prison cells, after a peaceful and prayerful Good Friday procession among the different churches in the Hillside area. It was months before their threatened punishment was abandoned. The rulers had a loyal following among some more dubious clergy, generously rewarding and manacling them to the gravy train.

NINETY YEARS TO REMEMBER

When Father Kevin returned from his leave in America, the first thing he asked was, "How has he been doing?"

Life returned to a more normal level again in a parish that had partially gone into remission, with the effective absence of two such vital men. Their returns coincided and with his recovery he was able to do more and more again.

It was such a pleasure to have Father Kevin back as well, and suddenly new life was being breathed into the parish by this pair of very different Mariannhillers.

Max Weeger and his wife Clementa arrived from Germany on the Friday, after Father Odilo's Rotary Club had wished him happy birthday and honoured him for his service. Holy Mass was celebrated for the parish and many invited guests on the Saturday evening of his birthday.

Archbishop Pius Ncube made it back specially for the occasion, having been at an ordination in Hwange that morning; he slipped quietly onto the altar to join in the prayers of the consecration. Father Odilo noticed him and his face lit up with a happy smile of greeting. At the supper that was held in the Elmar Schmid Hall, the Archbishop spoke humbly but with great clarity and conviction about the great calling of the priesthood, and toasted Father Odilo as a good example for all.

On Sunday, he again celebrated with those who came and stayed on after the ten o'clock Holy Mass. At these occasions, everybody was clamouring to speak with him and wish him well.

He took great pleasure in having his nephew, Max Weeger, and his charming wife, Clementa, as visitors, all the way from Germany. He had a special affection for Max, who had been to visit him in Africa five times before. The younger generations of his family were far away and he had forsaken them as Jesus had asked, in order to follow and serve more fully. However, they were always in his heart and prayers, and Max was a strong physical reminder of that bond, the link to all of his family and loved ones.

It was impossible to avoid politics, which to some people—especially the rulers—was not the done thing for priests. Father Odilo did not hesitate to criticise some of the excesses and the causes of the suffering, even though there were obviously parishioners of different political parties and views. He never spoke viciously, and always prayed that God's guidance and a change of heart would bring about justice and good leadership.

The gentle Father Kevin took up the call for justice and accountability, as he spoke on the sermon of the healed leper. Today's 'leprosy' could be AIDS, or other damage of body and soul, including the arrogant unwillingness to take responsibility for what is being done to damage the country and its suffering people. Jesus certainly wants to heal everyone, but the leper had come acknowledging his illness, and knowing that God could heal him.

TSHONGOKWE MISSION TURNS 50

He drove up with Dr Davis, in John's car, to stop over at Tshotsholo and go through the next morning to celebrate Tshongokwe's 50th anniversary. People came from all over and he was greeted by Sithole and Ndhlovu, two men he had baptised he had worked with years ago after he had established this outstation. The rains had poured down briefly and refreshingly the night before while they sat chatting in the lounge at Tshotsholo.

Now the clouds hung in the air and briefly sprinkled the tarpaulins covering the altar and much of the crowd. Bishop Robert Ndhlovu celebrated Holy Mass with the mostly Spanish priests who came from as far as Kana Mission and Hwange. The young girls, dressed in beautiful white dresses, danced in unison as they brought in the offertory gifts. Mothers sat with their children, clothed more fully than 50 years ago, but still poor. A few babies were discreetly being fed, soon silently at rest in their mother's arms or comfortably returned to the blanket on their backs. Several men wore suits, and you could see the committee and teaching members of the community by their sashes or other badges made for the occasion.

He spoke in iSindebele and raised many laughs with his accounts of things fifty years ago. He also described his great joy at working among them, God's gift of the many experiences he enjoyed, including a long list of animals, some of which were now so rare that the children had never seen them, or even heard their names mentioned. He praised his colleagues and helpers, and hugged old Sithole again; Ndhlovu had slipped away just before, so he missed the chance to be paraded and greeted again in front of his community. These men sat smiling in front and to his right as he spoke, fluent and accomplished in their language, respecting and loving them, as they loved him.

He returned to spend some time with his visiting nephews, Max and Otto, both rightly proud of their great uncle, and pleased to see how well he had recovered since Max's last visit when he was recovering from his hip replacement. At the Catenian Clergy Night on Monday, a noticeable spring was in his step again, and he was full of vigour and so much love and experience to pass on to the people he loved working for. Archbishop Pius had recovered from his Bell's palsy, and thanked these businessmen for this loving and traditional link with their clergy, especially at a time when the country was experiencing so much difficulty and oppression. The ladies received their usual kiss on the cheeks and he cheerfully remonstrated with most of them for being too skinny, which was usually quite far from the truth, in their eyes at least.

The next day, after 6.30 am Holy Mass, and his daily duties, he took a trip to Nungu with John and his nephews, no doubt wishing that he too could climb up to the Cross on the summit once again. They visited the neighbouring kraal, where he told the aged and partially unsighted gogo that she was a young girl! After all she was only 80-something, while he was a 91-year old. They loved his ease of conversation and asked him to pray with them in the dark little grass hut. It was decided that Mass would be at 11.00am next day, and they were invited to join in.

That evening, they shared a very German feast, with some of the Zoellner family's schinken and wurst, German Becks biers, ermentaller cheese and rye bread. After admiring the stars and singing a few festive songs, Father Odilo retired to the double bed up the stone stairs in the cottage built and disguised among the rocks.

The next day, Max, Otto and John left Father Odilo to lie in while they made an early ascent of Mount Inungu. After checking on the cattle dipping, they all had breakfast, chatted happily and prepared for Holy Mass. The ladies brought a box of their large onions, which Max bought for the Mariannhillers at Queens Park. Later they went to Gordon Park, where they spent the evening with the Maloneys and Norman Scott.

Father Odilo celebrated the Mass of the Resurrection on Thursday morning, for his friend, Charles Langlois, supported by Archbishop Karlen, Father Kevin and several priests. Charles' death was amazing; he had been with Edith to Mater Dei, where they had received Holy Communion.

At home, he had settled down with a small glass of whiskey beside him, and began to read from The Imitation of Christ for Edith. His chin settled down and he lowered the book into his lap. Edith waited a short while and then prompted him to proceed, but he was gone; he had made the most peaceful passing anybody could ever have wished for. His many prayers and the dedicated service he gave to the Church were surely rewarded, for him, and for the ease of his whole family. He described Charles and his many wonderful characteristics, one of the most outstanding of which was his total dedication to Edith—the two would invariably be seen holding hands, right up to the very last.

His time with his nephews soon had to end, and they hosted a large meal at the Cresta Churchill Hotel on Friday night, before taking their leave and flying back to Germany on Saturday morning.

A TRIP TO THE PAST

It was October, that month renowned for its dry and dispiriting heat, but this year it had been different. Light rains, heavy winds and several weather changes had occurred in a short time. With much talk and planning before it, a day had now been fixed and their trip details were agreed. After celebrating his 92nd birthday with his confreres at the Mariannhill Headquarters in Queens Park, he went through to breakfast and to meet with his three young engineers. 'Late as usual,' he soon began thinking, but was delighted to see the three of them and ushered them to places to catch up on the breakfast.

Plans were already being changed. Peter had become inundated with urgent work and was to leave them to go without him. At least that made it possible to stay out an extra night, as Angelo and John had both suggested. A jovial send-off was accompanied by photographs at the vehicle, and farewells from Brother Alois and Father Alphons.

The route to Nkayi goes past gold mines and farms and there was no lull in the flow of questions and discussions about what was happening and the people he knew and asked about. The narrow tar road had scattered pools of water alongside, and a busy stream of buses and other traffic, some of whom never seemed to look in their rear-view mirror, so that John was forced to find places where he could overtake on the right-side gravel shoulder.

Angelo was soon dispensing used tennis balls, as rewards for directions, and the dirt roads towards Kana Mission soon came to the Godfrey Huggins bridge over the Shangani River. There was a small amount of water among the fierce rocks that covered the riverbed, and the day was heating up.

At Kana Mission, Father Rozende was delighted to welcome them, and they ate roasted peanuts while they sat and listened to a radio broadcast of the almost unexpected but obviously correct acquittal of Morgan Tsvangarayi, the opposition party's president, on the state-organised frame-up that could have been used to hang him or imprison him for life. There had been a mood of tension, especially in the capital, and the relief was enormous, even hope-filled. Perhaps, after all, something sensible was happening behind the scenes.

Driving through Manoti, new powerlines were visible, even if the roads all remained gravel, and at Sengwa Mission father Angelo was equally delighted to offer his hospitality and some shared fruit from his gardens. He gave directions to Sengwa Gorge, and after crossing John's concrete bridge over the Sengwa river—with its two predecessors sunk or sinking further downstream as a result of inadequate understanding of the sandstone geology's weaknesses—they drove all the way around via Chief Sai's area until they eventually reached the Gorge. (John had always travelled by bush shortcuts before.) Almost immediately there was a challenge about the depth of the gorge, where the whole river squeezed into a narrow gap, sliced over the centuries through the sandstone. A rope was lowered to settle the controversy and at the mini-bridge crossing it was only about 10m deep.

From here, the roads became more and more difficult, weaving among the old fence posts, from which all the wire had now been stolen, and cutting through bush and fields in the general direction of Lusulu. The sun was setting and the last dry but sandy riverbeds were crossed before coming onto gravel roads and picking up speed. Too much speed, it soon turned out, and a tyre was soon punctured in the dark, on the sharp rock-strewn road. After fitting one of two spare tyres, they drove past the Kariyangwe Mission turnoff, deciding that it was late now and they needed to make for Binga as soon as possible.

Another tyre suddenly succumbed, totally ruined in the short time it took to feel it going flat; but fortunately John had two spares. The spare was quickly fitted but on driving off, the car was pulling strangely and they soon found that their front right tyre had gone down as well.

That was it! Now, how would Father Odilo react? A ninety-two year old man who had endured a long hot day, travelling over 450 kilometres already, some of this on the worst possible bush tracks.

While the two tyres had been replaced he had walked and felt the state of the road in the darkness. He had offered up his prayers, of thanks and of supplication, and he had enjoyed the evening bird and insect sounds and the familiar smells and the feel of the bush that he had traversed so many years before on foot, by bicycle, and sometimes, where possible, in his old Model-T Ford.

There was almost no possible chance of another vehicle coming this way now, and it was probably 12 kilometres or more to Kariyangwe.

'Well, there is not much we can do,' he said. 'I am delighted. God works in wonderful ways.'

John and Angelo were intrigued and quite relieved as he went on. 'I wanted to spend another night under the stars in the bush, so my prayers are answered!'

'But will you be able to manage?'

'Of course. I will simply put my head back in the front seat and we can sleep until morning, when we will get help.'

A chicken and salad supper was washed down with a few drinks and a bit of star-gazing in the dark African night. Angelo met some resistance to his heavy tots of brandy, but they relaxed and soon settled down for the night, John and Angelo in sleeping bags at the road side and Father Odilo in the front seat. The nearby dogs barked occasionally and cow-bells could be heard clunking in the distance, but there was no sign of a fire or any other form of light or habitation. The ground was hard and rocky so it took some time to nod off, but they managed.

Out of the darkness a strong light appeared in the distance. It was like a bright moonrise, but it drew closer. Suddenly, John knew what it was—a vehicle. He sprang up and rushed to the side of the car, to ensure that they saw people and who knows what other reasons? The truck pulled up, and out jumped two men, one with a quart bottle of beer in his hand. It was soon clear that they were well-meaning, and miraculously, their vehicle was also a Land Cruiser; they kindly agreed to lend a spare tyre and to follow behind all the way to Binga.

Once again, God's ways are amazing, for these men had diverted to this road for some reason that they themselves did not really know.

Much more slowly now, they made their way carefully over the remainder of the gravel road, onto the smooth tarred surface that seemed like a bit of heaven. They were able to wake up Rick's caretaker at the Lodge and to retire into the luxury of fresh and soft bedding in a well-fitted out house at the side of what had been the biggest man-made lake in Africa, Lake Kariba.

While two still-repairable tyres were being mended they came back for Holy Mass and breakfast and then went back to visit the two American priests, from Toledo, Ohio, with their magnificent and huge thatched church on the hills above Binga. Father Odilo took in every detail, and admired everything, from the tall thatched roof to the locally carved wooden tabernacle. They drove back towards the main Bulawayo-Victoria Falls Road and crossed the wide and rocky Gwayi and Deka rivers on recently built concrete bridges. At Deka, on the banks of the Zambesi River, they stopped for a picnic lunch at the Wankie Colliery's fishing camp and pump-station.

They didn't stop in Hwange town, although Angelo checked in with his office to see if they needed anything taken back to Bulawayo.

A brief stop at Saint Mary's, overlooking the Lukosi river reminded Father Odilo of many things, including the time he had walked on the northern ridge to find how suddenly it had turned green with the oncoming rains, and the time he had found people beating fish to death as they leaped out of the sand and water that preceded an upstream storm's flood-wall as it coursed down the semi-dry river bed, losing enough water into the sand as it went, to travel at a man's fats walking speed.

They drove into Tshotsholo as dusk set in, and were again warmly welcomed, now by Father Angelo. He allocated them rooms in their modern pastoral centre and after freshening up they enjoyed a festive supper in his humble kitchen.

The next morning, they had coffee before heading off to visit Tshongokwe Mission, where Father Odilo had joined them a year before to celebrate its 50th Anniversary. They took photographs of John's high-level bridge over the Shangani river, and Angelo's weir that dammed the Shangani River for the first time along its course to the Zambesi. Waiting at the car, Father Odilo was attacked by swarming red ants, an indicator of the impending rains.

At Saint Luke's Hospital, Dr Hans Sharlaz was delighted to chat, but as Father Odilo was due to visit them for their feast day the following weekend they soon took their leave and headed home. He teased the married men, who loyally insisted on turning down a wonderful lunch that was waiting at Queens Park, in order to rejoin their wives.

WINDING DOWN

Father Odilo had continued to serve as parish priest and later assistant parish priest at Christ the King, when Father Kevin O'Doherty returned to run the parish. Now, even at the age of 93, there was no understanding of the word 'retirement'. He drove himself around in the Audi that his own brother, Father Joseph Weeger, had bequeathed to him several years before. He celebrated Holy Mass daily, heard confessions, presided at weddings and baptisms, visited the sick in hospital, attended a wide range of community and ecumenical activities and performed most of the duties expected of a young and active priest.

He always loved the Matopos Hills near Bulawayo, and had a cheerful group of friends with whom he would head out on regular Wednesday afternoon and evening visits. He often used to say that 'the eye also needs its share of rewards', and the beauty of nature was one of his great consolations and interests.

He was actively interested in the Matobo Conservation Society, whose work with the National Parks was rewarded when the Matobo Hills were declared a World Heritage Site in July 2003.

He could not avoid becoming increasingly distressed at the misrule that brought the country into a state of almost total economic ruin. At first he avoided criticising, and the Church was caught in a struggle between what it saw as its role to stick up for the poor and suffering, and avoiding being drawn into party political issues.

However, the deliberate assault on the legal system and on some of his own friends, like Chief Justice Anthony Gubbay, Judge Fergus Blackie and Judge Simba Muchechetera, upset him greatly, as did the way that the disastrous "land reform" simply became a process of wealth transfer and looting by a clique who were enriching themselves by the actions and policies of what was then the ruling party.

He saw suffering and loss all around him. Great injustices were done to the farmers, for whom he had great respect and empathy, and he saw how pensioners had their savings and income rendered totally worthless. He understood and felt deeply saddened by the desperate plight of the increasingly unemployed black population, whose incomes dropped in real terms by huge percentages as the callous and tangible consequences of inflation and devaluation made them poorer with each passing week. During all this he never ceased praying 'that our leaders may become enlightened and do what is right for the good of all the peoples of the country.'

Far from such a miracle coming about, inflation had risen to nearly 1,200% at that time[xxvi], the currency had dropped to a tiny fraction of even its 1999 value and over three million Zimbabweans of all levels and much of the country's most vital manpower had fled to find work elsewhere, often becoming the only source of support for their families. The toll of AIDS was leaving children orphaned and adding to the burdens on relatives and society generally. An environment that enabled greater levels and types of crime to enter into Zimbabwean life had been well established, and a 'culture of impunity' was enjoyed exclusively by the favoured clique who lived off the patronage surrounding Mugabe and his former bush-fighters. In contrast to their subjects they had become enormously wealthy, flaunting it and remaining determined not to release their grip on this system of government.

Meanwhile, the Catholic bishops' statements were becoming more clear and better heard. Less-easily manipulated bishops were showing leadership for their flocks and the mainline Christian Churches were uniting. Neighbouring countries began to see through the party-propaganda and world bodies like the African Union, The European Union, the United Nations, The British Commonwealth and others could not fail to see what was happening in a country that had every reason to be a model of success and harmony in the troubled continent of Africa.

Faith, hope and charity were actually growing stronger, and perhaps it had been necessary for bountifully-endowed Zimbabwe to experience how bad things can become before it would wake up sufficiently to act for itself, so that people can live together in harmony and mutual respect, with a primary objective of establishing and nurturing an 'enabling environment' that encourages honest production, employment and development, for the good of all its people.

(Later, a violent and dubious election enabled Mugabe to stay on in another coalition of sorts, but some of the mechanisms of looting were curtailed. However, the confiscation of one of the world's richest diamond discoveries prolonged the agony for the people of Zimbabwe.)

In January 2006 he was driven to Johannesburg where his replacement hip joint was checked and found satisfactory by the surgeon. The doctor who treated him so charitably and cheerfully, Dr Dalby, advised him that the battery on his pacemaker was running down slowly and should be changed before mid-year. While there he went to assist at the Victory Park church services one Sunday and ended up as the main celebrant, as the priest already had four masses to say. People got to know he was in town and his hosts found him being phoned from all over South Africa and being invited out by past parishioners and their families.

MOVING OR NOT MOVING

The time came for his superiors to require that Father Odilo move to their headquarters in Queen Park. He knew it was bound to happen, but it was hard for him to leave behind the parish and the people with whom he was so familiar and in whose love he was comforted in his old age. The parish's plans to extend the presbytery by adding two small rooms downstairs had been approved but very little had happened so far. For a man of 93, and his fellow-priest, Father Kevin, the upstairs living quarters meant frequent climbs up a steep wooden staircase. The downstairs rooms would relieve this, and make room for an assistant priest that the large parish needed more and more.

Pressured by a letter from his superiors, he called in John and Sheena and over a period of several weeks commenced the enormous task of sorting through accumulated paperwork and notes. "I cannot be expected to complete this before about October," he stalled, "but at least we can do the best we can for now."

He had sorted through some of his many cards and letters and directed, "just throw these out now, unless you know somebody who can make use of the lovely pictures."

"I think Margaret would be able to use them for the Christmas cards she makes," John suggested, so that was duly agreed. "What about the other cards in these boxes?"

"Oh, you will have to look through and see if there are any to keep, but dispose of them as well, the same way. So many memories . . . . ," he mused, as he looked at one or two. "What wonderful people. I have been so lucky in my life."

"This will not be of any value or interest at Queens Park," he said sadly, as he handed over collected news clippings and the numerous articles and readings he had accumulated. "History is simply not appreciated by my new confreres. It is not a failing in them, just a reality of people's priorities."

He had kept on file or in folders and envelopes records of most of the meetings held by the parish council and the various societies. After agreeing on what needed to be kept in the filing drawers for parish purposes, there were many other documents to decide upon. "Of course, I understand; we have a new young priest who will need office space and does not want to feel my shadow over him all the time. Keep what you think may be of use, John, but throw away the rest. There is far too much here."

"Father, you know me too well. Let me sort through first. I shall certainly preserve things that have historic value. Even these letters you are throwing out; let us check through and keep some of them as well."

Africa Day—Holy Mass celebrated at foot of Cross

A new pacemaker battery was ordered but delays caused a postponement of his scheduled operation. The Sunday before surgery he gave a happy sermon, but with a message that he was looking forward to being able to soar above the eagles, free of his earthly body and to be able to join his Creator one day, hopefully.

Despite all the troubling issues that he was constantly exposed to, he was invariably cheerful, inspirational and optimistic in outlook. Even Zimbabwe's rapidly accelerating political deterioration was something that would not normally cause him to crumble; in fact, he seemed to be managing well, even though he almost seemed to physically share in and endure the suffering of his parishioners and friends.

He had been anxious about some things, among them the unpleasant nature of the pressure to move him to Queens Park, to make way for a replacement priest. There were aspects of this that prompted him to write a response about respect for senior clergy and some attitudes in modern clergy that he thought should be corrected. He was trained in an era of discipline, commitment and obedience and he wrestled with each of these issues—his was a moral dilemma, to speak up or to simply acquiesce. He drafted a stern letter, and he pondered greatly before adapting, completing and sending it. "I am not concerned only about myself," he explained. "I hope that what I say will help our new Superior, and be of guidance with attitudes of specific priests."

The surgery went well and he resumed full activities, including immediately afterwards celebrating his regular monthly Mass for the Scouts at Gordon Park in the Matopos.

The annual pilgrimage to Mount Inungu had been on the parish agenda for a while, but it seemed that National Parks were insisting even more strongly than in previous years that they should charge those travelling through the Park their normal entry fee. For most people this was simply unaffordable, and for several years the authorities had listened kindly to his personal plea for their consideration, often only at the very last moment though. It was always a taxing process and this time he left it to the parish council and eventually said, "Well, if they do not allow us, we must simply cancel our trip!" This gave him great pain, and he was disappointed at the failure.

"I am fine," he insisted, when he gave John and Desmond a special blessing before they left on their long-planned pilgrimage to Lourdes. "May Almighty God bless you and be with you and may Our Blessed Mother guide and protect you on your way."

His strong hands gripped both of their hands, transmitting the warmth, care and hopes that he shared and wished them in their visit to Lourdes. "Please greet Father Paul Horrocks for me, and of course, send my love to Max and Clementa if you can get up to see them in Germany. I will miss you, John." The last thing the travellers thought was that he would not be there when they returned.

Although the pacemaker operation had gone smoothly some local sepsis developed in the surgical wound. In his typically independent fashion he tried to deal with this himself. He made a full round of visits to almost all the Mater Dei hospital patients but two days later Sister Gemma and another Mater Dei sister came to visit him at Christ the King. They had become concerned that he had not been well.

When they were told he was uncharacteristically in his bedroom, they sensed something was amiss. "Hallo, Father Odilo," they called out from the lounge below. All was silent. Anxious now, they climbed noisily up the wooden staircase and knocked on his door. They heard his weak response, to come in, and they opened the door and peered around the corner, over his crowded little desk. Under the tied up mosquito net, on his humble old bed, lay Father Odilo, with his large feet sticking out at the end, in a pair of his favourite old socks.

They were very worried now. "How are you, Father?"

"Oh, I'm alright," he intoned deeply. "I just feel a little tired and I have a bit of pain in my abdomen."

Sister Gemma felt his forehead. It was hot and he was clammy to the touch.

"Don't you think you should have it checked?" Sister asked, and immediately went on before he could give an answer, "I think you should come with us."

He offered no resistance and they knew then that this was not a minor problem. Together they helped him put together a few things. His room had two old wardrobes and a filing cabinet, plus his desk and some bookshelves crammed with old papers and notes. His drawers held a large assortment of old socks—he never threw these away, it seemed. He had also kept his German traditional clothes and clerical wear dating back from a long time ago. They found his simple old suitcase, with his shaving necessities, always ready, with plastic bags wrapping up the individual items of toiletries and clothing. He was frail now, and going down the steps, he winced in pain from time to time.

They drove him in their car to Mater Dei Hospital and he was quickly admitted and given the best of care to treat what appeared to be an abdominal infection, seemingly with good success. However, the pain in his lower abdomen developed more acutely, and when its cause was hard to find it became necessary to operate. A lesion, or ulcer, was discovered and dealt with under partial anaesthetic, but the problem did not abate. A second operation under full aesthetic was performed to clean up an infection. Peritonitis had set in and by now he was considerably weakened.

Teresa O'Dea was a frequent and concerned visitor. "I wish John was around," she said to him.

"Yes," he agreed sadly, "and Ian McCausland is away as well. He is in a far more serious state with his cancer. I think he is visiting his daughter in Tanzania at the moment. I miss them, but well, we are in God's hands. I hope I recover, but who knows?"

"Don't say that, Father. You will be fine," Teresa assured him, but a deep sense of foreboding made her turn aside as her eyes welled up with moisture. It was impossible to imagine being without him, a priest who had been so much a part of their family and lives. He knew all about each one of them—everything. She knew how he had visited her husband, Patrick, after he had been blown up by a landmine, and he always asked after his damaged leg. He had also been with the family to marry Patrick's sister, high up in the Drakensberg mountains; and he was simply always there whenever she was at Mass, or helping with St Vincent de Paul and the other parish duties that she did. It was probably mainly due to his influence that she had gotten so involved in hospital visiting. Now, it was he who was the patient, and this time seemed different. He had bounced out after his 'battery-change', just as he had shrugged off the hip replacement operation and the revision a year afterwards.

Few people were allowed in to see him now, to help him and keep him from over-exerting himself. However, Larry came in with Wallis one day and tried in his own way to share and comfort this priest who had known him and his family for nearly 50 years of his life. He would never have dreamed that he would live longer than this amazing man. However, with age comes acceptance and wisdom that does not co-exist easily during our youthful years of certainty. He knew that this good and holy man was near the end. He was able to get the message to John and his three children, who were at that moment driving from Lourdes to Italy on a journey to visit the Weeger family in their home village of Arberg in Germany.

Father Odilo's faithful nephew and friend, Max Weeger, flew out as soon as he heard that Father Odilo was admitted to ICU. Max was with him constantly, as were his great friends, the Franciscan Sisters, Father Kevin and other priests, and Archbishop Pius who arrived back from a trip in time to give him his final anointing.

Max was able to obtain a response by hand pressure for some time during this but towards the end he knew Father Odilo was slipping away. Prayers were being offered from all who knew of his condition, in South Africa and also in Europe and America. Two of his close colleagues, Father Martin Schupp and Brother Alois were in Europe at the time, and many other people who loved him and may have been of comfort at this time were also far away.

Father Odilo slipped into a coma and died peacefully at around noon on Thursday 8th June 2006. The readings for that day were so apt that they reflect the acclamation, 'Your words are spirit, Lord, and they are life; You have the message of eternal life.' He would have heard them in his subconscious and also his nephew Max's words in German, as he reminded him that he had lived his life fully and well and that he was free to go now.

St Paul told Timothy[29] he could rely on this saying, 'if we have died with him, then we shall live with him. If we hold firm, then we shall reign with him . . . Do all you can to present yourself in front of God as a man who has come through his trials, and a man who has no cause to be ashamed of his life's work and has kept a straight course with the message of the truth.'

---

[29] Tim 2:8-15

Mark's gospel[30] tells how Jesus answered the honest scribe, '. . . you must love the Lord your God with all your heart, with all your soul, with all your mind and with all your strength. The second is this: You must love your neighbour as yourself. There is no commandment greater than these.' It is hard to think of a more fitting commendation for a man who lived his life like the candle he often used as a metaphor in his sermons, giving light and warmth and consuming himself in so doing.

The following Monday, 12th June, a day when the majority of priests are in town from the outlying missions, he was laid out in a coffin for viewing and the Mass of the Resurrection was celebrated by Archbishop Pius with his priests and clergy and a crowd of thousands that had managed to be there, from all over Bulawayo and further afield.

With his nephew, Max Weeger

---

[30] Mk 12:28-34

Epilogue

Father Odilo was truly a man among men.

He died in the Mater Dei Hospital on Thursday 8th June 2006, after a short but painful illness; surgery was unable to staunch damaged intestines. We received the news while en route from his home village of Arberg as we drove to Paris. It was very sad news, knowing I would not see him again, with so much to tell him and so much more to discuss and watch unfolding in our beloved but beleaguered country, Zimbabwe.

The Catholic Church has been enriched in a solidly spiritual way by his life and service and thousands of Zimbabweans have benefited in their religious growth, their access to mission education and the benefits of mission hospital care.

Father Odilo had deep admiration for the founder of their Mariannhill Missionaries, Abbott Francis Pfanner, who took up the call in 1879, with his famous response to start a Trappist Monastery, 'if no one is willing to go, I shall go!' The Mariannhillers evolved from their parent order in response to more practical missionary needs and celebrated their 100th Anniversary in 2009. They will come to reap the fruits of Father Odilo's contribution to their own spectacular growth, from small beginnings as a Trappist Monastery in Natal, South Africa.

He had a great love for the people of Zimbabwe and for its natural African beauty and challenges. He expended his life in working to uplift and convert people, bringing the twin gifts of knowledge and faith.

Although he met Robert Mugabe as a junior teacher, he was slow to criticise the growing abuse and misrule. His was not the political arena, and like Our Lord, Jesus Christ, he kept his focus on the human and spiritual world. This did not mean indifference or unawareness; he felt the pain and suffering of people and always supported services and meetings, where people gathered to pray and speak about the Zimbabwe We Want.

Before my trip to Europe, in May 2006, he had already begun to tidy up and pass me documents, news clippings and material that he knew would be treasured. His archives are a mine of historic and spiritual material, going back to university years and the shorthand notes he kept then. It will take many more books and future scholars to do justice to those records, and future books could be written with much more detail.

He leaves behind a rich legacy of experiences and achievements, but most of all he leaves a worldwide trail of people whom he knew and cared about and who knew and loved him in return.

APPENDICES

1. Honours and Awards

- ❖ German Cross of Merit, First Class
- ❖ City of Bulawayo
- ❖ Paul Harris Fellowship, Rotary International
- ❖ Order of Saint Lazarus of Jerusalem
- ❖ Boy Scouts Association:
    Matabeleland Province's highest award,
    Silver Elephant, on a dark blue ribbon
    Zimbabwe's highest award, Silver Eagle, on an orange
    ribbon
    Golden Lion Award, for dedicated service to
    Scouting—2005

Receiving the Silver Elephant by the Scout Commissioner,
Norman Scott, in 1999

2. Glossary of terms and words Abbreviations
2.1 Abbreviations
- CMM   Congregation of Mariannhill Missionaries
- NC   Native Commissioner
- DC   District Commissioner
- TTL   Tribal Trust Lands
- BSAP   British South Africa Police
- RAR   Rhodesia Africa Regiment
- CMED   Central Mechanical Equipment Department
- UDI   Unilateral Declaration of Independence

2.2 Zulu and isiNdebele Words
- Piccanin   young child
- Duzi   close by
- Nkosi   the boss
- Baba   father, older person, used respectfully
- Igusu   sandveld forests
- Ingwe   leopard
- Ipamba   vines, creepers in forest
- Ngwenya   crocodile
- Mbejane   Rhinoceros
- Madoda   men
- Mdabuliwesinanga   the one who dashes through the bush
- Nkomoyahlaba   the cow which horns/gores you
- Dwala   rounded, onion-skin granite mountains
- Bayethe   royal salute, highest praise
- tshongololo   millipede
- balekile   ran away
- salibonani   hallo, plural
- sibongile khakhulu   we thank you very much
- hambani kuhle   go on your way well
- Makiwa   white person (used derogatorily mostly)
- uMdala   old man
- uNkulukulu   God
- yebo   yes

2.3 A few German words and places
- Gasthaus   inn, guest-house
- Gymnasium   grammar / high school
- Eichenlaub   oak wreath, medal, award
- Riem   leather, strap, belt
- Was ist los?   What's the matter?
- Schwan   swan
- Sauerkraut   pickled cabbage
- Schlusselblumen   cowslips
- Landratte   'land rat', not an experienced sailor
- Limes   Latin for boundary, where the Romans drew a line in rock, unable to conquer the German tribes

2.4 Afrikaans Words
- Kopje   small hill
- Boers   farmers
- Stoep   patio
- Wag 'n bietjie   wait a bit, a double pronged thorn tree

3. Flora and fauna
3.1 Some Trees:

Marula	sclerocarya birrea	umgano
Mukwa	pterocarpus angolensis	umuvakazi
Fig	ficus Capensis	mukiwa
	colophopermum	
Mopane	mopane	mopane
Paper-bark tree	commiphora marlothi	uminyela
Pod mahogany	afzelia quanzensis	mukamba (Sh)
Snot-apple	azanza garckeana	uxaghuxaghu
Buffalo-thorn, wag 'n bietjie	ziziphus mucronata	uMphafa
Silver terminalia	terminalia sericea	umsusu

3.2 Birds:
Black Eagle   Verreaux's Eagle
Go-away bird   Grey Lourie
Honeyguide
Hoopoe
Yellow-billed Hornbill
Ground Hornbill
Kingfisher
Yellow-billed kite
Nightjar
Lilac-breasted roller   efifi

3.3 Fish
Barbel catfish

4. The Author

John Sullivan was born in Bulawayo in December 1952, the eldest in a family of five boys and two girls, and has lived there all his life, apart from time spent acquiring his degree in civil engineering at the University of the Witwatersrand in Johannesburg. A keen rugby player, he also enjoyed playing squash and tennis, and ran the Comrades Marathon—once!

He married Wallis, a chartered accountant, and they are proud and happy parents of three sons and one daughter and their grandchildren tally is growing happily.

After graduating, he was commissioned to serve in the Corps of Engineers, and went on to work as a resident engineer on road and bridge construction up until Independence. Then as a businessman and owner-contractor he built factories, bridges, sewage and water works, houses and a wide range of structural steelwork and manufactures pinch valves for the mining industry. He served terms as chairman of the Matabeleland Chamber of Industry, and president of the Bulawayo Catenian Association and the Bulawayo South Rotary Club, and he has been keenly involved in his community where he considered he could be useful.

He has travelled extensively, but this has always filled him with greater appreciation for Central and Southern Africa, in which he believes strongly. He loves walking, climbing and observing things like the birds, animals, insects, rocks and trees of the Matopos Hills31. In 2001 he drove up to Tanzania and Kenya, and climbed the icy 6,000m Mount Kilimanjaro with his eldest son, for a brief view over Africa from the highest free-standing peak in the world.

He is resolutely confident that African misrule and turmoil will end, especially in Zimbabwe and he always urges friends and colleagues not to give up. "This is our home, and one day when history is written with more perspective, the good things that we and our forefathers have done will also be acknowledged."

5. The Illustrator—The Artist

Ashleigh, (abbreviated as Leigh), Hogan was born in Bulawayo, and attended the Dominican Convent before going on to Rhodes University, where she graduated with a BA in Human Movement Studies and Geography. Leigh is a teacher at Girls' College in Bulawayo. Her two older sisters, and her mother are teachers as well.

She knew Father Odilo all her life, having been baptised by him, and spent many happy days hiking in the Matopos, as his "pack-mule" with her sister, Bobby. They often attended his weekday early morning masses at Christ the King. Leigh is a keen sportswoman and loves the outdoor life. Father Odilo suggested her as a volunteer, and she willingly agreed to John's request that she do the illustrations. She is married to Graham Edwards, who has many similar interests.

TRIBUTE BY AMON MPALA

Friday 8th June 2007

Delivered after the Memorial Mass, by Amon Mpala, Eucharistic Minister,
Christ The King Parish, Bulawayo

" . . . . One year later, we still feel saddened having lost one of our most respected and extraordinary advisors in Fr Odilo. We miss him because he was a trusted, consistent source of support and wisdom, as well as a wonderful friend to many of us. He had a reputation of being honest, sometimes making polarising statements that stirred controversies, but for those of us who truly understood him, we benefited immensely from his uprightness.

He was a great and noble defender of righteousness—a fearless warrior in his own right, not afraid of taking unpopular stands—all in the name of integrity. We will remember him in history as a decisive figure in our religious life.

As Eucharistic Ministers, our association with Fr Odilo did not start and end in the sacristy. It went beyond the boundaries of the church.

A perfectionist in his own right, he demanded commitment and dedication from us all. He did not hesitate to tell us when we were wrong—and in the process, he also provided guidance as he tried to mould us into good ambassadors of the church.

It is an open secret that his willingness to take unpopular stands and to advocate on behalf of unpopular positions led to him being judged harshly in some quarters. His commitment to the community was a long-term commitment, for he was not overly concerned with short-term popularity.

When we were on duty, he placed emphasis on time management and the need for utmost respect for the Eucharist. He expected us to conduct our duties in a Saintly manner—his way; a deviation from his set standards attracted a tongue-lashing, and for the altar servers, it was a combination of a tongue-lashing and a flick on the ear. Of course, all this was done in a loving manner to help us perfect our ways of doing things.

In short, I can describe Fr Odilo as having been humble, passionate, industrious and highly intelligent with very good memory—a man full of wisdom, which he was always willing to impart to others, and a disciplinarian in his own right.

> To know him, was to love him and to know to love;
> To know him, was to know the truth and believe in justice;
> To know him, was to know commitment and learn to be dependable;
> To know him, was to know selflessness and to learn to be there for one another.

.....During Lenten period his emphasis was that: if it's a sacrifice, it must hurt; if it doesn't, know that it's not a sacrifice.

And his other challenge was that we should all be like a candle: for it gives warmth and light while consuming itself in the process. His message was that we should light each other up because a candle loses nothing by lighting another candle, but will enable the other candle to also give light and warmth.

This humble tribute is intended to stimulate an appreciation for a remarkable priest, an extraordinary advisor, a devoted preacher, and a spirited Christian.

We are truly thankful for his life and works. His way of life remains a challenge to all of us who want to grow in faith. He left us a rich testament that should deepen our faith and should continue to be revered by many of us who truly wish to come to grips with the beneficial realities of our Christian faith ....".

Mount Inungu with its Crosses

Relaxing with Elmar Schmid and other confreres

A Youthful Father Odilo

ENDNOTES

i.   The underside was engraved, 'Gewidmet v.m. lb Angeboerigen, (dedicated by my beloved relatives), Arberg 8.V.1938. P. Odilo Weeger, CMM.

ii.   Matthew 28:20 and Mark 16:16

iii.   Rhodesia Railways 10th Class locomotives were very successfully developed for the route, and had a 4-8-2 configuration and its 20" pistons had a stroke of 26"

iv.   Albert Giese, a German prospector, heard of the black stones that burn from the local people, and explored the geology, pegging his first claim in 1894.

v.   Pepper ticks are really the larvae stage of the tick, an acarina order of the arachnida class of life. When they first hatch they only have three pairs of legs, like insects, but after they moult they have four pairs of legs and go on to become adult ticks; their purpose in life is to mate, engorge, reproduce and die.

vi.   His brother was Sir Patrick Fletcher.

vii.   Barbarous acts like these cowed the local community into silence, terrorising them into submissive helping. Official resistance to their terrorism was fostered in those who saw them as paid or coerced communist puppets. In military dispatches a fighter was referred to as a 'CT', an abbreviation for 'communist terrorist'. Whatever may have motivated them, their memory will always be stained by the record of their cruel methods.

viii.   The wartime efforts of Pope Pius XII were initially acknowledged but he was later badly slandered by certain members of the Anti-Defamation League and others, until after the laid-down time-lapse, documents in the Vatican archives clearly revealed some measure of his and the Church's efforts to rescue Jews in the face of the seemingly invincible Germans.

ix.   IIsrael Zolli converted to Catholicism on 13th Feb 1945. He wrote a book about Jesus the Nazarene; this prominent conversion provoked great concern and opposition among his Jewish colleagues.

x.   Arberg was only about three kilometres North of the Limes, a Latin name meaning the boundary

xi.   It seems that the terrorists who attacked New York and Washington had this date in mind when they planned their attacks on America on 11th Sep 2001.

xii.   24th Sep 1957, Vol. 1, No.2

xiii.   Kariba dam, completed in 1959, is a double-curvature concrete arch, 128m high by 617m along the crest, and took 1,105,000 cu m of concrete. The gross capacity of the dam is 185 cubic kilometres, (185,000 million cu m), with a full surface area of 5,577 square kilometres

xiv.   From 1970 to 1982 he served as provincial of the Mariannhill Missionaries in Zimbabwe, and thus had to move to Christ the King, Hillside. (He served 4 terms, whereas usually the maximum was 2 terms.) He also ran the parish for the CMM.

xv.   This is a sort of spinach/cabbage whose leaves are harvested from single stems, and is grown for own use, by most homes.

xvi.   Memorable Order of the Tin Hats—for British trench veterans of the First World War

xvii.   Although the trail went cold, the culprit was eventually caught and brought to trial—he escaped from custody in Victoria Falls. An otherwise reputable journalist repeated an allegation that this was the work of a Rhodesian force, in his book, Against the Grain. Spurious and insidious opinions like these are definitely unfounded and rebound against people who try to write the truth out of history.

xviii.   The Requiem Mass was held at the Cathedral, with the Father General, who had been in South Africa at the time. He concelebrated with Bishop Karlen and Father Odilo, in his capacity as the Provincial.

xix.   19th April 1988

xx.   He was in Father Vincent's parish at Luveve, and he even had words with him in the 1990's. It seemed then that he still showed no remorse for his deeds.

xxi.   Bishop Henry Karlen CMM was the brave cleric who presided over Matabeleland through the terrible war years and then confronted President Mugabe with the evidence of the post-independence atrocities being committed by his Fifth Brigade in Matabeleland. There was no appropriate reaction and eventually the Church and the Legal Resources Foundation released their report, Breaking the Silence. This brought together many carefully substantiated and recorded massacres and atrocities committed by the army in order to terrorise and humiliate the Matabele, perhaps fearing them as a strong enough voice against the policy of single voice and total control that the then ruling party wanted to enforce.

xxii.   Lumen Gentium, 8

xxiii.   In Cape Town. The world's first heart transplant was pioneered there after tests on baboons had been successful.

xxiv.   Father Odilo kept a diary of mass intentions, which records exactly where he was any day. This is a fantastic record, and can reconstruct a whole life history. He celebrated over 26,000 Masses.

xxv.   He actually 'fell', a cancer victim, some months later on Friday 1st July 1999.

xxvi.   It did not take long before the machinations of the Reserve Bank and its attendants drove inflation to the highest level that any country in the whole world ever experienced. In the process, though, many of those with the right connections were able to take advantage of the differing exchange rates being maintained, including an 'official rate' available to the 'connected ones' which resulted in them being able to enrich themselves and impoverish others; they could even import a brand new Mercedes from Germany for the outlay of a mere US$100, properly rotated through the system!